MW00810643

Collected Poems

Alexander Theroux

Collected Poems

FANTAGRAPHICS BOOKS

Seattle, WA

Fantagraphics Books
7563 Lake City Way NE
Seattle, Washington 98115

Executive Editor: Gary Groth
Editor: Gavin Lees
Indexers: Daniel Germain and Daniel Johnson
Associate Publisher: Eric Reynolds
Published by Gary Groth

To receive a free full-color catalog of comics, graphic novels, prose novels, and other fine
works of artistry, call 1-800-657-1100, or visit www.fantagraphics.com. You may order
books at our web site or by phone.

ISBN: 978-160699-802-1

Library of Congress Control Number: 2014959871

First Fantagraphics printing: April, 2015

Printed in Malaysia

for Sarah
and our two beautiful children,
Shenandoah and Shiloh

Many of these poems have appeared in: *the Yale Review*; *the Paris Review*; *Poetry East*; *Conjunctions*; *Graham House Review*; *the San Diego Reader*; *Exquisite Corpse*; *Denver Quarterly*; *the Literary Quarterly*; *Urbanus Magazine*; *Boulevard*; *the Michigan Quarterly Review*; *Rain Taxi*; *Review of Contemporary Fiction*; *Image: A Journal of the Arts and Religion*; *Helicoptero*; *Seneca Review*; *the Recorder*; *the Journal of the American Irish Historical Society*; *3rd Bed*; *Fence*; *Anomaly*; *Subdrive*; *Sahara Sahara*; *Nantucket Magazine*; *Gobshite Quarterly*; *Gargoyle Magazine*; *Italian-American Mgazine*; *Bomb Magazine*; *A Celebration of Poets: Showcase Edition*; *Provincetown Arts*; *Green Mountain Review*; *the Hopkins Review*; *Apology*; *the New York Times*

"Then the Lord answered me and said: Write the vision; make it plain on tablets, so that a runner may read it. For there is still a vision for the appointed time; it speaks of the end, and does not lie."
—Habakkuk 2:2-3

"If you're going to say what you want to say, you're going to hear what you don't want to hear."
—Roberto Bolaño, *The Insufferable Gaucho*

"The purpose of poetry is to remind us,
how difficult it is to remain just one person,
for our house is open, there are no keys in the doors,
and invisible guests come in and out at will."
—Czeslaw Milosz, *Ars Poetica?*

CONTENTS

CONTENTS

CONTENTS

CONTENTS

Tulips in Green Paper

Tulips in green paper teach
color is as much brocade as hue
in my dreaming-room of you,

whose red flowers in the light
wetting part of me in folded shade
to darken my heart with lust,

spreads such green paper in me
that I am red and ready to succumb
whereon me you softly lie.

Firegreen Cake

She whom I loved was everything to me,
the splendid alternative to all the people
who, next to her, seemed barren brown.

"You're too intense," she cried
and pronounced me angrily a firegreen cake,
too embarrassing for common eyes,

neither popover, pal, nor passive pet,
but one who in displays of love-born color
flamed in my feelings for her,

aching mistakenly to give her gray,
not merely something here or there, but all.
Everything. Always. In firegreen.

The Way to Cedar Rapids

"We carry with us the wonders we seek without us; there is
all Africa and her prodigies in us."
— Sir Thomas Browne, *Religio Medici*

1

What Cedar Rapids waits
for you depends on who you are
and what you want.

2

Imagining the way
that Cedar Rapids is
is not to have to go.

3

Not to have to go
to Cedar Rapids and being there
is much the same.

4

Among the more irritating
ideas are that those who go
whistling off to Cedar Rapids,
like small retailing Nebuchadunsaw
with his train schedules,
grow large.

5

Do you have to know
by white anemic maps the way
others go to Cedar Rapids and return
with rodomontades?

6

A better way to know
Cedar Rapids is often not to go,
as if going there mattered
more than not.

7

Two plus two equals four
discovers exactly nothing,
merely restates it, megadick,
even in blessedly feathery Cedar Rapids.
You have not seen a city or a soul,
neither transfigure nor adopt,
only verify.

8

In your dreams
the way to Cedar Rapids
is not the way to go.

9

What would you co-opt
when you take out your loupe?
Cedar Rapids is a pratfall of facts,
no more than someone who makes a wish
scorning necessary acts
necessarily is.

10

Nor is to go to Cedar Rapids
the way to know, no more that source
than the solution of whatever attributes
beautiful fancy feeds us.
Are we the world we walk on?

11

Only in the mind
can we tell Cedar Rapids
how when we've been there or never been
we're never wholly through with
what we've seen.

12

In real Cedar Rapids
a spirit that is stricken
makes the bones dry, too. My gaze
is for that grace unaware of itself,
imagining pale alexandrites,
say, in skylight.

Pavane for a Dead Princess

I love you, dear heart, but am not in love.
And when you try by stealth to make it more
By fevered hope, love ebbs by such a shove,

For often hearts that burn too hot insure
In what they'd seek for warmth a kind of cold
That turns a tropic heart to frozen waste.
I offer all except where ardor bold,
Inflaming you, appropriates a grace.
There is in passion's nature an excess
Throwing embers, as it were, upon a pyre,
Whereby we curse what most we hope to bless.
If therefore love intense is your desire
Which asks that I a deeper love express,
You burn with heat but kill the flame by fire.

What Was The Peach To Nellie Melba?

Since you won't be my lover,
I refuse to be your friend.
It may be vulgar, this
Hideous female trend,

But I'm one, like God, in number,
Choose to be unique;
You're with me or against me.
I all or nothing seek.

Don't ask me to be generous.
Pragmatism's me;
Show me love and friendship?
Antithesis I see.

I'm a modern woman,
Of this please have no doubt:
I stick around with someone
Only if things work out.

If nothing's finally in it,
What's a visit or a drink
To a woman who wants marriage?
I go by what I think

And can measure in a man
Who'll commit himself to me.
I go by what is solid,
Not by what I see.

No dyads or dichotomies
For such as me, my friend;
To me a value's what
I'm holding in the end.

Don't talk to me of grace,
You go from bad to worse.
Winter's round the corner.
Put money in thy purse.

No parts for me, come round
When ready with the whole.
Bugger drinks and dinner.
I want to own your soul.

Jack and his Jungle Jacket

I wish that jacket could be made in green,
muggy, heavy, lazy, threatening, loafish, leafish,
to remind me I'm myself part jungle,

with arms like hollow looping tendrils
that stir like the breath of capricious men with fever.
No signature blazers with plackets for me.

I'm no China cat, eyes farded with kohl,
but hot as two hells I am, wilder than wet Dambulla,
Sigiriya, Anuradhapura, and Polonnaruwa,

dripping, spirit-filled, a bamboo-bordered welter
of iridescent ridiculousness, crazy caws, tank drums,
noises worth postcards of scorpions in green.

Why Mow?

That's your analyst's couch?
Lie on it then, if you must, underneath
    the golden sun, and smile for fun,

Mr. Veedol with your oily clanker,
marching feet, chin determined as a Hapsburg,
    and psychotic drill-bit gaze

at that part along the flowerbeds.
Trim, trim, trim, you neat nitpicking putz,
    kill the Montenegrin shepherd

in you, as surely a form of lying
to yourself as hiding everything it is you hate.
    I dehort any fool for shearing.

It is no delight pushing that thing
across latitudes of lawns, moron of conformity,
    leaving swathes that in the end,

by autumn, reveal but strips of crottle.
Cut lawns are nothing but a form of television,
    maintained by coercive communities

who hold you up for style. Grass.
Isn't it but lovelily there as such for us, spread flat,
    not curst like cows with crumpled horns?

A human chew toy is any plaything
made a trinket by whatever severely barked directive
    knick-knackers one back and forth.

No shepherd folds by what weather
waits for him or winces when he must stand forlorn
    in driving rain, and he is thin.

At least he stands, poor wretch,
for something in those pointless driving mists.
    Something solid, something real.

We are put in chains by anything
we have to do by what anybody else insists we do
and cannot freely tell of all we feel,

a bed I have never lain, I will never
lie, and let me pleadingly exhort that you yourself
never lie, upon. Never mind in.

Eli's Daughters

"Now the sons of Eli were base men"
— I Samuel 2:12

Two sour faces, lined from bitter old scores,
Wishing to death all men clomping the library floors,
Editing theses, scowling at windows and doors
Constantly banged.

Grad school prats, piles of fat books beneath,
Foul your cold hair, pencils drawn out of your sheath,
Huddled together, barking for silence with teeth
Almost befanged.

The Justice of Babe Pinelli

It was the fourth game of the Series in 1947,
Yankees versus Dodgers, and on the mound was Bevans,

With two gone in the ninth, and the Bums extremely bitter,
For Billy B. in pinstripes was throwing a no-hitter.

On first was Al Gionfriddo, who suddenly took off,
Sliding into second with a mouthful of dust to cough.

The crowd howled execrations in hopes he was erased,
But umpire Babe Pinelli called him safe at second base.

"Safe?" screamed Phil Rizzuto, who swears unto this day
He had put the tag on Al by and finished off the play.

But what of Bevans' noble stint? Worsens now the story.
For Lavagetto doubled then to ruin Billy's glory,

And with that single hit did Brooklyn toll the bell
And manage in the process to win the game, as well,

For two that B.B.'d walked scored quickly on that riff,
And Babe unto the Dodgers had made his Christmas gift.

Ironic that a man named Babe could generate such hate
In rabid Yankee fans who Number 3 adored — but wait!

Let's jump ahead to '56, nine years down the line,
Not long in baseball annals, where memory's sublime.

The rival Yanks and Dodgers came face to face again.
The epic test of skill, that classic trial of men.

The storied Flatbush Bums did all within their power
To put paid to the likes of Mantle, Skowron, Bauer,

With Sal, Labine, and Newcombe with his legendary grease,
Along with Snider, Campanella, Robinson, and Reese.

Both teams had each won two and now was set to play
Out the stakes for number five on that historic day.

Bomber ace Don Larsen had found a perfect zone:
Not a hit or walk in nine long innings had he thrown,

He hadn't struck a batter nor committed one mistake.
Everyone stood breathless as if the spell would break.

Who stood behind the plate? Pinelli! The very man
Who in '47 cursed Billy Bevans, waving but a hand.

Should not some pity be given to an aging umpire's name
Who prior to formal retirement was umping his last game?

A million critical eyes instead on Pinelli were locked,
As Mitchell of the Dodgers stepped boldly to the box.

Last of the ninth, now, when Dale still wagging his bat,
Ate a couple of hot smokers and then readjusted his hat.

Fans bit down on their fingers, already badly chewed,
While down it came to a final pitch. Pandemon ensued.

Is it so strange a player be summarily K'd on strikes,
With Larsen on fire — very few had seen the like —

Throwing heat pitch after pitch? Bowling them over like pins?
Isn't it simply proverbial, a winner is someone who wins?

It plays so well in the mind, except of course that it doesn't.
Unprecedented! A perfect game! Except of course it wasn't.

Larsen's very last pitch was clearly a ball that went wide.
Any damn fool could see, it went sailing high and outside.

Was it remorse Pinelli felt for flubbing the one call as he did,
And so committed another behind which another Pinelli hid?

Was Pinelli guilty? Had he spent all those long years vexed?
Should what gets blacked in one age be polished in the next?

So the Yankees scooped the Series in being handed that bone
By an ump whose Catholic conscience whispered that he atone,

In the very same way that the Dodgers became a charity case,
During the bit of highway robbery in that forty-seven race.

Don't try to tell Pinelli two wrongs don't make a right.
"They do," he no doubt whispered, going to bed that night.

The moral here is this: when two parties ask you to judge,
If you should alienate one of them, don't the other begrudge.

Show the requisite latitude and continue to propagate sloth.
Don't stop at being unfair to one, try being unfair to both.

What Mr. Ambidextrine Was Told at Confession in the 31st St. Shrine

Any man is any sort of man,
at some time or other.
We aren't even our own friend
until in a disapproving way
we've *not* become our brother,
by which I mean we're bought
and sold in that crucial way
and found by what we've sought.

The Maroon of My Copper Beech

1.

I want that color for my life,
To make stately my soul of mouse-poor chroma,
Dyed anti-representationalist with habit.

Fashion for me plumulaceous kisses,
Soft as these smooth capacious tints of tree —
Born opulence and sweet enwrapment.

2.

I want that color for my life, not bright
red opinions, neither hair of auburn tint,
but something between the MIT sweatshirt
I wear to jog, slot-machine chocolate, for
sweetness is part of color, and the damson
boots a girl I knew in Paris wore along
the Boul' Mich laughing in the heavy rain as
we kissed by a tree.

Love, tree, candy, girl. I was too young
to know that freedom was theory, then,
and, unlike maroon, not deep.

Copper beech, smooth gray trunk,
I want that color for my life,
No overneedfulness for you, no
staring shades, no shiny
eye-killing color to
your blue-red leaves
that fall, coloring
the red air
they help
to
blue.

Two Heads

He is cue-bald. They became an item
only because she had dyed her own hair
monkey blue. Couples always forgive
what in the countenancing of necessity

they would otherwise roundly condemn.
Cripples badly need to seek out cripples.
Remember the murderer who when asked
"Why did you kill your wife,"

replied, "She wouldn't cry." I know
you far too well. When on the day
he rudely mocks your artificial helmet,
trust me, you will mimic a comb.

The Cabaret of Theresienstadt

When all our dreams are over
Will then be part of now?
Ask me that tomorrow.
I will try to tell you how.

Muss ich, ohne Ziel,
Bleibt immer herein?
Es war einmal
Es wird einmal wieder sein.

Will once upon a time
Be what will be again?
Wait, until tomorrow
For we will find out, then.

Muss ich, ohne Ziel,
Bleibt immer herein?
Es war einmal
Es wird einmal wieder sein.

When we awake tomorrow
What do you think we'll find?
That tomorrow is a place
If it cannot be a time.

Muss ich, ohne Ziel,
Bleibt immer herein?
Es war einmal
Es wird einmal wieder sein.

Polonnaruwa

Those who carved the statues
were not ordinary men. The caves are dark.
  The dirt below is not quite damp,

  not quite dry. Candles held high
reveal frescoes. Myths and mad-eyed monsters
  and a gold-faced king loom up.

No one is prepared for silence
such as now is found in that reclining Buddha,
  and then further in the cave

another seated Buddha with a face
is smiling. Because it's reclining? Or hidden in a cave?
  Because we're not prepared for it?

  Who is prepared for what awaits
of what is suddenly warm peace in warring hearts?
  We make prophecy work, first off,

  by being so predictable ourselves,
forcing the past onto a future we've contrived
  simply by, in our rough state,

  being but sadly what we are.
Stone is rock made smooth, its gray round
  wholeness immune to angles.

  But by incorporating soul
this serenity, those secret smiles, that silence
  are filled with every possibility,

  rejecting nothing, knowing all,
a *sunyata* that has seen through every question,
  mildly kind and kindly mild,

  saving me from unworthy desires,
polishing me for the tranquility of acceptance
  in a bath of holy kenosis.

  Oh, everything is emptiness
and everything compassion in that dark stone,
  purifying my eyes, my face, my self

  as stupefied beside that cave
I observe, not quite dry, not quite damp, rock
  become by pureness perfect stone.

The Many and the One

We're rum with days, multiple displays,

Old, tall, abject, confessing, vexed,
More, even as we stand alone, complex
Than when we act in the usual ways.

Society should be blessed because
It allows us to further complicate
Or evolve, one might state —
Our stranger unseen inner laws

And so study the gift of ourselves
Which upon examination may seem odd
Until we come to see, it's not the God
In us we notice, it's the elves.

Contrasting Fruitage

Would the girl I took to see
South Pacific in 1957, if she reads this,
Please try to contact me?

One rainy Saturday night,
We took my parents' old maroon Dodge.
I had two tickets in the loge.

You had on wicked silver shorts,
Were shy, wore a gardenia in your hair,
Whose scent went down inside me

Like a long white string.
Sitting beside your beauty in the dark
Gave me warm reflections

As full of Technicolor as the Jujyfruits
I was too embarrassed to pronounce to buy,
And when you went to the ladies' room

I wolfed the tub of popcorn that made
My cheeks far slicker than my oily hair.
You bought a box of Nonpareils,

Which you delicately pointed to
In silence and had the grace to eat them,
One by one, with finger and thumb,

When in the dark our glances met
Just as Liat and Lieutenant Cable kissed.
And so we did the same.

Your lips tasted warm as cocoa,
A tropical heat in the bold blush I felt,
Leaving me a joyous deafness

I ascribed to thrumming theater speakers
When those lusty sailors burst out in choral song.
How unlike the morts I met in later life,

Crude Camilles and Creepy Cathys,
With shapes like pears, fists like powercats,
No conversation, and big hair,

Their tits deader than bagpipes,
Never mangoes, not those swollen flowers,
Rose and white and heather,

Which in the Polynesia of that Paramount
My buttery fingers tentatively unfurled to pat,
When magic gave to mystery

What more informs my memory
Than any lovely place named Bali-Hai.
And I can't remember your name.

The Rubber Face Above the Size 17 Collar

Mr. Onosmodium's penchant for caramels,
and the intensity he brought to food, finally did him in,
suffering a sudden heart attack,

as awkwardly swerving on the toilet,
while reaching back with difficulty to wipe himself,
mishandling the rolling bumph,

he noisily pitch-poled sideways
with one gasping attempt to snatch at the towel rail beyond.
Overeating's not a trick or a lie

or a lame excuse for something else,
for a fat or fleshy man feistily fights a famine in his mind
and is as solemnly evangelical

in his goals as any holy prophet
with wagging beard insisting on the primacy of God.
He resembled Herbert Hoover

toward the end, brick-red of face
a squarish ham of a head that looked awkward in a collar
stiff above it. Men as bulk

have made an effort, give them that.
Who are we to begrudge that man his gingersnaps, buns,
pot roasts, cheesewheels, lavish pies,

crème renversées, babas, duck terrines,
oysters, chocolate profiteroles, boar's heads, taramasalatas,
all of the blue trout he packed away,

or have stinted his delight with menus
as he lolled over in his mind meals for the Holy Redeemers
which was the way he saw the world?

Was Ezra any better flapping over scrolls,
fussing over cold pronunciations in the Torah, erasing or replacing
rabbinical dots and wiping them away?

A table, a toilet; a scribal tool, a shrimp fork,
whoso brings intensity to what he does makes a rubber face
a rule, call it a ruse though you will.

Adam and Eve and Pinch Me

Love when it's offered breeds little success.
A woman adored often couldn't care less.
Fidelity guarantees only redress,
For loyalty causes rifts.

You want to get rid of a woman. Then try
Not keeping a distance but being nearby.
Say, you'll be with her until you die.
Offer her lots of gifts.

The more you give, the more she'll demand.
Say, when to let her pass you stand.
She'll mentally give you the back of her hand
And consider you only weak,

You're always despised when you show care,
Because you are available, honest, and clear,
Once you are won and brought to the lair,
Another man she will seek.

Her fingers are shaped to the grab and the snatch.
Who gives a fig for what she can catch?
Trying to show you two make a match
Only turns her heart to stone.

Possessions are lost in the having, it's said.
A woman needs debits to be in the red
Prove your fidelity and you prove you're dead.
She wants what she doesn't own.

Betrayal sits deep in the female soul
As fire in a furnace on burning coal.
It's not what's been given, it's what's been stole
That's added up in the end.

So pretend as a pair you make perfect rhyme
And you can pull off a perfect crime:
Seem kind and ditch her at the very same time.
Then get a dog for a friend.

Cradle of Pine

There was nothing in you of faithfulness
  To place in this cradle of pine,
Nothing of fruit but of barrenness
  To give it of yours and mine.

But yet in its gaping emptiness
  a memory rocks the soul
Of what in its aimless movement seems
  like you perpetually cold.

I remember you in that absence there
  But an irony's all I can save.
How a tiny cradle of wood for a baby
  Evokes a perpetual grave.

Litany for Lubricia

Maine is an island in Egypt.
Wales is a river in Spain.
Coconuts grow on a mountain in snow.
Deserts get hammered with rain.
Crocodiles come from Chicago.
Silver is mixed in a mill.
Grass is quite rare,
The equator is square,
And Kansas is south of Brazil.

You are exactly where you should be.
No one's more faithful or true.
You'd never try to tell a lie.
Whenever I leave, you are blue.
Honesty shines through your face.
Vows have made holy your breath.
A heart that is pure.
A grip that is sure.
You'll stand by your word until death.

Postponeless Creature

Was it your view I was hesitant
about getting married to you,
despite the fact that of husbands
you've already had quite a few

and seemed dead keen on another
by remarks you made when we met
although it seemed passingly odd
to me we hadn't shaken hands yet?

You spoke of a pool and a dog
and a babe in a nursery room
in words that neatly suggested
all that remained was a groom.

Won't you forgive my annoyance
in finding it thus a wee
bit peculiar you had these ambitions
before laying eyes upon me,

who sitting there on your left
and seeing your hands knotted white
felt your option if I declined
was the chap sitting there on your right,

although by the law of averages
and from local gossip I've caught
the chances are probably good he'd
already been given his shot?

Victor Herbert's Toyland

How the world was never pink
like your soft nursery notes
and nothing like the joyland

reflected in the celluloid
cyclorama of that revolving
top with music given to me

at Christmas, which left me
unready for a breaking heart
that went crack in the real

world from real love, whose
borders, once you cross them,
let you never return again.

The Rings of Edith Sitwell

"On the day she died, December 9, 1964, she drank a double dry
martini for breakfast and stated, 'I'm dying, but apart from that I'm
all right.'"

— Geoffrey Elborn, *Edith Sitwell, A Life*

She loved large rings, chose big stones,
for they shone to great advantage on her long fingers
even if emphasizing her papery skin,

and yet those bold cat's eyes, onyxes,
obsidians, citrines, tourmalines, amber, malachite,
carnelian, sphenes, aquamarines —

she was particularly fond of aquamarines,
and also coral — topazes, idocrase, turquoises, lapis,
and sunstones did what all artifice

is supposed to do, mime or displace life,
shift a visitor's unconscious, the better to accept her
without obvious conscious criticism,

but then why should not a shy poet
find sanctuary in exotic costumes like a young abbess
or palatine in a dramatic wimple?

Her acrid profile needed wild bird hats
to offer a defensive façade for a woman who declared
  once, "I am an unpopular electric eel

in a pond full of goldfish," or sometimes
high silk headdresses, concealing her mad hair so that
  it was never known whether she had any,

although to judge by photographs taken
in her teens she had, and yet efforts to crimp it thick
  only made her look as weirdly angular

as that long deformed Plantagenet snout
which like her spine had a kink in it, the squinting eyes
  of a Vilnian *shroff*, her pointed feet

often slippered or covered, bony, hidden
by angular drapery, just as those elongated fingers
  were knuckle-bunched by rings,

although her hands were often hidden —
in the unfinished green portrait by Wyndham Lewis
  she is painted with no hands,

a dour Vorticist virgin (she knew neither
man nor woman carnally), for she fled the studio
  after being lunged at by the artist —

and yet those rings, sapphires, opals,
beryls, star garnets, rhodochrosites, amethysts, rubies,
  spinel, bold jewels, as sharply-faceted

as her features, were worn to deflect
the eye as much as they attracted it, a crowd-source
  of indirection worn, like a magician's

sleight-of-hand, to sparkle and so
dissemble as art always has, less as a comment on
  than a chosen alternative to life.

Undermountain Road

The jittery woman, not bred to grace,
smiles into polished men as mirrors
and, unladylike, interposes her plans
like a foot to hurtle into their lives.
These men are always the same to her,
never one different enough to merit
he be allowed the choice to accept
or reject (God forbid!) what she is.
So she plays her big black piano alone
in the dark and, convinced herself his,
waits by the telephone.

You never let
me come close to you (I couldn't mean
what I said, though I promise I tried,
reflecting only your hopes with regret)
for you filled the space in between.

Rider in Red

What terrible rider
in red, an offense against
what military beatitude —
the blood the martyred soldier shed? —
makes the sight of red ritualistically wrong
in the officially-folded triangular
American flag handed to his widow
and children, when irony,
like him lying there,
is dead to red.

Childless, Dogless, Manless, Empty

Q. "Have you ever been obsessed by anybody?"
A. "Yes, long ago. I remember the obsession more than the person."

— Lucian Freud, in an interview

I.

I love the way you think you know
What in all this vast round world's the best
For everyone you keep in tow,

Constructing destiny and fate by will.
Whatever you choose to want you get; who fails
Of a sudden by proscription's sent away,

Leaving you a mad and midget queen,
Howling in your hallway, swatting at the walls,
The portcullis of your wagging mouth

Banishing the lame and halt off island
Who've had the bold effrontery to live their lives
The way you hadn't planned for them.

Dark island, as much a refuge as a lair,
What is told of truancy is those sequestered hearts
Who seek you out to hide their lives in ferns?

Are they bitter hearts, old from assignations
Of other men and other islands who come like ghosts
To whisper hints of adultery and sin?

An isolated house, wet peaks in the mist,
Childless, dogless, manless, empty, circumscribed
By air. That's your boast? Your claim to fame?

You light candles. Cold hearts find hope
In candles lit against the sentimental night
To fight the shadows of their lives.

Cold hearts, however, never look for hope
When something else is there for them to kill,
To maul by supposition, hearsay, lies.

Don't you recognize that famous flame?
Shallow now because before too high, high because
Cold and empty hearts, though ruined by it,

Live by snatching fingers, pushing hands,
The way demented royalty has always served itself:
"Don't call, no explanations, I know all."

I lay down with love and wake to accusation.
Cowardly was what in Anchorage you called a letter
Written by the pusillanimous to say goodbye,

Which is precisely what you did, but worse,
For you the drumhead court, execution without trial,
Your judgment mere presumption, nothing more.

The whorish never weep. No apologies.
No contrition, mother's milk, not even breasts,
Never tears at final separations.

How desperately for reassurance you
Vamp strange men, fools, frauds, and carpenters,
New neighbors, lawyers, others' friends,

But always fail, getting rid of men before
They you. The speed with which you act, of course
Convinces you you're right as rain

In everything you do. Pilots drive,
Unlike poor benighted passengers who have to ride.
You shape the way you want to see

Exactly what's to happen will, so does.
Calculators always know by how their candles gutter
beforehand any thief will utter,

And if a lover has to feel the pain
It must be your idea of what it's like to be alive,
In spite of loss and hurt and cruelty

You leave behind. So proud you are
Of your swift inviolate professional decisions
Rendered so neatly, with such ease.

We deserve ourselves. What we do
Is what we are. From your high and mighty throne
You send down your directives,

Don't write, you say, don't phone,
But who is there to listen, who to heed your voice?
Can't you see that everyone has gone

Of those once gathered there by choice?
So, tell me, why if you're so clever, please,
You're always so spectacularly alone?

II.

But not alone, it was my luck to see,
When aging desperation whispered to your lust
That many men in value exceed one.

Roundheels in the terror of loneliness
Are always exposed: even show a longing for it,
Your striving tricks having been revealed

In what always you'd police in others,
Hypocrite! Remember that bald man who visited
You that day when I was also there?

You went white that Sunday, your face
A rheostat of muffled fury that before he came
He didn't call to clear the way.

Deceit always fit you well, where honor
Was a perfect stranger when you were left alone,
Your native state. Deception isolates,

For though there you are at forty
Plus turning loopy gray-haired somersaults in slow
Bombast, no one except those casual guys

You shine on out of your despair
As if, while one again you prove your shallowness,
Anyone remotely cares. You *are* your sister,

Crammed fatly in your own bad cannon,
While your reedy voice barks against the sparks
In inconfident denial of what you are,

As if you are set alight to soar,
But never do, but come whistling down a stick
Instead, a small ratoon of failure

Like your small perpetual schemes
To be adored, Lilith, by every passing herbert
To whom you're introduced.

Do you always whisper at doors?
Assume that worried face at ringing telephones?
Ungum by sticky algebra the lies

You're forced to have to tell to cover
Others you've committed in order loudly to deny
Truths too thin to see yourself?

How odd, men are so familiar with you,
Know where you live and when in that island heat
Moulage impressions can be made

Of your obliging self, aviatrix,
Mistress of portals, escort runt, hair-sprayed tartlet
Rentable for any bid emotion.

Xeroxed persona, yours is a mask
For all seasons. There you eat. You there abide.
And in those big dry rooms where sun

The clapboard bleaches, never souls,
Mix your cocktails for whomsoever sits on sofas
Just at dusk to keep the shadows strong.

Your gray hair dyed a plastic helmet,
Wobbling thighs, flaccid body, half-made leg
And over-perfumed self revolted me

And all that makeup, cakehead,
Did little to unmottle your burnt complexion
Coarsened by the heat of hate.

You're neither young nor honest
Which fathers in your empty bedroom facts
You need to keep around, old girl,

Facts indeed, but fictions, too,
To foster that lowborn belief we're all like you,
Nimble with midnight messages

No one hears but the empty men you need,
One going through the window, one out the door,
Who enter you like weapons

And sit tumorous like death inside.
"You're no different than I," you bray accusingly.
Comfort yourself. Old age will bank

On such revisionism that cellar
Of cancerous cobwebs where I'm sure you will be sane
Awhile, before the final pills.

III.

Consider, finally, the monstrous fakery
Your costumed self arrays in colored photos
Adorning that old bureau in your room:

A farce of faces, mostly family,
Not a one who doesn't hold you in contempt,
And yet they pose in your charade

Like rows of cherished friends.
But all your lies in fact, making forgeries
Of tact, allow in meeting newer men

For a newer, truer you,
Breezing through that soulless atrium of oak
With bowls of sauce and shrimp

For some new cack-handed candidate
To sire on you in mindless superfoetation
The baby you aborted years ago.

And there you sit, revealed a dunce
Not so much for half a life ignoring books
Or howlers ungrammatical and sad

As for the vulgar way you dine,
Your fork out in your mannerless fist
Shit-shoveling your bad cookery

Like a Hottentot in a hut.
But when had manners in the self-deceived
Anything at all of grace?

For one who buys annulments?
Turns the church with cash into a car wash.
Making nuptials a joke?

You have for stupid suitors
Plans more serpentine than your own guile,
A cat's cradle of some size.

The hotel soaps and stationery you
Compulsively steal to give as gifts to impress
Your Brant Rock friends was odd.

In childhood, I don't doubt,
Some cherished thing was snatched away from you
Whole mothers can't replace

And within you left an orphan
Found both in the hapless youth you squandered
And now in the postureless crone.

Humpbacks, or so the legends say,
Are evil in Ireland when they walk abroad.
Is it your assumption then

That when you cheat and lie
A physiology's involved, and the universal
Crippled all behave as you?

Is it possible that someone
By having come to know you even for an hour,
Would think of making love

To sprout some witch in a womb
And by fate's intimidation wreck his life
As patron of your petty genes?

Nurturing is not your gift,
Nor can that Egypt of unguents in your bath
Ever hope to sooth a soul

Flatter than your breasts and bum
That seem to me more metaphors of barrenness
Than that island cul-de-sac

To which only skulking types,
The surreptitious and the shadow sort
Who mostly act by night, are led.

You don't so much abide on islands
Half as much as you embody them yourself
Isolation. Separation. Reed.

You are truancy, island, isolato,
All at once, echo calling back to hollow echo
But in the noise a Judas grief,

Born of the adulterous father,
Dragon mother, and crude siblings you compose
Merely in the act of being you.

Why Can't the Wood Be White Tonight

Why can't the wood be white tonight,
as a window for my eyes

that I might recall my wedding night
and a memory that lies?

Two empty chairs there simply stood
waiting for her to come,

but the old furniture, only slain wood,
sat deadly mocking and dumb.

In vain now as then am I staring still
into deep immemorial night,

and my single thought is the only sound:
why can't the wood be white?

Can a lie be told in the moonlight white?
Can the wood of the moonlight lie?

Can a moonwhite bride lie in the night?
Can true love ever die?

***

I waited for hours pleading with fate
to put white thoughts in my mind,

for the moon was high and the bride was late
and a ghost in my dreams, not kind,

rose with her face from a shadowed grove
and whispered that love had gone.

As the long night passed, I never moved,
but waited there all alone

with madness descending dark as the ground
though the moon was pale and bright,

and my single thought was the only sound:
why can't the wood be white:

Can a lie be told in the moonlight white?
Can the wood of the moonlight lie?

Can a moonwhite bride lie in the night?
Can true love ever die?

***

They found me that night in silent despair,
nor a syllable since have I said.

Forlorn here I wait with two empty chairs
and not a thought in my head,

but the dreams I dreamt when the moon was high
and I ached for her face to see

in the wood of white by the dead of night
that she might see love in me.

Now with only the wish of my wedding night
and the memory that lies,

why can't the wood be white tonight,
as a window for my eyes?

Can a lie be told in the moonlight white?
Can the wood of the moonlight lie?

Can a moonwhite bride lie in the night?
Can true love ever die?

A Sonnet for Petros

Composed on the Occasion of his Birth, June 12, 1994

Beauty in a child foremost is hope,
Allowing us the chance to live again
By what later fulfilled in promise and scope
Is born of his own bright dreams among men.
To that hope a love is also brought
That crowns the possibility in youth
Of what elders often give away as not
Applying to a senior's need for truth.
So may the hope we have and hold for you,
The love we bear for you but need as well,
All truths required to ourselves renew,
Peal in the sound of your baptismal bell.
Remain forever the gift to whom we give
The hope in you by which we hope to live.

The Mind That Moved The Hand That Broke The Hood Ornament Off My Mercedes

No block of cement, of whatever
Thickness, is short of mass inside.
Stones are stone all through.

What dipshit spelunks a yard,
Creeping about like a question mark,
Scuttling through bush and brush

In the dead of night to think?
Sweaty Esau had a brick for a head,
Outside to inside dead.

Suddenly there it is. It shines,
Bright medallion, mandala, tripartite,
Given an importance in the darkness

That devalues more than shadows
All it hides and dyes him dumb,
A doofus dumber than a bag of hammers,

Rocking the medallion free,
A primitive in such a semi-squat of need
It would be embarrassing to see.

Pushing and pulling as an act
Has more to do with sheer stupidity
In the frantic than merely greed.

But the thievery is all his own
No seminars, please, on elemental man.
A crook need merely be cryptic.

No, the dishonesty is all his own,
As human as only humans are, even if
Mountains are only morons.

Ghosts in the Rain

I saw in that black slant of rain
the rising ghosts of the sheeted slain
from all my recollected pain

and recollecting all that pain
that rose with all the blackened slain
slanting through the ghosts of rain

brought back like black to me so slain
in the recollected sheets of rising pain
all the ghosts in the slant of rain.

Inward War

"There never was a war that wasn't inward."
— Marianne Moore

Look in the pages
of whom you will
for such a rhabdoromantic
shiver, please,
as the children playing
inside my loneliness
that I might therefore
proceed to make
pages for you to look.

Peru

Lima, Tarma, Sureo, Chosica,
Chanchemayo and Paracas,
I fell ill in the tracks of a llama
And prepared to watch myself die.

Cajamarquilla, Ilo, Chimbote,
Casapalca and Libertad,
The sun like an egg was frying
in the blue oven of the sky.

Ticlio, Cerro de Pasco, Oroya,
Chaclacayo and Chulucanas,
St. Rosa suddenly came to me
and I rested my head on her thigh.

***

Lima, Tarma, Sureo, Chosica,
Chanchemayo y Paracas,
Me caí en el camino de una llama
Y me preparé a verme morir

Cajamarquilla, Ilo, Chimbote,
Casapalca and Libertad,
El sol friéndose como un huevo
En el horno azul del cielo.

Ticlio, Cerro de Pasco, Oroya,
Chaclacayo and Chulucanas
Sta. Rosa de pronto se acereo a mî
Y descansé mi cabeza en su falda

for Eduardo Galeano

Desert Space

I dreamt in my pain
you reckoned with mine
when my heart was broken in two

and hoped to see
as I looked for a sign
for what that happened you'd rue.

Who would deny
that's where you start
in hopes of remaining true?

But then again
if you had a heart
you'd be someone other than you.

Sipapu

An Indian badly needs a hole
as faith of course requires needful flight,
the soul to rise and over rise.

A hole that's bored of hope becomes
a distinct cosmology of roundness and of circles,
    recapitulating what it can of skies.

Cenotes are sinkholes, kill-hole pots.
The Maya held that water covered openings
    into other unwet worthier worlds.

Leaving home defamiliarizes us
with exactly what we need by exploration
    to see what has to be sought.

Riverless Yucatan has neither lakes,
but a soul needing puddles to argue holes
    prays, as an Indian's faith unfurls.

Helen Silencieux

At midnight Helen Silencieux arose
and wiped the sky for clarity with anxious hands
    as she peered with hope to see

if from her jumbleful of dreams,
from the wetness of her fear and sad foolishness,
    something she could have as soft

as the pair of leather gloves
in Mens at Bradlee's that she lovingly caressed,
    grief-shopping in the aisles,

tried on, inhaled. The rabbit fur
she quickly nosed when no one was around
    felt like god on her dead cheek.

The blanket of stars all seemed
despite their twinkle as emotionally unemployed
    as she, so often distant from herself

She recalled yesterday so well
and how deeply rich the leather smelt of men and horses
with the fur as soft as thistle-tops.

It had rained on her odd hair.
When she came home she squeezed her hands
and put the kettle on and thought

as alone she sipped her cup of tea
and sorted in mind through her fractured reveries:
Are we also where we're not?

Pull the curtain. As to prayer,
what awaits in the sky, she thought, is more like pie,
sold only when being bought.

Memories Are Motionless

Memories are motionless.
What of them is thereby fixed in space
a permanence achieves.

What child of nubile noblewoman
persists in goodness time cannot erase?
Children are thieves

of love, moving to remind us
that by every single act of stolen grace
moving memory aggrieves.

White Water

Water is silver where we splash
Whether in waters brown or blue.
By what in fear we choose to rue.
White awaits in what we hope for
Which is proven by what we do.

On Filleting a Copy
of *Gourmet* Magazine

A piece on Mexican food intrigues you
But what you scissored to save
Cut right through the verso side of
A remoulade sauce that you crave.

Fancy that spread on hot-buttered scones?
On the back is part of what stood
Of that northern Morocco travelogue,
But now it is gone for good.

You see, in the way of saving one
The other you have to forsake —
An African tourist's presumably
Not someone who wants to bake.

Chutneys, a goose, potato potage,
A short-take on Sri Lankan meats:
Snip any one of them out, and
Your table's covered with sheets,

For no logical order's apparent
In what *Gourmet*'s editors do;
One listing goes next to another,
Assbackwards and hindside to.

Where's page 35? Armenian kugle?
And who wanted this cinnamon thing?
I had specifically cut out how
To tie up a pork-loin with string!

Recipes continue for pages which
Go unnumbered when there is an ad:
To attempt to follow the sequence
You first must try not to go mad.

A full-page photo's always appended
To an article on the flip side;
So choose: you want the full picture
(And the half-particle inside)

Or that special recipe scissored out
As something you wanted to keep
And the lopped-off part of a castle
Above the river Dniepe?

Odds and ends start to accumulate
Which you somehow never can match.
A leftover snippet on fishwhip
Is found with an essay on thatch.

A March Hare dinner menu's in shreds,
And the proper way to get maple
Sugar is botched completely,
Which you set out trying to staple.

Why are all menus jammed up in front,
Their sequels all jammed at the end?
With what in the center do readers
So badly want to contend?

Scented ads in the magazine
Are meanwhile pervading the room.
So every recipe mentally reeks
Of the heady stink of perfume.

And who on earth can rip out a page
From that spine as hard as a ledge
Without it all tearing to pieces
Halfway through that merciless wedge?

Always the same old writers appear,
In-house pets tested and true
Whose tastes you've longed been bored by,
And predictable point-of-view.

Other complaints I could make. Your
Small news on nutrition's obscene,
Menus? Complex. Or pretentious.
And too many call for machines.

So no more recipes now do I cull
For rather than suffering bile
I've picked up the common man's habit
Of throwing them onto a pile

Or hitting my head with a hammer instead
At least to remind me with steel
That lack of logic is simple,
Not always expensive, and real.

Jonah Considers The Right Hand from the Left Hand

Falling out of love
becomes as delicate an act
and as necessary to attaining wisdom
in what demands it makes of grace
as the reverse of what now we feel
once called for a different face.
Nineveh was spared, for it repented.
It was harder for Jonah to forgive
than condemn that erring city.
We are all irate prophets
and kill in the way that often
love is only pity.

Hermitage Above Ghoom

A white crane with aimed beak
cuts like a knife through pellucid light
out of the green rushes.

What of the tantric of its pointed
head in relation to what you, traveler,
have come to respect?

Both know and don't know?
Have come to love and by a natural law
also learned to stand in awe?

Milarepa told us the human body
is infinitely better than a wishing gem.
It is poison to crave.

Learn well from that ornament.
of the flying crane with its incessant eyes,
waterbird as arrow,

slingshot of learnedness,
beneath the whole concept of knowing,
seeing all-in-emptiness,

dragging us along to Asia,
with its thin legs shaped to flight.
to dissolve experience,

to show us the sun is light.
And show us the pure white peaks are white
And show us the living God.

There is a far side of Kanchenjunga,
the side that has never been photographed
and made into pretty postcards.

When sought, the mountain fades,
diminishes. Christ told us, "I am the door."
The nailed door. The cross.

Was that door nailed shut by death?
"I am the opening," he said, one sunset.
Crane and God are the same,

so they are inseparable,
silk feathers, high flight over Unduwap,
toward Ceylon, out of cold country.

Through the pellucid light,
out of green rushes it comes to you, alone there,
in your mind-hut, above Ghoom.

The Game of Love

Snatch out
My heart,
Slope-skulled Maya,
And feed it
To your jaguar
God.

Cut off my head
Like a papaya
And punt it
About
The Uaxactun
Sod.

When was love
Ever meaningful
Or unique
When it wasn't
Also
Odd?

Seedless Trees

The tamarisk. A name
of obscure origin, is only used
for making brooms.

Barren poplars wear,
but never breed, a hollow cottonwood
for empty rooms.

Infertile alaternus,
eunuch buckthorn, is ornamental green
and never blooms.

What in prettiness
that's ever promised thrives? Sterility
breeds doom.

Shiloh

When in the twenty-acre peach orchard
soldier's fire destroyed the trees
who remembered in the petals of confetti
dying made a wedding of one's breath

to a phantom bride arrayed as death
which came like love with no one ready
and prefigured in the shadow of unease
a nuptial grave for both the wretched?

Winter in Pointe-Aux-Trembles

What do bustards flying south
betoken for winter in Pointe-Aux-Trembles?
A killing frost that falls

on fields like a funeral pall
under shrouds of clouds that form like bombs
white as a leprous mouth.

Joueurs D'Echecs

Louis XV in the Parc-aux-Cerfs
looked on beauties recruited from Paris
as so many filles de boeuf.
And if the clamor was loud
when one gave birth to a child
livres were settled upon her
in the Avenue de St. Cloud.

Mademoiselle Poisson, or Miss Fish,
who became Madame de Pompadour,
ate Spanish fly by the dish,
but who fucks in order to die?
Louis's sexual excesses were such
she became *maitresse en titre* instead
and ran the whole of Versailles.

Eternal Recurrence

Isn't it just like you
to say because I find you loathsome
I'm bitter at the world?

Don't you need me to lie
about you the easier for you to deny
you yourself are a churl?

So why not indict a world
in which a swine so mean and small
fobs himself off as a pearl?

Virginia State Song

Where the lovely Blue Ridge Mountains rise
   I made you a vow I would be true.
Under golden Old Dominion skies
   the song in my heart was for you.

Never in the waking dreams that stormed
   did that love for you once ever stray;
Nor did the heartfelt words that formed
   in my soul end after you went away.

Refrain: *But time must pass, it will, the days can never stay.*
    As the years unroll, we too often lose our way.
    Our dreams can end.
    Just how they do
    who, oh who,
    of us can ever say?

Now although I have come again to see
  everything I loved faded like dew,
in these hills of everlasting blue
    may my heart that was filled with rue
   prove by remaining true
    'twas always here for you.
      (music: Paul Ferlan; lyrics: Alexander Theroux)

A Thought on the Ballet D'Amore

My one thought in seeing
Romeo & Juliet danced at Covent Garden

was, love is too imperfect a state
for humans to live up to it:
Love can't find a way.
All those imprecating
thumps, fat thighs, noises, heaves and grunts
incarnadining soups and make-up
serve to undermine, not advance,
the beauty of ballet.

Everything's A Version

Those vivid takes by Claude Monet
put steel into the ways of what he saw,
not the whys of what he took.

I find whole reports earfuls,
fabrications, fantasies. What's an angle
but an eye? "Happiness writes

white," asserted Montherlant,
whose eyes in penetrating living colors
denied nothing they reflected.

A black shadow is nonsense.
A shadow contains all the spectral colors.
Light alone dyes it black

as your hat. So other lies accept.
Lies are versions, and the surest sign
of wonder is exaggeration.

Monet's mittened cliffs, those
blue-damson haystacks and hats, I love,
but they say little of a lot,

speaking not of wholes, but halves,
versions, in the way of loving someone, say,
we by definition limit love.

De La Tude

Poor De La Tude, a forlorn wit,
served 35 years on the rack
for writing a simple epigram
about Pompadour on her back.

He lived to old age and don't
his tales which made Jefferson roar
prove that wit has more power
than the vengeance of a whore?

Did The Big Bopper Go To Heaven?

He was Protestant and fat
and he had a libidinous laugh,
"You know what I like" was lewd,
and I was roughly half

his age when his record hit.
The suggestive lyrics I heard
on the R & B station in town
struck me as crude and absurd.

His going down in an airplane
in point of fact actually moved
me to hold the abiding conviction
that God had somehow approved.

For someone to actually dare
such filth in his heart to tell
made me know in my heart he was honest,
so convinced me he went to hell.

The Body As Costume

The body is a costume, worn like motley.
We are, in portrait parle, as different
As images and motion make for unalikes.
You're no speaking likeness, Dogberry,

With a face like a pariah Hop-On-Pop,
To me. And I with my s-s-s-s-s-stutter
Am no more like the lawyer who, muttering
"I'm no par*agle*gal" with his glottal stop,

Is from ironic sallow-complected you.
We are what we wear, do as we appear,
Whether cross-eyed, chipmunk-cheeked,
Owl-faced, with homely wens or shiny

Foreheads, dance erect or slumped.
It is not a question of what we dare.
Clowns with rubber noses and flapping
Feet are no greater figures of fun.

Take gaits. The way we walk, a shuffle,
Bouncing high like billybeduckets
Or country coons with their hair in spikes,
Makes a vaudeville most would pay to see.

Assless, as flat of bum as a back,
Or bubble-rumped as original bikes,
Our birthmarks tell a tale, making
Those distinctions real that say we're we.

No two fools are ever quite the same
In shape or color, as gal or feller,
In height or footprint or twist of ears.
Flaws define us as tempers do bears.

No imagination's mercies come to play
In the cruelty we bring to what we mock.
Crisco recipes for the Jewish housewife
Sculpt a fatness for her out of lunch

In ways no buck-toothed redneck knows.
The filthy thin delirium of his imago
Makes my pale skin crawl. We flinch
But recognize the costumes on parade.

Who's proportionate? Roll up the charts,
DaVinci. Forget equilateral man
Was anything but myth. All's imperfect,
Mouths and tits and bladders and clits.

We're pied like poppies, color cartoons,
Bald, bowlegged, bent, and badly scarred,
An upside-down smile, sagging as flat
As a flat rubber tire in someone's yard.

But hark! Are those shouts and voices
In the gallery for what now assembles
To be seen? Step up! Tickets, please!
Enter the big tent! Look who's there —

It's you. But will you admit to it,
Oaf, that scaramouche of lying eyes.
A domino of crowfeet, crazy hair,
That chin? Although no mellow blue

Or lemon kliegs can hope to throw
A softer light on it, let it live,
For isn't it flesh and isn't it human
And sad enough to forgive?

Amos and Amaziah

Why was Amaziah with his calf-worship
any worse than Amos who before he was a prophet
was a shepherd under sycamores?

Blackfeet Indians aren't the same
as Blackfoot Indians, in the very way a slotted
spoon is like a spatula,

pretty much in name alone.
Amaziah's false claims to King Jeroboam II
against his rival Amos

was worse than what Jehovah
through Amos wreaked against contriving Amaziah,
making his wife a prostitute,

killing his children, and
sending Amaziah to die on unclean ground? What
between us then makes sense

when differences in human kind
are made only of distinctions, and history
is but an artificial fence?

The Loneliest Person in Scituate

On the coldest night of December
At the wintry turn of the year,
When the hearth threw out not an ember
To assuage my increasing fear

That I was a creature whose friends
Had diminished with passing time,
Although I had money to spend,
Accrued in a lifetime's climb,

I was living — I can't explain —
In a house alone on a hill
As if in a dark kind of rain
That rarely left my heart still.

I heeded little of others
And cared little more for myself;
I reckoned no man my brother
And ignored them with conscious stealth,

For more than my own profane
Way of living, if selfish and small,
I considered that, even if vain,
Next to others I somehow walked tall.

I paid my way and walked on
And scarce bothered a soul I met;
Anyone's pain I looked upon
With infinitely little regret.

With the poor, the gimp, the benighted
Living on scraps handed out,
Any social reform so blighted
Increasingly raised my doubt

On one night rainy and gray
When it meant not a whit to care,
A truth I could always relay,
A stranger seemed to repair

From a doorway (it gave me a fright)
To pick me up from the ice
Where, slipping, I promised to fight
With every last legal device

The office of public works
In the Scituate offices where
Pretty much everyone shirked
Any strict obligation to care.

I rose but quickly released
My hand from his with distaste,
For I saw that he was a priest,
Inveterate symbol of waste.

A coin from my greatcoat I offered
Him there in the low archway light
In exchange for the help that he proffered,
But waving it out of his sight

He touched my arm with concern,
And he looked me deep in the eye.
What in me then started to burn
As if something started to cry?

Not a word did the stranger utter
Yet a voice I heard all the same.
Did I myself simply mutter?
Was someone calling my name?

Was he perhaps putting a curse on
My hand as he squeezed it so tight?
He said, "Pray for the loneliest person
In Scituate tonight."

Advice seemed never so stark
As I finally regained my feet.
I walked wordlessly on in the dark
Along the empty and desolate street.

I felt it but fair to the bums,
To the prostitutes covered with lice,
To the widows and beggars in slums,
To follow the prelate's advice

And just for once give them the pity
Of the coin I had managed to save.
What's a line from a pious ditty
A priest conjures under a nave?

And do you know something? I prayed
For the thing that he asked me to;
Even if somewhat dismayed
I did what he asked me to do.

A silence suddenly dropped
In the midst of what I had said.
My heart, once beating, had stopped.
My feet became painfully lead.

Is prayer in utterance echo,
The cause of what we must hear?
Does what we ask somehow beckon
Our personal ghost to come near?

Can absence be suddenly presence?
The whole forgive somehow the part,
Whereby is supplanted the essence
Of emptiness in a cold heart?

Like the world I was suddenly cold,
I was the beggar, the whore,
It was I now friendless and old,
The old drunken sot on the floor.

I'd become the souls I'd rejected
The drifter, the friendless whelp,
The lost, the scorned, the neglected,
The creature in sore need of help.

Tears for what I'd forsaken
Scalded my eyes almost raw
For in the single look I had taken
Was something deeper I saw.

You see, in my plaintive call
I was never prepared to see
The loneliest person in all
Of Scituate was me.

Old Man

Remember that old man I saw
And said that he looked like me
And asked you, as he limped,
Weaving in between the stalls,
to forgive me, when you asked
that I give him money, and I said
I won't?

Don't.

Ped Xing

What man, tell me, ever
crossed the street like that,
an angle boxed on a sign,
no hands, no feet, no hat?

With muppetless arms abrake,
he doesn't know where to go.
Is that raised arm idiotic
a plea for cars to go slow?

Its arms are not connected.
Nor is there sense at all
of motion in this patron
saint of perpetual stall.

Is he walking over a curb?
Or toward a thought or a thing?
Is he mute with frozen hope?
Or doing a buck and wing?

What with its detachment
from the neck is being said,
that something clearly half
alive is one half dead?

My vote it says in streets,
even if traffic increases,
Whether there's caution or not,
Man is essentially pieces.

Glenn Gould Goes to the Arctic

Wasn't blatant cold the enemy,
A black cold that made your fingers fish-sticks,
In empty large rehearsal halls?

What were you looking for up north,
Seeking out snow, mucklucks, elements of magic
At the tip of the magnetic pole?

Do we seek out things that hurt us
To confront what otherwise would kill us,
Like you insisting that F minor

Was in particular the key
That best expresses your personality,
But from the creaking piano

Sounded icy and flute-odd in woods?
I loved you more in Medicine Hat, however,
In the condom of your woolen cap,

Coats, two pairs of mittens, soaking
Your arms in hot water, than playing for tuxedoed
Fairies down front at Carnegie Hall.

Consolation of Philosophy

Why would nature choose long years
To give a creature is a riddle,
Like the turtle which appears
To relish it so little,

But now better deal with strife
When mankind's proven such a dud
Than squander two-thirds of your life
In stupor in the mud?

Mrs. Zechariah

Weren't those scary visions
Zechariah saw of an evil woman sitting
In an ephah, then two more

With the wind in their wings,
Their wings like the wings of a stork,
Wicked wings and wicked winds,

Carrying the ephah to Shinar
To build the house where it became
Lewd Babylon and raving Babel

Only Mrs. Zecharaiah in curlers
Hotly thrashing under her ceiled sheets
Then rolling over toward him

Like a tub or two of upturned meats
And asking with a wicked grin of shame
For a little bit of pork?

Satan is a Jewish Joke

Saul of Tarsus
landed on his arsus.

What hoodoo of vicissitude
saw he? Not Parnassus.

A horned Humababa,
wearing red rubber galoshes?

Dragon of the sea?
with carnival facial farces?

Fa fa fiddle dee dee
The devil is all molarses.

Mother On A Train

O please, leave drooling Zappo
or Doocey with his fancy pants alone,
you with your fussing fingers,
and tell that six-year-old in red,
kicking off the radiator templates,
that his piercing howls and snaps
everybody on the car can hear,
weary as his whines, and the window
he keeps bonking with his wrist
in rhythm is ready to collapse.
He's not tired, as you prefer to think
only fat and spoiled and short and twee
and it's not the rocking choo-choo
frankly he should fear but me!

Raveloe

Such dark insistence your bright eyes
Make upon the world that it attends
To your delight as though that prize
Lessens all its faults to make amends.

Your constant chatter is a kind of prayer
That wakens up the rest of us asleep,
A kind of youthful love that tries to share
What, in giving, it insists we keep.

No actor, mime, or jester could
Outperform the funny skits you do
With faces, voices, looks, nor would,
When twilight falls and play is through,

One never feels that fully you are met,
For when you are in bed and fast asleep
Somehow on that day the sun has set.

Why I Don't Believe in Man

When Pompey dedicated the first permanent theater
 in Rome, accommodating 400,00 people, and got
  together 20 elephants and 500 lions, the
   slaughter of these unfortunate beasts
    was so revolting that even the Roman
     populace was moved to pity when the
      elephants, seeing their escape
       cut off, seemed to beg for
        mercy, but no mercy
         came, only
          lions.

Suing Is Unchristian

for Ms. G.L.

Keeping short accounts
I promise, is a way of starting over.
Is. Is. Is. Restore yourself

With being, charity's best, gift.
Forgiveness, try to see, is not cheap grace
But a restoration we all need.

I realize that to get through life
Becomes a silly way of showing God, even
by implication, you've prevailed.

But the god of second chances
May proceed to cast you down, greedy
Gail with your buttocky need

To grasp to own to keep to hoard.
Remember for your health Barnabas of old
And, I recall, a few holy Jewesses

Who, unlike you, hadn't loins
Of pork for hearts or terrifying talion for tits
And came not from New York.

Bob Cousy: Boston Celtics #14

My first thought was: *gunslinger*,
Hired like a bold assassin just to kill.
Sport isn't fun. Basketballs, ballistics,
No less than fired shots or screaming lead
From a lightning draw, number fourteen.
Yours was a similar job, to shoot them dead,
And nobody, killer dressed in green,
Nobody better gave back the fear of God.
Black hat, black hair, black shoes,
Who can say what opposition feared the most,
Your shooting out the lights or throwing

Passes fast enough to goose a ghost?
Anxiety is the great destroyer of response.
Whole squads folded when you drew, shot,
Sent passes screaming death and fire.
There's a speed that truly one can't see.
You beheaded them with loops, spinning,
Then came ornate ones, from the knee,
Running left, right, picking, twinning,
Reversing hands, out, behind the back,
Configurations like a knight of chess,
Baroque in intent, byzantine with skill,
That made moronithons of other teams
And sent them to Boot Hill.

Everyone Exists in Order
to be Entertaining

When Lao-Tze himself asserted
no greater crime exists than exciting envy,
   did he suspect we yearn to know

   only to look better? Knowledge, vanity.
We learn facts as we put on faces and flowers,
   boutonnieres to fussify ourselves.

   No scarlet dragon which spits sin
worse than Yalies, plumulaceous profs with proofs,
   prelates with palates of quodlibets

   who make us cringe in ignorance,
poor by what we have not cared to know,
   merely fearful in our innocence,

   cannot fail to note just by hearing
any crude and contrived shattering spatter of p's
   — watching their p-p-paprika —

   that preening truth is hideous.
I hear Chinese music and sit dumber than stone,
   wishing exactly no one my vain self.

Thumbfumbler

Maracas are plain gourds
with handles filled with seeds and shot,
but when you to be true

to the rattle in you,
those thrumming *chika chika chika* jerks
that rub you hot,

shake it up a lot,
only to find the music makes you blue,
what's the big reward?

The Rape of the Carnival Woman
One Hot Funless Night By
The Muffin Boy, The Jobbing Tailor, and
Myself

One hot funless night
I ceased to be the carrot-man
Who grew so hot at noon:
And with my pals,
The muffin boy,
The jobbing tailor,
Raped the carnival woman
In her socks.
She tried to describe herself
To me,
All hands to her,
As she thrashed beneath her paint,
Under her enamel and her pennies
On the funless night.
The muffin boy was laughing,
The tailor was hysterical as bees,
But I pushed a stick in her mouth,
And found underneath the sequins
What I thought,
Funless and hot and one
One hot funless night.

Willow Tree

I find consolation in your sight,
willow by my window,
for your lessons of the night
like a kindred soul endow,

so softly do you weep at the whim
of fickle winds when they start,
so easily do you break in limb
just like a lover's heart,

Nakoma Yuccacandle of the Black Hills

Such sweetness in a face I never saw
That brightens even more than sunshine hot.
And but scorches when your heart is caught
Like mine by love and adoration's law.
Your lightness, laughter, wit and joyful tongue
Which unleashes like a flock of birds
In soaring flight wondrous bursts of words
Crowns like light your beauty slim and young.
You are so lovely in your every turn
That sight itself a glimpse of you does yearn
To have to please its eyes with bliss
And I can sympathize for when I see
You turn to me with looks so heavenly
My soul itself receives a gentle kiss.

Ballad of the Crusades

In the cold enchanted woods
Where the path goes by the laurel
In the shade of a red-bud tree,
With its heart-shaped leaves just falling
And in a branch a tiny bird,
I found alone in doublet green

One who shunned my company.
It was a girl of sculptured face
With tresses black and doe-bright eyes
And when I saw the bird take flight,
I picked for her a sprig of laurel
With the fondest hope that she
Would listen to my words
but then I saw her sadly turn from me.

Near the path she wrung her hands,
And from her heart she deeply sighed
"Jesus," she cried, "King of the world,
You are the occasion of my grief
For I am friendless and ignored
Since the best of all this world
In serving you must turn from me.

I am left alone with empty arms
In the shade of this tall tree
For never being seen, alas!
May therefore you someday in shade
Lean against a tree in turn
With grief like mine, alone like me,
And know the folly of lost love."

Jesus and the Cat

Jesus in Nazareth once saw a cat
that peered from shadows of a distant past
and he knelt to touch it with joy.

It was in Egypt when a little boy
where his family had fled that he often sat
and witnessed them revered like Bast.

He smiled a moment to remember at last
at the age of five near Heliopolis that
a cat was his only toy.

Dear Father

A Poem For My Father
On the Occasion of His Eighty-Fifth Birthday
January 13, 1993

Dear father, by whose good heart I long ago
Came to judge the worth of other men,
Though measured by your height all fall below
That mark, let me as a child again
Walk along with you as once I did,
Half in joy and half in admiration
For all the time you took to show us kids
What lit the flame of our imagination.
I want your blessed company forever,
Never to be parted from your side,
Though I admit in walking my endeavor
To hoard the love of my beloved guide,
For with your hand in mine, my heart implores,
My loving hand will ever be in yours.

Lucifer is Haunted by the Echo of his Last Goodbye

You made me just what I was
For what I tried hard to be
I saw was in spite not because
Of what was truly in me.

We have to be what we are
And be able to choose for this
For that can only mar
By not letting be what is.

And so what you were I saw
And chose the opposite plan
For if what in you is the law
Thank God I became what I am.

Amelia Earhart (1996)

my pilot

I have often dreamt of you in flight
where on vast wings my happiness of heart
soars to touch all I ache to hold,

and then my dreams of you behold,
through storm and clouds and darkest night,
what on high my lofty dreams impart

how hopes in flying, just like art,
are met, where sudden sunshine then unfolds
a love sublime above the common sight.

Marriage

"Any enjoyment is weakened when shared."
—DeSade

What holds down a carpet? Tacks.
Theory's nice, but not facts.
And while sweetness surely attracts,
Remember, honey makes wax.

Mutterance That's Song is Prayer

"My heart began thumping with a kind of terror, the terror
of discovering you're human, which is worse than any fear
of the supernatural."

—Dawn Powell,
What Are You Doing in my Dreams?

Cold is anxiety, not warmth.
Music and prophecy come from the same place,
interiors where we live and die,

atrocious as animal lairs and profound.
When don't we sing what we have to express?
It is deeper than language, that place,

darker than deepest confessions.
In order to sing, head and butt are squeezed
together, just poised to recoil.

Mutterances are as real as anything.
The very language cries those baleful days
we bid bye to those rhabdoromantic

shivers by silence, just as we speak
in diminutives, frankly, to dilute conviction
when otherwise we'd sing, and loud!

But isn't everything expressed
a deep surprise? A note of song, a prayer,
folded paper planes, and phalloi?

Our bacchic yelps are surely as wild
and gravely deep as what is mysterious when
witchily white in moon-soaked light.

every wail, bay, cry, and whimper
intuitive resolves beneath reason that, less
than reinforcing, question us.

What singing is was never rational,
but like panting purely from the hormones
where from a heart's prophetic moil

echoes boom that reach to depths
and hit hot heights even higher than light
that glowing within and wild awakes

what in having nothing to do with cold
by what as a sibyl it sings and so says
has nothing to do with fright.

Babs and Fred

If Barbara Frietchie wed Frederick Nietzsche
and a child to them was born,
he'd have little luck
and walk like a duck
and his characteristic quirk, no doubt,
would be patriotic scorn.

A venereal disease he'd inherit from
dear dad and his flesh would sag.
He'd be picked on by boys
and make terrible noise,
facts that may pall, though he'd stand up tall
with loyalty to the flag.

He'd be cross-eyed, drool, grow old, and write
his last book, look up and complain,
while he frothed at the mouth
as he headed south,
"Shoot if you must this old gray head
because I have gone insane."

Curst Cows Have Curst Horns

How in idle talk and vain
Except by turning from what's true
Can you speak of being free?

You will never know the pain
Of suddenly losing someone like you
When you are someone like me.

Manual Jokes are Clown's Jokes

A water glass is emptier
In a cold and lovely room by the sea
Than the room it quotes.

We write books to escape.
One must have the boredom to desire
  Badly enough to create

Fictive cosmoses, imagination,
Like plain vitrines, waiting, hoping,
  Visibly to be filled by what,

Surrounding us that's real,
Huger than we poor scriveners by much,
  Provides us the way out.

Of empty rooms. So we escape
But in the way of water must complain
  By what we have to measure

Of fullness without, which mocks
What we in fancy must of loveliness use
  To fill the emptiness within.

Dr. Baruch Goldstein

"Today a New York-born physician who had emigrated to
Israel 11 years ago shot to death 54 Palestinians with a Galil
automatic rifle, capable of releasing hundreds of rounds
a minute, mowing them down as they prayed at the Tomb
of the Patriarchs in the Abraham mosque in the Israeli-
occupied West Bank town of Hebron — or Al Khalil, as it
is known in Arabic. He wounded more than eighty others.
A 33 year-old graduate of Yeshiva University, he was a
member of Kach International, a group founded by the
late racist Meir Kahane. 'He was a wonderful doctor,' said
Helen Pach, a friend. 'Compassionate and honest. So gentle,
he wouldn't, hurt a flea. But he figured why help the enemy.
He refused to treat Arabs.'"

The New York Times (Feb. 24, 1994)

Under your expert hands
all were healed who cottoned to your god
of Israel, O Jew.

Then why not let Jesus, slain,
offer up his sacred life as an apt reward
for everyone but you?

Saturday Morning in San Juan

Nothing's open at eight a.m.
The humid amapola is up and red.
Streets in soft air sweat wet.
It's as if everything is shot,
with nothing in sight not dead.
A stillness in its heavy green
seems to suffocate each tree.
Radiator shops are everywhere
and shut. Not even sweepers
looking at *pajaritos* swooping
over surf you no longer see.
The Afro Car & Truck Rental
at 621 Ponce de Leon (724-3730)
is not open, like everything
else that Saturday shuts in
(as if brought down by a gun)
merely by what so shiftingly hot
is shot by the shunting sun.

A Garden in Persepolis

Persepolis was only half-explained
Under lion-headed mountains of such a blue
Theretofore I'd never seen.

Nothing there was recognizable,
Except a garden, no colors, no golden rooves,
No plinths, no platforms.

I'd come at last to the ancient city
And there was nothing at all. Fruitlessly,
  I stared upon an immense plain

  Where heat welled from the earth.
I saw Persepolis, but what I so imagined,
  Only vaguely half explained

  what I saw, a stretch of mountains
Bluer than what of elemental man's endured.
  A garden but remained to lie in.

O Rhages Desirée

  What of Rhages, older than Babylon,
Capitol of ancient Persia, now forgotten?
  The name's found in museums now

  On Seljuk bowls of blue and gold
Where haughty princesses on Arab ponies
  Cavort through blue poppies.

  Didn't Zoroaster say by law
That lying was the worst of crimes?
  Is therefore Rhages a fiction

  (As clearly as for Tobit.
It was not he who went there with his dog
  To find the gold his father hid)

  Or where for me a princess
More real than any bowl of blue or gold
  Clops pony-wise through poppies

  To bring elemental Rhages,
Capitol of ancient Persia, now forgotten,
  From moldy museums to me?

Study in Crimson

A Cinghalese lady in a magenta saree,
from where I sit in twilight on the bank,
is too amazed at the seething sun,

soft and soulful and redder than crabs,
setting over Hamagama, which is burnt itself
by elephants pounding dust in the ganga,

to notice down in the spoon-billed boats,
with bonfires on them, floating slowly by,
flushing out birds that bark like dogs

who go flying whip-like over zebu-carts
past the hump-like hills and into the sunset,
red hot couples doing oogly-doogly.

Paul Nosedocks

What novelist, tell me, ever
gets stopped in airports but you?
(And with China awaiting, too!)
I know fame creates growing attendance
but *books* can do that to you?

Up to this point I thought
writers were mostly ignored,
their humdrum faces assured
they would only be badgered and sought
by bums or tarts or the bored.

You are the major exception,
according to what you say —
to women just open prey.
You're sure it's not self-deception?
You're not taken for Johnnie Ray?

Is God Good?

Is God good? Won't then on the other side of death
be spread vistas of trees, lightfalls of the kind

of peace I recall from the golden Augusts of my youth,
characterized by the safety of my mother's warmth,

not a femme covert pulling at a neap through pain,
married to some hairy fescennine shouting at her

to save him, but one who let us disappear in her
consumed by a pentecost of saving flame and love

and the kind of hope we're told is absolute in God
— in short a world of promise so rich and motherly

it shapes at last for me an image of a perfect earth
which I basically conceive as my life without me?

Poor Sparrow

Do petals drift on wind unheeded?
What scroll records with a million variations
the way things grayly pass away?

Is any music ever lost?
Are our melodies and moans perpetual somehow?
What of old men crying

at the wind in the windows?
What part do they play behind those curtains?
Are they as dead as fabric

when they flap and blow?
Our dreams are odd shadows of a white rose
flashed in a silver mirror,

eaten by live light to die,
not to be born to live, to love, to flourish
where thrive and always thrive

those questions we must ask
to prove we can, and, being therefore able to,
   somehow prove we simply are?

Eric

He lumbered, hangdog-like,
scowling from a low-vaulted brow
like a Gutnish hulk from a dark thicket
in another time. He existed

to annoy boxes of books
he shifted about inside his filthy bookshop.
No brains he had, but for cozening monies
few were more adept.

Once he sold me a truck
he had stolen, swearing on God's name,
as he pulled his Swedish hair,
limp as abaca hemp,

it was fully paid for.
But thieves are always traitors
to the gospel of exactness
and you, fat boy,

bluey hunter, dacoit,
liar, drumbellied oaf, hosehead, yob,
greasier than a chandler's shopbook,
who dixied friends

and sucked up to enemies,
can yawp yourself hoarse for favors
when next we meet and you
won't have the price of ham.

Three Kinds of Light

Sun rises in mists unexplosively,
like wetness in a shirt can't hide flesh,
and young eyes even hurt.

Now I am splashed with designs
coming through the holes in the lace wall
of trees. Now earth sings!

The soft brown holy dusk
of the thirties, after supper, makes me,
remembering it, want to cry

Primo Carnera's Shoe

It sat in the window of Lepore's Shoe Shop
which we passed, holding my father's hand,
tugging it frantically to make him stop and
tell us of its bewildering presence there:
a wide, flat, menacingly square-toed 15 EEEE,
its wrathful heel and butting barge-shape
as long as our imagination could scare up
to fashion from fancy the size of the giant,
a wrestler, we were told. And had he died?

A single shoe by itself alone seemed weird,
oddly landing in a shop in Medford Square,
unclaimed, as, who knew, anything might be.
I suspected even then that nothing on earth
wasn't in some way threatened by desertion.
On its sole in small brass tacks, primly
spaced, read in two initials a huge *P.C.*
The rough leather might have been his skin,
so squat, outlandish, in something so big,
even Dad, I saw, considered it in silence.
And in that I knew that part of him was me.

A childhood's filled with secret places where,
though one may look, one has to look again,
not simply to believe (for everything's believed)
but only to verify once more those shadows,
and even shapes of those unshapely shadows,
as breathlessly we point and gingerly come near —
tower high enough above us that we may see
(as our faces on the window reflected fear)
menace is as dreams have made them out to be:
to know, and know again, that, unlike Dad,
in shape or shoe or shadow bignesses are bad.

Being and Becoming

Isn't being in love
merely loving the chance
to be able to love,

somehow to borrow
on earth to enhance
what's promised above,

the better to know
the feel of a trance
instead of a shove,

and so miss the hawk
by taking the stance
we're seeing a dove?

Dead Leaves

When young I thought dead leaves
in their crispness smelled alive
and when I raked them into piles
I would not jump into the jumble
which comprised for me a soul,

a holy leaf-meal muskiness that
struck me as a kind of mystery
given to be known by earth alone.
Then one November night at dusk
I boldly jumped into the leaves
and with a sudden sadness felt
such knowledge with a shock and
of a sort I had never had before.
I felt them claw at my color
and got a whiff of their decay
as though they were yet alive.
But I knew that they were dead
as part of me went dead myself
on that November night, when
briefly, just before the fall,
I was young and smelled alive.

Lit'ry Boston

Sean Carroll's a Boston novelist,
Jim O'Connell a critic and friend.
They've worked for years together
With this fond hope at the end,

Both reputations would flourish
And neither be seen as a hack;
So each became fully adept at
Scratching the other one's back.

Sean wrote the sort of novels
All agreed were a waste of trees.
He was far more suited to selling
In Filene's (bottom floor) BVDs.

Jim was a lowly teacher
In classrooms very like zoos
And for tiny handfuls of chump change
Scribbled abysmal reviews.

No ego's more largely inflated
Than a local celebrity's is:
But why not sell carbonation
By adding a little more fizz?

So a scam was quickly devised
Of the kind in Boston called "cute:"
Soon Sean was dubbed the new Tolstoy
While Jim was hailed as astute,

For Sean to Jim said, "Want
To see two wrongs make a right?
Publicize both of our names
By praising whatever I write."

Novel on shoddy novel
Then fell from Sean's grubby pen,
With Jim on the sidelines scoring
Each one a ten out of ten.

They did radio, TV, and Jim
Gave magazine interviews
Of Sean and his eerie insights
On international news.

They took each other to lunch
In pubs paddies alone knew
And grew maudlin over old Ireland
And made toasts to Brian Boru.

Why shouldn't Irish help Irish?
Bugger style, honor, and taste.
Integrity never wooed voters
Or won a mayoralty race

In a city as rancid as Boston
Where pols both fat and corrupt
Made these two dunces seem purer
Than the table whereon Jesus supped.

On Valentine's Day no candy
But gifts of a sort then came due:
Carroll said here is your novel,
O'Connell said here's your review.

All of it bore a resemblance
To a midway booth at a fair:
Focus enough on the pitchman,
Your wallet's no longer there.

Their wives tried eating together
At Doyle's in Jamaica Plain
Whenever a new book appeared,
But not without visible strain

As final goodbyes were made
In a cool farewell at the curb,
Mrs. C having spoke of the novel
Mrs. O of only the blurb.

It didn't stop either O'Connell
Or Carroll from working their bit;
Whatever wrote novelist Carroll
O'Connell judged it a hit.

Speaking of baseball, I've always
Thought it quite grossly unfair,
When a pitcher hurls a no-hitter
The catcher gets never a share

And rarely if ever is mentioned
In the glory of what was achieved
But who understands the concept
Of a battery can't be deceived.

I am trying to say that if Carroll
The Nobel Prize ever wins
Remember not only the bowler
But the fellow who set up the pins.

The Nobel? I know what you're thinking.
They've made big mistakes in the past
And given this matchless award
To many a pain-in-the-ass.

But think of the precedent set,
Although guaranteed to confuse,
When that Swedish prize ironically
Has to be given in twos!

Shadows on a Sheet

Logic is an octagon,
a space of nothing inside a silence
I can't use.

Who's to verify,
in what your eye reports of love,
plain facts?

As distance dims
the signs of life, so *la raison*
kills solid faith

by creeping closeness
to probe eight times for key removes,
as shadows on a sheet.

Susan Wrist

You are not nice, sharp-nosed feminist,
as blunt and blue as if you were a gun.

That hair is brass. The breasts are dry.
Dark is mind in all you claim to see.

What big teatro that grief-shopping
where you dress down produce-boys,

hemming and hawing over thin carrots.
Saturdays you swim. Your Big Yank jeans

you wash on Mondays. What sacrament
eats at table alone on wind-dried foods?

To keep from loud polemics against men,
cats, kids, modern art, godly interruptus?

Is the spite that you cherish in the screed of
Edna A. Proulx and her turnip-hoer fiction,

— rural rutting, repairmen, rutabaga meals —
the only fuel you run on when you rave?

When you bitch, crimson javelins the sky.
Men cramp with pain inside to see you,

wagging in your fist abortion pamphlets.
How much insistence can a person take?

Anyone who knows you is deceived
if he or she does not, and immediately,

fathom your contrarieties as, unlike
Cordelia, you prattled on and on and on.

What happened to grace, reticent and dark,
wetting true hearts with love, Ms. Wrist,

when beautiful bel canto voices smote
the hearts of worshippers, their souls,

children gamboled over grass to rebecs
enchanting verdant glade and hollows dark,

and slippered damsels in cone chapeaux
watched masques at dusk at Ludlow Castle,

then mutely danced for love in moonlight,
silvering buckles rings, shoulders, eyes?

Apes in Green Hell

When maribundas with human voices
cawk and call and cry *"Coata! Coata!"*
a vast night of trees wags
in the heart of the Matto Grosso.

What trouble sound explores
whether from apes or men thumming
spoon-long drums from dark Mambaca,
in the soul of the Matto Grosso.

But there are no apes there, nor
men thumming anything intelligent
in the mind of the Matto Grosso,
only green phantoms wagging trees.

Archaeopteryx

A cantankerous mix
Of scales but no flix
That's riddled with ticks,
With teeth just like picks,
Tail-feathers like wicks,
A head thick as bricks
Wherein little clicks
For its IQ of six.
It worries with tricks,
Wingbeats and kicks,
And raspy-tongued licks
The prey which it sics
With claws sharp as picks
Can shred into sticks
All its eye can affix,
And to add to the fix
With its name so radix
You can't spell it quix.

Twelve Apostles

"Aren't numbers only figures?"
— Sir Richard Burton

Number one's the Lost Man,
A desolate figure in a barren land.

The Cobra's number two,
As serpentine as a waving band.

For three, Niggerlips,
Full, widely-parted, fat, and queer.

Comes number four,
Which resembles an upside-down chair.

The Mark of Zorro's
Five, three slashes inspiring fear.

Call six the Fishhook,
Depending in silence a perfect snare.

Seven's the Gallows,
Where many will swing according to fate.

Eight then follows:
A tubby snowman, eunuchoid and elate.

For number nine,
A tadpole with small vivid head and tail.

To Thinny and Fatty
For ten, one hugely fat, the other quite frail.

Goalpost is eleven,
Which rises in concert, a parallel gimbal

Then Man with Pet Snake
For twelve which seems an adequate symbol.

The Ames Bros.

Nice Jewish boys with beaked noses
whose fierce feral faces on sheet music
gave them the look of jackdaws,

their face-photos always posed
together, stacked, like drupe fruit.
Ed became famous on his own.

But what of the others, Hawk and
Magpie and Raptor or whatever their names,
deli-owners, hecklish and jecklish,

who served up sandwiches of songs
to moony girls in the dull, innocuous Fifties
where "Undecided" was a way of life,

"You, You, You" McCarthyite pointing,
And plunky "The Man with the Banjo" each one's
own dull voice and moon-desperate head.

Imagine Black

I am what I deserve, blinkered, public,
Getatable, indecorate, with finch-like tints,
Neither black nor white but always grey,
Much as my weak internal self must strike

Who considers me in fact. Objects are smoke.
In myopes, posture tends to be extremely bad.
Yet who's not bent with failures? Who not
formed by shaven shapes? Identity's a joke.

We choose any sort of seeing, any sort of sight.
We are stipple. I am striped. You are plaid.
But what better calculated to drive you mad,
Than never solid darkness, brightest light?

Imagine black. A forest where you can lose
All of a thousand huntresses, coal-mine hope,
Reclusion, a blind, nightmare housed by sleep,
Death, a wall, color you can't even choose.

Phenomenology of Prayer

Like Mr. Chin on Narrow St.
lighting his opium chiboque
to revisit places in dreams,
can't I by merely anger meet
the gods who make my life a mock
by their jackdavian schemes?

Garbo's Voice

The slow husky tones caressed, nurtured
A passion Scylla-blue, your pleas to men

To forgive you for what in pleading, for
They had to be denied, so many there were.

It growled and purred and wept, a smoky
Voice, animating scripts too banal for words,

Low in register, like your deep-caverned eyes.
I loved your cheekbones in the theater-dark,

Swedish boy-clothes, body of an athlete,
Not the divine curves of a familiar goddess,

Shoulders big enough to swim the Channel
Or bear aloft a dead lover in your arms,

Grief in marble at the prow of a ship,
Your flowing cloak, the long cold folds

Framing and exalting, your white austerity
That matched the pointed nose, curled lip,

Hitler raincoat, simple flat-heeled shoes,
When you vhispered to me in aisle four,

"Darling, don't, don't, don't, puhlease,
Doooon't —ohhhh, do so if you vahnt."

The Ravens Of Mt. Denali

While purple ravens croaked their quorks,
the way death interested them above the spruces
made me always think of you, alone.

Ravenstone is an ancient English term
for a place of execution. And frozen Anchorage
seems always you as hunger is for birds.

I heard *"gruh"* and ringing *"klongs,"*
as hopping corvids, turning over empty leaves,
crying *"djong,"* tasted cold shapes

with beaks sharper than your scorn.
I loathe winter. Mt. Denali was never colder
than you in your best kindnesses

were calculating in whatever you poked
and prodded to have. In your bedroom on a wall
hung a violet poster of that mountain,

your bed below a Ravenstone of lies,
where your own cold shapelessness recalled for me
as much a place of execution as a waste.

Scarcity wants feeding on a kill.
I watched ravens who, to stave off death, raced
above the spruces, flushing voles

from their subnivean holes, and they,
quorking on that cold and purple mountain,
always — *always* — had your face.

Mother and Daughter

You love my mother in a weak attempt
To repudiate by your contempt
The very woman who gave you birth
Who of all the people on this earth
You most despise, and so your plan
Is to try to deny her all you can
By shows of bounty, smiling lies,
And win esteem in your own eyes.
How blacken a mother you've come to hate?
Find a double and with it mate,
As the cuckoo's manner will attest,
Who seeks its home in another's nest.
In your mad desire for validation,
Your craven need for recreation,
You actually steal by what you give,
Never forgetting, you never forgive,
Wickedly wishing your mother pine
For every flower you give to mine,
Finding in notes to my mother sent
An added joy in what you prevent
From giving she who gave you suck,
Whom you blame for your bad luck.
Whatever you do to seem so kind
Shadows reveal of a darker mind.
You shape two mothers to be of use,
Both to serve your every excuse,
Mine for approval of what you hide,
Yours to kill, whom you can't abide,
In this double act of treachery
Is a kind of daughter's lechery,
Wherein the need to cozen two
Mothers, *neither* close to you,
Reveals in the act of lying to one

Another's loss, so you have none
By honest faith on either side,
Only old women to whom you've lied.
Under the stone of your devotion
A serpent lurks of black emotion,
Guileful, for any attempt to say
Simple words only serve to betray.
Words? Not words. Words are human,
To vows attest, the truth illumine.
More apt with you to speak of a hiss.
The Judas way. You kill with a kiss.

Salomé

Your father was your uncle, Herod Philip,
whose own half-brother Antipas your mother
also married, giving Herodias dual claim
to both these men and also one another.
Each scheming uncle had to swallow bile.
King Herod Philip never measured up
in siring you. And Antipas, out of spite
for being second, sent Pilate Jesus Christ.
What hope who danced for Antipas had you,
when prodded by lewd Herodias to ask
for John the Baptist's head, to feel delight?
The feeble joy in taking sanctity to task?
To prove the which before your life was through
you wed your great-uncle, Herod Philip II,
son of Herod, Tetrarch of Trachonitis,
yet another Herod of the horrid Herods?

Beppo

"Better is open rebuke than hidden love"
  Proverbs, 26.

How I loved to quarrel with you,
to swing in your awful rage
as if in a hammock where only you could sit.
How I loved to hear your scorn,
running jive upon you,
like coats you wore that never seemed to fit.
How I always came to find
whatever your problem was
I was instantly made a miserable part of it,
but I was above and you were beneath
in your howls of whorish greed.
You meant never a word you said.
So Beppo me no Beppos, radio teeth.
Scream words as black as a funeral wreath.
I want what is real to read.

In Your Shirt

I know all the moves of the overfamiliar
Visiting hack with a camera to kill you,

Sent by some slick to give you some play
Or rag where facts never get in the way,

Like the Boston *Globe*, a true oxymoron
In a newspaper's name if I ever saw one.

A request is made for a brief interview,
The Q and the A and the old parley-vous.

An old guy appears, half-lost and absurd,
And sees his visit as a favor conferred.

Within five minutes, he is using your toilet,
Selecting green tea, pouring water to boil it,

Sorting your mail with circumspect eyes,
Asking where your favorite manuscript lies,

Denoting the house ("Do you have any lemon?")
Is sorely in need of the touch of a woman,

For the library leather and panels of wood
Seem heavy ("No muenster? Mousetrap is good"),

Assaying the worth of the grandfather clock,
Opening cabinet doors to take better stock

Of those antique chessmen, miniature sets
(Not nearly, I'm told, as good as the Met's),

Low-rating the vase on the table in there
Which doesn't belong 'neath that chandelier.

"You still read Arnold? Any more wine?
Why aren't you married? Is that real pine?

Local booksellers tell me you're bats.
Could he go out? I'm allergic to cats.

Have you an ashtray? What about Poe?
The movement of your latest novel seems slow."

He can't hide he's jealous of all you have done.
A failed writer himself, he's a figure of fun;

He knows reporters on the food chain of writing
Compared to a whale are somewhat like whiting,

And so to belittle you he is suddenly keen,
To seem perceptive and make you look mean.

Discussing your house instead of your books,
he comments how gritty gray clapboard looks.

Wherever a fault can be shaped it's recorded,
many cans on a shelf, assembled, are hoarded.

My working-class dad with a humble position
Becomes an average prole with little ambition.

A painter, a teacher, my mom will be dissed
As a "career housewife" and simply dismissed.

He'll see my machines for four acres of lawn,
Write I collect mowers and am mentally gone,

Why hadn't I written a book these last years?
His research, like him, is well in arrears,

For my novels are sitting right there on the shelf
But he has drunkenly mixed me up with himself.

Long hours are passing while he's taking notes,
Wondering if every Cape Codder sails boats,

Stating reporters can't do so, wondering why
My prose style is so fulsome, academic, and dry,

Asking if authors — now he's peering at books —
like me can earn enough royalties to hire cooks.

The messages on my phone machine mount.
Of my hints to their consequence I have lost count.

It is August and humid and sunny and hot,
But would I be willing to pose for a shot

By that limp pachysandra next to the drive?
(Stieglitz, you're lucky to still be alive!)

"We've no time, I assume, for a look at the ocean?
A mosquito just bit me. Any calamine lotion?

Are your parents alive? Do you write with a pen?
Tut, tut, you're checking your wristwatch again."

Out come the books as a sign he must go
"Will you inscribe them, 'Best Buddy, Mo.'?"

An extended goodbye takes almost an hour.
Directions alone drain most of my power.

A working day lost, perfunctory thanks,
A feeling 'til midnight you've fought forty tanks.

Though the visitor's gone, have not a doubt
As to how these interviews always turn out.

(One half, my smartest, with a view to deride,
Is speaking to my other vain half inside)

When the article's printed and mailed off to you
And the fishwrapper's opened to page twenty-two,

Where the depth of insight and worth of prose
Seem written by someone while touching his toes,

And what is the headline sure to appear?
"Alexander Theroux: Prick of the Year"

Irish Forgiveness

"The Irish, whose other creed is hate"

Rudyard Kipling,
Something of Myself

I thought when lovers lost their path
love always sought the earliest renewal?
It was your betrayal caused my wrath;
you were unfaithful, it followed I was cruel.
In the silence of the aftermath.
Reaction after action is a rule,
Born as much of loss as born of fear —
I showed a mercy I also asked you share.
How false to feel that love's enough,
That wanting someone makes them soon appear.
Irish hatred thrives on its rebuff
And burns a century as well a year
And calls forgiveness stupid stuff
And never again, *ever* again, will care.

Richie the Third

Bald, unshaven, lumbering
you, that Frankensteinian scowl
under your peculiar manchet of a head
made a face as commonplace as a bubble
in biscuit dough.

I find it truly fitting
with your nose so crooked and cruel
that no chosen slob or lout could better be
for husband three, only just more stubble
who come in a row.

Mrs. Fishcrane Caught Again in the Act of Betrayal

"Memory is the enemy of friendship."
— John Milton

No serpent's head was ever pulled
Into more tapering a point than at that moment,
You were caught. He looked up, dumb

At first, without comprehension,
But your nose went white and grew a dowel,
Bluing your lips, like rubber bands.

What swallowed in your eyes,
Misleading you to believe I was a phantom?
You saw what you are, is all,

What others have known for years.
The sudden fright turned your night hair ratty,
Making twisted fingers of those knots,

You who claimed to be so expert
At showing control, your face now bag-lady old,
Caught cringing like a dunce.

The closer to the counterfeit, I saw
With you and that dead unshaven bald companion,
The greater the genuine I missed.

Your low idea that everyone's a sneak
Revealed how the thrust of your scoliotic soul,
Warping all your forward motion,

Gave you the sidewinder's moves
I suspected from the first. But you at last
Were apprehended in the glare of day.

I saw your first and only thought:
What can I say to lie to try to shift the blame?
The very way a quarter century ago

You, for Billy on his birthday night,
Deserting another husband you no longer needed
For an assignation with another man,

Cunning in the way you slid about,
As the cold and guileful snake its sinuous wake
Leaves in all it courses over

To confess to its dire length,
Slithered out of the hole of his broken heart,
Betraying another you once loved.

I promise, I will see you there forever,
Caught in your deception, as to me you turned,
Exactly from a text of Scripture,

About to be trodden on, shit-low,
Looking out of those mendacious beads for eyes,
Too stunned to flick your tongue.

For Lubricia
St. Mary's Church,
Scituate, Mass.
Nov. 27, 1994
Thanksgiving Day

Christmas Eve, 1994

To seek forgiveness is to pray.
It is a place where, in malicious rain,
Wait broken hearts, alone.

The refusal to forgive darkens.
It is deformed, not to be human beneath
Appearances. Devils make people

Wait, in purple snow, praying
With frozen eyes, wait out leaden hours
For months while passing time,

Squeezing a creature's soul,
Catches its shrieks in cups of coal
And watches it die with glee

The silence this cold night
Of my disappointment let me ever remember,
Oh Christ, for my cold sins.

I used to close my eyes to pray
But after a while no longer dared to do,
Lest God be blamed for you.

Mother is Certissima

"Mama's Baby, Papa's Maybe."
— Hortense Spiller

Your mother was a nightmare of the stick.
She beat you with, and so in raging black,
By which you came to call your birth a trick
You sought to pay that faithless lady back
Whom you claim refused to give you love,
Ousting you from what little place you had.
Still you call on vengeance from above.
By maternal lies and cries made mad,

Having been betrayed by her at birth
Who lives and thrives by what inside you dies.
Your fury kills what's left in you of worth
Forcing you to shape a faith by lies
With needs revealed by what you must deride,
As drums by nothing evoke a noise inside.

Scoundrel in Humarock

Anyone who whispers please can have her,
the way, merry, always with a worldly malice,
Joe McCarthy fed himself with mockery.

Toads sprout. A cold subpoena asks
only what it knows solicitation cannot do
In the way of gaining entrance.

Mrs. Graziadei with her pagan parasol
turns from her rock garden on Hanover St.
to request you make less noise

exactly the way you whispered yes
to that bald, penalty-faced lout who waited,
dumber than a bag of hair,

but who knew enough to whisper
questions to your former husband over breakfast
in hopes to find you warm enough

from Humarock by moonlight to invade,
driving over silent marsh, flintrock, garden,
in order in the quiet to get laid,

While you, your desire to explore,
choosing to be flattered, waited, peering
through the fanlight on the door.

Book Thief

A bibliosclerotic with hand out
steals from long black shadowed shelves
fat volumes under his surtout,

avoiding spies and library elves.
No Talmuds, zines, or crowpoled books,
no works into which an idiot delves.

He looks askance with copper looks
and when no one at all is up and about
hops away like a fearful rook.

Gertrude On Top

It is extremely difficult to picture with grace
Miss Gertrude Stein with hairnet in place
Mother-naked showing slabs of bluefat
Mittens on her feet by a snoring cat
After wolfing five pounds of beef
At one sitting in hungry relief
Her huge bum glowing piston red
Lying on top in a creaky bed
With poor Alice B. Toklas
Utterly out of focus
With flailing arms
Calling alarms
In pajama fur
Unable to stir
Suffocating
Beneath
Her.

Rev. Elks in His Midden

Rev. Elks who sips chartreuse
knows Iowa to be basically greenish-yellow
  by way of his wet drinks

  and not by harking back
to his simple life as a Keokuk barnboy,
  rolling in leghorn wheatishness.

  Is it for him to discern,
sitting in his midden, rooster-right,
  miniature diminutives of thought?

  Exacting truths of brilliance,
showing off on a front-porch atrium
  with flagitious quotes?

  Obscure and heteroclite prophets
knew the Gnostics called our bodies sewers
  and preached a stupid doom

  amid the noise of the world,
presided over by forked-eyed Satan Ialdoboath,
  captain of the Archons.

  Give him his Sunday afternoon
and drinks freshened by soft meadow green
  and yellow wind. He knows

  when lovers kiss, a church is made,
and cranes and flying crows and shadowed elks
  renew in spite of peevish sects

  the blessings of moist nature
that world-haters and Baptist obscurantists
  despise, but only the lonely love.

Tourist in Kyoto

In the warm summer of Kyoto
peaceful Mr. Hidayaki slows down to sleep
while outside a shaggy banana plant

does not sweat in the garden.
The continuous drone of cicadas compose
sounds that penetrate the rock,

while a constant *mi mii miim,*
that is the equivalent of sound in whirring
by the orangeaceous heat,

faps in the palpable stillness for me
to ponder. White-wristed geishas sleep late
and acolytes in Zen temples nod.

I hear the tinkling bells of a temple
in Horyugi, where ripe rice is heavy-headed,
and rising out of the shallow river

white herons wave and wheel.
Sorrow appears as a single spy, for always
I dream of you, as I have in shrines

where girls in tiny mitten-socks,
with fluid white hands, manage like thin herons
never to tread on skirts.

We enter the room where Kwannon
is nobly housed. It is a much larger than life-size
figure, delicately carved in camphor wood

and darkened with time and polish.
There rests one foot on her wooden thigh,
the other one soft on a lotus,

while one hand touches her cheek,
the noticeable Bodhisattva of compassion,
but she invites a fear of you.

I say she, for Kwannon is held
a goddess, but she is reputed to be sexless.
The curtains are half-drawn around her.

I take the ceremonial great tea
and under a sky toasted to a delicate crispness,
with heat shoving my heart,

return alone by road from Huryuji
without discipline in my eyes of mind and face,
carrying the memory of nunnish you,

past the plant, hum, acolytes, geishas
with fluid white wrists, and peaceful sleeping
Mr. Hidayaki, and alone I sweat.

Everything Smells Like Something Else

Everything smells like something else,
a fat lady's hat like chinchilla pelts,

trombone oil or trumpet grease,
chronic anxiety or deep unease,

a slumbering girl's extended arm
like streets in La Jolla of royal palm,

human armpits precisely like pencils,
old ladies blue hair like mimeo stencils.

British ashtrays reek of kippers,
unmade beds of bedroom slippers,

Your conversation, dry and tedious,
like the empty lobby of the old St. Regis.

Dust in the air when brakes are applied
recapitulates tanning hides.

Sniff real close any newspaper print:
that's not exactly the smell of lint?

What you can detect in the sensual lotus
resembles a pineapple's scent, ever notice?

Camel dung in the Empty Quarter
like the queries of a newspaper reporter,

An old man's forehead, pale and arid,
like the piano department of London's Harrod's,

Lavender carpet deodorizer,
a prom queen's purse with open visor,

Armenian food, sharp and exotic,
of things Caligular and strangely Nerotic,

Old leather volumes, book-glue and spine,
the open mouth of an abandoned mine.

A chicken's feathers to me seems most
(push your nose in) exactly like toast.

The hint in cooking of cardamom
like the empty shelves of a thrift-shop room.

Metal is sour inside large bells
the way a room with a sickbed smells.

A young girl's breast in every way
has the sweet milky scent of a *crème brulée*.

The phenolphthalein we burned in beakers
gives off the stench of a teenager's sneakers.

A nun's black habit, eerie and stark,
is odorific of movie dark.

An old man's robe, overly thumbed,
has the bready smell of stale old crumbs.

Having just eaten, a cat's awful breath
is exactly the way I imagine death.

Coke Upon Lyttleton

Mr. Coke met a girl in Middleton
Whose body wasn't a riddle to him.
Miss L. took a passionate yen to the bloke
Whose thigh he peremptorily started to stroke
And all night there was Coke upon Lyttleton.

I Knew A Girl White as A Gardenia

I knew a girl white as a gardenia
Whose bangles rang along her arm like song.
She jangled as she walked and her demeanor
Gave a ding to day, to night a dong.
She smiled and crimson javelined the sky
With lights that flashing fire in her eye
Bounced dishes off my soul, and made me die.

I knew a girl white as a gardenia
Whose electric eyes shot like flash would glow.
She giggled as she talked and her deportment
gave to day a high, to night a ho.
She flirted and the world exploded like a gun
While shafts of fire orange as the sun
Ran through my heart, and I was done.

Afternoon of Regret

Rouault's figures are broken by lines
I recalled that afternoon with sadness.
I had not seen your face in 138 days.
We met in a dark Chinese restaurant.
The booth we sat across in forced our
bodies to face each other, fecklessly,
the way we would a future. Echoes
made the silence noisy. We were alone.
You sat like a conspiracy theorist,
spreading out a Christ-bitten pamphlet
and the purple faith you'd turned to
as, what, insurance against yourself?
I was talking too loud, you exclaimed.
No kiss, no hug, not a single question
for me, like "Are you seeing anyone?"
(Self-pity is, foremost, unawareness.)
Stark , heavy contrast is what Rouault
is all about. I sat in the black contours.
The gifts I'd wrapped embarrassed you
because you carried no like thoughts
for me. How in having many men can you
expect love from one? Lines separate,
as love is discrete. You find no love
because you fail to distinguish men,
blaming them, after seeing each other,
for the faithless acts of leaving you.
Doubt is an aspect of suffering. You
worship defeat, believing in miracles
of God but not for you and me. I saw
you brighten with a smile that afternoon
but only once: for the Chinese waiter
who came to fill your water glass and
who then quickly walked away.

Paris, April 12, 1995

Curse of a Dying Harlot

On the eve of her self-immolation —
By means of a dive from a plane —
A whining cadaver with lots of palaver
Wrote a will and appended her name.

To the husbands who sought to abuse me,
By making demands I be true,
Who refused to sublet me and so to upset me
Their vows simply wouldn't renew,

To the priests I sought for approval,
Who extended annulments to me,
Who let me disparage the concept of marriage,
But demanded double the fee,

To my fully dysfunctional family,
Irish and stupid and cruel,
Not one single gene even close to the mean
In the whole biological pool,

To my fanatical wide-bodied sister,
Who snatched all the love of our mother,
Whose hair was dyed brass but the size of whose ass
Gave people to think her my brother,

To the brother I kept as my lackey,
Who camped out in my house half a year,
He had an I.Q. the size of screw,
And a body the shape of a pear,

To his spoon-headed son with a head
Which performed every function but thought,
Who ate and who dribbled and who constantly quibbled
With a brain the size of a dot,

To the many men I have traduced,
By deceit, outright lies, and false tales,
As my sexual skills were like cod-liver pills,
I had to develop fish-scales,

To the ball-boys, mechanics, and pilots,
The drummers, ham-boners, and cops,
I fellated them all, the short and the tall,
And proceeded to lap up the slops,

To Bruce, Captain Dick, and the doctor
Of something or other he said,
To all I let suck me and lick me and fuck me,
Enticing them to my bed,

To Billy the husband I jilted,
So little money he made,
Who made me a harlot and never a starlet
By the piddling sums he was paid,

To Richie as bald as an egg,
Whose fun at the commonwealth dump
Was poking for bottles and discarded throttles
And dead cadavers to hump,

To my several lesbian girlfriends,
Who are homely as old winter pears,
Who were never a threat to the men that I met,
And I myself can change gears,

To the penniless slobs that I've bedded,
So dim and fat and inordinate,
I married down so that I'd wear the crown
And always have a subordinate,

To those I deluded with presents
Who laughably chose to believe
In me as a queen but what was not seen
Is I only gave to receive,

To my philandering father,
Whose grave I with flowers endow,
You'd not have a part of a jackass's fart,
If my mother weren't such a sow,

To God who created me ass-less
Who also flattened my tits
I offer you hate though you're at the gate
To hand out the final permits.

I leave you years full of nightmares,
I leave you gross ulcers and boils,
I leave you confusion and hatred,
I leave you chaotic turmoils,
I leave you the plague of the dying,
I leave you decades of pain,
I leave you the worst I can give you,
I leave you unbearable strain,
I leave you my undying promise
To appear in your lifetime again!

When I Fell In Love

When I fell in love with you
I felt so famous in my own eyes,
  filled with such a force

  and famished for the size
of the fame of falling fullness,
  finally finding love,

  I could feel almost faint
with force and as filled with fame
  as love is with surprise.

  When I fell in love with you
I felt equally frail in my own eyes,
  filled less with force and fire

  than famished for the feel
of the fearful force of falling in love,
  fat with a filled feeling,

  almost faint as famous,
and as fully frightful of falling is
  when I fell for you.

Desert Hermits

Dryness is loud, strangely
the way bones are cracked for marrow.
 Religions are born in the desert,

 in the very same way we listen
is actually a kind of digging for food.
 Oases live, sand is sterile,

 but empty deserts boom in fall,
shoot when the shimmering summer heat is gone,
 which is a way of hearing questions asked.

 Sunset colors are a kind of tears
and scorch to black the fire prophets' faces
 as rocks expand and loudly crack.

 Who would not think silence
would prevail where so much desolation waits?
 Not those whom wind whips sad,

 for whom slack air at other times
leaves no downwind audibly to crouch against.
 Noise, wind, heat, sand, emptiness

 reach us alone by what we ask,
from what we alone have learned to suffer,
 strain by way of need to hear,

 reach us in the way they will
and if we choose to listen teach us to hear
 that all trails lead to water.

For St. Teresa

 I dreamt I saw your love
in the shadow of your tears,
 the way repentance proves
a changeful hope can be,

so I can stand above
what in my soul of fears
a growing love removes
by what you dream for me.

Sicilian Girl

I sent you bright oranges from Cefalù
That flamed like the love I offered to you.

Purple wine from Pachino I sipped,
Like kisses evoking the mist of your lips.

You sat in the hot Agrigento sun with me
At a tiny white table under a tree,

And the Saracen dark in your level eyes,
With their secret power to hypnotize,

Flooded my will. With a sudden start
Golden doors opened under my heart.

How urgency calls up the color red,
Where what is shown is all that is said.

A shaft from the sky of Tyrrhenian blue
Bolted through me just as I entered you.

Small yellow blooms went flat as we rolled,
Invading each other, body and soul,

And as I began kissing your soft breezes out,
A spectrum exploded, and colors poured out

for Lynne Pacitto

Fat Lady, Why Do You Peer

Fat lady, why do you peer?
The swirls in the sky,
that buttermilk horizon,
is reflected in your own
billowing bathing suit.

Look inward for everything
that blue can be, and is,
surrounding you and yours,
not to the horizon,
that flattened faraway line,

for meaningful blues, big
be-circling butting blues
you can never quite see. Didn't
Duke Ellington say of Mme. Zajj
"A lady is a drum"?

> Craigville Beach
> Centerville, Mass.
> June 20, 1995

Families

A family member rarely comes to help.
Each hopes the other fails at crucial times.
Brothers float along like so much kelp.
Sisters give each other looks like fines.
You want to take a trip to China? Creep.
You badly need some money? I'm asleep.
Blood is neither thick nor red nor deep.

No victory with brothers ever matters
Or can be understood as truly sweet
Unless one sibling's failure flatters
Another's need to savor his defeat.
The face of a family is a family mask.
A request of any kind becomes a task,
A burden by the very fact you ask.

One's own height is relative to what
Can be maintained by keeping others low.
Therefore seem to give assistance but
Never to the point where others grow.
Each one mimics what the other mimes.
A criminal knows a criminal's crimes.
Nothing familiar can ever be sublime.

Cliques are formed, never of affection,
But merely as the means to shun a third.
No sense is ever had of real selection,
Rather thinning out the family herd.
A family is only people together alone.
What is thicker than water? Only bone.
Blood is what you can't get from a stone.

The Chocolate Hills

In the Chocolate Hills
during the months that are dry
I sit alone eating *bagoong*
waiting for verdant July.
O iloilo, O iloilo
I look up when I cry
I so love the doves,
I yearn for the doves,
Seven-colored doves in the sky.

In the Chocolate Hills
in the way of a desolate scene
I sit in Bohol in the sere and the cold
'til the hills again become green
O iloilo, O iloilo
I look up when I cry
I so love the doves,
I yearn for the doves,
Seven-colored doves in the sky.

A Crowd is Always A Fat Man

A crowd is always a fat man
Too fearful in size to appease.
It does nothing according to plan
And sways with creating unease.

Feeding it gives it dimension.
It sweats in its groin to devour
When something gets its attention
Whatever the day or the hour.

Its surges are its insistence.
Its affirmations are howls,
Hooted with loony persistence
In long and unadorned vowels.

It must be fed, so it orders
Victims be brought out like food,
But notice when after it murders
A distinctive change in its mood.

Fairy Tales

I marveled at stories when I was young,
lying upsidedown, of hideous Magotines

put to unrelenting trials like dupes,
cuffed, forced to wear tiny iron shoes,

of lost Ursulas, wilting in dungeons,
having to separate millet from barley,

of tasks, to cross a bridge of knives
for proof of love. Chivalry is hope.

Lying is always right and always wrong,
where right side up is only point of view

and irony in simple story, simple song,
teaches what alone by lying can be true.

What hobbling malignancy stumps forward,
like cats, frogs, trolls, does not last,

and Hidessa, kissing a mottled beast
but finding a sudden prince in her arms,

made red-and-blue cloth books for me
what real life in brutal battles never was.

Alexander Cups

No cheat is a buffoon the way he steals,
For guile in all the darkness it portends,
The way it takes advantage of its friends,
Lies and wounds and hurts and never feels,
Is never clownish, so is not absolved
Of traits that it prefers to think it shows
That indicates by wit it something knows
And therefore from a species rare evolved.
You are a thief, a thug, a food stamp cheat,
A lackey sucking up to authors, hacks,
Servile, patting Klub Kids on their backs,
A failure, hitting women in defeat.
And yet how darkness irony revokes!
For all your mal you're still the butt of jokes.

Larry Tucker

I know an oaf who changed his name from Larry,
Ate far more than he could lift, was on the dole,
Stole money from his girl, wrote very scary
Prose as scrimp and nugatory as his midget soul.
He published trash in 'zines but came to find
That while even using a fake name as a blind
All storms of great applause were in his mind.

Cape Cod Cats

They run cranberrybogward
and can find the wind in humid shade
by merely smell.

They smell like seasails,
green pinefur, sand, wet boxwoodbreath,
and merry hell.

They sit on waiting hills
perfectly aware that fishwhite chowders
sort of yell.

The Threat of Loss Revives Desire

The dire threat of loss revives desire
In those who once considered love a game,
Who turned away while others burned with fire
And stood aloof and untouched by the flame.
A lover spurned can suddenly go numb,
As if an executioner perforce
The unloved victim spurned by pain becomes,
And loses passion, loses all remorse.
The wheel of fortune, lo, turns fully round,
Reversing moods that neither pleas nor prayers
Nor vows nor time nor succor ever found
Answered by the loved one's prior cares.
Now, let her attend, not shape, her fate
And stand beneath the window green and wait.

Kirillov

In memory of Vera Ivanovna Zasulich

There is no loss of sun
As I hold this gun
Filled with empty dreams
Should I use it? Why can't I abuse it, as a toll?
Let God alone allow for someone else's schemes.

Although my hopes have ended
I have befriended
As a simple means
A real solution to the revolution in my soul.
Let God alone let someone else make scenes.

Leon and Traci

How love in making one of disparate souls
Unites by passion two and binds their hearts!
An infinity of hope enrolls
Each to each, and loneliness departs.
We can say with lovers in a way
Always east meets west, as short meets tall,
A serious in a loving soul-mate play,
With always one to hear and one to call,
As fire relies on wind and air to flame.
No couple is not made of elements
Diverse, yet always something of the same
Is found by love in Cana's sacrament.
Love's the mystery that's first begun
Of two diverging complements made one.

Mohel with his Mouth Open

Overweight from salty lox, I come
with a sickle, approaching the reality of evil,
sharper than shrapnel.

I am unfederated as Burma.
No weenie can withstand my numinous energy
    as I trundle house to house,

    keen in my wide black hat,
no versicolorings, no coat of many colors, only the
    acoustic shadow, dark,

    of what once was there, untribally,
offending G-d, like my protuberant belly,
    fire-hot with rollmops, schmaltz herring,

    honeycake, schmeers of cream cheese.
A bris is a taste of blood and ugly howls. Please,
    celebrations are as much the cause

    of my professional fat as weakness
for food. Stop feeding me kugelach, friends,
    no more cakes and fluden!

    A raised knife is a tool ascetic.
my fat and froward fingers were designed to cut,
    not cruddle kreplach.

Culver City, 1930

for Pola Negri and Lya de Putti

There was an odd community giddiness
in that orangeade-stand shaped like a pagoda,
but I must add a fabulous wittiness.
A cuckoo man with a head like a leek
served me a squash with an Ecuadorian odor
in a glass that was wearing a beak.

Two Toucans

Two toucans per dead tree
seems to be the jungle rule. They perch
clucking yellow-mottled beaks

— no wingbeats — like castanets,
"Hi-kyuck; kyuck! Hi-kyuck, kyuck! Kyuck!"
They shift warily on the trunk

of two dead stubs, wicca-like,
but risible amid the ropy woody liana vines,
black-bodied, with hues like uproars,

birds who in clucking twos
from big bright beaks held straight ahead
by sharing views make laughter.

All Roys Are Fat

All Roys are fat but tubbiness can't hurt
in everything that life presents of choice.
Don't push away that wet dessert.
Doesn't size allow a fuller voice?
Portliness by definition makes a ring.
I say eat the head off anything.
If a belt's too short around your waist, try string.
What is comic usually can sing.

Obstacles

Rose Cullen: "What you want and what you settle for are not often the same."
Luis Denard: "And often what you want is no good either."

The Confidential Agent (1945)

Obstacles reveal
desire by what we fear prevents
success. What we desire often
masks the desire of the obstacle,
cold unlike the fire of miracle.
Don't we tend to use obstacles
because we badly want to forget?
Or to make what we don't do
simply more exciting? Surely
we love heroes because
they're brave enough to succeed
in living than for having first
been willing to die.

Desire is but
a mystery, in the way obstacles
create desire. Why would we need
to wish if nothing were in the way?
Desires don't reveal the obstacle,
obstacles reveal our desires,
in the burning way we all suspect
that loving is a way of being sold.
Coldness may be the way we need
to find we require fire. So much
for the heat of dreams, so much
for desire; with heat we plead
but forever identify with cold.

Titters

"...and his pharmacist, Titterington,
whom King Farouk called Titters. Titters was
the official food taster for the wary king."
William Stadiem, *Too Rich*

Talk about a full-time job! Try working for Sr. Fatty Farouk
As taster of gourmet delicacies and primary kitchen spook!

I pity you, poor Titters, than whom no one had more to ingest.
Poor tummy, colon, sphincter, to say nothing of heart and chest.

He turned down almost nothing that came in sight of his head,
Yalandji dolmas, salade Gauloise, and along with garlic bread

Things like *dinde de Fayoum rotie froid á la gelée d'or,*
Often wagging the while to amuse a tart a libidinous petit-four.

For the bald and gluttonous Egyptian King food was a way of life,
a passion reserved for the table most other men kept for a wife.

Tubby often began a repast with a *soupe de mer à l'Orientale*
Or *consommé de volaille froid* swimming with handpicked dal,

Followed by two or three cutlets, *poularde de Bresse Lamberty,*
And a superbly delectable *galantine de Faison d'Écosse truffée.*

Nothing left the imperial kitchen, not a crumb or crust but that
It had the health and benediction of your gastronomic *éclat.*

Three hundred pounds plus of royalty could eat a cow or an ox,
Adding platters of *charlotte aux fruits,* crusty bagels and lox,

Then crisp *agneau de lait à la bergère, baklava pyrimidal,*
Asperges en branches sauce jaune, an *amuse bouche* of ginger ale,

A wipe of the brow, wet *friandises, glacés assorties,* and then
Fresh tronçon de saumon (on a platter of gold) *à la Vénitienne.*

Were you not tempted to tell us what of all foods most pleased
Sire Farouk? The truth? Orangeade — and macaroni and cheese!

Of sucking cigars in a dirty cloud? Of eyeaches like *mal de mer*?
Of getting sick and stomach sore? Falling asleep in your chair?

And how could he find the energy to toss tiny pellets of bread
Aiming to hit fellow diners (they say) right on top of the head?

I have a question you must have been asked more than once
By petty gossips, court inquisitors, and every passing dunce:

What food did you fail to sample during that last dinner in Rome
In the Ile de France restaurant when he was in exile from home?

The word is, many assassins were lurking about in 19 and 65,
When Nasser, ruling the country, was angry the king was alive,

And that some spook with alacontin, on food prepared before,
Killed the fat king the second he tasted the lobster thermidor.

I don't doubt for a minute, dear Titters, you bear a lot of guilt
When you reflect (a) on the milk and (b) the way it was spilt,

But few would contest the staring fact, if not without a sob,
That, although you suffered yourself, you did a thorough job.

What in death, I wonder, might be justly inscribed on your stone
That would summarize for posterity a way that you should atone

For leaving so open to mortal peril one you were sworn to defend
Even if only by tasting a giblet, some figs, or a single celery end.

Of many saws suggesting themselves one perhaps most rings true.
I can see it in yellow marble, "To Titters: *Chaque á son gout*!"

Bigotry is Ugly

"Dear Georgie! Screw the Arabs - but for God's sake, stop
saluting Generals! Love Jackie. 4/21/69" — inscription on a
book to George Jessel from Jacqueline Susann

"Arabs and Other Animals" — Erica Jong, a chapter title in
Fear of Flying

"Arabs are Dogs" — Rabbi Meir Kahane

"Every house owned a Koran, but almost no one knew how
to read it." — Leon Uris, *The Haj,* the novel as calumny, a
600 pp. racist attack on Muslims

"I get very nervous when — Arab-Americans, fine. Just
show me where it says, 'I want to live in peace.' That's all I
want. I want you to have a good time. You believe what you

want, I believe what I want. But I don't want to hear that
you're out to get me. And that does scare me."

— Joan Rivers

"They're stupid. Their religion is as ugly as they are" —
Rabbi Ovadia Yosef, the ultra-orthodox Jewish spiritual
leader, on Muslims. "Non-Jews were born only to serve us."

Jewish women are bilious cranks
Who'd step on God to score a bargain hat
They have profiles long as foot-long franks
And will squeeze a narrow dime 'til it shits fat.
They utter not a word they do not whine,
Rush with delight to every goy malign,
Spit at every Arab face in Palestine.

Jewish women are mechanical banks
Who all devour money when they fuck.
They ring like bells in comic thanks
And grow in value buck by added buck.
Push your coin into the metal groove,
Iron arms and legs begin to move,
One clanging hump per clanging shove.

Jewish women prefer to marry wanks
Who are as servile and as bald as eggs,
Carry cash and scurry at their flanks,
Race to buy them gifts, yip about their legs.
They are sexless as a burlap bag unraveling.
They have two right hands for grabbeling.
No railroad train is louder traveling.

A Kiss for Cynthia

There sits Cynthia
Cold as Corinthea
Her vulva big as a store.
With far less etiquette
In the state of Connecticut
Than your average ten-cent whore.

Staring is Black

Staring has an awful gust of force
that participates in fact in something physical
in that it emanates, radiates.

Stupid Susan, flat as Winnipeg,
with her molrowing lack of grace and style,
loved to try to look you down,

but who fell for it? Not me.
Bad manners gave her away, slow but urgent,
as convolvulus smothers a buss,

and her precipitate fascinatio,
hot, crude, well-known ploy of the sociopath,
brazen, like her muddy eyes,

when it tried to cookie-cut you
only left her glaring, atrociously and dumb.
No, that black, black staring

had nothing of the jararacussu
serpent despite the toxic way she fronted me,
other than its fanged persistence,

although blackness in the world
for all its improcreance never doesn't matter,
even, stupid staring Susan, yours.

Boston Girls

(song lyric)

I'm never more awake than when I dream of Boston girls
I goggle every skirt in Copley Square.
When a beauty with surmise
Smiles at me with lowered eyes
I click my heels and dance like Fred Astaire.
And when perchance I board the street-car
And the bell for Boylston squirls
You will see me crane my neck
Checking — what the heck! —
For the lilt, for the tilt, for the gilt
for the lovely guilt of watching bouncing curls.
Should I spy a girl I like
Whose skirt I'd like to hike
I would reconnoiter without pause
To enlist among my cause — *caaaaaaaaause* [altogether]
I'm never more awake than when I dream of Boston girls.
I'm never more awake than when I dream of Boston girls.
I am never more *awake* than when I dream of Boston girls.

Zoroaster and Mrs. Titcomb

There is an ancient tale, told over ale,
In the village of Breadville many a night,
Of a mysterious stranger, darker than danger,
Who once inexplicably came into sight.

He appeared all in black to a vicious old hack
Who sold fish from a shanty down by the dunes,
Some say cursing and some say rehearsing
Weird, indecipherable, uncanny runes.

Looking quite tubby, less wife than hubby,
Oval of face and spinnaker fat
— the floor always shook with each step that she took —
Titcomb always unhooked the slat

On the door of her shop, bidding all stop
Until her pet ferret she punted away
Whose hideous shriek seemed to come from the beaks
Of gulls by her windows who darkened the day.

A fish-shop in Breadville can be like a treadmill
When winters keep you from walking abroad,
So with footsteps unerring we purchased the herring
That slovenly Titcomb threw in with the cod.

Of our foul little village, harbor and spillage
(A troughway that ran through the center of town),
Old Tits was the bitchiest, by far the witchiest,
Sow who could make the sun even frown.

She was given to farting and endlessly carting
Barrels of sprats to the edge of the quay,
Where tikes without waists pleaded for tastes
But she'd pitch the lot right into the sea.

According to rumor, told not without humor,
She had sliced her old man with a fish-knife she wore
In a cold rubber liner swinging near her vagina
Under a smock smeared with entrails and gore.

Old townies say, stare though you may,
That one night out back by the traps and the mesh
What once thought was haddock out on the paddock
Had the rank fetid odor of real human flesh!

She gossiped, she lied, she cheated, she spied.
For squinting at scales her eyes were adept.
What sort of strapping did she use for wrapping?
Sheets from a King James Bible she kept!

No laws of a mayor nor minister's prayer,
Nothing could stop the hideous fact
Of a malevolence that crushed the benevolence
Of everyone simply by her every act.

She sold squid and pike, rockfish and tripe,
Complained that people stole fish from her place,
And during one sale a stranger turned pale
As she wagged a clam rake an inch from his face,

Who'd question the cost of fish eaten by lice?
But something was different in this dark exchange,
The tall man's dark eyes clouded over like skies
And over his face came a terrible change,

Which odd condition, with his inquisition,
Brought from her every invective and curse.
He was a magician and with your permission
Now comes a significant turn in this verse.

A stranger, I say, who came by the way,
Someone whom Breadville had never quite seen,
Wearing jet black from the front to the back
And bearing a raven with uncanny sheen

On his tall shoulder and what seemed even bolder
A long pointed feather stood aslant in his cap.
"My name's Zoroaster," with a voice like disaster
He whispered, his face an inscrutable map,

And said he was needful of fish but, unheedful,
The bitter old hag was typically cruel,
"I am here to perform — by magic, transform —
A miracle rare for those yearning for gruel,

Which I do out of care on this earth once a year,
Gathering all those who for the truth yearn,
Fish multiplying and bread for the dying,
Asking only a change of heart in return.

Always I choose, without bruiting the news
Of what is my mission and what is my hope,
One single creature of no definite feature
Whose acts must determine my annual scope."

He stared at the hag, the nasty old nag,
"But what find I here of worth or of merit?
Here is no kindness, only the blindness
Of a fat and fatuous fool and a ferret.

Is Breadville the world? Evil unfurled?
Are you alone the despair that I see?
Do poor men still labor? Neighbor hate neighbor?
With misery everywhere, mercilessly?"

And then with cold fire he pointed a dire
Finger at Titcomb who exploded in bits,
Like a fragmented moon, a broken balloon,
With a noise like sound itself losing its wits.

Within a mere second, as if he were beckoned,
The snarling ferret leaped but was caught
There in mid-air by the dark stranger's stare,
Which killed the scarlet-eyed beast on the spot.

Nobody then saw the stranger again,
Though a banquet was held the following day
With much bread and fish piled onto each dish
And peace and goodwill holding sway.

Decades have passed, but thoughts are still cast
Back to that horripilant hour of fear
When a generous feast followed on the decease
Of two beasts for whom not a soul shed a tear.

One thing is mentioned whenever conventions
Of folk in Breadville sit down to drink,
A tale of suspicion, involving contrition,
As if people fear to say what they think.

Had real bread been threshed from real human flesh?
And fish from ferret, as is commonly told?
Was the strange rumor true that the man somehow knew
What his visit to lowly Breadville would hold?

A very old sentence we hear in repentance:
"From dust man is fashioned and thus into dust
He soon must return," although we would learn
The final meaning of why it was just

For a phantom so rare thus to appear
In a village of such dissent and disunion,
Kill two useless souls, like emptying bowls,
And serve them up as a kind of communion.

What of the bird who never once stirred
But looked on as if it were having a treat?
It was later repeated it watched smugly seated
With all of the pomp of a black Paraclete.

What can be said of this tale of the dead?
Let me pose to the riddling reader, forsooth.
A symbol? A story? A dark allegory?
A fable offered to tease out a truth?

Where Zoroaster in the form of the master
Of a dark universe coming down from the sky
By an act of mystery as a fact of history
Leaves you a problem to figure out? Try.

Dr. Seuss's Eyes

Dr. Seuss's eyes were U's,
Whether painted greens or blues,
And whereas grammar this defies
Truly all his U's were eyes.

Dr. Seuss's U's were eyes.
This the Golden Rule revives
And Mr. Buber's wish renews!
Dr. Seuss's eyes were U's.

Black Booty Blues

Headin' down to Memphis
Find me a high-steppin' brown

Headin' down to Memphis
Find me a high-steppin' brown

Slip on my crocodile shoes
And go truckin' that jit round town.

Gonna put on my porkpie
Be like I used to was

Gonna put on my porkpie
Be like I used to was

I wanna jellyroll my mama
Like them sports on Beale St. does.

+

Where be that yola who
Lookin' to a bang my drum

Where be that yola who
Lookin' to a bang my drum

Plan to rotate that child 'til
She be moanin' under my thumb.

+

Need me some redbone,
Spotlight on Sassy Sue.

Need me some heavy redbone,
Spotlight Miss Sassy Sue.

When that fryer she turn up
Hope to did what I gonna do.

+

Had me a taste of some satinin
Chocolate drop supreme

Had me a taste of some satinin
Chocolate drop supreme

A shag and a shot of sugar
In the arms of a laundry queen.

+

I seen me a mess of fine women
In this world far and wee

O, I seen me a mess of fine women
In this wide world far and wee

I tell ya, black booty olny
Be gettin the job done for me.

Football Star

An oaf in a helmet's an American paradigm.
Women cream to see his bulging buns.
They bow and scrape like craven slucks for him
Whose baleful stare is like a set of guns.
So they create in him what they demand:
When not a fat fuck waving to the stands,
A killer in the dock with hanging hands.

The way we love to give away our freedom
— and who are bigger dunces than fans,
Including all the tarts who fuck and feed 'em
And all those tubby owners to a man? —
To ogle dongs without IQs at play!
How paradoxically that we betray
The very selves we freely give away.

I loathe the refuge that we need in crowds.
A uniform by definition kills
An individual who put in shrouds
Is oddly waked by monkey-howling shills
Who root for some giganto with a ball
Don't dwarves revere anything that's tall?
Filthy in the mud and white with spawl.

Save me from those cretins in the stands
Who madly chant as if they're seeking prey
While always making gestures with their hands,
Clawing all they wish to rip away.
Calling this a game is purely fiction.
A din is reason's dereliction.
There is joy at every crucifixion.

Postcard From L.A., 1937

I am squinting at Los Angeles!
What cheekshine! Round peach-colored mirrors!
  Lobbies paneled in black glass!

  Sunshine heats me like the boil!
Who could not see me with this bowl of clafouti,
  flaring cherries, melonballs of green,

  and not — in this galaxy arcade
shadowed only by a Hebrew hairer than you,
  wolfing down a hot tagine,

  a Joses whose ugly gabardine
shines bright as floors, lapels, men's shoes,
  ladies' gowns and slicked-down hair

  of Vitrolite, Catalin, and Bakelite —
yearn to peep through Grable's crystal plastic heels
  and howl hello to Hollywood like me!

May Sarton Never Had A Baby

I am no maximalist fatso, besides
my cat has a bladder infection. And woman's
  share in ontological reality is fraught

with loud tromboning males to wet you.
A clairaudient confided to me once in Maine
  to start to write gynoecious verses,

all lovelily à propos to me.
When Garbo said she would die a bachelor
  in film she spoke to me.

Then, my garden takes my time,
of indigo loosetrife, parsley, dock, and whin,
  with its blue electric stare,

reminding me of my uniqueness,
even if by fools I badly tend to be confused
  with May Swenson and Margaret Yourcenar!

Don't you see my *poems* are tikes?
And so what dumpy cassowary of a mother can ever
  match in me what I feel of fire?

Milkfeed whom you will and bake
quoit pies for all your dirty rug-rats in mid howl,
  vaticides at the breast.

Vissi d'arte! I have my pen
and dunk it in *my* ink for *my* own words, thank you,
  all round and beautiful as quim!

Catherine Linton's Love

If Heathcliff had not returned a gentleman,
elegant in that sharp frock coat for me,
since grown used to life far better than
idle vows pledged underneath some tree,
love had failed, precisely where it lacks.
Where is comfort when missing in a life?
A tragedy, you say, but it exacts
the proper toll on one who'd be a wife.
And so I fell in love when he achieved,
in his becoming lord of an estate,
without which he'd not have been received,
but yet he proved a master of his fate.
His wealth rubbed clean his youthful dirty hands.
I needed him *successful*. There it stands.

Canadian Names

Westbrook, Otway, Davis, and Stith,
MacDonald, Pearson, and Smoot,
Ryerson, Robertson, Massey, and Smith,
McWilliams, Frye, and Canute.

Cameron, Hardwick, Thompson, and Vaughan,
Stewart, Ridley, and Ross,
Inchbald, Ramsay, Dobson, and Strawn,
Parkinson, Newbald, and Voss.

Arbuckle, Murray, Renfrew, and Jones,
Bryant, Wallace, and Bennett,
Espy, Gardner, Campbell, and Stones,
Jowett, Jarvis, and Sennott.

Kingston, Urquart, Guthrie, and Gride,
Snavely, Brawley, and Powell.
Wouldn't you think in a whole country wide
One name would end in a vowel?

The Anza Borrego Desert

In the heart of the Anza Borrego
where heat flames up out of hell
I smell premonitions of demolition
Like echoes where noise itself fell.

Nothing beckons, nothing is fixed.
An ocean of greasewood and stone
Stares up at the sarcastic sun in a silence
That in dryness is whiter than bone.

Thin men with haunted eyes
And shoulders hunched like a rook
Wear pig-stickers strapped to their legs and seem
To throw them at you when they look.

Badlands, scoria, rockledge, and sink
Reveal there a curious weave
In which curious shadows and scorpions
Vie in the night to deceive.

There is neither dark shade nor direction,
Only ocotillo studded with thorn
That seem with the mountains like altars to say
One needs to be slain to be born.

So I enter the Anza Borrego
With a hope as for something to save
But look into the heart of that emptiness
As I would stare down to my grave.

Chapultepec Crunch

Candy in Mexico is shaped like a human skull.
I have an imagination arrow-long and still.
No black words screeched by a poverty trull
More sharply defines the earth and its kill

Than being allowed to eat our common head,
After fleshly pudding and pulp is gone.
So smack your lips of powdery, sugary thread,
White like the orts of horrible, gnawable bone.

A Fat Woman's Blocked My Passage All My Life

A fat woman's blocked my passage all my life
As if Satan put this bolo there to try
My patience, waving as somehow would a wife
Always at the corner of my eye.
I see her geometrically a loop,
A dirigible, a fucking tub, a hoop,
A peridrome, a monstrous fruit, a drupe.

What does she impersonate by hair,
Bristling like cacti with sharp thorns?
Dumb as a box of rocks she bulketh there,
Immune to imprecations, shouts, or horns.
What keeps this person rooted to the spot?
To be so round yet never roll a jot?
Don't women need to use the john a lot?

Won't some creature please remove this stone
From before my sepulchre so I
Can resurrect and so proceed alone.
Instead of waiting here with her to die?
Move it, porky! Shift that fat caboose!
I've a gun! And you're a grazing moose!
Want to learn the meaning of a goose?

Where is she going that she has to put
Directly in my path that massive bum,
Shifting mindlessly from foot to foot,
While adding, to my discontent a hum?
Her inability to move resembles NATO.
As she squats there like a huge potato.
Going where? Who knows, including Plato.

Christmas Card Malice

Their Christmas card, postmarked on the 23rd,
is to guarantee — lest having been deferred

or sent far too previously upon its way —
that it be mailed precisely on that day

that you receive it, exactly on the 24th.
A nasty mind, as frigid as Santa's north,

conceives this as a way, let it be clear,
that the Tartuffe who sent it may appear

to be the soul of kindness and concern,
in whom the blazing fires of friendship burn.

But what in fact is being said is this,
that you, whose card they looked for, were remiss

in caring just a whit that they exist,
even as a simple item on a list,

otherwise they'd have surely heard from you,
even if only a season's obligation to renew.

My point is that final postal day is proof
that once again *you* have remained aloof,

while they have proved they're loyal to the end
by simply pointing to the Xmas card they send

to show that, while they are loyal, you are not.
So you in turn are sold by what they bought.

Giving, you see, can be an act of spite,
the gift that kills, a kindness to indict,

allowing for your "loyal" friends and true
to mail their great Noël salute: "*Fuck you!*"

Everyone's Head Describes A Bum

Everyone's head describes a bum.
It seats you for the life you have to face.
In the way it beats you it's a drum.
I own up to mine with some disgrace.
Bounce it down the stairway of the years,
With its wrinkles, buttock cheeks, and tears,
Born of bumps and thumps and slaps and fears.

Signor Križevac At the Met

A Croat in a cravat,
sings his mandatory "boola boola,"
standing in blue light,

as gladness runs above
in boxes where opera buffs madly clap
to sweeping vibrations,

like a silken scarf
undulating up and down in waves. A swap
is made in spangled light:

both are only noise,
a *strozzapreti* part going and coming.
What is offered in song

is returned in applause
to go hooping round like that cravat,
round and loud and black,

on that singing fat Croat
who, on the run from grabbing claps,
sweeps off the stage,

having gathered in a
spotlight on a blue and spangled stage
his mandatory "boola boola."

Ceylon's Isle

I dreamt I had a glimpse of you
as if with the beauty of a child
running in the blowing soft
wind of Ceylon's isle.
But when I woke, I came to see
as though I'd seen a child depart,
the blowing wind on Ceylon's isle,
had blown away my heart.

Babe Paley Passes Away

"She had not a glimmer of having a soul."
— an intimate of hers

On her deathbed, clawing her gold evening bag
toward her, Babe selected a cigarette and puffed.

She regarded her Japanese bronze monkey
holding a peach-shaped box where she used to stash her pearls.

At night she still wore makeup. The Cushing sisters,
Betsey, Minnie, and Babe, owned Corots, Louis XVI chairs,

emerald rings, ceramic crab tureens, rich leather bags,
expensive dogs, candlesticks shaped like porcelain frogs.

Mother Gogs had warned all of them to marry well,
which of course to all of them meant marry wealth.

Babe dined at La Grenouille wearing her hair
plumed like a parrot, sent thank-you notes from yachts,

and dreamt of idly walking barefoot across clouds
in a black Mainbocher dress with everyone agog.

She sipped wine that sparkled in tubular flutes
shaped as thin, as frail, as asparagus shoots.

Once, she read a book. "She had enormous sense,"
recalled Diana Vreeland later, who knew important

people had good bones and always set the social rank
as internationally best-dressed women always do.

Time however passed in its own way — and *now*
rising from Porthault sheets soiled with diarrhea

and needing her bidet in the shape of an elephant,
Babe yanked the owl-head bellpull to call her nurse

but up rolled something entirely else, all lacquered
black and ominous in the shape of a waiting hearse.

A Sonnet for Margot

Composed on the Occasion of her Christening, May 5, 1996

A third child always has a mythic sense
Deep within that others never see,
Certain gifts, legend says, from whence
Mystic attributes, like lock and key,
Together work to solve those mysteries
Others of less prescience fail to do.
Legend also says a grace and ease
In such a child's attendant through and through.
Sweet Margot, as in splendor tall you grow,
By your mystic birthright intervene
For us when lost that we might better know
Not a puzzled state but one serene.
Enchant us as today we you caress,
And know, bewitching us, you also bless.

Truro

I felt the wind from Truro
As it blew across graves and graves
With all the grief of a hopeless tomorrow
And the sorrow of passing days.

In misty dusk it awakened
The bell of the ocean buoys
With a sound as if God himself had forsaken
Me with the saddest noise.

A darkness vast as a cloud
Shadowed the harbor like pain
And the empty and desolate sky wept out loud
In sheets of ruinous rain.

No comfort found I or cover
For the wind and the sky and the sea
Without mercy repeated over and over
You'd never come back to me.

I felt the wind from Truro
As it blew across graves and graves
With the promise of a hopeless tomorrow
And the sorrow of passing days.

Hebrew and Jew

Which do we choose between Hebrew and Jew,
Select one or the other or something new,

Deem by a faith or judge by a nation?
The Young Men's *Hebrew* Association,

Official name, was formally given.
So explain the Council of *Jewish* Women?

How distinguish one from the other?
Judaeans don't walk along brother to brother?

What's the right term, guy with the beanie,
Please say which (I know it's not sheeny),

Israeli, Judaean, Hassid, or Ham
Goes best with Benny, Heimie, or Sam?

Jewish cooking's the proper phrase,
And never once in all my born days

Has Hebrew cooking ever been seen.
(Maybe some variant like "Polish Cuisine"!)

How can equally both be acknowledged,
A place called *Hebrew* Union College

But then as if out of perversity
The *Jewish* Theological Seminary?

Don't blame me, I didn't invent it;
I'm looking only to circumvent it.

Want a fact that will blow your mind?
You can find both names combined

At the same time! Both of them used!
Now try to tell me you're not confused.

The American Hebrew and Jewish Tribune
— a name as redundant as lunar moon —

Is a principal weekly of that very race,
So why not simply choose one as the case?

Isn't redundancy always illogical
In things avoidably tautological?

So how then explain the multiple name?
A trick? A joke? A riddle? A game?

It sharply points, this odd condition,
To that people's penchant for acquisition.

Remember when once Jack Benny was asked
For his money or his life by a man in a mask,

Getting radio laughs from Denver to Dover,
He paused and replied, "I'm thinking it over"?

What he wanted to say, which isn't as funny,
As gravely he pondered life without money,

Was clearly what every Jew would have said
Who wanted both cash and not to be dead.

The thief he'd survey and, as if by rote,
Then cagily ask him, "*Vi kent I hef bot?*"

The Katabasis of Lizzie Borden

Fall River assumed she was bugfuck,
Smug with her thrash-metal hair,
As she sat in the dock watching the clock
With a most pathological stare.
In ten minutes she was roundly acquitted
And dismissed as if with a push,
But townspeople lowly tortured her slowly
As convolvulus smothers a bush.

At the Congregational church,
Surrounded by vacant pews,
She prayed alone in her stays of bone
As her neighbors tightened the screws.
So she quickly threw over religion
To feed birds and squirrels instead
And spent her Sundays as if they were Mondays
Idly sipping oolong in bed.

She bought a house with the money
The death of her parents allowed her
Sister Emma moved out which followed a bout
Of queerness that started to crowd her.
She wore mittens when sipping her cocoa,
Attended the opera at night,
She was heard to squeal with a friend Nance O'Neil
And wore hats as black as a kite.

A further alienation continued
From neighbors who called her inept:
She came up with a sketch for a workman to etch
The house name on her front step.
"Maplecroft" she denoted it
And once on the front porch stood by;
Beangooses passed her with looks of disaster
But she never batted an eye.

Living on after the murders,
In years more than three times eleven,
She departed this rubble with gall bladder trouble
In nineteen and twenty seven.
She spoke never a word of her terrible case
Before taking her final trip
But left scads of money on a June that was sunny
To someone named Adelaide Whipp.

Crucifix and Circle

Eratosthenes configured
the circumference of the Earth,
knowing the solstice would work well
in relation to zenith and girth.
He thereby explained the circle
and Cyrene was his place of birth.

Simon was also there born
who, conscripted by Roman force,
to relieve the Dei Genitrix
was ordered to carry his cross.
We connect him thus to the Crucifix
and no small amount of remorse.

Two earthly shapes elemental
can consequently be traced
to this singular city of old:
a figure round as a face,
a line horizontally bold
to a vertical one interlaced.

Christ died upon both of them,
the cross and circle, as well.
He was nailed to a cross of wood
to buy us salvation from hell.
To earth he brought only good
and by us he was murdered pell-mell.

I See Only The Roses Of Shadows

I see only the roses of shadows
and the somber lilac of shades
in a garden where recollection
with your face like memory fades.

No green was ever as hopeful,
nor gold, as our passionate love,
in that garden where once your eyes
shone as blue as the heaven above.

We walked in each other's angles,
to trouble we both turned our backs,
for we would taste nothing of white
and would touch nothing of black.

A change soon came upon us
like the close of a perfect day,
followed by violet weeping,
and then there was empty gray.

I see roses only as shadows
and lilacs as somber shades
in a garden where recollection
with your face like memory fades.

Van Gogh's Concept of Crows

I sat in the Café Tribulaix,
    sipping my citronade,
when a pie-headed tart in black sable sloped by
    with a nose like a blending blade.

I breathed a quip as an African guy
    with acidulous caricature
posed unembarrassed before her table
    and said he was Mr. Lohr.

She smiled at his face round as a *boule*,
    Titine and this blackamoor,
him with his feet limousine long
    under that Levantine whore.

An apache sprouting a scarab ring,
    flinging off his black cape,
stomped across the crepuscular light
    and angrily called him an ape.

The paint of the woman's muscat eyes
    in the loudness started to smear
when the coon was shot and dragged away
    by a sable-plumed carabinière.

I wobbled home drunk and from my box
　　selected a stick to compose
the canvas that made up my final effort,
　　Wheatfield With Flying Crows.

Mercuria

She gave thanks,
like the Mussolini regime reconstituted depleted banks.
She said honey,
the way he credited depositors with 20% of their money.
She was loyal,
As he to the trusting populace ultimately proved royal.
She disappeared,
So please may she be treated the way the Duce was spared.

The Weird of the Wanderer

I'll kill myself at Grasmere, very near Wordsworth's grave,
Where the woods with trees are clawed so sharp
That my merciless soul as it tries to depart,
Torn as cruelly as you tore my heart,
May serve in shreds to make strings for a harp
That I might seem by song as something God would save.

Meadow Glen Drive-In

As tenderly I cradled your head in my arms,
guarding you against the cone-headed monster

in the closet in *The Brain That Wouldn't Die* (1959)
both of us, frankly, profiling lust in kind,

me and the hairless freakazoid, I mean, not you,
smelling of hot puffs of hair wash and perfume,

a *maja* in a semi-crouch in my Dodge backseat,
dizzying me with plumulaceous kisses, always

greasy pink, I myself yearned to ravish you,
soft-center bon-bon with your cheap scent,

far heavier with promises than any God,
sexier than those rare and musky unguents

by Pitou worn by such old tarts revenged upon
by giant bats, trained to sniff strange lotions,

in *The Devil Bat* (1940), with Bela Lugosi,
Dave O'Brien, and Suzanne Kaaren. We saw them all.

The Embalmer (1966) where in the murky sewers
of Venice beautiful girls were snuffed and stuffed!

The She Beast (1966) where sexy Barbara Steele
transformed to an ancient sorceress — in color!

On those summer nights, more humid with greed,
oh, far more heavily humid with purpureal need,

than any shanty tramp in the sinister cinema,
what deep noirissimo thoughts I had of you!

Were the hair-fetish murders in *Violated* (1954)
foreign to me? Those mutt-faced bikers with VD

in *Savages From Hell* (1968) haunting that poor
foolish girl with truncheons and testosterone,

possibly any worse? The rutting rapistoleros
in *The Beast of Yucca Flats* (1961)? Not a bit.

I was *The Screaming Skull* (1958), headlong
into swollen fantasies, crepuscular as my old car,

dirtier by far than those howling Hottentot
blimp-bulbs in *Terror of the Bloodhunters* (1962)!

Trust me, I was miniaturized by a base intent
no weirder than those by creepy old Mr. Wacko

in *Fantastic Puppet People* (1958), who, keeping
his victims in small glass tubes, occasionally

took them out, as on our date I did with you,
to stem the emotional strains of solitude.

I was wet! I was wild! I was *Black Torment* (1964)!
The Creature From the Black Lagoon (1957)!

It was I! The ravishing rampage of crawling fury!
You remember, moon-breasted babysitter, don't you,

the screaming telephone calls to warn you that
some twisted and perverted droolie, hot to attack,

was in fact upstairs???? I must confess to you
now, in diabolicolor: *He was there in the car!*

To the Poetry Editor of *Yankee* Magazine Ms. Jean Burden

Were the poems I sent too scrimp,
or just too rich, making allusions
  Cow Hampshirites can't fathom,

  or was it simply, sitting there
with woodshed pencils, you computed
  that you simply had to pay

  for them, always a sore point
among folks widely known for being
  tighter than a duck's rectum?

  My guess is something else:
you merely wanted more pie poems,
  nice didactic things

about farmers fabricating
hog-proof fences and grey rocky walls
   as metaphysical shrines

to ingenuity, or of Miss Bump
down there in Henniker having soulful
   dreams of finding apple-weather love.

Editing's no easy task, I know,
I know, you with your fussy hairnet
   and red plaid anklesocks,

but, really, having taste,
although, I realize, not a native gift
   is something you should try.

Lavinia Miloşovici

A gymnast with a tulip face, so young,
   with every daring turn my heart you steal,
   you move so fast as if by nature sprung
   across the mat revolving like a wheel.
I love your pony tail, your pert doe eyes,
   the tension as you wait with powdered hands,
   your boyish nates and buttocks no disguise
   against the love your girlish grace demands.
But whether on the parallel or high bar
   or standing on the balance beam before
   you do a perfect somersault in air,
I must confess, fawn-like Olympic star,
   there is no way that I could love you more
   unless a leap into my heart you'd dare.

Mao

No one born in the reaches of subtropical Hunan,
alert with inner rage for the bite of spice,

a forking bite with heat that never fails to fan
a heat that like a demon can envenom rice,

won't often fail himself to fan with inner rage
with just as hot a breath in everything he teaches

those in need of heat tramping through an age
who then become infected by everything he teaches.

Mao adored red pepper, like other Hunanese.
He shook it on his eggs, on soup, and once upon on a cat

he ate when starving, skin and bones and grease.
He shook it on a star and put it on his hat.

146

Mahogany Trees

Mahogany trees, desolate and bare,
forever dropping dying leaves,
look stark, the way a lover's stare
betrays something that it thieves.

Mahogany trees with empty eaves,
in being stripped and always spare,
recall the way a lover grieves
when learning someone doesn't care.

Should we find consolation fair
that our broken heart retrieves
solace where nature so bereaves
or should it blacken our despair?

Among Tears

(song lyric)

Why do I love? Why bother caring?
What do I have? How am I sharing?
When will you feel the pull of my heart?
Where is the logic in standing apart?
I hear you say, O, I hear you say,
Like a child at play,
There's a touch of display among tears.

What is the answer? Why am I living?
When shall we meet? Where is the giving?
How in this desolate world can I care
For a sweetheart when she's never there?
I hear you say, O, I hear you say,
With uncaring delay,
There's a touch of display among tears.

When can I hope? How will I make it?
Should I give up? Or just try to fake it?
I ache for your love and the beautiful way
You in my dreams can turn night into day.
Yet I hear you say, O, I hear you say,
As you wave me away,
There's a touch of display among tears.

Lynn Fontanne

How often was Lynn Fontanne
forced to re-spell her name
for the general throng who got it all wrong
even in the flush of her fame?

This odd name can only portend
with a superfluous E at the end
an odd situation like planning vacation
when you have nothing to spend.

Her surname did not contain,
at least to the lexically sane,
one single crotchet for people to botch it,
but how did they say it? Fontaine.

See, no one addressed as Fon*tahn*
could have ever been raised in a barn,
so with Lunt and that nom she hoped to become
the essential quintessence of charm.

But no one managed the name right
although it seemed chic at first sight
for what looked arranged turned out quite strange
somewhat like a misaligned bite.

With both ends exactly symmetrical
making each of the names highly metrical
a sound's mispronounced like someone just jounced
by having touched something electrical.

The vowels also tend to confuse,
where the jaw must make three distinct moves,
ih awh ahn said in sequence, never mind frequence,
is like being entangled in clews.

To desk-clerks in best bib and tucker,
not common or crude like a trucker,
how often each week did she still have to shriek,
"*Five* N's, you dumb little fucker!"

And imagine how dreadfully often
the dancer her voice had to soften
when asking some sage who was having her paged
would he like to try out his coffin?

A show business truth to abide
when giving your name a big ride
is that every inflation is clear indication
of the minuscule talent inside.

You were lucky, even if tony
E's and N's added a share of baloney,
  to find your name squeezed on any marquees,
  for you were strictly a phony.

Tibet; or All Journeys Are Vertical

  Trekking high is a way of saying yes.
I'd been lost without anything like promise,
  marching horizontal in the sun

  with no end of advertised nostrums
and all those calumniating humans by your side.
  I lit a thousand butter-candles

  in Chaurikharka for an answer,
no map by my side, as if I could read anything
  through the smoky fishdark there.

  I am in eerie Tibet in quite the way
I find myself, alone, and querulous in a cathedral
  or stone I can barely comprehend

  in the boisterous air outside this hut,
flicking the flames double-shining like my cheeks,
  the small gold figures of Buddha.

  The shape of my hands in prayer,
futuroidally in a shaping point like ready rockets,
  teaches me less about what to say

  than where to go. There is no glory
unaligned with soaring, which is always mapless
  as is air and as bursting bright.

  Give me eagle-height, darkened rooms,
the possibility of answered prayers in a silence
  crowds hatefully have never allowed,

where candles, buttered for brightness,
aiming to the dicey verticals howling up your hair,
   point out the right direction.

Kiowa and Buffalo

A Kiowa holding up his bowl
divined from its leathern orb and smell
   the academica of buffalo,

who kept him warm, as well,
as his purposive hide allowed of soul,
   letting his spirit grow.

It was a creature, we know,
of faith into whose dead mouth was told
   matters of heaven and hell,

never an enemy, never a foe,
round as seasons in which he could tell,
   as they came round, his goal.

Punk With a Red Mohawk

A punk with a red mohawk,
   even with that horrible hardness of head,
   reveals something of fire.

I love the determination of red,
   anguish that by a chromic attitude alone
   registers anger even in hair

red as good corned beef,
   boldly iridescent like hard fishy scales,
   when they get cured just right.

He need not seethe in order
to wear hard-fought hate in his hair to tell
what color alone does best

but bristle iconographically
and merely glare into passing windows,
ready with an angry chop.

A Trace of John Wilkes Booth

"I will tell you the God's honest truth"
— the mob's standard opening for a lie —
"your talent defies processorial laws."

Yet cannot cruelty also show ruth
when others ask that you descry
such praise as protocol applause?

A trace of Mr. John Wilkes Booth
shadows both, and when you sigh,
believe me, there is probable cause.

When Vilma Banky Married Rod LaRocque

When Vilma Banky married Rod LaRocque,
bottling up Pomona St. with a camelcade of Cords,
fans cordoned off by the chowmeinery

drawn from filmdom, crookdom, turfdom,
even girls in pelican hats from the washeteria,
all the whoopticians from the Hollywood,

stood with fists of rice near the drink
stand in the shape of a lemon, by the hot pink
doughnutery of enormous sugary stucco,

and they mattered on this special day,
gathered by that ice-cream stand wittily built
like a freezer with a handle, they did,

as did the waiters with water-parted hair
peering from the white-and-red lunch wagonette
fashioned in the contour of a weenie

at wacky flappers in felt cloche hats
bouncing up and down under the theater awnings
of *Ben-Hur* to view the honorees,

but it was the big stars from the studios
dancing jittery ambulandi at the Cocoanut Grove
in the Ambassador Hotel, monkeydoodling

vixens wet as fog and as lubricious
as the bounders riding their irony and thighs
in howling heat at the reception

who, because they didn't care a whit
and couldn't care and wouldn't care a whit
in the year of nineteen twenty-seven

gave the day the very shape the age
required when heedlessness was all in style,
unlike the simpletons in movie-love,

and without the rice, the hats,
the bouncing up and down or any of the zilch,
made Rod and Vilma's wedding real.

Singing Beach

Its slips of fine white sand
give off an odd tune from its hair,
something like a whistle,

but whips your face
as raw as any stinging nettle
   ever made it bristle.

   How accurate that pain
reveals from such fine whiteness beauty
   beauty sharper than a thistle.

Prayer of a Fat Man

Fat is aroma.
Snowshoe toward me with bags
of what, white

as toilet porcelain,
makes frozen ice-cream creamy,
red meat juicy,

dumb cheese bright.
No mad games of flashlight tag
by avoirdupoisettes

at Stop & Shops
can match my greasy snores at night
for real meaning

in a world
so already badly dark and fallen;
what is one more

porky corpse?
We are the other white meat.
Fuck broccoli.

A Chinese Girl's Reflection Upon Wearing a White Barrette in Her Hair

Taboos forbid desired behavior,
according to Sigmund Freud,
but is it not true
that what is taboo
creates what we savor by mere disfavor
of what's likely to be enjoyed?

What we should rather choose to avoid,
like the Edenic fall,
is not the taboo
forbid me and you
of what is enjoyed or makes us annoyed
but the urge to desire at all.

Moon Rainbow

I loved you out of all reason
and vowed as the wind blows free
that we remain one
while rivers may run
If hope means promise, can't everything be?
Are there two sides of a rainbow
and will you be waiting for me?

I dreamed in my heart you left me
to sail a mysterious sea
as grey as the years
and my falling tears
If hope means promise, can't everything be?
On which side of the rainbow
will you be waiting for me?

I saw one night a moon rainbow
for those in their misery
whom love must redeem
in their lonely dream
If hope means promise,
can't everything be?
If there aren't two sides of a rainbow
will you still be waiting for me?

Twice Shy

Why is it that water will not burn?
Water, first, is dihydrogen monoxide,
Which results when oxygen in turn
Combusts wherever hydrogen resides.
A chemical fact is therefore learned.
Water stays wet in the matter concerned
Simply because it has already burned.

Can this somehow apply to lovers who
Are wounded by emotions of the heart?
Should they another interest renew
Or from the world of lovers stand apart?
How can a heart again burn steady
and tall in winds that blow and eddy?
Only because it has burned already.

So what of love compared to water pure?
Must an effect always have a cause?
Does fire nullify? Inflame? Inure?
Passion, sadly, follows changing laws.
We may discern a hawk from a dove,
Determine below from high above,
But never which is water, which is love.

Richard Simmons's Hair

I can look into your small potato mind
by seeing what is missing in your eyes,

or, worse, is much too scarily there,
seafog-grey and tiny in piglike intent.

No one should sweat into a nest.
Droplets in your bulb of furry hair

seem all wrong for an exercise guru
such as you in twee tanktops and tutu,

doin' dipsies and howlin' thlipses,
"Sweatin'," "Tonin'," and "Groovin',"

such phony intimacy, transparent lies,
with studied friendliness arranged

to shake down Miss Lactating Harriet
with poofwarm hair, all those meese

who snatch at your fleecing fingers,
and weep on your blue sepulchral fat

because they feel you don't judge them.
Confess, you want men to see France

when up and down you bounce like Baby
Bright and not these tearful hambas

with their endless wolfing-Raisinets
and wanting-to-end-it-all stories, right?

I can detect in someone so cardigan-cuddly
that your raised collar is a kind of hug

you badly need. I only say your hideous
hair is topiaried out of all proportion

with calves toneless as tonka beans,
loose gut, and snailsoft shoulders.

even if that hair is (such is my objection)
the only thing about you that's in shape.

A Postcard from Tijuana

I rubberbounced in cathcarts
to buy switchblades and pointed shoes
in uncooperative Tijuana,

sweating with uncalculated noise.
How even these little goals went nowhere
like those striped burros in hats,

factrix beasts resembling me,
so reproduced by my many Americorporeal
habits, overweight and hot,

as I stood there knifeless
on the corner of 5th and Revoluçion
in my awful boxy shoes,

not knowing which way to go
unlike a zillion billion hip pancheritos
or whatever they're called,

all with blades and pointed shoes,
who, looking cool, allowing them to walk
and talk with style, weight,

made all the others sweat, man,
gave others noise who, seeing pointed blades
and shoes, opted to cooperate.

Wilhelm Reich's Law

"Willy loved to hear Ravel's 'Bolero.' Once,
  after the record had been played, he told us about
  a dream he had for the future: he saw himself riding
  into Berlin as a triumphant king mounted on a white
  horse, while the band played Ravel's 'Bolero.'"
  — August Lange, a Norwegian friend

In a long sheet-iron tub at windy
and wet Mooselookmeguntic Lake
you expensively soaped your fatness,
with a milled and perfumed cake,

dreamt of being a great conductor,
better than Brahms whom you hated,
of more money for Organon Institute,
that your enemies be berated.

Shouting through Teddy Roosevelt teeth,
you bullied your three poor wives
and, mad with sheeny jealousy,
chased them about with knives,

imbibing your freakish energy
from the orgone sensed in the air
that you claimed to harness in boxes
and for cash were willing to share —

"mouse-accumulators," you called them,
linking science to sexual trips,
got you more funding and grants
and honors and memberships

than entire colleges and schools,
so loudly you banged your drum!
Oh, how badly stung you were
when Einstein refused to come

to shiny, piney Maine and bless
your clockwork rigs and ratchets,
made to capture energy's air
in canisters fashioned with hatchets.

Was it your fear of outer spacemen,
do you think, that put him off,
whose ships' black air you insisted
gave off such deadly exhaust?

Or that you thought you were Christ,
meriting church group and altar?
Or yearned to stand on a podium
and pretend you were Bruno Walter?

Or the theory you once advanced,
if a person breathes well it's OK
— and you claimed you were a physician! —
to smoke more than four packs a day

as you did, thus giving your heart
along with its rolls of pink fat,
the 300 insane beats per minute
of a tachycardiac!

What scam in American history
can beat a man who would dare
to promise sexual happiness
and get rich by retailing air?

I say Congress should draft a law,
and then pass it without delay
to be named after William Reich
and this is what it should say,

"Resolved: in matters of *bullshit*,
whether sold outright or on loan,
the word must appear on the label,
and the label must clearly be shown!"

The Irony in Our Prayers

"Tell all the truth but tell it slant —
Success in circuit lies...
The truth must dazzle gradually
Or every man be blind"
                                    — Emily Dickinson

Those of us who find it difficult
not hearing irony in our prayers
wish that hobo in the aluminum hat,
waving at imaginary birds, were God,

if only to give one's own mutterings
believability. Please let me hear
instead of echoes of my self-contempt,
something, anything, of faith, for

isn't mercy always well-deserved,
whether when eloquence, becoming
earnest, proclaims like a sober saint
or sadhu or sage skilled with psalters

or some poor thumb-tongued fool?
I fear as I pray to God His response,
straight, direct, undeviating, true,
will impose on me what I deserve

Poets can't be made from pain
nor agony fashioned for lyrical
tributes to thrones so very high

that distances become too vast.
We can be eloquent in consequence
of what we are allowed to *dare*.
That is my thought, this my prayer.

Godlight

for Johannes Kepler

Starlight, shining from points
unnumbered leagues away, away,

hints in high cold space
parallel lines by night and day

share a mutual point
at far infinity where they converge.

This doesn't tell us that God
awaits where time and eternity merge?

Krackles for a Girl

Katrinka, bless you, I cringe
when you appear in crisp winter leggings
like one hundred twenty flames

setting me alight like coals.
I love you sufferingly, hot as Boca,
writing mad chia like this

with words cripple-crooked
and widow-empty next to your every
waking wonderfulness, yet

my fardels of notes, unmailed,
are even sadder where they're boxed and
sitting on cold shelves.

You are my faith, not God
or his hooded priests breaking flat prune
hosts of chrimsel.

I risk consummation in hellfire
lacking sufficient faith in it, or need,
  ironically, even as I burn,

  biocoveting your curves.
Cook me, later! In hell I shall crackle
  happily in skillet grease

if my snowy dreams can but include
you Katrinka in your leggings cocoa crisp and
  as long as I can hear you coo.

Opossums Love Persimmons

Do opossums love persimmons so,
because their name is fluent,

the way grassy graves grieve
and fire incarnadines flame?

Snakes have dinners in the dark
without benefit of eyes and yet

cannot fail to love the taste
of sound that makes a meal.

Willow leaves whisper, poplars
furiously prattle, conversations

with the wind that wooing them
nominates in such a truant way

what they are supposed to be.
Are we then consoled in praying

the very same way, at least so
we are told, God needs to hear?

If opoponax isn't partly perfume
by the splendor of its name

then prayer is only foolery,
its unreachable strength a fake,

if on these stones and boulders
we cannot believe in kneeling

we are given by what we name
everything we expect to know,

which is why, in my opinion,
serpents hearken as they eat

and merely for the fluent name
opossums love persimmons so.

Mother Hubbard Blues

God is like a mean bitchawful mother
    with too many chillun' to spare

God is like a mean bitchawful mother
    with too many chillun' to spare

Too many spilled out of that apron
    to show any single one care.

All of they starvin', thirstin', dyin',
    fallin' on bended knee

All of they starvin', thirstin', dyin',
    fallin' on bended knee

How with such a passel of chillun'
    can be heaven lookin on me?

Like Ol' Mother Hubbard in de shoehouse
    scoldin' her chillun' for sass

Like Ol' Mother Hubbard in de shoehouse
    scoldin' her chillun' for sass

You lookin' less to feedin' my mouf
    than puttin' a boot up my ass.

Our bellies soup to soup always achin'
    ain't no single sign of a bowl

Our bellies soup to soup is always achin'
    ain't no single sign of a bowl

Only bad hunger moanin' to miseries
    only miseries bein' told.

For us not a single day different
    from bein' jess zackly the same

For us not a single day different
    from bein' jess zackly the same

Like a hollerin captain in cotton,
    betcha don't even know my name.

If God you a bitchawful mother,
    don't plan on devotion, too

Hey, if God you a bitchawful mother,
    don't plan on devotion, too

Cause theys too many women around here
    be takin' the place of you.

Mad Economo

Mad Economo, peering up,
for blue is the favorite color of the insane,
wags a rose to heaven,

as if to appease above
for its miseries down below and in so doing
fabricates a sacrament

by how in his patient way,
observing all the rubrics of common liturgy,
he is more than willing to show

God need not be blamed
for condemning him to madness and a love for
blue that requires red from thorns.

Vultures la Chopmist

Vultures are black and blue
like razors, and like fearful razors sharp
claw the seaside stair.

where, gathering to carp
in rainy Chopmist with their cries of rue,
they flap above the weir,

bleak in the seawet air,
and echoes seem along that gloomy tarp
to shriek a death is due.

Mother Cochin

for J. Moore.

If sulkiness is the midget of emotions,
you're the dwarf queen of cacklessness,

Mother Cochin, fashioning all sorts of
plots and schemes from age-old gripes

hatched from your own spiteful attitudes
assembled under you for years like eggs.

What brooding! Doesn't it fatigue you,
fuss your sad old feathers, Pertelote,

scowling on your perch in San Diego,
left high and dry by some angry rooster

who also learned that queer hate in a hen,
long past laying, boxed in with her idea

to claw and scratch and peck and bite,
resolute to never, ever set things right,

can only make it look a fitful fool?
Isn't bitterness unbecoming in one

so prone herself to bad behavior?
But when that bird is small, a dwarf

barnfowl, its eyes gone red with wrath,
how fatuous that hen appears who sulks,

sitting on emptiness in bitter thatch
long since bereft of anything to hatch.

A coop's a place to breed. In your own
you brood and like a fowl now sourly find

no one any longer pays you any mind,
for happily having long since flown.

Haggling

In Mesopotamia now called Iraq,
where deals take place in the dark

by wily little Iraqis
with duskier skin than darkies,

you don't stand a ghost of a chance
to salvage so much as your pants,

and regarding neighbor Iran,
which is also a mercantile land

one time referred to as Persia,
file honesty under inertia,

but in Israel, formerly Palestine,
policy is to steal you blind,

and no swap's transacted of treasure,
unless as a sign of good measure

on the heap of extortionate gold
you throw in your Christian soul.

Lauren Bacall Selling "Fancy Feast" Catfood on Television

Coupledom is a farce
if Lauren Bacall, now selling cat food,
holding up tiny tins

in old red claws no longer
soft as pussy fur, not as once they were,
smooth and handjob warm,

can't uphold the ideal love
she and Bogie supposedly alone held high.

What kind of cash can with

no embarrassment ask of us
such blindness, presume such memory-failure,
that we ourselves in what

we have to turn away from,
whistling, putting our lips together and blowing,
won't be also catty?

Celibacy

I watched girls in Chalcidice,
darker than olive birds,
as I wended my way to Mt. Athos,

and in mocking winds I heard
the words of unchaste Eurydice
calling to me without pathos.

President Mobutu at Table

Mobutu clacked at his bowl
for the last toothsome traces of kasha
and then let out a fart

into the cushions of mole
where he lolled in his fat like a pasha,
then suddenly gave a start,

feeling a pull in his soul
for a dish of banana Afrique in focaccia.
He wolfed three, plus a tart,

which left an uneasy hole,
and so, since his very long reach was his art,
he gobbled up Kinshasa.

To Mickey Hood Who Travels the World and Visits Monasteries on His Motorcycle

"Raise the bridge, my friend is sailing by."
— St. Augustine

Wheelman, pilgrim, who finds God
as much in wind and wet and wandering
  as any holy pale renunciant

eating black radishes by night
in the desert of his prayer and self-denial,
  no rear-view mirror for you!

What do you see beyond your glasses,
Mick, how many rose moons, sad roads, bent trees,
  dry hills, cold hands, night lights,

and thin as a druid, greasier with lube
than a wart hog's dug, didn't you conventicle
  everywhere with holystoning monks

speaking fortune-cookie English
only to feel bone-dead sleep quicker than one
  can say never late than early?

No misomundist travels in his head
as far as you in pursuit of monastic solitude.
  It is never unfeelable form

in merely biking — how lost
in remote dorps you must often find yourself
  seeking the spindle of a spire? —

but patching vow to vision.
It is not necessary to change, you well know,
  rather necessary not to change.

Remember how Lord Krishna
in the Bhagavad Gita, holily contemplating
  the nose, sitting cross-legged,

prescribed the "mystic squint"?
I see only you on your motorcycle of a night,
not Krishna, riding Godward so.

Dreams Do Not Make Noises When They Die

Dreams do not make noises when they die,
like hypocrites who try to bring you pain
preponderating as an open sky
that blackens of a sudden and brings rain.
A soundless dream emptied me of them,
several irksome brothers with long snouts,
rattling with bile, filled with phlegm,
who badgered me with self-regarding shouts
and voices that while feigning true regard
cursed me white with spite behind my back.
Their asses were as fat as baker's lard.
Their souls were hard as coal and just as black.
I heard nothing when, awake, they lied
and nothing when my dream for them had died.

A Bogo Speaking Bilin

A Bogo speaking Bilin
with an inexplicable grin
of a sudden as if he were king
flashed an enormous ring

blacker than Barbarossa
and raising his tribal karossa
insolently poked out his bum
along with a gesturing thumb

as if by matter of fact
to show that the ebony black
of that steatopygous moon,
round as an African spoon,

matched in color the stone
worn on his knucklebone;
one complemented the other,
as color blended with color.

The value of blackness he saw
in the ring delighted him,
for the sable that nature had dyed
was quoted on his own hide,

confirming a logical link.
Or is it foolish to think
we can love (as lovers confess)
what we in fact also possess

it is rare to love what one has;
by a paradoxical jazz
we tend to value by tar
mainly not we are —

and so was this inky bauble
hard and round as a cobble
which made the Bogo feel tall
not part of himself at all?

I found the sepal far firmer
than the inky nap of his derma
(I wabbled one of his cheeks
while he made hideous squeaks)

and saw in less than a minute
a further argument in it:
what we want to add as a plus
is what is missing in us,

meaning that man's only eager
to seek what makes him less meager,
as opposed, say, to being inclined
to love as a person defined

by what he has in profusion
without adding further confusion
to existing body and soul —
in short, a man who is whole.

So which motivation rings true
between the alternative two:
is love as expression a vaunt
or a declaration of want,

the way the ring or that Bogo
understood as a logo
either extended by art
what he felt was a missing part

or merged with his sense or who
he was by dint of his hue,
thumb, bone, knuckle, and bum,
with nothing else to become.

Is the Bogo speaking Bilin
looking from outside in,
with diffidence, with doubt,
or looking from inside out?

But does it matter? Ego
like need is just a stratego
both an expression indeed
of uncircumscribable greed.

Love is always a riddle
where one is put in the middle,
tasking me therefore to try
to proceed to state as to why

a Bogo speaking Bilin
with an inexplicable grin
flashed an enormous ring
of a sudden as if he were king.

Bloubergstrand,
South Africa

On Seeing Edward Keinholz's *The State Hospital*

I can tell by the wind on the bamboo
as to the storm's direction. Thoomps,

booming like terror in my heart and
effecting changes there like toxic

greens on spiky, unfamiliar bushes,
send messages of an exacting death

as if I'd read whole volumes on it
by dint of merely flat-headed fear.

Fear has the white of a corridor,
empty and sudden and cold and long.

Trees, cracked in two like bones, are
being snacked on while being drowned.

Our asylum is on a north/south axis,
so one side is 0-180, the other 180-360.

Is it wrong to watch doves clump air
out of their wings for landings

during our blackout drill, exploding
against the tall windows like frappes

and leaving whitewash on the panes?
I yearn only for what I hope to flee,

a way of avoiding what the wind wipes
white to warn the patients once again

we are the inhabitants of storms
repeating in our souls like needs

that leave us helpless in our rooms
by way of wind, trees, dead doves,

acid greens, shapes of rooms, axes gone
all wrong, and, like all patterns, fear.

Dropping Fleas into a Glass of Water

Wet fleas are three-fourths dead.
The way they despair is, oddly,
by activity. I find the way sunshine
illuminates their last agonies
by adding irony to pain the way
when desperately we try to pray
in struggling to save ourselves
our imprecations quickly take on
disbelief so used we are to God's
suffocating silence as we drown.
Their minuscule bagpipe bodies
brown and tiny as tobacco flakes
with snouts like Bosch's horns
as crazily they scissorleg and
thrash, bite for air, eat water
the way leaves gulp red light,
experience with each abdominal
exertion in the champagne night
of frying, sizzling bubbles
the dreadful fact that jumping
does not work, just as prayer reaching
for a similar height does not
in our despair. As to beseeching,
kicking, thrashing, madly humping
fleas in water likewise is our lot.

For VP Richard Cheney
and all monsters everywhere who advocate
and delight in torture.

Voltaire At His Climax

Only when Voltaire became
impotent and felt the same,
according to Renoir,

did his work prove truly great
which no one else could imitate,
although somewhat noir.

Nothing not ratiocinative,
and only fluids definitive,
went into the pissoir.

King of the Golden Mountain

I never pined for a glass of Sangiovese,
paired with a slice of Spanish goat cheese,

expected tannins meant for long term aging.
Who in my life knew whites are drunk young?

The euphroe of my head let in other air,
no intermezzi making me cultured or important,

no shiny Bechstein standing in a glossy room.
My windfalls were round about my yard, near

bloviating neighbors, street trams, yard noise.
We ran through old streets — not Dog Town.

with niggers in hats with faces like vireos,
but we looked for, as if we needed, "stuff,"

and went ash-barrel-picking like Ashkenazim
of a Saturday morn in goofy, mooching shoes.

What grey-green afternoons can I collect
from boyhood with paladins roaming anything

like fenceless prairies? Long-pondered
seasons found me gathering my tiny joys,

like tossing jacks and whipping bumming-tops
and flipping aggies into heel-dug holes

and wolfing webby Concord grapes snatched
from backyard vines on cold autumnal nights

when the loamy smell of earth and leaves,
bringing dreams, gave another kind of light,

illumined like the grins of jack-o'-lanterns
or the wheels of Wintergreens we crunched.

Finding words and music to motion and shadow
as every passing season whistled me along,

I recall finding odd that the four things
Eisenhower boasted won the war for us,

the bazooka, the jeep, the A-bomb, and the DC-3,
excluded radios which blaring all those years

fueled my dreams like coils of autumn smoke.
Neighbors, noise, streets, girls, grapes,

horizons long that, for their suitability,
were never less for me than solid ground.

The function of memory is strengthened
by use. I am a living slave to recollection

whether of girls and schoolboy crushes,
ocean waves, or a doping of sheldrakes.

When finally I go exiting through gift-shop,
holy angels will have to shake my skull

free of all the fables and flora, and fauna
I swept into dustbin of my head for use.

Robust syllabi, like shafts of sunlight,
sweetened recognitions in my rising heart

which joined ferocious alphabets to songs
and stanzas I suspected only I could sing.

Collecting is confession, just as clearly
(and obviously) as selecting any choice

is making a disclosure. In our assemblages
we repeatedly show what for us stands

in the way of mercies for our dreaming lives,
regarding objects that, as we gather them,

paradoxically give us away. It is all of it
less, far less, an aspect of acquisition

than it is ambition, whether cold or warm,
but ambition's also inexact. Try simple hope,

for dreams for me were of a smaller scope.
Ambition's rarely found in any healthy form.

Allen Ginsberg

(1926-1997)

You wrote a last zany letter
to President Clinton from your deathbed
    seeking a medal of recognition

and to your agent at the end
because your *Selected Poems* was not reviewed
    in the New York *Times* Book Review,

"Can you do something about it?"
A Jew has to succeed in this particular life
    since he knows there is no other.

You browned like rotten celery
and died at 70 at 2:39 a.m. on a Saturday while
    everybody else was asleep,

    except me who was pedaling back
from a party on wet Riverside Drive celebrating
    a friend entering the convent.

Compulsive self-promotion is
a nasty occupation in Gotham City and canniness
    its orthodox religion.

 "Holy the crazy shepherds
of rebellion," indeed. Your deliberations
    were as profane as your guile,

    ragged whiskerando or not.
Being bopped-up on bennies and be-bop
    is frankly no more mystical

    than I am King Panto,
neither is blowing strangers holy or clouds
    of jumbled run-on screed,

    but self-promotion is an ocean
of waveless wind and foam. As my friend
    entering the portals of grace

    goes without fanfare or medals
hung like fruit about her light, I say to you,
    Go, dead, to the darkness.

Mujahaddin

No arms are left in Afghanistan,
only quirt-tongued harridans
crying for tons of guns.

What is more darkly memorial
than repugnatorial
bitches swart as nuns

hairily hot on murderous heights
madly hurling atrocious nights
into what once were suns?

All Soul's Day

Didn't Lucian explain that when we die
our shadows turn into our accusers?
Who better to know our many faults
than those inseparate from them,

such as shadows on a foggy night
where they themselves can hide
in darkness, never to be seen,
like blackest midnight, Hallowe'en?

Where shadows are concerned,
thrown across the way we see,
nothing should be asked to learn
the miracles of mystery.

Those souls who preach that
shadows lead their separate lives
will never know unmirrored peace
nor Independence nor release.

Transylvanians insist that shadows
of living creatures can be built
into houses, captured by the mere
terrifying fact of being there,

by their proximity to shed or shack,
like soot or smoke. I fear stones
can be inhabited by eating ghosts
which can extract the souls of men

whose uneasy shadows fall on them
like hovering, like baleful hosts.
When Basutos say that crocodiles
can drag a man's reflection under

water where in crepuscular light
it drowns the man who casts it,
know we stand above another self
like a shadow in the way of shade

replicating what it cannot hide
of all we've made it can't abide.
A question like a shadow might
murder anyone who asks it.

Thousands of Short Shadows

Juries, merely for being average, are morons.
I would not trust the fate of my pet pig

to one or them. Thousands of short shadows
cross the waking world to blacken my idea

of Man: figuration is a valid means to use
in delineating the real from the ideal.

It is *people* in the landscape who kill
any dreams we dream of what we will.

White crucifixes, notice, hang in whiteness,
in the aura of open emptiness, and blank,

while ignorant bigots, fools, and churls
with their hypnotic faces, mask-like heads,

show up in colors one can identify as uniform
and, gathering together to conform with spears

below our lonely battered Christ, scorn Him,
in the same way average people, made average

by the laws the common muttage of this race
follows by indifference to despise originality,

execute, like juries, never changing pace,
the innocent in order to conserve banality.

Red Persicory

Who gathered wind in his garment?
Who supported all the ends of the earth?
Who is the "eater" out of whom

came something sweet to eat?
I have no valid answers and remain dumb.
I would only like to solve

the insistent hothouse riddle of
this red persicory and the attendant problem
of its oblong thumb.

Thai Silk

Silk is as cool as teak is slim
as shine is bite and light is fire

and hung on a frame to wonder at
frail in the way that panel grain

plain in relief as a solid could
pass for fluid in the nap of wood

like flowing hair even if tight
may seem hard though soft as musk

alters by dint of sudden mood
the way by day a slant of rain

changes angles by dark of night
as sizes often with shapes conspire

like silver dawn to somber dusk,
solid and liquid to each aspire

as teak is cool as shine is bite
and light is slim as silk is fire.

Chiang Mai, 1992

Scarecrow

For L.M.

"Every scarecrow has a secret ambition
To terrorize" — Stanislaus Lec

No more incongruous a figure
ever crossed a yard, thin as nailed sticks,
  than bumless you, plural,

  walking in strides like a camel,
pick 'em up, put 'em down, your victim's hips,
  one higher than the other.

  How you never belonged to a landscape!
Who could ever find that one anomaly lingering
  in your many that, were it not so sad,

  makes you such a figure of fun?
What sharpened those crow-feet by your eyes
  if not hatred dark as body hair?

  To pick some basil, mow a hill,
tie a garden stake, none of your multiple selves,
  ever included an efficient one,

only jittery incompetenta in comic
clothes, pants too short, long flapping feet,
  breasts flatter than flawns,

  that face of low pedigree making
your crooked smile a Venetian carnival mask,
  silly as your purple fingernails.

  When you smile, your high red gums
seem basically your foolishness, although
  I fix on your long dowel nose.

  And so a scarecrow with tiny eyes
stands in my yard, even if it never worked,
  its bat-lug ears, always dirty,

  a semaphore to reckless ravens
who, immune to body odor, fly in circles
  over all your witchy selves

  that compose one crooked figure,
useless utterly, except at waving off all life
  not from any healthy garden

  but that patch you soil of dead
black vegetables in which suitably you stand
  the tallest, deadest one.

White is Nevertheless Visible

No reveler in green, yellow, red
  at Guadeloupe's Carnaval de Pointe-a-Pitre,
  wet by his drunken optics,

  or those doing half-naked soca
  dancing with pelvic thrusts in hot Tobago,
  torturing a circle of dirt,

or coons drumbumming merengues
in feather hats on woven mats in Jamaica
with tuberoses in their teeth

are needed to prove that white
as a color is ever emptier than idle hope
or in any real way alive.

A Christmas Poem

When 1 B.C. went to A.D. 1 what techniques
could muscular Recordato still not use,

fabricating piles of striped clay red pots?
Did no steeplechase on wide strategic roads

fail to thunder? Whiteness and purity not
seem covariants in she whom we would love?

Time, being is its own friend, recognizes
its own contours, going out and coming in.

If what was lost need not be forgotten,
the way a rigid bowl anchors fluid mud,

its form the shaping hands memory makes
as bold as any blue water it can hold,

or some color by merely glistening aphric
prove all we need to see to summon dreams,

the way the recollected air impends
the ebbing echoes any galloping portends,

time cannot be said in its enduring flux
not to be the friend we need to change

our hearts to welcome Christ the very way
by repentance we ourselves can rearrange.

the way in recollected air resounds
the galloping hooves on grounds

Semi Bi, Demi Twi

Since the term bi-monthly means
every other month — six times a year

and bi-weekly alternative weeks,
although semi's a synonym still,

why, then, if bi means the same,
is semi-monthly therefore defined

by pedants, who to great confusion
have always been greatly inclined,

as a cognate term for bi-weekly,
which in English we equally share

for anything issued that every
other given week must appear?

Should double phrases exist
(words should chaos forestall!)

for defining a single fact?
Prefixes fix nothing at all.

Why then employ bi if semi
will perfectly well suffice

when we can't even determine
if both mean one-half or twice?

Since semi-monthly displaces,
Demi, which means the same thing

although demi's entirely ignored,
any attempt at bold reckoning

with any chop-logic that states
bi-weekly is twice in four weeks

(like semi, but, notice, not bi-
which like two dissimilar cheeks

on a face have not the same hue)
could drive a person to drink,

who lost in the midst of the muddle
finds that he's unable to think

anything through with coherence,
for while semi bi-weekly means,

what denotes every two months
is a far different can of beans!

Do you find all this creating
a murderous migraine, as well?

Proof somehow of original sin?
A torture in verbal hell?

Don't think you're losing your mind.
It all reverts to scriptural Babel

where language became as corrupt
as the rude, multifarious rabble

which speaks no clearer today
in promises, oaths, or in vows.

Any hope? Avoid conversation —
no whats, no wherefores, no hows

and desist from purchasing papers
or sleek magazines. Save your dough.

I've said it once and a thousand
times, pal, "L'enfer c'est mots!"

Chang

Chang is the most common name on earth,
but four other definitions add to its worth,

different meanings, all spelled the same,
as this spectacularly popular Chinese name:

constantly, mountain, open, and *bone*.
What fun to get some Chang to intone,

"My bone that mountain open always"
making word-sense, not merely word-play.

I realize to dong like a bell is demeaning,
but he would convey the following meaning:

my bones always ache climbing high as a bird.
The thrill of this all being told by one word!

What a singular sound if this Mr. Chang
clangingly sang, "*Changchangchangchang*."

not only making full sense in a sentence
about some mountain-climber's repentance

but pulling off a classic show-business dream —
a Chinaman imitating *all the Supremes*!

Solitary Thought

"Hang yourself, brave Crillon! We fought at
Arques, and you were not there."
                    — King Henry IV of Navarre

Memory, an act of love, is a sexual
act. I wanted to remember what you preferred
for your own reasons to forget.

Loving acts, thoughts, spoken words,
creating desire by giving worth to drive,
alone create memories to hold.

Sex for you, as you surrendered,
was kept vague and so remained not love —
yet what you refused to face.

Who cannot say she loves you
can always suddenly never see you again
by the contrivance of a fate

that refuses memory its place
by what is never passion. Who was it said
that sadness is close to hate?

Amnesia is very like a death,
in that wiping everything away renders
any search for worth too late.

Christmas Alone

Oh, lessen, Christ, the dunnage on my heart.
I am not fit to handle battens and boards,

planking of such greased and terrifying lengths
their noise when falling enters me like swords,

but far worse is the weight as heavy as my sins
stacked high on me like piles of wood in cords.

You who had to bear the wood our wickedness
heaped upon you, help me bear my own, my Lord,

suffering, but not like you so cruelly raised
upon that cross, nailed and pierced and gored.

Please ease my pain that I may say my prayers
this frozen night and not find hollow words?

Welsh Englyn

A good englyn must have four lines, of ten, then six,
syllables, the last two lines having seven syllables each.
The first two lines are called the *Toddaid Byr*, the second
two the *cywydd* stanza. In the first line there must be
a break after the seventh, eighth, or ninth syllable, a
detached section called the *gair cyrch,* which may consist of
one, two, or three syllables, and the rhyme with the second
line comes at this break; but the tenth syllable of the first
line must either rhyme or be in assonance with the middle
of the second line. The last two lines must rhyme with the
first rhyme in the first line, but the third or fourth line must
rhyme on a weak syllable. The englyn is an ancient verse
form that originated from Welsh imitation of the Latin
epitaphs on the gravestones of the Britons.

In foul New Haven sits a school—called Yale,
   Beyond the pale and cruel;
Want to learn to be a fool
   In a place to ridicule?

Then to Connecticut please come—make haste,
   Be two-faced, even dumb;
The general faculty here is scum
   All winter, spring, and autumn.

Webs

"I haven't even been feeling human lately.
  No, there's no one else. I want to learn to be alone."
               — Laura Sparkley

The spider was you
waiting until we had a disagreement,
and then you moved

like a white bite,
ending my life with you in an instant,
suddenly drooling

to scutter back
across your hang-line to that thing
in the other web.

Ratios

"I met this guy who works in a record shop.
He has been singing in a rock band for 20 years, is poor,
probably alcoholic. Worse, he is married. Obviously, it's
foolish for me to become involved with this person, but
I can't help it. My mother spoiled me, and I mostly did
whatever I wanted when I grew up. Because of that, I just
do whatever I want now and don't bother about the
consequences."

— Laura Sparkley

But don't you see why we studied ratios
in school, or didn't you pay attention?

If that record-shop slacker you vamped
with your blue fingernails and thorough

knowledge of Cheap Trick's old LPs
("I had a wicked crush on Robin Zander"

you can squeal with mirth at thirty-four!)
is even close to half good-looking, even

if a woeful alcoholic, bleary with lies
and versions of the wife he's betraying

while he ruts with rabid you in a room,
you don't stand a chance, let's face it,

you're far too homely to get the guy,
even if blowing him under the counter

gets you a couple of free CDs and lunch.
But if, *if*, he is some ratty wolverine

with a pony-tail, pimples, and lots of
lore from being twenty years in a band,

immune to your constant mink-sour breath,
pipe-thin arms (one with that hairy mole),

and bat-lug ears that jut from your big
hair like monstrous handles from a jug,

you're good for many more CDs and food
and cassettes for years and years to come.

I say, the guy's as good as landed only
if he's homely, drunk, divorced, and dumb.

Laura Sparkley Takes Her Sketchpad to a Café

"Our greatest pretenses are built up not to hide the evil and
the ugly in us, but our emptiness. The hardest thing to hide
is something that is not there.
— Eric Hoffer

You who had neither the talent nor the temperament to
draw became instead a lifelong cartoon pretending that
you could.

How everyone had to suffer for it! It galled you in the way
that spite remained your basic rule for judging all the arts

and bonded you to every loser, slacker, punk, and slouching
dunce who played guitar or drums. Failure is a way of life.

Any loser wins your heart! Any crippled attitude or anti-
social fuckrod immediately redeemed the time for you.

Anything inartistic won your love. The falsity, the fear,
the foolishness you showed by impromptu games of taking

up a pencil and looking at a tree or bike or head with a
faux-deliberating eye, while it all revealed you for a fraud,

infected you with a sympathy for fraudulence, mothering
a need for loss, dead-ends, empty sex. The bad drawings

you screwed up became in life all the losers like orphans
who came your way for blow-jobs, took you to dim cafes,

where you drank coffee, scratched off letters, discussed
European movies, grinned at rockabilly riffs you loved

with that simpering high-gummed smile of yours, so red.
Those reechy guys, not friends, were symbols of your loss,

your failures, the drawings in fact you could not do.
Real dunces in your world replace your awful sketches,

are the scrimp and mucked-up sketches come to life!
Which is why at Parsons during all those wasted years

you sought mainly to connect with freaks and frauds
instead of making art and planning for a life of such.

It was the roach-small way you hovered over anything
you drew, or "rendered," to employ the art-school term

you much preferred in order to aggrandize what you did,
and all those inferior false-starts and muddied duds,

anatomical balloons and howlers with infinite erasures
you angrily ripped up that made you so envious a girl

with an unforgiving hate for everyone successful, most
notably good-looking women, but truly any healthy soul,

that transformed art imposter into desperate fellatrix.
That elongated nude your mother kept above the stairs

in her cheapjack apartment howled with the crippling
waste of money used to send you to New York to study art.

Whenever I see Egon Schiele's *Nude With Crossed Arms*
you yourself pencil-thin and homely descend to cry again,

"I should do more sketching," whereupon you trundle
off, bowlegged, sulking, to a remote corner of my yard

to waste another afternoon doing foxed and foolish
pencil-drawings With crutched anatomies and softball

heads. "Yeah," you used to say, feigning a Manhattan
accent, only one of your pretenses to look hip, "yeah,

I want to do some sketching," but oh how wistful you
returned, your pad clapped shut with shuck and shit.

You are the living counterpart of Schiele's nude,
a sickly, sexual, soulless stick with spindle nose,

as you snatched your grudging parents money and left
that hick-town life, as if you were Mary Cassatt.

Whenever someone asked if you painted, how sadly
white your crooked nose grew upon the realization

you could not manage tuck with chalk or charcoal
but made the hopscotch grid your wasted life's become.

The low esteem you always feel by failing in your art
attracted you to the kind of creeps who also failed

in the copycat way that you do in your wastrel days.
aimless and repellent muttjacks just like you.

And so your hackwork has forged a kind of population.
Compensation has an eerie way of making ends meet ends.

Art, in short, has rendered life for you — I hope you saved
your awful drawings. They were in fact your friends.

Laura

Your vagina is as black as night.
Your heart is smaller than your age.
What you choose is how you bite.
The mind in your head is a rat in a cage.

The dwarf in you feels bitter as sin.
You list as you walk with uneven gait.
Jealousy gnaws your gall within.
Gorgeous women you instantly hate.

Your face resembles an early Braque.
You reek of the odor of yellow milk.
Bonking oafs is your life-long mark.
You have the complexion of dirty silk.

What joy to awake on some distant morn
To a life in which you'd never been born.

What Rhymes With Horror

for Laura

"I have no friends, so I fuck,"
 is the way you conceive your life.
And because you look like a truck
 that swerved in a highway jackknife

flattened you out on the road
 with a body orthopteron thin,
(add the sour reek of a toad
 as you breathe out and breathe in)

who wonders sporadic affairs
are all you get late and soon?
Your ass is as flat as the stairs.
Your corpus the shape of a broom.

Your profile resembles a vulture's.
You sport a huge hairy mole.
Doctors ought to take cultures
of odors that come from your hole.

Your nose is always crab red.
Your snatching fingers are cold.
You've got a misshapen head.
Your eyes with crowfeet look old.

You once said that possibly AIDS
was in you, but you wouldn't check,
only continued your humping parades
with what losers you could select,

kowtowing for any companions,
suffling them for mere drinks,
jerking them off under stanchions,
hustling them with crude winks.

One guy who sang in a rock group
with a wife who was pretty and blonde
you hurt like a mad hairy *loupe*
and her husband proceeded to con,

until he smelt all your scheming
and got a good look at you close,
which put an end to his dreaming
as he woke with a unlucky dose,

And you're surprised he ignores you
after banging you for a week?
Why aren't you taking the whore's view?
For him it was taking a leak!

How could he love such a phony
with a mental patient's careers
of parapsychotic baloney
and a scrubber's crocodile tears?

How ugliness seems always unlikely
to the person who's vain and not bright
enough to know she's unsightly
especially in bed and at night.

Still you insist you're abused,
always bitching about your sad life,
while proceeding to selfishly choose
to cuckold another man's wife!

You claim your father molested you,
your mother is always on drugs.
Whenever your own sister tested you
(though retarded) you were a thug,

slapping her in your insanity,
pinching the hapless girl's arm,
and with characteristic inanity
indifferent to anyone's harm

excepting of course your own
which you bleat about night and day.
I've seen you steal and you're prone
your closest friends to betray.

Gail you wrote was a prostitute
in a letter I'm looking at now.
Fat Larry should be destitute
for which you pray with a vow.

Eurydice, Mary, nutty Phyll,
you rake every chance that you can.
You belittle, you hate, and you kill
and whisper behind your hand.

You're also hairy and cruel
and cheap and deceitful and pale,
your body tricked out like a fool
in the masquerade of a nail.

A dogface filled with self-pity
with thirty-four years of ill-luck,
you bore your tricks with this ditty,
while haunting nightclubs to tuck,

"My mother spoiled me," you said,
"and let me do what I want,
and so until I am dead" —
imagine this as a vaunt? —

"I follow my whims to this day
and don't give a shit whom I hurt.
Whatsoever I desire to say,
whomever I dish and what dirt,

That will get me anything free
and some sucker keep on the phone
is what I will do just to be
protected from living alone."

It is true you could never bear
one second of facing that ghost
who glares with a hideous stare
from mirrors with nothing to boast

of beauty or softness of form
or kindness or nurturing love.
coldness alone keeps you warm,
your heart like an empty glove,

for sourness none can surpass you,
real bitches need badly to brood,
your scowl reveals how vast you
can envy, your primary mood,

for everyone, all who ignored you,
lovely girls you loath on the spot,
the stylish you claim always bored you,
the worthy, the handsome, the hot.

You are a true time-bomb at fury
whom life has blithely passed by,
unfavored, ungainly, a drury
with curses for all far and nigh.

But all your byzantine plotting
to revenge yourself on the world,
all your trashy trend-spotting
as you fellate churl after churl

as though proving yourself a success
or some new creature of luck —?
Hey Laura, just up and confess,
"I have no friends, so I fuck."

Women have always disliked you
who intuit you don't give a damn
for anyone up, down, or through
any person not also a man,

yet men all eventually smell you
and see into your wrinkled eyes,
then conclude some bumless Gorgon
has appeared in mid-30s disguise,

bowlegged, listing, and rude
with bad teeth and fat lower lip
and manners unthinkably crude
and a woeful imbalance at hip.

No, keep your panties on, friend,
just to feign being someone of worth,
and, trust me, you'll see in the end
you'll not have a friend left on earth.

Nutcracker

for Laura

Your wide mouth as red as a schlong
matches a beak that's as long
as any firehouse hose
so whenever you smile
in ridiculous style
you look like you've swallowed your nose.

The Gospel According to Laura Sparkley

Varla: "Go get her!"
Rosie: "So I have to get all wet because the Lady Godiva
wants to swim?"
Faster, Pussycat, Kill! Kill!

Breakdown the sonnets of Donne.
What was his secret to sound?
Teach me to understand Shakespeare,
Hopkins, Yeats, Stevens, and Pound.

Cook me Mongolian beef again.
Lend me twenty while I'm in arrears?
Will you give me a ride to Boston?
The supermarket? Then Sears?

How does one write a novel?
Is this dress pretty on me?
Thanks for the lift to T.J. Maxx.
What is a catalpa tree?

Can you help me move flats again?
(I know it's the second time.)
Let's swim in the ocean on Sunday.
Mt. Washington's still there to climb.

You took me to Martha's Vineyard,
Gave me necklaces, earrings, and such,
Bought me bagels to take to work.
I depend on you so much.

Why would my father write this?
My mother queerly say that?
What is the nature of graduate school?
Exactly what is a ghat?

Thanks for buying my spectacles.
Is mine a serious cough?
Friday's my dentist appointment.
Could you kindly drop me off?

I'm grateful you pay for my dinners
You've been doing so for three years,
And bringing breakfast in bed to me,
Consoling me in my fears.

Remember you took me to Plymouth Rock,
Those thrift shops, and many plays.
And all the gifts from Mexico,
When you wrote to me every day?

All the books that you gave me,
Stacks that now fill my room,
Presents at Christmas and Easter,
Our visit to Henry James's tomb.

I'm forgetting the LA *Times*,
When you let me do book reviews
Because you kindly managed to see
The money I badly could use.

Should I take this job or not?
I've come to you time and again,
Asked all the essential questions,
Rehearsed all of my pain.

I have met a lot your friends,
I'd say hundreds of them since we met;
I'm sorry I have introduced you to not
One of mine, and yet

I have been seeing another man
And for you feel no longer the same.
So I have therefore decided
To let you carry the blame.

Stop taking over my life!
I want to be on my own!
You're so fucking judgmental!
Like a king on his fucking throne!

You pompously tried to take over!
I've let you dominate me!
Don't be so hypercerebral!
Why can't you let me be free?"

Anthropophobe Beach

"I am going nowhere in life. I've always known it.
 I'm a cipher."

— Laura Sparkley
in a letter 6/27/97

It was lying out on the white beach
where your dishonesty showed up,

like the ovals you stirred in the sand,
ciphers that symbolize your soullessness

to me. Your long black feet stand
on the sand like two open graves.

"Crummy," two passing guys mutter
 seeing you in your cheap blue bathing

suit. While shadows replicate you
in the bent fries you never share,

as if you leak bad lotion, you have
a real gummy smile for the boys. Zeroes

comprise your low-bred imagination.
Who thinks you know what to hope for

of worth is himself abidingly naïve.
Your homely head is an empty disc.

I find watching you walk to the sealip,
awkward and bowlegged as pliers,

a manifesto at crippledom. You list
like a bad lie, walking diagonally,

like bad geometry, when I recall
the old rule: "Anything plus 0 is itself!"

A Quaker on Nantucket Visits a Store in 1859

As bright colors are excluded
from the dress of Friends, what creation for a
Quaker can you quote,

general purveyor? An unshaven
behatted man barters briny quahogs for cloth
white as sail and black as tar,

potatoes, corn, radishes, fresh
tomatoes with undiminished cheeks of red,
for twill pants and a coat.

Black like extremest white
codifies the simple prayer that we be nothing
but what in fact we are,

not the way that, shamefully,
we by guile to others proudly would appear,
that garish colors riot.

What in simplicity by way
of what he wears makes a statement
of what he would forfend?

No plush pink or purple
for him whose solemn God prescribes he pass
his sober days as quiet

as a dark October night
or bleak afternoon in the gray dunes Quidnet,
where even stripes offend.

Sunyolk

for Marilyn Monroe

I love because I ate
the golden sun like that chick
just before it hatched

drew into its stomach
the flaming yolk of the egg,
providing itself with food.

It sits like you in me
warm as a yolk like golden food
until I resurrect.

I adore you as the sun
warmed the yolk the peeper ate
and made for it to take,

the way we all eat love
as if to warm ourselves to hatch
an inner flame as food.

Winterreise

Remember at the beach the sun,
the funfare, bumping cars, lights,
penny arcades, shooting galleries
and the machine with the Gypsy woman
who spit out your fortune on a card,
the big head of a laughing clown,
going ho-ho-ho? How far we walked.
At one point we got lost. And scared.
It was gray at the end of the esplanade.
The wind came up. And it grew cold.
We could no longer smell the beach.
In a dirty parking lot filled with broken
glass, an empty oil drum, I sat
and waited for a long, long time.
I knew what Dad would have said,
"There are no more rides." Now he's dead.
So's Mom. And you were everybody.

A Sonnet Written Written on the Occasion Of Louis and Nancy's Wedding

July 13, 2012

Just as east and west compose a whole
every union requires each be each,
for a mutual union in separateness,
while it gives integrity a soul,
allows in love a space apart for both,
where loving partners flourish in their space,
though never unaware that each is half
in which sharing makes a total troth.
When you see you both are incomplete
unless fulfilling what the other needs,
your love will grow in bounty like a land
where coasts, although they never meet,
strengthen what they join, like soul and heart,
and by such bonding never grow apart.

Hope Q. Anderson in Misty Oregon Explains Her Life

Passion is a mood I fear to feel
for all it asks of my suspicious heart,
so wounded in the spirit, to reveal,
and so my rule of thumb is stand apart.
Reason's equally, as to mistrust,
part of what I equally abhor —
flight is what I choose, and frankly must:
closing is easier than opening a door.
I can't, for safety, take the chance to try
to learn what wordy lovers say is true.
Let eloquence be silent; it won't lie
the way the nature of my fears can do,
and I'll look brave, even if my acts will
look like motion though I'm standing still.

For Sarah Son

"It must not be just a fleeting moment but a physical bond
between the varying events in life. Not exactions. But
abstractions. Abstractions that are like nothing in life in
their manner of reacting."
— From *Abstraction-Création, Art Non Figuratif*, no. 1, 1932.

When two people meet by way of the heart
With but a premonition of what's to be,
A bond is made that never lets them part
As after darkness one more yearns to see.
So destiny has played in our two lives,
Muses to each other's hopes and dreams.
A lovely artist paints, a writer strives,
Connected as our yearning lips would kiss.
It seems predestination carries weight,
If loving me becomes your hope, and this
My eager heart shares equally that fate.
May the love that gives us each to each
Show destined love infinity has reach.

The Dreadful Reality of Being Oneself
Eventually Becomes A Comfort

When you're different from everyone else,
a variant, the black night is never your enemy.
You sit in a low boite in Hypoluxo

in the darkness, watching yourself go by.
Your shadow, oddly, shares the vectors of,
because it is, your destiny, as is

the wont of shadows. When death comes
lubriciously to lick your ears, as is her wont,
all stupidly selfish people — listen,

please — try to concentrate with will
to note the immunocompromised fact for us all
that blues are the mother of sin,

and night is that mother's mother's
threat, unless you in your art or guile or pride
are hardened enough not to care.

A Poule at Pavillon

At Pavillon, that shiny poule
indelicately swirling a fork among tiny *crevettes*
knows rouged shrimp from the shapes

of pointed pain that paid for them.
Her mahogany red nails, as flash and sharp as tines,
are really black as night.

What clacking from that table!
Plates, nails, forks, shells, tongs, the shaking
of jewels by her swirling shine.

Color characterizes a state of mind
in whatever women wearing white batiste and gold
with shaping shears for fingers

as it does the noise she makes
working those intractable *crevettes* around in all
  the rouge they need for taste,

  her shine, that noise, inviting
the disapproving look of three quiet hateful ladies
  at a nearby table at Pavillon,

  exchanging looks in total silence
as sharp and flash as tines that say they well know
  rouged shapes from silly shrimp.

Sarah Son's Eyes

  I sailed a ship to ice-cold Japan,
wistful in the grip of myself, I remember,
  under desolate winter skies,

  but that curve of the bay,
its strange *clarté* that frozen December,
  the way of its gentle fold,

  made me yearn to return to you,
and so with the heat in my heart of an ember,
  the flame within but bold,

  I turned back to you in Korea
how easily passion can reason dismember —
  drawn by the shape of your eyes.

Around Borneo

  Borneo, O Borneo, what round heads
  you have, like your circular script,

  ovoidal noses, circular smiles. What
  cyclic motions everywhere you look!

I heard phrases in Sarawak, orotund
as the far funny face of the moon,

pocked, light, clock-round, bulbous,
white, drenching the trees at night

in fantastic opalescence. The wheels
that carry everyone everywhere here

incarnate every Borneonian whose hot
skin, glabrous, brown, surround him and

her, as if to say any hoop is human, not,
I feel, the way I go round about myself,

circumferentially in angle waywardness,
so dumbly linear, woefully, unohfully,

walking around, lost in the moonlight,
unforgivably western and so square.

Wat Po

My waiting alone in Wat Po
meant in the way I waited with a mouthful
of humid prayer

everything. The Emerald Buddha
resembled a small boy, high above the crowd
of kneeling Thai. In thin shirts

and rubber thongs who drifted
in from the brown klongs to bow and say prayers,
shoeless, their tiny white socks

so innocent for the delicacy,
like small flags themselves, all pointed away
from small Gautama, gold

and green, who revealed to me
that the round world is miraculous by the way
  we must see past it, past it.

  I saw offerings of tiny birds, ribbons,
punk, a red bottle of cola. The Buddha is not
  the object of prayer, only the means

  to love. That young jasper face, old
as stone, sitting high on platforms invites us
  higher, to look higher, up,

  past its mystery to miracle,
through miracle to those simple truths that
  are the most difficult to see.

  I later walked through dark Bangrak,
like a candle myself in the incessant heat and
  traffic, mad tuk-tuks. scooters,

  a humid prayer myself, my mouth
filled with fumes, but I also felt walking with
  the crowd of tiny Thai, everything.

I Bought My Baby A Baby Buddha

I bought my baby a baby Buddha
along the Sukhumvit Road,
and wasn't it my joy to find
as across the night I rode

that Thailand girl waiting for me
in the Temple of Wat Phra Keo
like incense under an Asian moon
and with as richly smoky a glow.

O Siamese moon, O chakra of love,
Around, go round, looping all lovers
in a sensuous circle of sound

I bought my baby a baby Buddha
along the Sukhumvit Road,
and when I sat it in her hand
our love began to flow

in the quiet there of the waiting dark
for two lovers suddenly knew
a god in ourselves is given to see
that god alone is true.

O Siamese moon, O chakra of love,
Around, go round, looping all lovers
in a sensuous circle of sound

I bought my baby a baby Buddha
along the Sukumvit Road
and how in my anxious heart of a sudden
was lightened a heavy load

as every kiss created an ache
for the blessing of only one more
as we prayed for love from God above
and he quietly opened the door.

O Siamese moon, O chakra of love,
Around, go round, looping all lovers
in a sensuous circle of sound

Damaris

In Acts 17:34
the name of a woman appears
who is alluded to once, but more,
no history ever shares.

We know her as a friend of St. Paul,
and a woman of Athens, as well,
a Christian who was given the call,
with not a word more to tell.

Not a single mention again is made,
only that reference flat
of that simple name in simple display
like a button on a hat.

Who she was and what she did,
if old, how pretty, and why
in ancient Greece she never hid
among scholars or acted shy

Holy Scripture never has said,
except that the woman was there.
(I say a woman, but was it a maid
with locks of honeyed hair?)

There high on the Areopagus hill
as Paul outlined the Good News,
the gathering crowd was content
until he asked his listeners choose

between Jesus Christ and pagan gods,
when all of the arrogant Stoics
and debunking Epicureans gave odds
such fables were empty heroics.

A human being? Who rose from the dead?
Turned water into red wine?
Wore a crown of thorns? Like a goat he bled?
On loaves let multitudes dine?

Claimed to be the King of the Jews?
Then asked the Jews to convert?
To assume a new, their old lives to lose?
Forgive who suffer you hurt?

Only a babbler could offer this cant,
mad fairy tales to a one,
and anyone who subscribes to such rant
must stand out a figure of fun.

Amid such intellectual scorn,
this woman never gave way.
Her faith continued as it was born
and never once did it sway.

So can a name be memorialized
but given mention no more
with nothing more editorialized
of pious or saintly lore

in simply citing a person's name
regarding someone so small
when the praise of perpetual fame
was always reserved for the tall?

Can glory in one citation reside
when kings and princes of note
in countless volumes as high as the tides
have won the historians vote?

Forever her name will exist as a fact
as if a biography full
duly recording her every act
provided the sacred pull,

for we are ultimately judged in the end,
in this world we enter and leave,
no matter what fortune God chooses to send,
by finally what we believe.

Jugâya's Dream

Jugâya draws with a fir-needle,
putting cherry into a blossom

and on the paper a tiger yawns.
A lotus blossom floats as if

watery poetry could be real,
a vein of truth, to be sure,

in all these whites and reds
by which we want to swear,

hoping against all hope, that
delicate Jugâya with making mind

is able to construct in kind
even with a tiger in his lair

what ultimately cannot be false
that we may pray our prayer.

A Sonnet Written on the Occasion of the Christening Madelon Kelly Palandjian

May 15, 1999

What dark beauty's revealed in this newborn
that lets out light as if she were a star,
her lovely eyes the dark of early morn
the moment dawn awakens from afar?
How is it light and darkness can so play,
such deep and serious extremes they seem,
in one as young and fresh as newborn day,
as gentle as a star's precocious beam?
But light and dark are whole, in union form.
If one goes missing, lo, the other must fail
Fully to be; serenity we know by storm.
What is dark depends on what was pale.
Oh, like constant sun and moon at play,
Dear Madelon, embody night and day!

On a Photograph of Mia Farrow in a Stone Garden

As you peer through those glasses,
it is as if cognition, even in a perfect face,
seems to say intensity is needed

in order to know. There's a certain
solitude to anyone in a cold stone garden,
but here, where your chiseled

cheekbones among the sculptures
give us only another biomorphic angel,
I wonder if you don't wear granny

glasses as a shield against your
burdensome beauty? Do you lean not to come
close, the way that chubby *putti*

to your left, fearing sky threat,
reacts as if to guard you from the same?
Your black coat, with its yards of

buttons hugging you the way I would,
makes you more chaste than the statues
which nevertheless depend on you

for a grandeur that convinces me
that a human can be as beautiful as art.
Black coat, bent body, that full

intensity you wear seem worn
as a sort of refuge, the way our tears
actually mourn for us and laughter

acts as our applause. Your glasses,
scholar, nevertheless, as unadorned and
chaste as the stones you study,

those severe geometries, covered
with lichen and birdlime that photograph
makes stark, your eyeglasses

hide nothing of your beauty, only
show that intensity like certain solitude
born of a cognitive stare

as chiseled as your cheekbones
in a gardens where humans walk with angels
only perfect your lovely face.

Miniature of a Nephew

"He to whom God gives no sons, the devil gives nephews."
— old proverb

A person at a beach, naked to the nines, is a dropped persona.
It was not so much your spottiness, I thought, as the estimating
blank eyes with which you watched nothing as we watched you.
Horizons close us in like shutting traps and prove with ice-cold
certainty we are going to die. Human temples are white dent corn.
Blueness in the limbs seems phthisic. The way a human wrist
is such a mortal hinge, especially in geeks, and how you turned it
aped the flattery you always smugly thought we bought as real.
We all saw through your obsequious maneuvers, Master Craeml.
How you cozened! There is a prancingness to every arrogance.
There is a tidy etiquette that makes hatred in its malice mild.
Youth is relative. You were also enough of a hypocrite that by
the foolish conviction you saw more than we made any knave
seem actually to age to the degree one could never fail to see
it was but a matter of time before that grim guy in the sheet
with the scythe, always watching nothing, swung off both legs.

Joan with Horns of Hair

That movie house of your head,
dark, a rattrap with a thousand seats and
a lingering odor of dead burlap,

got me to go inside and sit,
fiend-bitten with anxieties out of number.
You with usual panfuriousness

always ran the same skrawky films,
the one where you complain 'til Tuesday,
interrogating the sky above,

about the nature of your life
double-featuring with it that other one
where men are all bastards,

including those in the audience,
gripping their overcoats, dying to leave,
but thinking it rude to butt past

others in their row, disturbed
themselves but like me feigning interest
lest you typically unspool

by the simple act of someone
leaving in the midst of yet another drama
screened by wild-eyed you

with your Theda Bara horns of
hair. During the inexorable spate of cartoons
I saw my chance to bolt,

flinging up the slanted aisle
with an eyeache toward any ruby exit sign
I saw that would let me out

through all that wasted time
in the space of your interminable darkness
into bright sunshine again.

Squirting the Monkey

When to Nantasket Beach on altar boy trips
we went, what we all first sought out to play

at the noisy penny arcade for only a quarter a pop
was the row of tin monkeys who edged to the top

by the volume of water each sweaty contestant
accurately aimed at his hole, a pissing contest

it was, invariably won by the steadiest stream,
and always reminded me of the way nuns told us

in Catechism class that instead of snarfing bags
of niggertoes or playing *salugi* with someone's

hat pulled off his head, driving the victim nuts
— a sport howling boys in the summer streets

called "monkey-in-the-middle" — we should all
kneel down and offer our thoughts up to God

and how, by means of our dedicated prayers
or pious ejaculations (with straight faces here

all of us always comically nudged each other)
or good works, like shoveling snow or banging

fat erasers clean on a window-ledge at school
or rolling ash-barrels out front for your father,

poor souls slowly advanced out of purgatory
solely by the merit of our fervent intercession

and eventually got to heaven, exactly the way
the monkeys advanced, in jerks, up fake grass

— they were all affixed to a north-running rail —
and the winner who managed the steadiest squirt

walked off proudly, laughing loud as Nantasket,
with his prize, a red-gold ceramic crucifix, its

cross-eyed corpus all covered with neon spangles,
manufactured in New Jersey by hustling Jews who

shipped them up the interstate by the truckload
but as real to us and as much a pious sacramental

as those poor jerking souls dependent like tin
monkeys on the theology of our mad attention.

Sunlight, Shadowlight

Never can summer seem the same
for I had seen in your belovedness a dream
that lifted my heart with song

but then as in some ancient game
or trial a cold seeping mist that made it seem
as if the sudden sun were wrong

fell across your lovely name
clouding with shade its previous golden beam
once so youthful and so strong.

You then one night appeared to claim
my love and my doubting soul by that redeem,
whispering to me that love is long

but only will or can remain
to thrive alone in such faithful hearts that deem
a similar world to walk among.

Now summer burns again with flame,
for my beloved taught me in a lessoning dream
how a heart to sing its song

must see how, very much the same,
sun and shadow oddly share a common theme
and both to love belong.

Queen Lear

for G.V.

I much prefer your coldness to your kiss,
exile from your loopy court,
stricken like your husbands just for sport
from Queen Paranoia's wishing list.
Banish everyone you can't enslave.
Murder anyone who dares refuse
what you decide they should want to choose
and in your homely presence how behave.
No wonder how in your infertile bed
you sleep at night with open eyes,
staring into space with all your lies
pressing down like coverlets of lead
but don't you see that in your muffled
screams *you're* the nightmare of your dreams?

No Jews Can Actually Be Found in Japan

"You can never fail to find what you always fear."
                              – Charles M. Doughty, explorer

No Jews can actually be found in Japan,
only mutts in gabardine with fishy eyes

whose fatness finds no comfort from a fan,
according to the ratio of greed to size.

All cheat, fry offal, suck their fingers,
scratch arithmetic in black and heavy books,

proving to the Japanese a demon lingers
in such hairy monsters with such horrid looks.

They badly slouch, look as soft as snails,
and on splayed feet walk on spongy shoes.

Their cunning smiles show teeth like nails
as deals are closed and major cash accrues.

Their oily handshakes always lack a bite.
They smell as if they all had eaten ants.

You see them on the Ginza every night
selling cut-rate diamonds from their pants.

But whether they exist in fact or mind
everywhere a fear of them creates a sound

of true alarm unless beasts of such a kind,
crummy or crude, rude or real, are found.

Waco

The red wolverines in East Texas died of rage,
it is said, while they were snagged in a trap.

What thing with iron teeth awaits in the sage
from which no escape is found through any gap?

Empty howls with claws tore the night to shreds.
The moon, a smoking shape above the night, was mute.

Nothing interferes with death, it is also said.
The beasts' white eyes were husks of eaten fruit.

Their rage lies only in their indignant scats,
the way that any trap about to snap a leg or face

of wolverines, their dripping snouts like rats
bitten by the steel without a sign of grace,

is as empty as the open sage, as immolated eyes,
as East Texas, as those woeful cries ignored above

that just-as-empty moon where they say heaven lies
and precisely where, it is also said, there's love.

Frida Kahlo, Sipping Strong Black Coffee, Denies The Color Exists

"Nothing is black. Really nothing."
— Frida Kahlo

Not even that monkey, that prehensile cat,
that dead sparrow, dead wings spread wide,

worn round your bold, inquiring neck — and
what about your atrabilious eyebrows, Frida,

a sudden crowflight from your beetling brow
borne from that nest of black blazing hair?

I see a gory retablo in that accidental body,
missing toes, broken walk, surgical incisions,

cropped tresses, dolls you keep in formaldehyde,
mad *La Pelona* taking amputating bites of you,

the headaches tubby Carascapo's infidelities
cruelly give you in unrecuperable succession.

Isn't your corset, signed like a guest book
and oddly decorated with snapshots, also black?

What universe is not bleak and Tophet-dark
when human feet have been replaced by wheels

which even that Tehuana skirt, spread about,
cannot hide from the smile of sugar skulls?

You regard me quietly, diagnosing nothing, sip
your coffee chastely, don't flinch, and smile.

"It's so horrible it's beautiful," you primly
say of a tourist ashtray sold to the gringos

and of course never deny life to other colors,
red, yellow leaf green, brown, blood magenta,

the intoxicating blues of this cobalt house
lighting up your street like spectral jewelry.

I offer you a tiny flower, shaped like a hand,
flor de manito, for your scars. What suddenly

do I now feel, in this commiserating moment?
Oh, is that what you meant here in Coyoacan,

that the rays of light one sees can only come
from what is always only black and so is not,

the way that *molé* sweetens meals of chicken
in hot cast-iron pans as black as Satan's eyes

and that a person has no real fame unless
he or she can be recognized from the back?

Artist With Red Sticks

A Cro-Magnon man with a mouthful of mammoth
sloshing above the meltwater and the pebbles

began to see by way of the bloody bones he spat,
the way ice moved upon the surface of the land

as a crude kind of decoration with odd rumblings,
how a funny skeleton can also dance along a wall,

mimicking like unmunched sticks what he also saw
became another mammoth, red with fur and tall,

and now he began to race to munch his mammoth,
rumbling like cracking ice through bone on bone

so he could spit forth visions stick on stick,
tall and red with fur, making bones to decorate

the walls and ceiling of a cave he marveled at
after heaving up a burp wet from what he ate.

The Windy Injustices of God and Bob

It was one rancorous midnight
when Hurricane Bob, roaring up from the
straits of rumpled, coal-black

Africa to sleeping Cape Cod,
a bleak poor land to a favored preppy one,
breaking onto my property

and snapping eleven locust
trees into splinterwood that I understood
suddenly like a light coming on

God's unalterable edict that
a woman actually cannot have a baby unless
she is also pretty.

Foxlight

A silver fox is actually black
wearing night in its fur as if to try
to take away from the moon

something of its shine. Unlike
the moon, its darkness is its primacy
although in the midst of night

like silver it can be lit by light
by way of the reflections in its hide.
It is not correct for another

to wear white at a wedding which
like the shine of the moon on a fox
blackly so insults the bride.

Winged Monkeys

What frightens little kids
about the flying monkeys in *The Wizard of Oz*
  is never their faces,

  demented, hideously elate,
pressed flat like those shiny plastic masks
  on 1940s childrens' dolls.

  Eagerness is terrifying
in anything. What runs, chases. And I hated
  what in their filthy fur

  we had to accept as
aeropteric by way of a warty witch's wishets.
  I know, I *know* they flew,

  another grotesque anomaly
along with things tailed wearing bellboy caps
  with, my God, *chinstraps*!

  My question is what moves
behind what makes us move in what we choose,
  accomplishing fates

  concerning which, may I ask,
who is supposed to be aware, me of my life,
  you ignorantly of yours?

  The truly real, the Hindus say,
is *neti neti*, not this and not that, and I admit
  to walking on ground

  as precarious as my mind
that the booming clouds that rose overhead
  seemed comparatively firm

  when of course I learned,
years before hordes of snatching monkeys
  gibbering with evil

could pursue me, they weren't.
Who was being served in what those flapping
   raptors chased was horrid

enough. But far, far worse
was the skin-crawling fact that, set in motion,
   they were so *willing* to fly

What terrifies little kids
about the flying monkeys in *The Wizard of Oz*
   is their obedience.

Greek Beauty

for Diana Aivalikles

I had a dream that the passion of blue
with the silence of white makes a sky,
open to those with hearts that are true
for something on which a heart can rely.
A life is not full unless many dreams
are pondered in the depths of the heart
to stop our pain, our lives to redeem,
comprising the comfort that dreams impart.
Please know that as this life passes by
those remain close who keep their sight
on their dreams as they look to the sky
in the bright of day and the dark of night.
So blue and white like the flag of Greece
brings to us the constant hope of peace.

The Umbrellas of Baw Sung

for Leila Hadley Luce

There is no bicep in an umbrella,
operatic, each an expressive face,

muscleless and presuppositionless
but with enough of visible jointure

to sprout like a laughing buffoon's.
In Baw Sang, the umbrella village

east of the Ping River, where damp
heat gives way to sudden downpours

all biscuity paper hand-painted
umbrellas are never raised or wet.

I wondered spinning one, watching
it spin, if there was not a vacancy

in roundness I had not seen before —
in hoops, hats, hoopoes, highballs.

Squatting men, curving hands, parasols,
Baw Sung itself by Ping, the way it is

arranged in such green leafage among
those cyclic mountains of Chiang Mai,

all are loops in the way my questions
pose empty problems open as my mouth

before this spinning whorl, a world
eternally recurrent: *whin whin whin*.

Do round people produce square babies,
as the proverb says? How explain then

glad, biomorphic Thais, with sponging
brushes making circles upon wet waves,

I see red and yellow crescents at dusk,
green and blue umbrellas in a riddling

row, the falling light giving shafts
long important shadows, making them

bigger, no longer bereft of meaning.
I see in each parasol a *mappamundi*,

the world-map of an age, blessing us
with the understanding of circularity,

with the comfort of seeing returning
is the way of beginning once again,

the beginning once again not renewal
merely but staving off the final end.

Franchot Tone

Actor Franchot Tone with his smart breloque
and shoes gleaming like the roasted light of Italy

looked much more essential than a floorwalker
but had that nifty breeziness and slick hair.

Do you recollect, for instance, how talk is song?
He had a sly way of showing with a secret smile,

those thin curved lips making mockery a mood, how
conversation with oneself is like a gripe,

one like patience we with irony all understand.
His was a patent-leather neatness. He'd never

have bonked lovely Shirley Temple or Betsy Drake who
pronouncing s's like f's was even cuter, only

because sexual paraphernalia did not apply to him,
like extra-large pockets or cheap wrist-watches

or tallness or rubicundity of cheek like tole,
not with a name that fit him like a wine label,

not with that knowingness, those tailored suits.
He spoke with quizzicality, tending not to blink,

and always folding his arms when speaking proved
with something of mockery through thin curved lips

a mood like nifty breeziness can work to show
you can acquire integrity just by talking about it.

The Tao of Patti Smith

Every time I see a godwit on Monomoy
I attend one of your concerts, where you worked
with wristlets, Rasta t-shirt,

beaky directness, flagration,
standing your ground. No Hollywood sexpot I know
can quite match your sexiness

in merely pulling a skinny black
tie off, or were you yawning in that photograph?
Your face has noir beauty.

Tina Modotti would have stood you
by a wall in Cuernevaca with groups of poor people
for you understand them

and care and by caring sing.
I love your innocence in revering heroes, looking
for the original line-up.

You in your thin tallness
remind me of January — are bracelets cold? —
for in watching you

in cold and wet Monomoy I tend
in pondering thin and beaky birds to think of death
as a kind of horizon,

for its pecking interrogation
in the cold is brave and tall and seems so daring.
The way you aim your guitar!

Three Yemeni Chewing Qat

Do those three Yemeni, chewing qat,
fat cheeks bulging with wet green plantchew,
  spitting into the Sanaa afternoon

in the vast Hassaba market,
where the stacks of high brown baskets lean,
  dry as those discarded leaves

which sucked of their own spit
and strewn upon the ground remain yet green,
  happen to know what goes round?

What is ground only leaves
a country running out of water, dry, brown.
  Chewing is a kind of thought

by which we also show we act
as much upon Sanaa as on the satisfied self.
  If through the afternoon then

those chewers *slunch, slunch*,
aren't interpretations true? And if that's so,
  can't we say that those who chew

water out of leaves and spit
eventually replenish what they have sucked
  out of the land by way of qat,

snatching more bundles of leaf,
grolching the wetness while growing fat,
  wiping a mouth with a hand,

with cheeks as round as baskets
dry and empty fill to spill and stimulate
  once again a fat wet land?

Heidi Bivens Waking Up in the Morning

Heidi Bivens, whirling,
revolving in a misty dream
in light both dark and pale,
    spins on her toe
with a finger on top of her head,
    light as nightingale,
    soft as a plume
then wakens in a golden snow
    of sunshine and spume
    and rises gently
like winking bubbles in ale
    with a golden glow
    out of her bed.

Sonny Rollins Playing Sax on the Williamsburg Bridge

Crying was a way to practice pain
up there where the horizon goes from melange
to black and cooperates for you

doing all that X-material on your horn,
no conversation, no ooftah, no shuck, a lot
of bat and catch and *moooooooood!*

You quacked into the night, you
who believed that records were commercials
only to bring people to concerts.

The roux was ragtime and blues
with every wet wail containing the ruin of
something close to a symphony,

echo-booming down the big struts,
rivet-rails like cartilage, long iron supports
and up again from the water.

Aloneness is nearer God, up there
with cold mice, suspended high above traffic,
your shoes wet as hyena shit,

where wasting music in the wind
is a mild revenge when you are that high
making with solitude a marriage.

Delacroix in Tangier

As no human endeavor is compatible
with infinity, or so found Gene, why not
let color itself create a world for us?
Like wax in the sun, his brushes
dissolved by day, solidified at night.
He dipped his brushes in wet avocado,
swam them in oranges, in green endive,
in blue and purple plums, rendering
sketches in scratchy pen-and-ink
in those Moroccan journals of his,
fearing they might vanish otherwise,
pictures in oil that dissolved by day
and then solidified at night, pictures
of men in deep blue caftans, women
in pink throwing wash from apertures.
When he died, dissolving by day and
solidifying at night, his many pictures
well remain, compatible with infinity.

King George and Queen Caroline Do
Their Rounds

It was an afternoon of spitting wet
as Queen Caroline walked past her tall white mums
in windy Richmond, pausing

to look over her witty bonnet
at the late dispersing sun at the river, saying,
 "Time for 'Maid of Honour' cakes,"

 cream-filled, toothsomely sweet,
and round as the wind around the mums, around
 the bonnet, around the sun, while

 George II, lusty from hot soup,
pushing away from his pewter bowl, gamahuched
 pale, curvaceous Henrietta,

 his witty meriodonal mistress,
unbonneted, toothsome, naked, and cream-filled,
 who was astonished how sweet

 her dispensing sire had become
in Richmond by the river in the falling dusk
 and how windy and wet he was.

Nantucket from the Air

 Look at any aerial map;
the isle of Nantucket clearly resembles
 an odd, jut-jawed boy

 who has just taken a bite
out of a lengthy piece of crunchy celery
 and is munching it with joy.

Vermont Driving

 There is not so much a way
 of driving in Vermont along those roads
 with rural single-lanes

as a driving need to find
a way to survive. Major highways there,
not merely old roads, allow cars

rarely to pass. Cut-offs
are also few as a way to turn and come
up fast, the way abruptness

does, as long and narrow lanes
in constant closing aperture prevent
anything like a wider view.

Hectoring road-signs warn
that penalties are especially enforced
at points where men are working

when and where you are assessed
double the fine. So speeding is out,
while lengthening lines behind

you, a mile of smoking cars,
are cursing you blue for being slow,
who've seen your Mass. plate

with its enervated color white,
so vividly not forest green, indicating
you're probably a Jew and lost.

"Where's the logic?" I asked
a farmer on a tractor one morning as he
bent forward to give directions

and leaning back thereupon
commenced to hand out wisdom of his own
which basically amounted to

what R. Frost once said: *The
purpose of plowing's to learn to follow.
Nothing to do with philosophy.*

Just plain common sense.
And so if and when you happen to see me
failing to go to fast

the next time you're driving
up that way, and at the very same time
needing to go too slow,

not looking for a cut-off
(not daring to take a moment to try)
so much as avoiding blame,

picture like plowing
that I am merely learning to follow and
you can do the same.

Two Empty Lawn Chairs

What does it say about a couple whose
two chairs on a lawn sit side by side,

facing toward the sea? That they stare
away in silence and not a word provide

each other in a kind of waiting scrum?
Or do they share a deeper need to know

— I see them at twilight sitting there
as some ritual to watch the setting sun

slip past the horizon as if it drowned,
maybe zippering a jacket at a sudden blow

of wind — that some unity can be found
for two in a conjoining point of view?

There are crucial silences profound,
having not a thing to do with rue.

Or by having lost a certain affection
had they chosen to live facing away?

Where had they gone? Shall we say that
a quest, if valid, must be taken alone?

Isn't need a form of love? Or its rout?
Do hands which join reveal that hope

is sought instead of felt when doubt
is all that's left with which to cope?

By failing to share do we fail to say?
By dividing dreams do we cease to live?

The empty chairs like questions asked
offer only answers one alone can give.

Is one's strength increased by using it,
or by ignoring wherein that power lay?

Where in independence by abusing it,
does silence hide what we refuse to say?

What does it say about a couple whose
two chairs on a lawn sit side by side,

facing toward the sea? No one is there.
So questions, like the chairs, abide.

For Sarah Son

(a sonnet)

A sweetness in your face I saw that day
Was shining with the brightness of the sun
Whose strength revealed in radiance the way
That light and heat can co-exist as one.
As much as we need light to follow fate

To see our dreams, becoming real, come true,
In warmth the fecund sun provides its mate,
And, Sarah, both of these I found in you.
Disappear, and it is as if in gray
I walk in shim and shadow. Nothing burns
Within, yet when again you rise the day
In glorious sun, the waking day, returns.
But nurture me like sunlight from above,
And I will thrive in corresponding love.

A Poem in Honor of Sarah Son's Self-Portrait in Bronze

A naked girl is shorn and waits,
poised at a moment to see
something far less of time
than eternity.

Her arms are extended for compassion
as though for solace from above,
in a state of suspended passion
for love.

A crucifix forms in supplication,
redemptive in the way a plea
shapes itself in a prayer
of humility.

The eyes are closed in serenity
with an endurance also implied
in which something also
Has died —

died not in the way of actual death
but to vanities of empty life,
forgoing as by a vow
every strife.

Such strength in a delicate figure,
her body in balance, at peace,
part at rest, part in rigor,
part release.

The elemental posture recapitulates
the essentially Christian one,
that only by losing our life
is it won.

Thanatopsis

What's the shape of pain, crushedness, no doubt.
It is rare to find a cultivated garden or landscape

in which the Japanese artist-gardener has not,
say, stunted trunks or twisted trees to suit

his taste, rearranging rocks for desired effects
and replacing natural grass with sand or stone

for purposes wholly non-utilitarian in character.
Shaped gardens, shaped green, shaped fruit.

But artifice is by nature only temporizing fun.
We live not in a garden but in a cold stone quarry,

blue-chipped relentlessly under skies and sharp.
We are all heading into an uncultivated world,

bank on it, as clueless as we entered this one,
screaming, naked, blind, salted, wet, yellow.

We will all be crushed by pain as to be undone
and all begin to whine and then begin to bellow.

Confucius said that jade, with its sharp edges
that do not cut, hangs down to the ground —

like humility. Learn now that what is crushed
is a lesson that unambiguously applies to us,

whether any gardener twists his trees or not,
rearranging rocks, replacing grass with stone.

We are clueless. We are twisted. We are dirt.
We are bone. We are gone. We are done.

Thelma Ritter

It is clear she was born to look homely,
an appliance to brew coffee, fix a meal,

or iron shirts, while looking up frowning
at the ways of the world. Shapelessness

qualified the actress by exempting her from
passion precisely to give advice about it.

Whatever she did on screen, she always looked
as if she were about to go food-shopping or

had just done so. She often did errands, only
upon returning to flop into a chair, hat askew,

woofing air and shouting, "I'm bushed!" or,
squeezing a foot, "Strictly a trip for biscuits!"

Antidote to the befuddled: not girl gets boy,
not girl loses boy, but mophead spouts irony,

slyly quipping out of the side of her mouth,
as wide as a letter box, eyes slit and snide,

rebuttoning one of her shapeless dresses or
snatching at her hair, xerophytic vegetation,

her face cross and as white as bad ginger. "If
I had a bad leg and a guy was crazy about me,"

I'd say I was lucky," she yamphed at Susan Hayward
(*Wasn't she always folding clothes at such times?*)

said similar things to Marilyn Monroe, poor froggy
did, to Grace Kelly, to Bette Davis, to everybody

pretty. Everybody else. She wore dull cloth coats,
shrugged and smirked, smoked like an old trucker,

her cigarette wagging up and down realistically
to add to her wit. Did she really count as human?

"Whaddya gonna do without money?" she asked
Frank Sinatra whom she felt had a hole in the head.

Sometimes she picked her teeth with a card. Always
she slouched, one arm back-flapped on a sprung hip,

but wherever she was, no great miracles happened
there. She was trustworthy because she was plain,

homely as an empty glass of buttermilk. She'd been
around, OK? like comfy slippers, went by ambiguous

bulldog film-names like Clancy and Josie, knew what
males were up to and what they wanted and, you know

somethin', so what, life's like that for everyone,
face it, missie, and by the way who are you anyway

that you think your shit is strawberry shortcake?
Recovery remained uncertain until Thelma shoved

that pulled face, dull as an elbow, into the heroine's
life. "That's why the lovelorn always come to me

for advice," she told Jane Froman. "You wanna
coffee? On the double. Whazzat? You wanna talk?

When you should be takin' a rest? To talk about
what? Lemme guess. Romance? O boy. *O brother*!"

Kissing Sarah

"In the wee wee hours, that when I thank of you."

— Chuck Berry

It did not seem planned,
only part of a gentle surprise,
the way a bright sky at sunset foretells a wind.
Do not look, do not press. Pausing
To look into her eyes, with a greenness
to melt you.

Need is the adventure, as you
feel the light in her beating heart,
the way a pale yellow sky foretells early rain.
But the rain is your love. Fate, as
you inhume her sighs, their hotness,
is dealt you.

The Writer As Figurine Baked to Sell

"There is not theory that is not a fragment
carefully, prepared of some autobiography."
— Paul Valery

Don't we simply say to seem, present
ourselves as a way or advertising what we seem to say?
I am a signboard, you wackos. Wake up!

To hear ourselves talking words in high
report is to defang them. Do we not in a sense
get rid of what we give birth to?

By emptiness, do we not prove
by definition that something elsewhere is full
of meaning as a pail of water?

But what is missing is what's there
— presence as a kind of absence — for all to devour.
Crafty intent absolves nothing, friend.

A figurine, baked to sell, taken
from its mold, creates perforce a hollow shape in us
as the rubber mold serves to show.

Any rhyming metricalist unburdens
himself with dash, simply serving to show he means
a good deal more to himself by words,

oh so carefully prepared, tapped out
by notes in clicks like code and then he is empty.
Better silence? The Good Grey Poet

fairly agreed: "Good-bye my fancy —
(I had a word to say, but 'tis not quite the time —
the best of any man's word or say

is when its proper place arrives
and for its meaning, I keep mine till the last.)"
Words, words, words.

Isaiah is filled with commentary, saying
not so much that terrible iniquities have separated
even hopping fools from God

as how twaddle and empty argument
must take place only where no one calls for justice
or pleads with one's integrity.

Photo Infringement

A photo in an unforgiving way
reminds us with unforgiving candor of what
invariably we thought forgot.

When Steiglitz blithely proposed to us
that his pictures of cloud formations were
   equivalents of his inner feelings

and mental states, didn't he know
that all photographs also mirror the viewer
   whether he desires it or not?

Is the past by definition embellished?
No one is in sight but ourselves, candidly shotlit
   to dog us later like unconfessed sin.

I in my mind wait in the Rue de Choiseul
with wrong thoughts, wrong shoes, wrong hat,
   persuaded in the morning light there,

a fool, not a graphic muscularity worth
art, in my slovenliness not whole but only part
   of my own fragmentary failure,

that I far and away best replicate my faults
by what is seen of grim, glowering me caught
   by a camera for inflexible eternity.

The hand-held camera makes the photographer
with his ready plates and mobility a kind of freak
   who with cunning snaps our souls.

How truly disenfranchised we are
by anything that memory, like sin, reminds us of,
   whether beside, below, within, or above.

A Poem Written On The Week Of My Engagement

On an Advent night and cold
the Eastern star so bright and clear
   I find with the simultaneous

musicalizing branches in ice
which freeze-click in the darkened trees
above my beating heart,

so very like your beauty,
Sarah, midnight, mystery, bright, clear
mystic, dark, a firmament star

yourself, I find such joy
in knowing that the Advent season
with its penitential grace

brings you into my waiting life
just as Christ is born into the world
to try to put an end to strife.

We are redeemed as well
by those whose saving love adorns us
as whom we choose to love,

and so on this Christmas night
of starlight and darkened trees with long
and icy branches numb

I call upon the infant Christ
to hear, like Sarah, what is in my beating
heart and into it may come.

Stony Brook, N.Y.
Dec. 20, 2001

Metonymy

I remember back in the 1980s
during the craze among women for carrot cake
— formulas were top-secret —

thinking not so much *women are*
truly crazy, fighting the urge to disclose
　　how much cinnamon or mace to use

or if to include them at all
nor how it all seemed tied to original sin,
　　avarice then, avarice now,

though that, but about *baking*?
And what to leave out and what to throw in,
　　with cunning and guile the ruse?

No, what I thought while I ate
during that craze, fighting the urge to say why
　　made me only say *I see, I see,*

for I knew as surely as fate
(another formula but never said with a sigh)
　　that marriage was not for me.

Brevity

Light is disappearing,
even as it's seen. That's why Popes
　　earn no salaries —

they're ready to die
when they are chosen. Didn't Balzac
　　try to tell us that

fame is the sun of
the dead? Hope is quite as brief
　　as wit in a human head.

Blindsight

If in our body we construct our mind, our mind
is a body image. We shave its feelings like stubble

and wait for its approval. Amputations by leaving
a phantom left hand make one mysteriously real.

The brain mapping a surface of the body makes it
a strip of cortex we need to know. A sensory signal

is basically a need to activate another missing self.
A face wakes to a wince the way neuropathy fabricates

a kiss. Pain is created by our need, a construct of
something there. Blindsight. Our brains in short

run our lives in the way we decide we will not talk
to someone unless she puts that cigarette out, now.

A Lion Can't Bite Through A Pangolin

Death is a contraction issue in the way
that we come to learn if it intends to stay.

A lion can't bite through a pangolin,
whose body of horn, as grey as slate,

can, it is reported, repel a rifle bullet.
Is a lion therefore given to conclude

a pangolin is stone in the very way,
after chewing a zebra's softer flank,

finding the wild wet revenue to taste,
that a bite through a body not horn

repels nothing? At the terrible moment
a rifle bullet bites into a lion, turning it

as gray as slate and soon enough to stone,
does it not realize it is not a pangolin

the way, say, a bitten pangolin knows
a zebra's softer flank is never his?

Death is a contraction issue in the way
we come to learn if it intends to stay.

Louise Brooks and Greta Garbo Spend the Night Together

Let imagination be a form of memory
allowing, by denying time, two beauties

to caress, celluloid lovers in a room
— it actually took place one night —

a whispering detente with two Hollywood
exquisites, a world above even A-list

types, never mind lesser actresses of
the was/then pricing sort and no end

of dress-extras lolling around sets,
big-bummed, hair like hatcheted flax,

who had crushes on the two themselves
and kept posters of *Camille* and *Pandora!*

Who was the matchhead, who the match,
when potassium chlorate whipscratched

red phosphorus? Was it Greta caressing
Weezie's legs like beathing a beech bowl

or Louise spoonroasting lovely Greta's
pale cheeks with her wimbling tongue?

I see them eating with their hands, Louise
in bluesilk pajamas, naked from the waist

up, neither for the Double-Talk Express
(information leads to misinformation),

getting right to the point initially with
plumulaceous kisses, ear-rings taken off,

an hour smelling bottles of Mohn perfume,
glasses of aquavit with a 21-gun salute;

when each fed the other creams, no trace of
rubber taste, the defect of lesser chocolates.

Greta then slips out of a crystal nightgown
into the soft vair in which she mutters love.

Mirror to mirror is not quite the image
you want, not just black helmet hair as

opposed to brown wispy bunting or Sweden
trying cluck-talk to Cherryvale, Kansas.

Garbo whose forté was intuitive éclat, not
thought, had nothing at all like Brooks' brain.

Wordlessly, as naked as Bronzino Venuses,
they express in the Monadnock formation what

I would do, you would do, he, she, or it
would do if memory were not required and

imagination were real enough to allow time
to give us either beauty to caress (or both)

like celluloid lovers at midnight, sublime
in bed, aflame, ready to pledge our troth.

Martha Graham and Agnes DeMille

Misses Martha Graham and Agnes DeMille
never performed on a double bill,

two horse-faced women in New York City
with nothing to give in the way of pity,

for fame deigns never to share a stage,
not with bold artists advanced in age;

two bright red rubies held side by side
will stain each other and cannot abide

each other's flash. And so the two of them,
danced alone until their feet turned blue.

One raised her leg like the letter L,
the other did giddy-up steps to tell

of dancing cowpokes and pioneer man,
of which the other cared nary a damn.

Martha once wore a Cantonese tunic
to play Katerfelto in the suburbs of Munich,

which yawning Agnes dismissed as soma
when compared to her dances in Oklahoma!

Agnes confided to friends of Graham,
"She choreographs the utterest mayhem"

and managed not, which was her way,
to stifle the urge to let out a neigh.

But Martha's friends asked Agnes DeMille,
"Are your dancers moving or standing still?

How dare you speak of a show's renown
with a hero dressed like a rodeo clown?

Find a nut from Fall River a subject fit
— an axe murderess! — for the stage legit.

These two yentas who changed their names
would each for glory have set in flames

while everyone watched in a public square
each quivering quim of their pubic hair

but done it alone, and this is my point,
refusing to share their work in a joint,

perform the same benefit or even attempt
to share a marquee without contempt

or say a good word or think to try
the merest rapprochement, which is why

Miss Martha Graham and Agnes DeMille
never once performed on a double bill.

249

In Tunis I Walked Through Halfaween

In Tunis, I walked through Halfaween,
a slum quarter, trays of sweets, impudent
spiels, toothachy candy, Bedouin in

from the *bled*, streaks of children,
urchins pandemonic, coffee vendors clacking
cups in your face like castanets,

liquids as yellow as pencils, red as
medicine, green as dye. I solve a riddle
under the white sun, while I watch

at noon under a minaret and courtyard
of mosques erected by the Aghlabites. A man
who kisses his forefinger in greeting

at a table gathers a woman to him,
surrendering to whispers. All cities are
founded in fear. What are the Tunis

afraid of? The sea. I watched them,
as I saw Byrsa, Dido's mountain, recalling
in her loveliness loosing his lust,

while she drew her *ha'ik* tight
across her back and under her buttocks
which to the Tunisian male

is the focus of voluptuousness,
how colorfully candy-like a lovely woman,
like Dido, won't be trifled with,

for colors, red, yellow and, green,
her impudent spiels, her castanets, ringing
in the air, make not just magic

of her but unsolvable mystery,
giving her unquestionably an aura of
real danger like the sea.

John Brown's Music

I once read in a musty book
John Brown loved Schubert's "Serenade"

and suddenly saw the old
Puritan weeping to the air disconsolate.

F.B. Sanborn had seen him
in Peterboro, N.H. in February 1858,

old hands in his lap,
jimmy-jawed, wet eyes, and stretched

to hear him speak. Who recalls
he wore red slippers at his hanging?

They surely served
on some level as part of his music.

May I Say Why I See I Finally Saw Why?

If white is expected of a ghost,
for example, as oak in a Cabernet
or a Merlot or Chardonnay,

giving it being, as it were,
colors it in the very same way that one
tends to regard water in Monet,

defining by scent or texture
or shape or body or hue or size what a soul
in a body's supposed to say,

I finally see why, may I add,
when everything is finally said and done,
that you seem made of clay.

Sound and Sense

There are so many sounds that make
so little sense in the silences of night
that all-night vigils of spirit

become the only prayer I make
against those silences, so to sweep away
at night the very sounds of sense.

Sarah's Hair is Like the Night

"Beauty is the experimental proof that the Incarnation is in
    fact possible."

— Simone Weil

Sarah's hair is like the night,
touched with glancing starry beams;
such a face as drifts through dreams,
this is Sarah to the sight.
And the touch of Sarah's hand
is as light as milk-weed down,
when the meads are golden-brown,
and the autumn fills the land.
Sarah: just the gentle echoing
of her voice brings back to me,
from the far portals of memory
all the loveliness of spring:
Sarah! Sarah!
Such a face as drifts through dreams,
this is Sarah to the sight.

Bird in Winter

A black-and-white day in winter
plagued me when a painted bunting flew by
black red green and yellow

with glistening beak, was there
for me alone, and a terrible answerlessness
silencing me that day just went.

Clearance Sale

After all her chores were done, washing,
wiping, waiting for a buggy for a time,

young Miss Culp, of the Old Order Amish,
saw a primrose ribbon at the five-and-dime

and, looking at it longingly, picked it up,
for it was an adornment she could not have,

as plain-sects cannot. She dreamt of a boy
sitting alone in the jewelweed and thought

of being married, probably in November (less
farm work) on a chosen Tuesday or a Thursday

in the clean red-and-white house she copied
on her quilt with patches from her piece-bag

where she stitched in thread the light blue
rain she often watched pattering her window

when all her work was done. How that wet pane
seemed like her heart waiting for the sun again.

Capharnaum

I was waiting there
in empty Pottersville for you —

grimoires of fog looping around
railroad tracks the color of sarcoma

Surely nothing is
too awful not to be true

A Mick at Nantasket Beach

"You don't expect anything decent to come from an Irishman."
— Margaret Thatcher, British Prime Minister

An Irish yob, typically pink with white hair,
spooning up a strawberry soda, pictorially

embodies his very drink while nosing the foam,
growing as passion pink with wet satisfaction.

The way he plaps his tongue serves to show,
cold reverberations in a sort of runaway face,

complacent, with a kind of stubbornness he
in a heartless way might coldly show a son.

A slurping gluttony puts piggishness in the eyes.
He pauses to stare, an empty glare, spoon high.

Part rubena vase, part large crackle-glass cruet
comprise a head, with crimping and crizzling

and wine-bud ornaments stippling the cheeks,
he clacks the spoon around for a few last bits.

How that dumpiness, those mis-rolled pants,
popcorn hair, as he smugly smacks his lips,

makes him belong to nothing like the sea, as if
he had bought his treat alone to feign some fun.

How dry and shapeless those etiolated shins
contrast with that flaring face as pink as pop,

so oddly out of synch in sun. No sun, no sun.
Or really fun. No wonder the Irish hate blacks.

Shear Madness

That's why they want to cut your hair,
women, no, not pushing for "inalienable rights,"
not *sovereignty*. Fat Chaucer was right.

Isn't it socially inept to wear new leather?
So why then let her mis-sculpt her talentless
and hacking asseverations on your head?

Doesn't newness alone intrigue her,
although any garden should look ten years old,
an experiment in rearranging

to work up a supplemental man
as if by her mad clucking tongue and cutlery
she's fashioning another fuck.

Idleness bores her rigid. Samson more.
She loves to hear the slashing *snitch snitch snitch*
and no nasty corrections. I say enough!

Hands off the secateurs , you hear,
If blinders, reins, and tackle I won't wear.
Join a local topiary club, you bitch.

Presidential Candidate

A child signing the steamed
pane with his pressing nose and fingerprints
wishes for glory, the way

fascist fuckers yearn to salute.
See foxes in the vineyard. *Füchse in Weinberg.*
Talk about long rifles

makes a rightist badly pine
ostentatiously to drape himself in rainbows
of medals and stiff gold braids.

It is his main attraction,
like a greedy shroff wish-washing dry hands,
aching to sell you furniture.

How I wish you could sew
that wide Mussolini mouth of yours finally shut
and go perennially mute

but predictable you
insist on marching out parades of clichés,
sanctioning your lies.

Chant and Lament for the Union and Confederate Dead

Alabama, Chattahoochee, Susquehanna, Tennessee,
Bull Run, Mississippi, Mills Springs, Pamunkey
Flow with blood through every stream,
Steam from beneath in incessant mud,
Flood as they run as if in a dream.

Roanoke, Ball's Ford, Rappahannock, Rapidan,
Potomac, Mississippi, Big Black, Ketchikan,
Flow with blood through every stream,
Steam from beneath in incessant mud,
Flood as they run as if in a dream.

Chickahominy, James, Totopotomoy Creek,
Cumberland, North Anna, Ohio, Warwick,
Flow with blood through every stream,
Steam from beneath in incessant mud,
Flood as they run as if in a dream.

Twin Towers

Again,
In our history,
Shadowy signs of
Messianism. Weirdly,
Vertical becomes horizontal
In a paradox of worship:
What's that black odor?
I distinctly recognize
Religion
There.

September 11, 2001

The Nowhere A Person Meanders To

The nowhere a person meanders to
invariably becomes real for them.

When and where a real place exists
makes meandering both matter and not.

Matter in a way opposes meandering
which is what nowhere is all about.

A real place tends badly to require
that we find a nowhere to meander to.

All persons who meander to nowhere
deserve the real place it becomes.

A real place can become nowhere when
meandering means nothing to a person.

Nowhere in the matter of meandering
makes a real place possible in fact.

What nowhere is and a real place is
not become the same thing in dreams.

Airing is the Least Dangerous

I spoke when my turn came,
finally, of what in you I detested,
aware in what I said

that nothing was requested.
Not colorfast, rumpled, heavy when wet
like the nap of textile,

your flatness left the image
and drape of a slept-in coverlet in me.
I absolutely lied

precisely and with guile
when I pretended to try to tend to see
in seeking to understand

you didn't need a thorough
cleaning, brush, beating, to be freshened;
for airing a thing can be dicey.

So now for you, to be just,
I do what follows the one cardinal rule
for cleaning a quilt:

do not do too much;
only to avoid later feelings of guilt,
do only what you must.

Winter Wounds

Imagine the moron
Who is loved
Thinking she deserves
By looks or fame or fate
Another's heart,
And so reserves
Part of what she thinks
She shouldn't give
To her less-deserving mate.
You can take the time,
Queen Pig, to spend
A lifetime as a fop?
We deserve nothing,
Unless everything —
You are certainly
Not enough —
To compensate for all
The lies we're told,
Your haughty huffs.
If someone in the world
Should ever be chosen

To rage against the cold
At the last minute,
The pall of coming death,
It won't be me;
I'll welcome it,
Without deliberation,
Without a reservation,
Winter wounds and all.

Israel

A couple with pouched
cunning eyes, and sharp,

while the black-hatted
bearded jeweler in a wheel hat

surveil a box
of estate diamond rings

impatiently waiting,
peers through an old curtain

in a small dark shop
on crooked Kite St.,

to a distant hill
it occurs to him to build upon.

A Sonnet On the Occasion of the Marriage Of Will and Alison

May 10, 2003

In the fancy of his sweetest dreams,
Smitten by passion, stricken by song,
For a huntress brave as Ali seemed
To wake in anyone a challenge strong,
Will hoped to win (and did) what she by loss
Submitted to for love, yet he was caught
Like the stag who yields. But no remorse
Is felt by lovers true, for what is taught
If anything in matters of the heart
Is, strangely, that when most we yield,
By proving we command our better part,
We then become the victor in the field.

The paradox all lovers should believe
Is that by giving they in turn receive.

Fessenden: On the Occasion of its 100th Year

for Peter Palandjian

What memory extols, prevails:
At Fessenden School on its hundredth year
a century past speaks of a century to come,
another hundred years of growth,
for a promise of continuity is made
where teachers, masters, taking unformed boys
in jackets, ties, and emblems red and gray,
— youngest, it seems, among the very young—
instruct those whom they also guide
both in classrooms and on fields of play.
"Receive my instruction, and not silver,
and knowledge rather than choice gold."
we are told in Proverbs 8, Verse 10.
It is on these grounds and in this place
of excellence, of boys becoming men,
where character is built, and where
our feelings for this school, repeatedly told,
truly constitute a kind of faith.
for it is here, by what we were assigned,
that we awakened to a better mind.

****

What do we seek as we return today?
We walk among old buildings and old dorms,
eager to see what we might discover,
stand in the doorways of old rooms,
looking back the way we look ahead,
to find what we essentially uncover.
When other names at school on doors we pass
to find our room as, older, we re-awake

to schoolboy dreams, we tend to find
less of what we wish to know and feel
of what once we did and once we said,
than our school's old dusty histories.
How a door frame is a kind of riddle,
open to little more than mysteries
of looking back, indeed of looking ahead.
Fessenden a hundred years ago
was no less real than this small school
we celebrate today. Other boys
who knew its sacred walls, echoing halls,
were also surely prone to try to find
meaning in what they sought to know
of teachers, stewards, study, laughter, play
and yet the years have also passed for them
with names on doors, frames on doors, all new.
No elegy sir low us all. we need to say
of what in our hearts we need to bind.
Not lightly does the whisper fall today,
"Where does a century go that's spent?"
I simply say to you; it never fell away.
Nor is what we seek truly lost in kind
of what of ourselves we yearn to find
that coming from the past to us is sent.
We stand in doorways of our old rooms
eager to see what we might: discover,
looking back the way we look ahead,
to find what we essentially uncover.
A door frame, if a kind of riddle, says
as well that we can also look two ways
and in so doing find what we would seek
"Where does a century go that's spent?'
I say nothing that awaits us
is ever essentially more,
nothing basically less.
What is thought, to me, is but rethinking.
Life, more than anything, is lent.
The finding is in the seeking.
What we seek we possess.

****

What memory extols, prevails:
At Fessenden School on its hundredth year
A century past speaks of a century to come,
another hundred years of growth,
for a promise of continuity is made
where still the portals of those rooms remain
through which, for a century again,
considering the past, pondering the future,
by what, learning here, we took away
we may measure what we were and can ever be,
with instruction our silver, knowledge our gold,
I evoke this spirit in memory's name,
a legacy true for both young and old
to cherish in values that ever remain,
May our school ever endure! I breathe it
into my own sons' lives when they enroll,
schooled to honor and manners we all know,
that it may continue for other generations
who with God's help and in perpetual grace
will at his dear school flourish forever.

I Got A Christmas Card From Kreskin

I got a Christmas card from Kreskin
on a late gray December day,
not even something my best kin
with idle compliments to pay

at this lonely time of the year
would frankly deign to send
who to me are neither dear
at the start of or at year's end.

He had to know who disliked me
and of course whom I abhorred,
thoughtless uncles I forever flee
and aunts who leave me bored,

two sisters hypocritical and fat,
brothers as slippery as grease.
Yes, he might foresee all that
and divine the need for peace,

of course, in times like ours,
know as well what I am thinking
and how leaden are the hours
that keep a person drinking.

My only thought struck like a dart
is: where he's from, dear Lord above,
who so can pierce the human heart
and know which of us needs love?

Sardines Laced with Anti-Freeze

Two fat sisters, one with vague maladies,
the other the abstract vice of instincts,

had been fleecing their mother for years,
visiting her, as if with love, for checks,

all this before the murder and the trial
you've read about in the *Globe* for weeks.

Of jewels there were none: but they stole,
before she died at 103, most of my mother,

money, mind, finally racing about the house
(each in different rooms) for sheets, a lamp,

old photos, a leather sofa, clocks, stuffing
pillowcases with what tag-sale magpies call

"smalls" — had they been eyeing each other
at that time and had grudges then begun? —

good knives, one brand coat, a leather bag,
two cans of anti-freeze, in the pantry tins,

and a leftover cake both wolfed down, coldly
eyeing each other's fat bags for spoils, or so

it was brought out, as you well know, in court.
They'd screwed out the window-locks, as well,

and boosted every tool from the back shed.
(Big after small is always comic, a spoor

of silent movies, like hippos wearing hairnets.)
No books for them who did not like to read

except their mother's bank accounts, as empty at
the end as the bureau drawers of deal scoured

of all dead papers, letters, records, notes, stubs,
an out-of-date insurance policy in rubber bands,

lest anyone discover what they had bilked her
of, tens of thousands of dollars, thousands more,

to redo their kitchens, invest in funds, and
spend on food, including, no doubt, that one

can of sardines fatally laced with coolant
that one of them ate as another played fate

in who knows what kind of defining scrim?
Necessities disintegrated their certitudes,

but it was greed made up their necessities.
Can hate then trump acquisitiveness? The dog

in each win out, snarling over improportions?
Did one, descrying her schemes in another,

seek justification in rubbing out the blot?
Was it finally envy that infuriated them?

Or had their children or husbands fought,
snarling over who got what and why and how?

Is prevention of another's happiness more
a force than the celebration of one's own?

Do rival monsters in coming to recognize
another monster demonstrate? Who cares.

Covetousness itself is ever a god of scorn,
a solid guarantee to look under your word.

Greed like these sisters, much alike in shape,
let them copy each other to exactitude, and so

one would perpetrate always do exactly what,
simply perpetrating, the other always did.

So, who killed whom, to bear the shame?
It does not matter. Both were the same.

A fat woman arrested, a fat one dead —
part of each other, like a neck a head.

Coward McCann, Inc.

I used to make faces of the Cs,
by making them Os in my school textbooks
when coming across that name

which appeared like a producer
of movies as a cocky endorsement virtually
on every page and spine,

a buffoon emerging in my mind,
devising loopy cartoons, mostly of him
whom I believe I saw and knew.

He was a coward, yes, and fat,
Irish, and wore big dumb shoes. Being
literal is a kid's prerogative,

but a weird publisher's name
might have been a foreign country or a
freighter beckoning me aboard

or, by an authenticity I chose
to create, some porker in tweeds offering
lots of Cs to fill for fun

in books covered with oilcloth,
yellow and ugly, smelling of kerosene,
with the sheen of mucus

and threads that came away
at the margins, that on sweltering days
were inclined to stick,

unlike my attention which,
when I should've been figuring how long
it took a sailing ship,

heading north at 15 mph,
from Norfolk to Portland, Maine
at high noon, to arrive,

I was alone in the back row,
day-dreaming, one elbow stuck like glue
to the nap of another book,

giving Frankensteinian life
to an overweight man with oodles of Os
or maybe doodling sails

but, unlike that ship, busy
and plying quizzical seas, yawning
and going nowhere fast.

Sarah Son's Portrait of Alex

Christmas 2003

Sometimes I'm the watcher
and sometimes the participant. Here I'm both,
an actor, wired, waiting.

trying to classify a fact
or interpret one of the frenzies of the world.
Does that gamboge complexion

reflect the enervations
of my working too hard? Intensity of vision?
Or is that a cyperpunk,

defiant with his divinity,
who boldly believed the girl who painted this,
intrepidly ready to see

I could be this dilated,
restless, unverifiable, hungry to know, tut-
mouthed, advancing without

and with convictions, also
loved me from the very first time I saw *her*?
She rescues my negligence

here, knows what I imagine.
There has always been something of the crow
in me, perched to peer,

jittery to jump about
whatever space I can to own what I might,
black feathers and all,

numbering several selves,
concentrating mostly on the lyrical skills
this most intensive face

promises I am capable of,
with me only hoping, as actor and acted upon,
with such a noble stare,

that, when looking at me
in such a valued state, I deserve to be as well
the valued me who's there.

Malcolm X's Food

Blackness, to some, is damp and white,
nothing nurturing, only desiccation.

Or is whiteness wet and darkness not,
the way snow suckles earth to health?

Malcolm X who consumed a quart of milk
with every single evening meal he took

also never failed to pour it in his coffee,
whitening the oily blackness to his taste.

A weakness for banana splits gave him
butter-fat and strength, he also felt,

for fasting three full days every month
which he did with solemn Muslim probity;

yet no chocolate and whipped-cream
combo was ever lost on him for fun,

the way his pilgrimage to holy Mecca
taught him that such and such a thing

are one. "Don't play with your food"
was just what he did *not* do to find

at his meals between sips and bites
a kitchen comment on civil rights.

Whiteness, to some, is sweet, and black
nothing nourishing, only innutrition.

Or is darkness wild and whiteness not,
the way rain distributes its wealth?

Marian Apparitions

I throw my crutch
at psychoneuroimmunological
creed.

I wish to shun
any paramysticotheological
need.

I hope to curse
all semiphenomenoecclesiastical
greed.

I hate to grow
most preteromiraculoabnormal
weed.

I refuse to eat
all physioparapsychological
feed.

Sylvia Plath at the Cinema Watching
Oklahoma!

"It is hot, steamy and wet. It is raining. I am tempted to
write a poem. But I remember what it said on one rejection
slip. After a heavy rainfall, poems titled 'Rain' pour in from
across the nation"

Sylvia Plath, diary entry

August 1, 1950

Alone, she ducked into the cinema
to get away from the pressure, out of the cold, her rooms,
London traffic, rain, black memories

as recent as yesterday, when a rent
rise made writing hateful poems ridiculous, and
was now watching musical cowpokes,

muttering dark words to herself
like those that irked bearded Eli the Hebrew priest
who, hearing barren Hannah's pleas,

confused her desperate prayers
with the hyprerfrenzied rant of any ravening drunk.
Sylvia had two children

and wasn't praying. All that yellow
American sunshine seemed not so much wrong
as simply not applying to her.

Masquerade rules all the living,
votaries in printed calico who dance to costume pain.
Farmers! Cattlemen! Vacuities!

I crave anonymity, she reflected,
slumped down in her doubts, puffing on a cigarette
but exhaling only fatal regrets.

She who had read 1 Samuel 13:15
would have pleaded with Jehovah to shut her womb,
had she been praying instead

of sadly watching hokey hoe-downs
in mellow Claremore in June weather no fat smiling
Stoic would dare to conceive!

Community is corny, prayer just talk.
for when did any colloquy ever yield the truth?
I want anonymity, she thought,

for not only nothing I remember,
but *"Oh, what a beautiful morning"* represents
   exactly nothing I know.

Hope was a lie, and Hannah deluded.
Fuck Elkanah who farcically claimed he loved her with
   extra sweets. Men are old music,

black beasts who knife your heart!
Foolish Laurey falling for all that shopworn rubbish!
   Curly was Jed. No warm sun

can impress me, she realized, nor
whooping idiots who go on shivarees, dumb enough
   to communicate by thought-balloons!

To be betrayed by American sun,
light, dance, those incessant lassoes, cowboys. Corn.
   I prefer to dematerialize, by gas.

Satan Traversing The Earth

"And Jehovah said unto Satan, 'Whence comest
   thou?' Then Satan answered Jehovah and said 'From
   going to and fro in the earth, and from walking
   up and down in it."
— Job 1:7

Do you fly, walk, swim, perhaps cycle,
a sierra of teeth clenched against wind?
Are you hunched? Call yourself Michael?
Visit solely those who have sinned?

The picture instilled is you burrow
   doesn't moving the earth imply simply that?
— a stinking mole be-snouting a furrow
   or skitting dryly through cane like a rat.

But when you confess to walking I see
how being deliberate's also perfidious
as you pause to rest by a wall or a tree.
(The horror of being efficient is hideous!)

When Jehovah inquires where you have been,
and you reply the earth you've traversed,
do you know who is doomed, do you mean,
already judged who among us is cursed?

How strange He had no idea where you were,
implying ignorance of where you are going;
if unseen by Him you can horribly stir,
what chance have we ever seeing or knowing

how swiftly a devil can trot, walk, or run
backwards and forwards, now up and then down,
going down to burrow, bobbing up to come,
all helter-skelter without turning around?

Your evil disclosure yet makes us alert
by the casual words with which you boast
of the devious way you can levy hurt
traversing the world from coast to coast,

whether hastening to or fleeing from,
so we above all must hasten to know
there are no customs whenever you come,
there are no borders wherever you go.

Your reply to Jehovah's question makes clear,
not as a foreigner but a native you go,
crossing earth's borders without any fear,
Satanic heel turning, Satanic toe,

wherever you travel finding free reign,
with demon to demon, fraternity strong,
encouraged no doubt to come back again
to be greeted in covens where you belong.

What in Jehovah went missing that day,
wondering how you your actions renew
in spreading evil along your dark way
and allow you simply to do what you do

as if this dominion's your own to traverse
walking its rim like a landlord his land?
Was that a blessing and not a dark curse
called down upon you by His holy hand?

But Jehovah's question still teaches us
what answer in turn to Satan declare
who confesses the way he reaches us
in his dominion of earth and of air:

You who can freely wander this region
where sin gives you such sanction to selve
must find suitable souls which are legion
in whose blackened hearts you can delve.

Yet your evil candor makes us alert
by the casual words with which you boast
of the devious way you can levy hurt
crossing the world from coast to coast

whether by your going or coming from,
so we above all must hasten to know
there are no customs whenever you come,
there are no borders wherever you go.

Open-Road Endings

No one vaguely heading nowhere
in particular, positive though he may seem,
is going on a picnic, OK?

I remember how in so many movies
I walked out of the theater feeling cold, more
or less convinced, squinting

as the lights came up, blinding
me, that nothing was resolved in finales
where figures trundled away,

merely. What was Chaplin saying
with all those open-road endings? Showing
all of us the way to Shenandoah?

Some other life? Another face,
another name on another head in another play
for another fate to pursue?

Regarding *The Kid, The Little Tramp,
City Lights*, what's insured by walking away
where the black-eyed susans grow?

Does being worthy of salvage
always mean crossing over a hill, turning
a corner? *Moving*? Should

a vanishing point galvanize
old dreams that seem less like hope than
an ungratifying pelerinage,

something we tell ourselves
of an aspiring sort (swallowing) when, say,
a child of ours has drowned,

and we weakly hug each other,
biting our lips, with, "Don't worry. He's
gone to a better place"?

I am not saying a better place
lies at the end of a road leading somewhere
in particular, let me add,

or a better land I know, in the
words of Old Black Joe, rather a spot that
when you come to it that road

reaches its end, that's all,
comes to a final ineluctable stop, I say,
    to let you put down your load.

Foul Air

Fat Ann Marie Prayless
in order to weigh less
upon going out to eat
carried a snack
to take home to attack
with an expeditious retreat.

She would land on her bed
with portions all spread
between chubby ankles apart
and call it a diet
in the midst of the quiet
by expelling a trumpet-like fart.

Two Sisters

" And a man's foes *shall be* they of his own household."
— Matthew 10: 36

There were two sisters, looking like a misters,
    cunning as misers of old,
whose bottomless greed outreaching their need
in their black scheming hearts planted a seed,
    already unspeakably cold.
After their father's death, their mother
wrote checks to each, as each told the other,
    for visits they made (for show),
so as time went by their mother they fleeced
by the cunning they hid and the guile they released
before any money the quite-nearly deceased
    could possibly elsewhere bestow.

No whores on the street whose penchant to cheat
　　were hungrier than these tubs
for in girth both were big as an Arkansaw pig
who in the trough, grunting, continued to dig
　　while dealing their siblings snubs.
Week after week they would drive in their car,
claim (what martyrs!) they liked driving far,
　　if for their mother's sake.
Five brothers, rivals, more honest than they
were no more deserving, they felt, than, say,
already big bullocks deserved more hay —
　　and, if so, let them eat cake.

The women got houses, to which their spouses —
　　for they were married, as well —
ascertained values and carried the keys,
walked off the acreage and counted the trees
　　for the option one day to sell.
Of course neither husband ever appeared
lest wifely wealth be seen to be shared
　　and so the enterprise blow.
The tuba swore to mother they'd provide care
if she fracture a hip or slip on a stair
and in every way her last days prepare
　　with no one to over know.

They managed by snatches to gather in batches
　　real property and cash,
amounting to hundreds of thousands at least
swilled down like pork at a twelve-hour feast
　　leaving nothing but ash.
The older of pirates, to establish a link,
washed the old woman's hair in a basin sink
　　to leave with a bigger check.
Still, their poor old mother hadn't a clue
as to who was the driver, who was the screw,
saw only both daughters as shiny and new
　　and morally correct.

It needed no guess where all the largesse
　　was spent of the money they took.
One fixed up the house she was given free
and paid out her daughter's four-year fee
　　for college without a look.
She blithely proceeded to buy a new auto,
a Mac for her son, and play at the Lotto
　　to try for a little more.
The other rehabbed her kitchen, then bid
to annex some land and develop the grid
which in final expenses Blenheim outdid,
　　stairway, window, and door.

All the while they brought presents to say
　　how deeply their mother they loved.
A vase, cheap candy, some gardening tools
they'd offer with drama as if rare jewels,
　　feigning heaven they'd moved.
They'd then throw a small geranium down
bending to anchor it tight in the ground
　　with always a show of pain;
then home they would race with another check,
the old lady's bank at their call and beck,
all of that cash without risking their neck,
　　and who around to complain?

With the passing years, neither had fears
　　of ever being found out,
for who on the planet would ever be looking
for missing sums in books they were cooking
　　or what it was all about?
Their husbands meanwhile kept well out of view
lest they with their wives be seen to accrue
　　what secretly all put away.
To all house repairs they turned a blind eye,
simply living to steal and planning to lie,
counting the days for their mother to die
　　and irked a bit by the delay

But one day a brother to visit his mother
   by coming happened to see
some canceled checks on a desk in a pile
showing connivance and everything vile
   but nothing of mystery.
Hundreds of thousands of dollars they got,
houses, emoluments, jewelry, the lot,
   but further and further still —
one had her name on her mother's account,
to be near to her and so near the amount,
and became by going straight to the fount
   executrix of her will!

So brother revealed what had been concealed
   to another brother — the gall! —
who set out quickly from basement to roof
gathering stubs as positive proof
   to photocopy them all.
It turned out each sister was richer by twice
than their victim who still thought them nice,
   always helpful, and glad.
Let it be said in the midst of this murk
the sisters' husbands continued to work
as did each sister, never given to shirk
   with cash so easily had,

but who can thrive when an endless drive
   for money is never appeased?
The more they wanted the more unsettled
the sisters became and grew more nettled
   at the sums each other had seized.
The feckless husbands both joined in the fray,
defending whatever their wives had to say
   and threatening to sue,
while the sisters, reaching into their peeves,
confronted each other as jackals and thieves
of the type who, proving disloyal., then leaves
   the other party to stew.

When the final disclosure that led to exposure
    of both embezzling bitches
reached all the brothers they took for a ride
but not the old woman to whom they had lied
    to hornswoggle all of her riches,
the men sent out letters with documentation
pre-arranged for the sisters' humiliation
    when suddenly everything changed —
at 104 years of age to almost the day
the mother, with senility having its say,
in the small of the morning passed away
    and a funeral was arranged.

There was glacial tension at the convention
    at church the following days
when the two hoggish sisters as if by right
frog-marched to the front-row pew to alight
    on asses like airplane bays.
No one looking could fail to have caught
the venomous looks as each brother shot
    daggers of hate at their heads.
What were they thinking? Hadn't they guilt?
Doesn't scum seek release? Hypocrisy wilt?
Won't in the end even bad conscience tilt?
    Pomposity go to the sheds?

At the grave-site all stood as stiff as wood,
    cold looks never abating,
all had chipped in to see everything paid:
priest, gravestone, and a digging spade,
    including the coffin waiting.
But the spiteful sisters whispered complaints,
in regard to spending and lack of restraint.
    Why all the lavish taste?
Imagine those morons not trying to save.
A slab of real marble just for a grave.
And isn't a coffin finally only a cave?
    Wasn't it all a big waste?

A Song for a Ukelele

(sung preface)

A young man left with but dreams to essay
for whom handsome was more than a light-switch away
who knew he'd never find love as things fell out,
so ransacking his hopes and stifling doubt
packed up his bags and went walking out
traveled to where his heart could be free
beyond the land and behind the sea
singing this fantasy:

There are girls in Krematal and girls in Bolshoya Morskaya
    and possibly Volt Bani
        but the honey for my money is the one in a
chair of leather
who in passion puts together
green bean red curry for me
    in the shade
    of a glade
    underneath Snickersee.

(refrain)

"All chunkin' down. down the ravelin' river
Chunkin' down the wide ravelin' river,
All chunkin' down. down the ravelin' river,
Singin' as we go, oooooooo-oooooh...."

There are girls in Shanghai and girls in Back-of-the-Yards
    and no doubt far Phuket
        but the crumpet for my trumpet is the one who lolls
on a divan there
sexily connivin' where
she happily invites me to stay
    in the sun
    just for fun
    in faraway Botany Bay.
(refrain)

"All chunkin' down. down the ravelin' river
Chunkin' down the wide ravelin' river,
All chunkin' down. down the ravelin' river,
Singin' as we go, ooooooooo-ooooooh...."

There are girls in dirty Chelsea and girls in Schlegelville
    and of course on Mt. Rainbow
        but my pal of a gal is the one waking up
in the bright morning light
with memories of a wonderful night
    and plenty kissed she hopes to bestow
    on a grateful man
    with a tigerish tan
    in the sand of Cape Tigroe.
(refrain)

"All chunkin' down. down the ravelin' river
Chunkin' down the wide ravelin' river,
All chunkin' down. down the ravelin' river,
Singin' as we go, ooooooooo-ooooooh...."

There are girls in Johore and Trenganu and Gettysburg, Pa.
    and there on the Shanghai Bund
        but my favorite lookie is the cookie who will take me
by the hand
and sing me songs of love so grand
teaching lessons with her pillowy lips
    pressed to mine
    with warmth sublime
    joined by accompining hips.
(refrain)

"All chunkin' down. down the ravelin' river
Chunkin' down the wide ravelin' river,
All chunkin' down. down the ravelin' river,
Singin' as we go, ooooooooo-ooooooh...."

Objective Correlative

After learning that Sigmund Freud had died
from cancer of the jaw,
W. H. Auden promptly replied,
— lest any link be forthwith denied
of this logical law
by any corrupt denier —
"Who of us could have possibly thought
Sigmund was a liar?"

Pontius Pilate

If ancient wisdom recommended
bile as a sign of health, why is a teacher
rewarded if you agree with him,

just as Pilate, washing his claws
in a basin, is dismissively oppugned and
doomed as a lout for eternity

in the Apostles Creed? Are those
few deft rhythms we habitually invoke of him
all we are to know of his bile

or health? The politic worries
of a wife over a file of parading nightmares?
Fear of procuratorial damage?

Christ's biography is fat fact.
What do we know of Pilate's rummaging needs?
How he deployed his time? Solved

snailage in his gardens? Savored what
foodwiches? Did he love shrimp? Ocher art?
Catapults? Where was he born?

How did he himself spend a day
at the age of 12, yakking, near what mother
who wondered where *he* was

when they went to the Forum
shopping for a goat-ring, shoes, erector sets?
   If they all went to Daiae or saw

   the waterfalls of Tivoli or caught
miniature sea-battles in the Arena, did it not
   matter in the way of warmth?

   What do we know of his own pain?
Nothing over a life of thought? Of deed?
   Not a word. Not a creed.

   How is preferring one boot thief
over another different from choosing between
   two woebegone captives in a dock

   when, at least in the ragged way
life presents itself to me, almost nothing is clear?
   Soliciting opinion from a crowd,

   argued Pontius. would bridge a gap,
at least, even if you would insist cowards
   are craven and seek compromise.

   Why are no stories extant recounting
dirt-stained young women dragged by the hair
   as pitiful disrobed adulteresses

   and brought to him in shame?
Such backward adjustment, even if difficult,
   rarely occurs in those stories

   told by teachers who, I promise,
are rewarded only when you disagree with them,
   as when with the Apostles Creed,

   official prayer by official vote,
in the name of loyalty and faith and wonder,
   you in God's name dare inquire

what seems only fair to ask, even if
in the way of doing so, in rapid chant or rote,
who *that* man suffered under.

Sibling Rivalries

While we all share bloodlines, hula hoops, parents,
no one is raised equally in any family of siblings.

Major disparities exist, as to not only fat or thin
or rich or poor, touching on thousands of quibblings.

Each child, first off, inherits two different parents,
who determine favorites without any rhyme or reason,

quite casually feeding one and calmly starving another
according to no syllogism, according to no season.

No house in this hellish world qualifies as a haven
when guile gives to one a dollar, to another a dime.

Oldest and youngest at farthest ends of the spectrum,
raised as "only" children by specific sequence of time

and validated all their lives by coddling and pride,
are both held in highest esteem and always valued by

dandling, fondling, wheedling, over-attentive, and rapt
Mrs. Favorite and Mr. Inequity with an admiring sigh.

The luckless, there in the middle, commonly tend to fail
by being widely ignored in the process of growing up

for while feeding one and stinting another is a way
of judging who's worthy by whomever is showing up.

Fact: parenting skills address the will and the won't;
certain kids you like and certain others you don't —

merit has rarely to do with those who are preferred.
A gift is given one at the total expense of others,

with nothing made clear in matters of distribution,
youth or age, healthy or ill, sisters over brothers.

Parents are wooed in a way by their scheming kids;
nothing of logic obtains in the process of division

with kids like rising and falling stocks and bonds
and Mom and Dad chuffed by games of supervision.

Selfish parents (the norm) most often tend to reward
mainly the children whom they can therefore control;

feeling rebuked by stronger children inevitably they
cherish the weaker who by that make them feel whole.

Most siblings in their vanity tend never to discern
how rewards and dispersals are all about variation

until they come to see that each of them is raised
far less by logical rules than mangy manipulation.

Sisters often gossip, strive, and plot from early on
to acquire everything they've marked that can be had

with a view (I swear I've seen it a million times)
by viciously making their rival brothers look bad

or indifferent which in turn makes them look good
and by transparently running them down in ways

or showing them pity, to strive for added height,
or cagily praising them by using faintest praise.

The conspiracy is everyone's: parents, children, all,
with all made martial by a vigorous zeal to blame.

But wasn't inequality the serpent's charge in Paradise
against the God who brought about all mankind's shame,

declaring that everything was meted out by whim when
by chapter and verse he said that nothing at all was fair

but simply pre-arranged by the hostile facts of life
where justice is non-existent and never simply rare?

Families deal with envy, strife, jealousy, and greed:
one carries the stove-pipe, another carries the stove.

All precepts, founded not by decency or law, are feral,
with everything about competition, nothing about love.

When it comes to siblings, nothing is equal or close,
while kindness is a fiction and charity, in arrears,

is colder than any snow in the dead of winter days.
Parity, as to families, is not even found in pairs!

Norma Shearer

When Norma walked on screen, a warmth
dissolved from the sunshine. A huge head

gave her the peculiar look of a wok ladle.
Wearing all that big brown hair swept up

like a ziggurat gave her shortness thrust.
The hideous way midgets yearn to loom!

She turned down *Mrs. Miniver* because
she flatly refused to play the mother

of a grown child. Wherefore vanity, I
ask, in someone who walks constipated?

With her mis-mated eyes, was it possible
that, peering about, she could not see?

Hey, Turpin, how many fingers have I up?
I would giggle at her watching in the dark,

swivel-munching caramels, wondering how
and why she married Mr. Irving Thalberg

who was in the dwarfy department, as well
and why of course that fellow married her.

Was that my answer? Another case of myopia?
The looming way midgets won't be hideous!

As to her odd profile, she looked knifey,
jut-jawed, as thumbless as a bear, and

rarely walked across a set but tottered.
And was not her scream a whip? No lux, I

thought, going to the movies in the afternoon
like an Asian, thinking: there's lemonhead again..

"Hit with a fish club," grizzled one actor
about that face of hers that looked conked,

to me, it seemed her eyes were insect-like
like a crass vinegaroon. What is a quango?

(So brazen felt I watching her I'd pry candy
from my teeth which I'd never do with Rita!)

She surely had pull in Hollywood to work;
my judgment of her was what W.C. Fields

called "noxis on the conoxsis" — nothing!
She disappeared in the end, not even allowing

the good taste that sets yesterdays' bad taste
on something of a pedestal, which in her case

is to say too much to prove too little. Norma,
for a fan, please, don't look to me. (Get it?)

Indiana Rick

One never knows quite who he is,
struggle though he might
in pointing to himself the while
to seem to all just right,
but who in fact he claims to be,
body, frame, and face,
from what that I have seen of Rick
rarely fits the case.

Just be who you're supposed to be,
no tricks or coy deception,
instead of playing feeble games
to seem the bright exception.
It must be sad so late in life
to come as sudden news
for you to find that no one else
can fill your vacant shoes.

What kind of nitwit looks to others,
though they don't give a damn,
to tell him who he is and then
declare that's who I am?
I say to all you needy artists
looking for rapport
"Screw! — and hit the nearest
Salvation Army store!"

The Story of Life

Spank the baby to bring it awake.
Suckle it fat and give him a shake.
Read a book and try to search it.
Foster a dream and don't besmirch it.
Wet the meat and call it gravy.
Comb the hair and call it wavy.
Piss the bed and suffer the shame.
Welcome to the world of blame.

Kiss the rod as the symbol of fate.
Learn that greater failures await.
Cover the feet and call them shod.
Select a master and call him god.
Walk the earth and call it travel.
Study logic and watch it unravel.
Talk to folk in a world disjointed.
Listen to them and be disappointed.
Hug some girl and fashion romance.
Marry her and remain in a trance.
Develop a plan for the coming years.
Watch and wait 'til it disappears.
Write a book and expect it to sell.
Not to a public with brains of shell.
Take a position and call it a job.
Work your ass like a common slob.
Hearken the taxman, heed his demands.
Gape as your money spills through your hands.
Follow your shadow and call it real.
Heat your brain and watch it congeal.
Pamper your body, it still will mold.
Suck on the stick of growing old.
Dig a grave and call it deep.
Enter the hole and call it sleep.

Thom Gluegun

I knew the first time I saw Thom Gluegun
looking down is a way of owning something,

for the geometry of a giant's calculation is
gauged by height; others must make a claim

by exertion, as if to say: *I see by contrast*.
Thom needed to borrow nothing, merely moved,

not even interceding to reward himself big
glugging bottles of milk like blue Jupiter.

Protestants have become taller than Catholics,
I have read, because their families have fewer

mouths to feed. Wasn't there a German study
that also found a direct correlation between

height and the number of cows per capita?
Rapt, girls stood under Thom in brigades,

borrowing the red air; he positively laughed
above on stilts while nothing filled his ears.

In high school he knew at 6'8" which bubblers
worked by way of a hovering disdain. What is

above appropriates what in a different discourse
we all below must arrange to have appropriated,

the way mercy is naturally expected by the weak.
I who have always been blown about by commotion

had a wistful way of seeing how Thom looked down
simply by looking up, using that same contrast,

which is, I soon saw, a way of getting through life.
The way. Calculation. Without cows. Or kids.

Salmon

A salmon travels on its red muscle meat,
steel of mouth and whipping-tail fleet;

like a fired bullet at the point of flash
it explodes in colors in a sudden splash.

What is that gray edging looking like hide
found along the middle of the fish's side

under the skin that flashes when flapping?
It functions for power like iron strapping.

The white tendon is that burst muscle, used
for speed and virtually cannot be bruised.

Its skin holding fat is pied and flecked,
with a look of being pebbled and pecked.

As red, gray, white through water shoots,
slow for a mo, then like a torpedo boots

back up the blue channel like a racing knife
to arrive and ironically gasp out its life.

We find it hollow in death, an empty flue:
staring, immobilized, neutral, cold, blue.

Two Fat Pharisees

Two fat Pharisees
 upset by heresies
 began to weep and wail,
"Perdition's near, we sadly fear!
 The Christians are taking over!"
 They flapped their wings
 and tore off their rings
 and into the air did sail.
 Oy, Oy, Oy, Oy, Oy, Oy, Oy!

The two fat Pharisees
 forgot the heresies
 mindful of what they lost.
"That ruby's rare, that diamond pear
 of the rings we threw away!"
 On the ground they scratched
 and the jewels they snatched,
 mindful of what they cost.
 Oy, Oy, Oy, Oy, Oy, Oy, Oy!

Greed Personified;
or the Story of Ann-Marie Fartbox

Fatter by far
than anyone's been
who left bites in a sandwich
as big as Berlin
she fleeced her mother of ready cash,
wore muu-muus about
like a walking tent
and with upturned snout
as a pig rooting trash
wherever she went
could broadcast her need,
"What I embody is greed, greed, greed."

As her double chins
jiggled like Jell-O
with an unfalsifiable grasp
and a voice all bellow
she wolfed down seven dinners a day,
wore hideous hair
and filthy gym shoes
worn virtually bare,
while in bed she lay
reading three day-old news
but, saving money, would plead,
"What I embody is greed, greed, greed."

She died in grease
smeared with cooking oil
surrounded by open cans,
three chickens on the boil,
and was carted off like a garbage truck
on a massive rubber hitch.
When the casket split
as they lowered the bitch
a sign in the soil was stuck
on which the words were writ
to sum up her life-long creeds
"What I embody is greed, greed, greed."

Elsa Maxwell's Headdress Ball

"Don't you love it?" exclaimed Lady Sparkk-Plugg,
over what she had assumed was Elsa's headdress,

but it was only her fat bowling-ball-shaped head,
amid guests, incandescent with jiggery-pokery

on the posh Daniell Hotel roof in Venice in 1957.
When's a head a hat? In a big swilling crowd, that,

and when of course uproariously swelled with fat,
as was this wet hostess, bulging in a Mainbocher

the size of an Arab tent, tenacious at the waist,
by sweat and heat the color of ceramicist's paste,

who was introducing a septuagenarian *arriviste*
from Keokuk, Iowa to a Hollywood mogul-beast

and a *domina* whose face positively did her harm
to a Jew dwarf cutely walking fingers up his arm,

inquiring if by that fox-hat worn in a Baltic style
mister was, ahem, planning to win first prize,

asking him if there among the throng it wasn't odd
for her that night to be cynosure of so many eyes,

batting them coquettishly while revealing a trace
of something like satisfaction in her bulldog face

— here Elsa reached to grab a passing hand to kiss
of some thingummy resembling a mister in a miss —

when all of a sudden some judge leaped upon a desk
and throwing out his hands as if to shout to God,

for in Venice little as to balls hasn't been grotesque,
and screeched to Elsa, "*Your head won the award!*"

Why Do Homely Women Buy Expensive Clothes?

They even gleep into long mirrors badly,
criminatingly yawning hard to rein in fat.

Cannot they tell how an extra inch of nose
or double-chin, wobbling like a fruity gel,

invalidates an Ungaro? Is it like hoping
with near-cretin President G.W. Bush that

giving words full value proves you smart?
Ceremonial script invariably seemed to me

too off-puttingly ornate for simple letters
that to my mind were never worth the drape.

Why do homely women buy expensive clothes,
like the fact of putting chiffon on an ape?

Are they blind to what, by subjectively adoring,
an entire world's transformed for their memoir?

What is the arousal template of self-love?
Need as an ache is a convey. It *rrrrr*umbles,

and everywhere you look's a *mis*assessment.
Any question's valid, if no answer's wrong.

Sauté fistfuls of shrimp in Romesco sauce!
Hump walnuts! Make thick rich cheesecakes

and in a witchy frenzy lick the bakeware!
But if you do, Ms. Muu Muu Mama, no blouses

or cellophane for you! Neither full mirrors
except funfair ones. Elsewise, discover air!

Labor Day

There is that Jerry Lewis Telethon
on top of summer ending! September

is depressing. "Back to school" as
a phrase gave me a urethral chill.

Local TV personalities, grinning, said,
"You've had your summer, now give!"

Final harvest *would* have a buffoon
reinforcing stupidity's predominance

by mulcting any hypocrisy in sight
like laying around getting tanned

while God in creating people gimp
lets us be preyed upon by Mr. Mouth.

He pulled underwear over his head.
When Milton Berle yanked him about

by his jaw, at least he'd shut up.
Money is extracted from us just as

the sun is going in. How Labor Day
is so *not* a holiday. It often rains,

with leaves of chestnut trees, crumpled,
are blowing crispy yellow in the gutters.

A secular sorrow cannot even tease
us to feel joy. We are lame, we see,

as television itself, desolating in
its crassness, another empty vessel.

How loss falsifies our expectations
we should be thankful. We should cry.

Perpetual Motion; or Emptiness is Eden, Too.

That was a hateful decision
I insisted to myself once again to try to fix
  my 1972 Allis Chalmers "Big Ten,"

  its mower-deck battered black,
generator wires fried, belts getting severed
  by pulleys, reminding me of

  something we tell ourselves
of an aspiring sort (swallowing) when, say,
  a child of ours has drowned,

  and we weakly hug each other,
biting our lips, with, "Don't worry. He's
  gone to a better place"?

  I am not saying a better place
lies at the end of a road leading somewhere
  in particular, let me add,

  or a better land I know, in the
words or Old Black Joe, rather a spot that
  when you come to it that road

  reaches its end, that's all,
comes to a final ineluctable stop, I say,
  to let you put down your load.

  Junk junk! No ordinary passage
of time incorporates more of anything like it
  later. Emptiness is Eden, too.

  I am not saying blab blab blab —
I am fucking insisting it is fucking over.
  No perpetual. *No* motion. OK?

Mothers and Sons

In the Temple at twelve young Christ
first to the scribes and elders spoke
although not part of his mother's advice
but rather a mission his need to evoke.

Young Billy the Kid in Silver City
stabbing at twelve a blacksmith dead
who insulted his mother without pity
took his first life with nothing said.

And so Mother Mary and Mrs. Antrim
shocked no doubt at the way fate comes
either in New Mexico and old Jerusalem
discovered in seconds passionate sons.

Perspective alone is crucial here
no disquisitions on hate or love:
two mothers learning not without fear
lessons can go from below to above

and can of a sudden go wildly awry
with a single matter of consequence clear
as to the who and not to the why —
do mothers really know whom they bear?

Or does one see with a throw of dice
their Billy the Kid in a holy place
preaching the law and the other her Christ
with a fish-knife opening someone's face?

Life of the Mind

Will one's knowledge in eternity prevail,
that part of the self remain forever alive?
What good is wisdom if at death it fail
when all through life for truth we strive?
Our bodies from the dead will resurrect,

but have we similar assurance of the mind?
What singular identity may one detect
if mental facets do not endure in kind?
Learning surely leads to knowing God.
Capacity to comprehend's to worship more.
All cognition left behind is but a fraud.
Intellect and will define the human core.
It what that's gleaned on earth of learning stays
that much in heaven can we know to praise.

Torture

The brutal loss of reason in torture
is quintessentially what serves it.
Every person — by way of forfeiture —
who practices it, deserves it.

Watching pain calls forth devotion
involving the compulsion to connive.
It follows then who puts it into motion
forgoes the chance to be alive.

The irony of such a justice is, to tell
the truth, to torture somewhat kin,
that they should die in pain as well
to prove that everyone is black as sin,

where human stupidity again proposes
by actions we would otherwise avoid
how looking into the abyss discloses
that staring back at us we find the void.

Sparta

When duty calls and is severe
and even the gods are tied down, no walls
to any city seem required.

Sparta had a currency of iron:
No fairy coins to spend for soldiers in red
 cloaks and close-cropped hair

 who took black broth in barracks.
Laconia had no walls. They were its walls.
 Guys were like stones there,

 where comfort was unmanly, as was
compassion and art. Art to them, a fancy
 succubus draining strength, was

 opposed by Lycurgus who said,
"Keep new ideas out." Their minds needed
 no walls. Savage war cries

 were a way of pledging fealty
to cruel policies narrow and Peloponnesian,
 framing the cruelest laws.

 Black broth, iron coins, dark laws,
red cloaks, stone heads, cold and austere beds
 of stiff reeds, brutal games

 of the kind where biting flesh made
even bouldermen seem braver. Did they worship?
 Indeed. Savage war cries

 comprise boundaries enough,
but that branch of the hillbilly Dorians
 with filed teeth and fierce,

 bald in a hell of helots,
worshipped Enyalios, Spartan god of war,
 whose image had bound feet

 so that the tall red war god
could never leave the confines of Sparta,
 boasting of no walls.

Death is Hidden in Clocks

Death is hidden in clocks.
I know if no good works can take the place of
  Christ's substitutionary death

on my otherwise hopeless behalf
requiring faith alone of me and not good works
  that I am less a fool of sin

than time, tick-tocking away
inside my temporizing need to postpone hope,
  borne of unprogressive guilt.

I've trafficked in rumors —
watched, chained, wound up, fugiting tempi
  godless as Ingersoll.

Let whatever mind-inventions
open to the ploys of my extemporizing guile
  work for my poor salvation

when, where, as, and if they can.
LaRochefoucauld was right. There are evil men
  in this wayward world

who would be less dangerous
if there were not some good in them, and I
  who can make a sorry case,

as I am a begging screever,
for stumbling out in my forgettable English
  that I have certain virtues,

realize that the directives
of those sweeping hands condemn me outright
  while I crazily fob off

my good works for the faith
I've never found within to make that clock, that
  ticking clock, not cuckoo.

Sunday Worship

On Sunday Jews worship antiques.
Mr. Scripophilowitz who refused
to issue any building privileges
in the drama of his mind as he drove
snapped at his wife, "Faugh!"
when she suggested that New Hampshire, being old,
promised product.
A bell in a white church tolled.
His wife, baumeister-fat, wobbleheadedly
surveyed the fields of trees en route
as if they were per lot as numbered
and, adjusting her truss hosiery
and black lumpy Ethel Rosenberg hat —
her father, Reuven Sinkler, a junkman,
taught her value even as a girl —
she stared coldly out the window.
On their way to a show
another church bell tolled.
They stopped for gas in Maine.
"Any Meissen?" she asked of the attendant
with a plate for a face
who had a shed out back.
"Pattern glass? Jadeite jewelry?"
Good pearls? Engagement rings?
Staffordshire dogs? Vintage frogs?
Nothing Louis Prang? Art Deco?
Cuff links? Hatpins? Patek watches?
Anything in antique swatches?"

Mrs. Silvaticus and the Moolie

Mrs. Silvaticus in her caracul coat
flourished her cerise pelt for an African man,
a bog moolie with flip-top shoes.

Lace is a snare. He hovered.
His paraphemia bothered her, his long head,
but how uncomplimentary he could be

can be described at the Borghese
when he with howling displays accompanied her
and made her eat humble pie,

the nig-nog opening a cancelli
and speaking of wolfing fish at the rolling lagoon,
all of it cobalt-cold to her.

Calor defined that endless summer,
the old dripping eves of the San Gennaro Hotel
and those barcaroling gondoliers

below who'd seen his swab-bobbing women
and ogling them in the isle of Celebes, young,
firm porcellanas wearing chaperons

who sparkled like amaryllis.
But his merciless phlox seared her and the grappa
of his inky fingers.

Being terrorized thrilled her, like
that wrestling simplex when, slamming her down
and wearing a hat, he tore her panties

off and pulling out her tongue
made her promise while she nearly suffocated
to buy him a blue ring!

So they slurped juleps, long wet drinks,
now naked in the humid room, zesting each other
with rubs, wide delightful plates

of buttered broccoli and pearl onion,
gelées, timbales, partly sunny gins gun-sharp
raised to each other post-sex

on the floor where lay her caracul coat,
pelt and panties, as if they'd been torn apart
by urgent, unappeasable teeth.

Magpies

It is unlucky to see one — only
one especially— of them. (Take off your hat,
   quickly, and cross your thumbs.)

You hang around in nines,
bird of ill-omen. You refused to enter
   the Ark, cawing with spite

Caw caudate caw caudate
sitting on a ridgepole, looking sideways,
   with your question-mark feet.

I find hateful deliberation
in your long graduated tails and that long
   beakery of yours, so black

I feel you could kill me
with those claws like long Thai fingernails
   so shaped for snatching.

You are famous for your lust
of small bright objects which you steal
   to put to your own devices,

ornithological scrip by which,
surely made for it with noir accountancy,
   you screw all dumber birds

depending from any tree
for a closer look, you prove that nothing
   gathers with more confusion.

The Binding of Abraham

On Mt. Moriah in the book of Genesis
what took place was a murdering father
   raising a tablespoon of a knife,

or was it slate obsidian black?
Yahweh and Abraham never spoke again.
But did Abraham and Isaac?

Soon afterwards his wife Sarah
died, first matriarch of Israel. Was it
from gloom over such madness?

The crime was not infanticide
but Abraham's greed for land, building
his Sarah's tomb, all the while

demanding big money and a deed,
whenceforth all the Jews began pouring in
sometime after the Exodus,

banging up ranch houses and pools,
beauticians' parlors, kosher restaurants,
and endless apartment complexes

for almost 3000 years, and so why
would a God who sought faith and obedience
reward the cunning of some realtor

in spongy shoes and a shekel bag
on his belt hustling hot Florida property
with wintry, Winnipeg guile?

A Parable of Java

Thunder darkened the Java skies,
rising over the emerald green tropics of Bogor,
A white travel boat was anchored there.

Mrs. Wheet, sophisticating chairs
received from friends, tall yellow bamboo ones, and
pouring fruity drinks in lovely flutes,

wondered aloud with disgust ultimately
who above was supervising *anything* in a way that
  appeased Presentists like her

  when Java clouded-up and rained
on much of what many women had perfectly planned,
  making them grim and nettled

  with no aspirin about, unlike ours
pried from willows. Faith, she failed to see,
  was not so much belief as a way

  of accepting the wayward means
the wacky world works. Moods quite darkened
  like the heavy thuds, not booms,

  echoing through the women's boat
when they, stamping, decided more than party plans
  do not work that include thunder

  which was proved again when Java skies,
dark and streaked and thudding over black Bogor,
  let would happen what would.

Womandrakes

  Womandrakes, bryony black,
  shriek and sweat blood when uprooted
  by hands with afrobrazilian meanness.

  I thumb my mind's own bestiary
  and find I am notching thoughts with insane
  roots shaped like no soporific

  whose erotic properties can whiten
  as I watch the drakes plucked and up-plucked,
  feeling oddly corrupt, prattling

about love with witch-draughts
in the kind of mind I now have by watching
what lets Rachel conceive Joseph

through Jacob. To sense detriment
by way of vegetables? How perfectly nuts!
But know you not womandrakes?

Sarah Son Painting at Scorton Creek

"The activity of the brush becomes the activity
of the water."
  —John Updike on Frederic Edwin Church's
       Niagara (1857)

To sketch a river is to bring into being,
inescapably, the land that it also drains.

What was originally whole with her deft
moves is suddenly, shockingly, in pieces,

water, banks, with no indexicality I see,
slopes, slanting plants, verdant grasses,

all the things she unravels, placing them
by transferal and a rapidly wisping brush

where one cannot quite grasp them anymore
as quite the way they were, including there

the rim of a small bridge by the river
near which she sits, separating grasses,

distant houses, water, banks, all in pieces,
small plants, nothing quite the way it was,

when all of a sudden reformed and reaffirmed
and more than whole they reappear on canvas,

brought not only into being but transformed
by the integrating beauty of a human hand,

and so at last we see, pleasure out of pain,
that she has put them back together again!

The Endpaper Map in *Winnie-the-Pooh*

Children make complete sense of it.
Its signs are continuous with our fancies,
like clowns stenciled on our cribs

or pastel colors, and show us
frankly the way to go home. No better clue
to where I felt I needed to be,

also convincing me I belonged,
left better traces. That ladder. Those
steps. The *location* of things.

Dark forests acting as an embrace
was something Wagner knew and Shakespeare,
legislating a syntax especially

all lonely children love for whom
any woodland vision more than anything
makes a drapery for their dreams.

Chinese Go Hunting Bears

Chinese go hunting bears
for meat, claws, paws, and gall-bladders
to pander to their health,

stopping jaws as they chew,
listening to hear if the cancer has gone,
the bladder not drumble,

then begin to munch again
those fat paws, patchwork saw in hand and
    probing foot-long fork,

    craving against the law
those smelly bear-claws and blue meat,
    afoul of law, cooked or raw,

    shooting the upright bears
right in the face right in their lairs
    for those hairy feet-paws,

    sweatily ingesting everything
but the howling, mad black roar to audit
    with clattering hardware.

    What they fail to understand, as
they pause, oily cheeks full of gout meat,
    is that sound stops for no death.

308

Flaws

    A silent man whose stone
in a ring it was wore a turban and carried a rug
    under his arm. How much?

    Did Mr. Cohen in his 47th St. shop
blaspheme? His suit had a bygone sort of smell.
    He dodged — scuttled — around

    the table the better to check
swap-angle from the other side. Didn't the earliest
    Marx brother, Karl, coin the phrase,

    "All that is solid melts into air"?
Unpicked-up-light-splatter in a white diamond
    bothered him. Isn't it fatal

to money to see a spot there?
"I want a selznick!" he pisht, screwing the loupe,
    squinting into the facets,

 "not dis heppy hooligan
 mit a tin ken on its head ent crossed eyes,
    fer fucking's sake!"

 he shrugged. "Two huntrit."
As to this *gorisht helfn* rug here? Beyont help!
  Vat do you vant from me,

   dipsy doodles? Thoiteen dollar, firm."
But the Arab yearned to *find* a flaw in his rug and
   ring, making Allah alone perfect.

Cloud Kukukukukuland

"As late as 1940 seven-tenths of
  New Guinea was unknown territory."

     — Jens Bjerre, *The Last Cannibals*

In Kiwogwonga, the Kukukukuku in that green hell
of wet jungle hunt more than white witchity grubs

but wolf human flesh with joy! What is announced
with those small bones worn through their noses

but that death can also provide an ornament
to anyone who will swap a pig for a life anytime

of the day? The terrified often become bullies.
I've seen those abos place fresh sweet potatoes

under the nose of an aeroplane so it could eat!
With warrior pusses, they will eat only enemies.

Any Kukukukuku can spin like a bumming top
in gibbering anticipation of any fleshly option.

The odd Stan Laurel-hair popped like corn
on men and women seems to whoop when

they out and out hump each other in the open
in cloudbursts as though ingesting a raw meal,

ripping off the tufts of grass worn in front,
examining the nap of each other's black skin

while pawing as if in prayer all that flesh,
that hair, those bones, those warrior pusses,

the ornaments that make the green jungle red
and wet as cloudbursts in dripping Kiwogwonga

until that winged thing comes again from space
and, unappeased, takes *them* into its dark maw.

Hyman Lubinsky, the Ice-Cream Peddler

was driving down Second St. in Fall River
the morning the Bordens were slaughtered on Aug. 4, 1892.
It was a Thursday, and he was a Jew

who, hawking ices, later swore in testimony
he "saw a lady come out the way from the barn to the
stairs from the back of the house,"

all offered in corroboration that Lizzie
at the time had been retrieving lead sinkers in the loft
in order to go fishing later, her hobby.

At the trial, pressed by the DA as to why
such a person in the low trades, a clown with bells,
happened to be rubbernecking there,

Hyman snapped, "What has a person got eyes
for but to look with?" — which did not go down well
   with the citizens in the seats, suspicious

   not only of that grammar *for but to look with*?
clearly an example of filthy low-bred slum-trade kiketalk
   but of some drummer broadcasting ices!

   Wouldn't he by trade chop ice with an *axe*?
Why was his idiotic wagon not checked by the local police,
   who also never checked the rolled-up coat

   beneath Andrew Borden's bashed-in head,
to see if, used as a shield, any bloody stains remained?
   I say that horny Hyman *lusted* after Lizzie

   and, coursing up and down that street,
sought to spy upon her female underpinnings on the line
   when not saluting her with crudities,

   which among her mad eccentricities
she in her loneliness may very well have encouraged,
   for who on earth can know the heart?

   On that sweltering August morning,
did she not call from the steps for a frozen-pudding
   that unctuously he offered free

   with whispers only to be let inside
with no one there if she would lewdly show him France
   which recklessly she dared to do

   (and more) when, lo, all of sudden
into the parlor marched stepmother Abby Durfee Gray,
   catching Hyman fumbling in Lizzie's shirt!

   As Mrs. Borden and Lizzie, then age 32,
never got along at all, mainly over inheritance issues,
   hard cash, that is, it was bad enough,

but with a stranger standing there
a knob-nosed sheeny in a white jacket with an erection
reeking with an odor of curdled cream

in the middle of that fucking room?
Upstairs tore Abby like a banshee, a cry splitting the room,
a shriek to shock the waking world

for the head of an ice-cream rapist,
whereupon Lubinsky in a panic raced out his ice-axe,
chased her upstairs, and killed her.

It was that or hanging, and he chose that.
An hour later Andrew Borden came home to take a nap
and was quickly butchered like a hog.

Had spinster Lizzie found revenge? Was she
caught up in sex? Dazzled by intrigue? Involved in a plot
to escape to the Levant with Mr. Whippy?

Calmly, they say, she ate three pears.
Was it done while the ice-cream peddler drove away?
A 13-day trial was held in New Bedford,

with Lizzie charged of double-murder
when the silent prisoner dressed in black, never testified
in her own defense and seemed not sad,

as a verdict of "not guilty" came down.
Nothing was ever heard again of or from Lubinsky
nor the sounds of his jingle-wagon

on the muddy streets of dark Fall River.
Years later, Lizzie hooked up with Miss Nance O'Neil,
an actress, and never saw a man again.

The Revenge of Art

Two greedy sisters is an archetype
in every folklore. Fable tricks them out as fat
and lazy to identify their cunning.

This is of course woodcut wit:
Chekhov, Hans Christian Andersen, Garcia Márquez,
all spun comic tales of them,

who always had chinless husbands
in the shadows enabling them by silent nods
and smirks and sexless consent

to fleece their ancient parents,
grab candlesticks, raid drawers, rifle cabinets.
Aprons are icons and wimples

here, trust Breughelese mooseness
in parochial women with huge cacopygian asses
along with facial hair and knob noses.

They are *pictures* of what they are,
as if they actually hired some Dutch dabbler
to trick the bitches out in paint!

Slovens are commonly careless
because their attention is usually elsewhere,
try on the subject of food, for starters,

and these cows left their bad odors
and chocolated thumbprints all over the *muebles*
they went racing out with,

as if to keep the spirit of fable
alive in perpetuating revenge that all remember
their failure and who they are.

Estonia: A Limerick

There was a man from Estonia
Who soberness couldn't be tonier
But when he conversed
His language seemed cursed
In a tongue that couldn't be phonier

Not Every Fat Fool with a Phylactery

"You are looking for me not because you
　saw signs but because you ate your fill of the loaves."

— John 6: 24-35

Not every fat fool in a phylactery
deserves the food of the Savior.

Can't we be proud in our prayer
— just as in our hunger greedy —

as we as lazy sinners position
ourselves to plead tor pity?

I imagine those Corinthians, cadging
fish and bread were not embarrassed

one bit, shoving, lining up for grub,
while telling Jesus they loved him,

all for the chance of a good lunch.
Mr. Klaw, old Cates, Mr. Shipnuck,

Abe Shapiro, the Kohns and Kahanes,
Edna Thalheimer, Mr. and Mrs. Schrift,

Sam Futz, Cohen the Jeweler, Spritzie,
the Livshitz Family, all the Clitskys,

Heimie Fox, Grandpa and Granny Wiesel,
hustling, heavy with bottles of seltzer,

toward their blankets spread out there
on the grass. What about all that talk?

"So we have to listen to bullshit —
They feed you good here, so *nu*?"

On Earth We Know That Hell is Near Heaven

"And in hell, where he was in torment,
he looked up and saw Abraham far away, with Lazarus
by his side. So he called to him, 'Father Abraham, have
mercy on me!'"

— Luke 16:23

Who is surprised? If heaven is near hell,
then hell is near heaven. Myth is concept.

No real comfort attends suddenness in luck,
can turn like a wheel within seconds.

"Afar off?" I thought there was only life
when there was inattention to life, which,

impossible, makes this living life a hell.
Are we not here daily to *witness* failure,

as God sees cruelly fit to make one man,
tormented by all that was taken from him,

have to watch what is given to another?
Isn't topsyturvification God's theology,

what life on earth is all about, horror
next to happiness as a pretext for fate?

How grimly sinister it is we have to see,
forever and ever, what we're being shown.

Is what we're deprived of. But is it new
for anyone who is alive to have to hear?

A great gulf is fixed, the Gospel says,
that they who'd pass from here to there

may not be able, and that none may cross
over from there to here. But I say *so*?

We poor creatures in shouting distance,
close enough to bitch or slake a thirst,

don't know those gulfs, preventing contact,
that also let us see what we don't have?

No gulf in eternity surprises anyone who,
living on earth, experiences it in time,

for hell is all we *have* to know heaven by.
My only point is someone should tell God.

Serpentine

Is nature warning us in what is rippled,
— rumpled, that line with no sharpness,

not straight, by definition, and so a sign
of something unpropitious, eerily malign,

almost worked as if predestined, serrated
as it were, like Robert Oppenheimer's hat,

lightning-strike, a moving serpent's spoor,
all crumbling fronts at the heat of battle,

roller-coaster rides, the cast of each hedge,
a boa's writhing mouth, or Harrison Ford's,

all impatient arms folded against belief
that in silent coldness refuse all relief

a shape to sharpen contradiction, the way
a crosscut saw, slipping, slices up a hand ,

everyone's grimace showing everyone's fear,
the signature of every rip and every tear,

— that irrationality, with its own geometry,
teaches us danger has no actual direction

but, squint-eyed, above all aims to impart
that indirection is indeed the devil's art?

Forgotten Kisses

Time does not end but proceeds
to fade away like the feel of a handshake which,
once pressed upon you, vanishes.

Baudelaire who said that touch
has a memory might not have been so cavalier
had he himself been witness to

the inflections always missing
from the lusterless kisses that you eventually
offered me are long forgotten.

What remains is but a memory
of what your touches wildly promised long before
they perished in passing days,

so that one may come to see —
was this not what Baudelaire meant? — that
memory is alone the touch

left for us to experience
of all that, after everything dissolves in time
we insist, *insist*, must stay.

The Scent of Jesus

Psalm 45, verse 8

We who always knew that someone who lived in the sky,
who walked among us until the day of his sacrifice,

working with olive wood, with saw, planes, and adzes,
the scented shavings of fig tree and arrow-weed thatch,

are not surprised you had the scent of wind about you,
sun, moon, grass, stone, sand, fire, ash, mountain,

sweet unshaven planks, joists, poles, bales of hay
in bays where animals laid themselves down to rest,

but we never thought to connect the delicate scent
of myrrh, aloes, or cassia with your hair, your body,

your fine strong shoulders or your comforting hands,
nothing rich, exotic, lavish, indoors, or ceremonial,

no matter how blest. How typically wrong we were.
I could weep on your royal strength, dear Jesus,

merely to reach to touch the thong of your sandals
that walked on wheat and goosewort and wild plants,

simply to feel the nap of that rectangular blanket
you might have slept on, a stitchless wool redolent

of grace and persimmons as fully comforting as wind
and sun and sky, but just as all the earth, redeemed,

has been touched with the odor of sanctity, why
should you not be? What not precious of all we own?

What not the rarest of all we have, and all for you
when such is what that night the Wise Men Three all knew?

Martha Stewart in Jail

"Thou shalt not suffer a witch to live"

— Exodus 22:18

I'm not part of the bedlam of non-humans, thought vain Martha
that snowy day she was trundled off and thumbprinted by police,

discovering suddenly she was unfalsifiably a rotten-egg lady,
humorless, domineering, incandescent with piggery, and hollow,

that cold bitter night studying her reflection in the cell window
in which a face with troll-eyes, slit and riddling, looked back

and spoke with the heartless truth, brutal to hear, that hers
was not gracefully learned but a scullery-maid's knowingness,

snatched on the run and read on television from cribbed notes.
She stared at the window which revealed an acquisitor's face.

Do I really grab? Steal ideas? Retail all that others know?
Beat, bully, berate poor people like puppets on a TV show?

Is it greed to own a magazine, with its title my own name?
Establish my own clothing line to put others to shame?

As she heard what the window spoke, she saw that her face
reflected nothing but greed where she had expected grace.

No adopted persona disguised you were at bottom a churl,
driven to have and to hold (it said)! A prig, a bitch, a savage,

cold as traprock! No billowing jackets to your hefty thighs
can ever hide by name-change a peasant has no manners.

Can't you see or cover up the cold disdain you mercilessly
showed to all those co-cooks you interrupted all the time.

No syntactic structure on TV of presentable or doctored hair
makes up for the inattention-blindness you cavalierly showed

to all lesser folk gathered around, as hired, to have to praise
your dim *feuillatage* as they endured your textbook rudeness

as with that flat-affect voice of yours, you bullied them all
and like a findfault snapped at them to hand you a whisk

and corrected the way they broke their eggs into a bowl
or screamed like a whip that you would not *touch* hot sauce.

As if, fatso, distinguishing a meat from a fishfork mattered!
You are Elena CeauÐescu! Your big back! Long ungracious feet!

You don't walk but lumber! That askew smile and peek-a-boo,
impish flirtation is that of the ugly aunt out of medieval fable,

the face of the homely older sister who with the rude fingers,
of a bellowing vergogna, with huge mouthfuls of gender-spite,

a bewhiskered chin, who always lost in love to a pretty sibling.
All these doom-dark things that reflection in the window said,

revealing to this cripple in the bedlam of that avaricious rut
that not only was her avarice an extension of her vanity but

reminding her that what she saw she copied with such need —
and so watching the *window* became a nightly form of greed!

Memoirs of a Midget

Did my childhood terror of the name Herodias,
lava, quicksand, and whirlpools, a minority

of one in my bedroom in which odd women and
water criss-crossed in dark mid-air, a sorority,

instill in my midget mind the habit of a fear
I might develop a crush on female authority?

Heinrich Himmler: The Cartoon

"Don't Dr. Seuss's characters all look like that
Nazi with the glasses, Heinrich Himmler, Mom?"
        — Alex Theroux, age 11, to his Mother

Do you believe this maybe applies
that funny Dr, Seuss got a tiny rise
— with his compulsion to satirize,
his nightmares better to minimize,
what an angry Jew might mobilize
the better to deride and criticize
(or should Ted Geisel we analyze?) —
out of drawing faces (a compromise
of the laws of all logic, I realize)
in his cartoons to characterize
their likeness, this is pure surmise,
to Heinrich Himmler's in pop-surprise,
blinking through specs with risible eyes,
pale, whacked-out, shining with lies,
cut with odd U's like knifed-out pies,
comic-book nosy but never wise,
with sharpened noses as if a disguise,
as if real madness can partly comprise
a vacant look where everything dies,
an inadequate chin of ignoble size,
a body as flaccid as one could devise,
an egg-shaped head as its booby prize
with something connected to pagan ties
— the epitome of a soul's demise —
where nothing hopes and nothing tries
to even acknowledge the terrible cries
heard in shouts to the overhead skies?

One last query on the subject of whys
if only to learn how it signifies
for its Teutonic echo no one denies
or its wholesale capacity to polarize:
wasn't Seuss as author surely unwise
to employ a pen name that logic defies,
even if trying to be one of the guys,
for of all the monikers to publicize
— "Theo LeSieg," a name to despise! —
that one is a doozy for all it implies,
never mind an allowance to authorize
any half-witted Bundist to theorize
that here was a person who typefies
any right-wing fascist who justifies
any goose-stepping loony to idolize?

Zebedee

"And going on from thence, he saw two other
   brethren, James, the son or Zebedee, and John,
   his brother, in the boat with Zebedee, their father,
   mending their nets; and he called them, and they
   straightway left the boat and their father, and
   followed him."
                                    — Matthew 4:21-22

A thought for the Hebrew fisherman,
Zebedee of old,
who heard little of charm but only alarm
in the voice of the stranger who
simply appearing out of blue
suddenly by mystic code
got the boys to drop their load
while hedging their bets to drop their nets
and ease on down the road.

One is amazed at the speed with which
Jimmy and Johnny decamped
from that little dhow, but may I ask how
that stranger, surveying all three,
in preparation to fish in the sea
with needles and nets in their laps to tat,
could leave us with such a mystery that
while seeking help from each young whelp
he left the father flat?

Double Indemnity

Walter Neff wears a wedding ring but has never been married.
He reveals someone falling in love can also feel quite harried
He reminds us that in L.A. drive-ins one can also order a beer.
He makes it clear that a part of lust also involves living in fear.
He is seduced by a cheap anklet worn by Phyllis Dietrichson.
He employs cold wit in repartee that we never feel is fun.
He in a strange rhetorical tic uses the odd word "oughtn't."
He proves that obsession is a vice that at its core is rotten.
He indicates his darkest depression by going bowling alone.
He is always smoking cigarettes and always on the phone.
He works a job in the Pacific Building on Olive St. in L.A.
He exudes more wistfulness than words can possibly say.

Phyllis Dietrichson's nutty hair does not belong to her face.
She offers up hugs and kisses but of affection nary a trace.
She is wife to a man whose first wife she clearly has killed.
She determines in merest seconds no man is ever fulfilled.
She immediately takes iron control of bachelor Walter Neff.
She is a classic opportunity whore and to ethics utterly deaf.
She looks dwarfish in her wig like Signor Wences's hand.
She buys five hats at a crack and shops to beat the band.
She resembles in eyeglasses a she-thing from outer space.
She discloses she is at ease with every phase of disgrace.
She clearly would kill her husband for any passing fellow.
She exudes a honeysuckle scent but in fact is only yellow.

Some Thoughts on the Movie *Watch On The Rhine* (1943)

If T. S. Eliot's correct in asserting poetry is not
an expression of emotion but an escape from it,

is it not the truth, as well, that poetry also
expresses the emotion it would escape from?

Paul Lukas who played the noble Kurt, an anti-Nazi
and WWII freedom fighter, won an Academy Award.

George Coulouris who played the sour, devious
Nazi Tech never came close to winning an Award.

In Hollywood only what you seem is what you are,
actors pressing their emotions to escape from them.

It is not defeating? Is it not truly bizarre?
Glory for how you appear, not for what you are?

Gold for what but seems and yet is not the case,
praise not for the written, only what is erased?

A Midget Ponders Sex With a Tall Woman

When I'm nose to nose,
my toes are in it,
but when toes to toes,
my nose is in it.

My highs are lows;
I'm short as a minute,
with vertical woes
as I begin it.

I have to disclose
as I try to pin it
no target's close
as a way to win it.

Who wouldn't be foes
in size obstinate
when everything shows
less than infinite?

For no one crows
trying to spin it
who has a hose
small as a linnet.

When I'm nose to nose
my toes are in it,
but when toes to toes
my nose is in it.

Two Architects Square Off; or Frank Lloyd Wright Goes Visiting Philip Johnson's Glass House in New Canaan, Ct.

That square sunlit box of glass
standing out clear on the land
reveals as much of simplicity as
proportion can satisfy and

of iron and wood shows but a trace.
"Should I take off my hat within?"
Inquired Frank with sardonic face;
"So am I outdoors — or in?"

"In" said Phil, with audible groans.
Of the adage Frank then took stock
Of when and where to throw stones,
stepped out, and picked up a rock.

The Man Who Set Out To Measure Jerusalem

"Where Jews are different than us is that guilt is not an
emotion that restrains them. It replenishes their contempt.
They feel it, but it offends them, so they insist on outfacing
it, no matter how crudely. By insisting they they don't
deserve it, that is fatal."

—Lord Shaftoe

When skeptical Jews begin to question heaven,
asking "Why was God absent?" with hideous contempt
of all that is sacred before that Nazi event
called the Holocaust, as if trying to get even

by a question invoking the worst heresy of all,
I immediately recall that loon in Zechariah
who produced a line of chalk like some pariah
— imagine the arrogance, consider the gall —

that he might measure Jerusalem, the city,
to ascertain in full its length and breadth.
Why not attempt by rule to measure death?
Where can be found a hubris more to pity?

Do you remember those Jews dying of thirst
who screamed at Moses in the desert heat
(Exodus 17: 1 through 7, for the exegete)
and threatened Jehovah while they cursed

their fate, insisting He fulfill their will
mocking the very God they tried to tame
with howling insistence he prove His Holy Name
who let Moses in smiting Horeb to open a rill

of water pure to placate the stiff-necked Jews?
Does not the pompous question "Where was God?"
regarding camps of death strike one as odd,
even if typically vile when Jews feel used,

to swap their faith with avarice and greed,
to hurl their insults at God's holy sky,
to stare upon His face with screams of "Why?"
to beg instead of pray for what they need

like those who try with tape to measure Zion
and by cunning to assure themselves of facts
and certainties to nail down tight with tacks
to attempt to learn the truth by lying?

Conjoin, we must, our free will with His grace,
not shift the blame to God for all our sins
nor test by rule what ends and what begins —
God Almighty *is*. What about your faith?

A Woman Who Wore Panties The Color Of A Glacier

I touched a glacier once in Portage, Alaska,
fluid in its turquoise as panties on a girl,

its aqua color a cross between the U.N. flag,
a Tiffany box, the frailty of a robin's egg,

and the glass of a bank window that the sun
hits just right in the way echoing ripples

of bluish-green run sideways in stuttering
scintillant shimmers. I see bluish ice-mint

in an image of a girl pulling on her panties
with a smart snap, almost like an ice-sound

cracking for attention as any mirror might
when someone saucy strikes a pose she likes.

Ice, shiny and gemsharp, is no less lovely
for its cold than soft surrendering warmth

in causing it to drip must make it tremble
first, and shudder, then with wetness flow.

Sheen polishes! I turn to seawater myself,
watching how a shape maneuvers into silk

in the lascivious way water whirls around
a blue glacier, tightening what it surrounds

the way elastic on a taut girl's panties
makes warm flesh kissing tightness hug

as any flesh in fabric, soft and saucy,
acting now together, simmers and is snug.

I touched a woman once in Portage, Alaska
who in her silk panties as fluid as turquoise,

cut aquamarine, polished as sheen, cracking
for attention as a mirror might with sounds,

surrendered warmth to show me how a color
like a glacier, wet, can also make a noise.

Witch Hazel

In the cold of winter witch hazel grows
Foi de riddle lol de riddle hing ling do

in the way with surprise betrayal does
Fol de riddle lol de riddle hing ling do

like a secret in someone no one knows.
riddle de lol de riddle hing ling do

Its blooms of gold and brown seem sere
Fol de riddle lol de riddle hing ling do

but what is, is rarely what will appear
Fol de riddle lol de riddle hing ling do

like the idle hope that love breeds care.
Fol de riddle lol de riddle hing ling do

I'll await on pondering why we're apart
Fol de riddle lol de riddle hing ling do

believing in vain the cold will depart
Fol de riddle lol de riddle hing ling do

holding like petals what's left of my heart.
Fol de riddle lol de riddle hing ling do

Yellow Grapes in Borneo

In humid Sandakan where the outdoors
is our only adornment, what is it about the air
that fairly sings with sudden tints,

the way a girlish body gives to the gold
of her bikini the whiff of need we feel in sex,
that being enhanced and not diminished,

smell evokes color? Is it from sunlight?
Dampness? Sheet-rain? Jungle? Wind? Is not color
the happiness we experience in scent?

Perfume blows out into the color of the
garden, sweeping up the damp breath of the humid
trees the way by blowing through a leaf

she subtly folds, eroticizes in me
the lust I feel by the force of the sound
I hear and not of the lips I see.

What scents blow in from the Sulu Sea
best tinge the air for me in swelling yellow grapes.
So, does its transforming chromo blue

or the murky green of the *nipah* swamps
or the cerise and purple in the wagging leaves
or the copper body of some Murut

depend in turn on what they take
from any frangipani and *chempake* and palm-leaf
adorning the harbor or Sandakan

in the way her lips are made not red
by any crimson *sireh* juice she might have drunk
but by the sweetness of her scent,

making a garden of color where,
in the dense and humid air of Borneo, I don't
doubt, she only meant to breathe?

Way of a Dolphin

A dolphin only laughs and fucks
not because it's got all day.
It fixes on one goal —
not cumbrances
nor mumbrances
nor questions like the soul
all of which it frankly ducks
— and that is just to play.

Screw Stanislavski

It is called acting because that character you are *not*.
What you may think has little to do with what's said.

Take the Barnstable post-office where I am often caught
by some bore who might be talking but mentally is dead.

I have never met a charming person wherever I have got
as even close to fascinating as the dullest book I've read.

Owls in California

You will not find owls in California.
Round wisdom there in feathered array

partners nothing it can find with day.
They don't do well with light, there's

that. Then, land is so *divulged* there,
with trees like voids, scant of bustle,

and nothing oval that ever sits in them
can focus on what it sees that's bright.

Who cannot consume what it cannot spy
would sulk as a solitary in that state.

No fat unblinking calandrius, pointing
its sharp beak toward a human sickbed,

no sober nigrolineatus used to night,
scoping out the mere rustle of leaves,

rats, fish, barnmice, or bunnies, wants
the kind of hot and brainless funshine

Pasadena adores. Owls as stern birds
of darkness, with facial discs acoustic,

shields that hear, prefer in the doom
and gloom to watch with eyes of light

which in a roundness like their heads
seek no sunkist misses, no heliopoli

but what, seen by shadow and shaped by
dark, is, more than fun, already food.

John Wesley and the Exegesis of Failure

God rest the holy preacher
John Wesley at his prayers
who thrice in life while pursuing a wife
found only a world of tears.
Sophia Hopkey of Georgia
from a Savannah family quite smart,
acting so grand, she jilted him and
cheerfully kicked out his heart.

So returning to England
from the far American shore
he developed a crush on seeing a thrush
whom none could have loved more.
He pinned his every hope on
Grace Murray from day to day,
but she poured scorn on how he was born
and, laughing, turned him away.

Poor John eventually married
a woman named Mary Vazeille,
who proved far worse in anything cursed
than words could ever reveal.
She heaped on him in public
abuse and brought him such shame
that as every tomorrow brought more sorrow
his life was never the same,

except in his life with God
by which he grew holy with pain.
On tired old knees he offered his pleas
in language Protestant plain.
May it therefore be requisitioned
of the Heavenly God above:
is the act of turning from women the burning
solution to finding love?

Ansel Adams at Prayer

When you have no faith,
lugging up your box camera to the highest ridges
  of the craggy Yosemite

  to shoot a waiting moon,
the way you see it suddenly appearing as a dream,
  paper white and awesome,

  mountains become mosques,
and you think "This is God" (snap), "That is God"
  (snap), for each tall peak

  rises a private Megiddo,
every vale and sloping valley that you spot is Kedron
  (snap) there for you alone.

  Flower and wood, a waterfall,
those pollarded trees (snap, snap, snap) all make
  testaments of sorts, chapels

  with ridges for naves with rites
and for readings the way you pray your proxy prayer
  Arizona Highways a kind of missal.

My Definition of Love is Sarah

(song lyric)

My definition of love is Sarah.
The way she looks at me,
That secret smile
Her eyes, her style,
Such entrancing mystery.

My definition of love is Sarah.
The way she smiles you see,
I feel the bliss.
Who could resist
Love's possibility?

[Refrain:]

When you're looking for a word
to fit something you have heard
or feel within your beating heart,
don't go searching in a book,
the answer's in her look,
the way that all romances start.

My definition of love is Sarah.
The way she looks at me,
That secret smile
Her eyes, her style,
Such entrancing mystery.

Edgar Allen Poe and Bricks

What is it with E.A. Poe and bricks
in the stories he loved to contrive,
simply one of his narrative tricks
in killing cats, doubles, and wives,
preparing of mortar and sand a fix
just to gleefully immure them alive?

We know that at an earlier time
he worked — with little else clear —
in a Richmond brickyard handling lime
which might have engendered a fear
of how enclosing walls can mime
a grave, but what a frightful idea!

Osama bin Laden Visits the U.S. in 1978

"A drawing is always dragged down to the level of its
caption."
                                        — James Thurber

Impersonating civilized people, at the airport
morts chewing sauce-drenched food shoved ahead

in line, Polly Shoecat with leopardskin chapeau,
angry George Grenadine, Harry and Vera Yellin,

chewing blintzes, old, fluffy-headed Leonard Eels
flipping his *Wall Street Journal*, despising them all

all, like those two loud barking rollmops, Edna Ratz
with chips and Ella Putz reading *Jump for Joy*,

but snapping at little Tommy Toomey, running brat,
while a Man of Achievement, gay, with a dun cat

wondered why that damn coon with the broom, Ambo,
had to go sweeping dust by his feet just then.

A gallery owner, Herbert Ferber, wolfed a hot dog,
disgusting Ethel Skull, next to him, who moved away.

When doesn't more mean worse? was not the first
question that had occurred to bin Laden and yet

was his most frequently asked. A mesomorph wearing
a green Dartmouth t-shirt, a mail-order harpoon gun

across his lap, kissed a braless blonde with a bow
as they said farewell. A drunk's hoot had scared her,

Mr. Weazel in his cups. They were Lance Tynan
and Prissy Wieck who had just pointlessly argued.

By the concourse everybody stared at tall Osama,
His Syrian wife wearing her black draping *abaya*

with that *hijab* or black head-covering as she held
their first child, small Abdullah, whose medical

problem was the main reason they had gone abroad.
Some rude Americans stared, some snapped photos.

Was it because that lanky man was tall at 6' 4"?
Sober, serious, honest, pious, guarded, puritanical,

a Muslim, he was only 21 and found he counterfit.
Were they retiringly pedantic, looking hunched

amid their baggage? Mrs. Klaw wearing rhinestone
glasses and reeking of *Joy* by Patou screeched

as she spilled her latté. Fatbodies gave room,
pausing with bagels-and-cream cheese held aloft.

When he saw Ethel Skull, filthy Mr. Weazel farted
and grinned, and Herbert Ferber motioned to a cop.

"Disappear," snapped Leonard Eels, panfurious
that overperfumed Polly Shoecat asked the time.

Waiting to go to Vegas, Linda Skirball was checking
out Lance Tynan, while Ub, her husband, disgusted,

wondered why fucksticks covered themselves up!
A wolf, Sam Spivack massaged his chick's thigh,

her tragic mask, rouged, scarlet with lipstick,
as she told him it would be her last adult film.

Harry, whispering, told Vera that she, Jaklyn,
was a whore. Edna Ratz and Ella Putz refused

to move over lest they be near filthy Mr. Weazel.
Wealthy Mrs. Sisyphus fed her pup Steak-Umms.

Angry Ub Skirball suddenly looked up and noticed
their flight was delayed; Linda merely shrugged

and began humming "When Will I See You Again"
by the Three Degrees and even winked at Lance,

coolly suggesting to Ub the pilot might have
crashed the plane because he'd proved impotent

the night before and grieved. When Ub, jealous,
hearing all that airport noise — angry George

Grenadine who was pissed at Tommy Toomey tried
to trip him — ground out his third cigarette

and turning a furious face to his wife barked,
"They don't purposely *crash* fucking planes, bitch!"

The Eyes of Wendell Corey

Was it the vacant eyes, the bayonet ears,
or the ghastly cast of that terrible smile

in a man who staring but a second gave
the frightful impression of staring awhile

that, so unsettling in what it conveyed
of unholy possession by hypnotic twist,

it seemed from some black portal of myth
a viper had suddenly entered through mist?

His blue eyes like a seagull's, scavengrical,
went dead in a stare-down, emotionally gone,

— like two uninviting windows, high up,
in a drab hotel with their shades drawn —

as black in disdain, sometimes tiny and red,
fixed like the glare of that mad bird's head.

He watched Joan Crawford in *Harriet Craig*,
gun-sighting her with that cold, baleful stare,

searching at times, then half-lidded, as she
was transfixed with her insanely short hair,

yet always that rigid face and jackal ears
appended like weapons to that rigid head

— motion never applied to someone who
so embodied in stasis the living dead —

but far more horrid than anything else
those eyes that any compassion belied,

eyes that threatened that anything live
which entered by sight immediately died,

soulless eyes, filled with nothing at all,
puff adder's eyes riveting one in a stare,

eyes that revealed in their feral intent
the judgment of death in a sinister glare,

as when the tall actor was Smiley McCoy,
watching and wordless in *The Big Knife*

with that duckhead of his, scarily square,
cold and robotic and walking through life.

Remember his character in *Holiday Affair*?
A conventional lawyer offering lame wit,

condescending, needing praise himself,
arch, ready to be jealous, a potential snit,

complaining of the string Christmas lights
as he trims the tree, making a fussy farce,

and, compared to handsome Bob Mitchum,
looking awkwardly odd and poker-arsed,

wearing an apron to help, a crashing bore
even back in 1949, getting in a stupid tiff

with a kid and Janet Leigh screaming, *"Carl,
keep your hands off my boy!"* a grim whiff,

that once more he would surely lose the girl,
but such was Mr. Deadhead's cinematic curse

to appear to give help in his dodo-like way
but end up — exactly! — making things worse.

In the film *Rear Window* he played to type,
an ice-hearted detective with cynical views,

secretively assessing in patterns of guilt
which of the suspicious options to choose;

often in shadows nightlighting those eyes,
unblinking, lidded, he stood coldly apart,

as if to show by remoteness and stealth
he was blind to pity and had not a heart.

Was it the vacant eyes, the bayonet ears,
or the ghastliness of his terrible smile

in a man who staring a second quite gave
the horrific impression of staring a while

that, so eerie the mood whenever he left
like something scrapped at a terrible cost,

it seemed the skin of a serpent was shed
on the desolate floor of a paradise lost?

Bo Diddley's Bow

Bo Diddley done invented the diddly-bow,
a one-stringed instrument he got to know.

More than anything he ever had to show
was this unlikely guitar that he made go.

Hambone, its rhythm like rum-tum-tiddly
and thrum between banjo and crazy fiddly,

has African roots which is never piddly
whenever strummed by the great Bo Diddley.

Pacific Overtures

In Samoa they are large and fair.
In Tonga they are stocky and dark,

although both sport similar hair.
One day in Tonga just for a lark,

adopting a decidedly menacing air
confrontatory and casually stark,

a Tonganese shaped like a pear,
a native, on a stroll in the park,

a pompous Samoan witnessing there
blurted out loud a nasty remark

to him who seemed a fat debonair
and was neither stocky nor dark.

"Pardon me, sir, must you stare?"
asked the Samoan hearing the bark.

Said the Tongan, "Isn't it clear?
Bum like you in Tonga be clerk!'

He heard the large Samoan declare,
"Because you are stocky and dark,

while I, a Samoan, am large and fair
you must turn yourself into a snark?"

Warned the angry Tongan. "Beware!
You show much too fat to put in the ark!"

To such evil threats without any care
how could the fat Samoan not hark?

And so without any further repair
a quick retreat he beat out of the park.

A Samoan may grow large and fair,
and Tongans quite stocky and dark,

but even a person shaped like a pear
can by evil temper turn into a shark

even if the two may have similar hair
and both taking up a stroll in a park.

When the Samoan came into a square
he all of a sudden took the mark

of a feminine vision beyond compare
who instilled in his loins a spark,

an American girl whose legs were bare
wearing in blue a brief cutty sark,

her skin so white with radiant glare,
flawless, without so much as a mark,

so hoping her to invite to his lair
he spoke out with a boastful quark,

but saying, "I'm fat but have flair,"
he grinned the wide grin of a shark!

It was then (as she was) the *au pair*,
bristling at his thick hide of bark,

with the ambition of clearing the air
spoke to the coon with an angry cark,

"In Samoa they may be large and fair
and in Tonga perhaps stocky and dark,

but to go with you I view as despair,
be it large *or* fair *or* stocky *or* dark!"

Wounded and in his eye a large tear,
the Samoan ambled back to the park

to find the Tongan just to be near
(whether or not it be seen as a lark)

a person with whom he could share
even a word, even if a furious bark

came from a person stocky and dark.
At least, *at least*, they had similar hair.

Three Rothko Poems

I.

Rothko and His Rectangles

They sit one above, one below,
vibrating against each other,
as if sharing what they know,
a union of child and mother.

Why are there always only two?
Why some brighter? Why dimmer?
And is it not odd a solid hue
can characteristically shimmer?

But then what is united you ask
in two faintly luminous shapes?
It is the viewer's dutiful task
to discern which of which apes

the other — or is it both do,
as placed there by the mentor?
(Detractors of a darker view
see a sandwich with no center.)

What may seem at first conjoined
in the end can be aligned
the way different sides of a coin
relate but are not combined.

Does the ocular trick of seeing
where two eyes one image make
apply to the strangely fleeing
forms Rothko's colors forsake?

Are the morphs strictly forms?
And don't the forms pull away
even if they are modular norms
in some close, indefinite way?

Aficionados are said to weep
upon seeing the paintings bold,
while some find nothing deep
and turn away camphor-cold.

Angry, he'd paint in a hurry
dark ochre, alizarin crimson,
cobalt violet, mournful murray,
Victorian front-parlor damson,

rudest yellow and mars brown
of the most unsettling hue
as side to side, up and down,
his wrathful brushes flew.

Shapes both fit and counterfeit:
while one or two looked dead,
others seemed from inside lit
by oxide green or angel red,

shell pink or smaragdine gold,
that seemed at times to throb
as if of a beat that was told
by a heart going *lob-lob-lob*.

A fat, dark-complexioned Jew,
Rothko used industrial paints;
peering at his work he knew
them to be infected taints

that would never weather time,
would peel, flake, disappear,
fade, as if treated with lime.
It was not him to shed a tear.

What may seem at first conjoined
in the end can be aligned
the way different sides of a coin
relate but are not combined.

He fashioned canvases to sell,
bought his paint by the tub,
came but then went by the bell,
knew what he sold by the stub,

used brushes wide as brooms
in a studio much like a lair,
and in those rectangle rooms
he caught a whiff of despair.

He would peer at his work,
but find nothing transcendent;
to paint, he felt, was to shirk —
and waste — any independence

from those melancholy blocks
so crucially interrelated
by the chromoterrible shocks
of what he saw he created.

Did he see in his work an abyss?
Are we what we do? What we make?
Can one's art rebuke, dismiss
one, and in a final way forsake

The artist? If so, why then stay?
He cut his inner arms and died
and disappeared and in that way,
as though his own art he defied,

but. bargain paint and transitory,
he confessed to a broken heart
— he could find no glory —
and went the way of his art.

II.

Rothko Unrevivifiable

Deadbent, an alcoholic,
in a rage over his own abandonment
by unfeeling parents,

fleeced by cagey dealers
who invaded his warehouse of paintings,
greedy as cormorants,

Rothko also sadly found
he could not move beyond his one image
quoting weepy rectangle

over weepy rectangle,
which imprisoned him. He was stymied.
Would that he could

simply draw a comical cat!
Could any of the Abstract Expressionists
crayon even a mere tree?

In the end, he became
his own father and abandoned himself,
slitting open his arms

at the very same age
his ponderous and grumpy father was when
that man abandoned him!

III.

Rothko Draws Red

Rothko flatly refused to accept good news about his health,
not when he had begun preparing to die for more than a
year.

For someone who badly needed and wanted to be in control
he saw the face of darkness, angry but not without fear.

Pausing over a sink, he saw a fat bald madman in a mirror
and knew exactly where the double razor-blade would tear.

There was not only a deep need in him to have the last
word,
there was absolutely nothing in this world that he held
dear.

Blood spread under him after he fell, a melancholy
rectangle.
It was blood, a study in red, his ultimate work, how queer.

Christ's Favorites

"I will look upon you with favor and make you
  Fruitful and increase your numbers, and I will keep
  My covenant with you."

— Leviticus 26:6

Can we in our frailties be loved? We can.
A woman in a cotton dress of faded blue crash,
  a man may in the cerements of the grave,

  a young apostle apocalyptic eyes,
all serve to tell us we are seen and savored
  by the Savior who has who died for us

  as *individuals* with fire, faces, forms,
and whatever fashion it may be that makes us real
  enough by Him to earn us special love.

  Since Mary Magdalen was the first person
to whom the Risen Christ spoke — "Mary," he gently
  said — may we not then revere the fact

  that He who held a special place in his heart
for the one who first saw (and passionately sought)
  his empty tomb, the first to tell the news

  to his disciples, calling it a miracle,
and know her as a true friend any man might have?
  I see no tribalism or trickery in a man

  prone to love one more than another.
We fail all by not with force and fire loving one.
  What human heart is not empty with need,

  does not select, by yearning, two or three
that fill one's soul to bursting with happiness?
  "Oh Lord, the one you love is sick,"

  cried sisters Mary and Martha to Jesus
who in Bethany raised his friend their brother
  from the dead — and he wept! — crying,

"Lazarus, come forth!" The two felt love
of the kind that, His own divinity aside, proving
   He could feel, from love, uniqueness

  in a soul, perfumes His humanity for us.
John, the special disciple "whom Jesus loved,"
   reclined next to him at the Last Supper

  and standing at the foot of the cross,
heard Christ in agony exclaim, offering his mother
   to him, "Dear woman, here is your son"

  and then to John, "Here is your mother."
A woman in a cotton dress of faded blue crash,
   a man in the cerements of the grave,

  a young apostle with apocalyptic eyes,
all serve to tell us we are seen and savored
   by the Savior who has died for us

  as *individuals* with fire, faces, forms,
and whatever fashion it may be that makes us real
   enough by Him to earn us special love.

For Albert

born February 14, 2006

On this splendid day a child is born
Whose name, a royal one, we call to mind
As any blown upon an English horn.
Your great-grandfather, a man so kind,
Is remembered in your name, as well.
No more splendid heart has ever beat.
Your noble namesakes, so evoked, will tell
When on the day you're Christened they repeat.
We pray the child on this important day

Awakens to the glory of his name
That one day he himself in turn may pray
For blessings on his son of royal fame.
This continuity of grace we bless.
No higher glory can the world possess.

Whenever I Walk I Cross The Street

Whenever I walk, I cross the street,
not to be bested, never to be beat.

It is never unwise to be circumspect,
avoiding a snoop who seeks to detect

where you may go and what you may do
to try crudely to trace the essence of you.

Whoever you are, you must not be blind.
There's always someone directly behind.

It is a way of hiding your ultimate goal
from one who'd blackly solve your soul.

I will walk forty feet then turn about,
pausing a mo in the grip of a doubt,

just stopping to check if anyone cute
might be behind to thwart his pursuit,

for anyone stopping will then be shown
to be the menace whose cover is blown.

I'll cross not once but recross again,
gaining the sidewalk but suddenly then

turn and in minutes appear over there,
provoking no doubt a threatening stare

from the evil face of a force so dour
it would spirit you off that very hour.

The sole way to live is by indirection,
lest those who try to make a connection,

of any stripe, if I must say it plain,
for cash, for luck, for power, for gain,

out of necessity or out-and-out greed,
lust, sheer nosiness, or desperate need,

to just pass the time, to get you to vote
to boast of his kids, to sell you a coat,

to sell, to hustle, to thrust some petition
in front of your face with this condition

that you sign it and then make a donation
to another benighted group in the nation,

to request on election-day you volunteer
to carry signs for some asshole's career,

to purchase a lot, for peace in the world,
to buy boxed cookies from some idiot girl,

to hear salvation from the Father above,
out of nothing but loneliness, even for love.

Man's vice is this compulsion to follow,
convinced similar souls are also hollow,

if hollow, then let him be part of a crew —
and so he assumes this right to pursue.

So as soon as I see him come, then I go?
Wrong. My crossing the street is a no,

a *not* to the hunter before he can aim
whatever fraud he is hoping to claim.

I zig and I zag and I zag and I zig,
maneuvers I would not term infra dig,

for such is the way I walk, and I say
it is my big secret to keep people at bay.

The sole way to live is by indirection,
lest anyone seek to make a connection,

so after I die and if you would grieve
with a sense of sorrow you need relieve

and visit the graveyard to pay respects,
checking if that stone is me or the next,

do so, but pay heed now what I confide
to you who may follow after I've died:

My tombstone may sit there tidy and neat,
but check for my body across the street.

White Telephones

What creaturely weakness, what need,
in old style Hollywood with its orange awnings,
  white linen suits, chapeaux of wax fruit,

  topaz rings that screamed with light,
and good wallets, thin wallets, leather wallets
  filled with many folds like labiae,

  leopard-skin panties and sex-slaves,
allowed its seal-sleek divas, programmed in their
  parvenuism, eating vanilla crêpes

  with berries in glitzy phony eateries
such as run by runty Prince Romanoff, born in fact
  ugly Hershel Geguzin, a tailor's son

spawned in Poland, whose sharp bent
nose could have easily doubled for an umbrella hook,
   to *marry* such posturing farceurs

   like simpering Prince Serge Mdivani
or Henri Marquis de la Falaise de la Coudraye
   with their patent-leather hair,

   perfect spats, and sharp-knobbed canes,
comic inauthentic girdle-salesmen all fobbed out
   like royalty in procession?

   "Reginald Earl-Everything-But greet
Count Waldo Balso!" sang Heshy. "Miss Pola Negri.
   You know Sheik Amin as-Soltan?"

   "Your elegant ring, Madame, so rare,
so poifectly oranch, oy, is not hef as irridescible as you!
   Where is Ramazani, the Iranian prince?"

   Did they figure, like the sleek furs
they wore that once used to be an animal fashion,
   style could fashionably be faked?

   Was it for those fat white telephones,
they craved to go on film? Lived, sweating, for a rank
   of pretext trying to be real?

   Erich von Stroheim added the "von"
to mimic a stalwart aristocrat, him a penniless Jew
   who, scratching aboard, sailed

   west trash-class on a bum-boat yet
thrived to drive a long white limousine imperious
   through the hollow Holmby Hills,

   past the Klitnicks, Mr. Wiggler,
Murray Nutkis and his pretentious *porte-cochère*,
   Heshy Clitorovich, the Fingerits

— posing as a copper-polished Prussian
gave him the face to fight a deeper shame he felt inside
  for hiding who he actually was —

  and all the hideous gonif-jockeys
with their polo mallets and coon batmen bowing
  in old-style Hollywoodland,

  under the zebra-striped awnings
toward all those seal-sleek divas in white suits
  and skimmers of fat wax fruit

  who with their creaturely weakness
and their craven need for oily wallets and full
  always looked for sharp-knob canes.

Mr. Mamzer's Landlord

  "My credentials? God wants me here!"
asserted Mr. Mamzer, an outraged Newark Jew
  sitting in his room in Harlap St.,

  savoring his *ulpan* with a burp.
"I walk to the wall at Abu Dis every day
  just beyond East Jerusalem,

  with my dog, you should know!
I'm an adventure rabbi, who takes people
  on tours. I love klezmer jazz.

  I'm here eight years." Poking
a cane on the deal floor with a rat-a-tat-tat,
  he bellows, "I sing *Hatikvah*!

  Don't toik to me of deserving,
whose fur business got me this land, OK,
  and a beautiful dollar?

You should be so lucky like me.
Look, this can of green peas. Made right here.
I got fruit up the keester, feh.

Screw the fucking Palestinians!
Israeli bulldozers will keep the goddam peace
and separate that Arab scom

from their *mieskeit* livelihood.
Weren't the fart-marshes separating us
from Manhattan over there?

You want to kvetch about it?"
he inquired, drawing back a curtain
with a shrug. "Toik to God."

The Four Unrhymable Words

"Young Hardin Macomb, recently involved
in a theft outside Golden was fatally shot on
Thursday and buried today. A close friend who
was with him, Solange Hawk, is pictured (left,
in orange sweater) putting flowers on his grave.
She quoted his last words."

— *The Denver Post* (4/7/72)

A cowboy who lisped once managed to *pilfer*
in March a nice pair of six-shooters, all silver.

He fell hard for a Colorado beauty, Solange,
who in colored frocks looked best in *orange*.

One morning he gave her a flower all *purple*,
which with a blush she took by the stipule,

never knowing, in that same dangerous *month*,
he'd be murdered, he said, "playing with gunth."

Henry Miller

A tall bald man with the odd plain face
of a Chinese peasant and a satyr's leer

who erotically demoted his living place
"a green house thatched with women's hair."

Parable of the Lime

A supermarket lime
cut in half through its equator
though it be cold

if adequately rolled
can taste particularly sublime
from the refrigerator

with you a creator
in allowing something not be old
by overcoming time.

Isaiah Was Sawed Asunder With A Saw

Hebrews 11:37

How awful to ascertain the holy prophet
was supposedly martyred by King Manasseh
to be later memorialized by every moppet
from B'nai B'rith to the ladies Hadassah.

Talk about getting a luckless draw!
Isaiah was sawed asunder with a saw.

A son of old Amoz, he was married to boot
and father as well of two strapping sons.
To say he could preach was never moot,
for this man blistered the crust off buns.

Talk about getting a luckless draw!
Isaiah was sawed asunder with a saw.

What, one may ask, had Jehovah in mind,
affording all sinners such a good laugh
by allowing a *mensch* of a spiritual kind
in full public view to be buzzcut in half?

Talk about getting a luckless draw!
Isaiah was sawed asunder with a saw.

May our consolation regarding the crime
of a brutal death no one would not shun
be that good Isaiah, the Man of his Time,
at least left two relics instead of just one.

Talk about getting a luckless draw!
Isaiah was sawed asunder with a saw.

Sticky Fingers

If amativeness is adhesiveness,
isn't familiarity diseaseiveness,

an inevitable aspect of eroticism
which may align to an exoticism

but end in polluting relationships
by denying personal vacationships

and render useless preconceptions
of love and lasting postreceptions?

Blue Potato Blossoms

When I had to look twice
at the soft frail blue blossoms there
above the tiny plant

I never suspected that
a small ball of a potato underneath
and so must recant

that colors gray and blue,
when it comes to living together well
as a concept, shan't.

Autobiography

My default reflex is to disappear.
My defect reflex is to default.
My appearance is to reflect default.
My despair appearance is to defect.
My reflex is to appear to default.
My reappearance is to reflect defect.
My refault defect is to reappear.
My defect reappearance is to despair.

The Truly Wealthy Can Never be Reached

"People are dangerous. If they're able to involve themselves in
issues that matter, they may change the distribution of power, to
the detriment of those who are rich and privileged."
— Noam Chomsky

The truly wealthy can never be reached. Pass by.
Driving, I never choose to speed, it is I who need not race.
It is you who have to run, slobs who have to try.

Autonomy is the kingdom of me, no access is my rule.
Go away. Nightcrawl. This is my personal manner, my pace.
All you yakking on the phone comprise a perfect fool.

I am down here in Orlando, thigh deep in hot sand,
phoning Lazard Capital with a bobo handing me bullshots.
Keep all *hoi polloi* away from polls, real facts, me

is my motto. Let them picket, howl, then go home.
Who was the wit said that on the outskirts of every agony
sits some observant who points? So I see no one.

No one can bawl me out, you see, no one can come near.
This is my richness. To eat, piss, smell, walk, fish, feel, write.
Anything I want, I do, I *dare*, free of the mob to steer.

By the way, who are *you* there at the end of my fence,
trying to breach my confidential cover for what to reveal?
I see no one, frankly, but yearn to get everyone hence.

Are We Running Out of Food?

When red Mrs. Mangold, puffing anger, rapped my hand
with a long tin ladle in line at the high-school cafeteria,
I was fat, yes, but reaching for another big baconwich,

my head swelled like a chandelier not for snatching
but because it came to me, all of a sudden like guilt,
that — everywhere, my God! — we're running out of food!

So badly scalded by the whispery information in me
I barged with almost near-sighted misery to eat all I could
against the cold horror of missing dinners I deserved

like my fat rapacious sisters who, hand-cranking food
in their blowsy housecoats, looked with measuring eyes
even as they swallowed every emptying bowl in sight,

pig-eyed with fear that the world will *just not wait*
around for them to consume the meals others meanwhile
were dispatching. Hot pies, pot roasts, whole cheeses,

wedges of cake, *jaune soufflés* — the sinking feeling —
and so this is my confession, you angry sabotaging pricks
who mock my fat, against the very day that happens,

when the swelling population at its dry waterholes
wakes suddenly to see no vegetables, no livestock, no wheat
or corn or even cooks but dark caskets everywhere,

blistered houses, and skies of gangrene. Look for me
a portly monarch intoxicating in my own air, with just plenty.
Why? *I knew, I saw.* I will have wheeeeels of Brie!

My Wife Always Tries to Find Habakkuk First

I don't need to win that badly, have always felt
that if I ever demanded fame it would be a self-test
so that I could see I'd gladly walk away from it,

but at church every Sunday when we are directed
by our zealous pastor to turn to a Scriptural text,
in a brutal irony aggravating me before God

my wife always tries to find Habakkuk before me,
flashing through the thin pages with a sly if secret
but detectable smirk like some samphire-gatherer.

What's exactly being said by what is being done
only makes me wonder what else I might be losing,
as she flashes fire, by someone of her stripe!

If gluttony is greed, is not such aggression
— and there in a pew we share! — somewhat,
I do not know how else to put it, *tigerish*?

There is a way of turning a page with grace
and equally a reticence regarding Habakkuk
or any holy text that in a casual way finds it,

like coming across a plant in a forest, say,
the way a lady would. Tigers have not only
striped fur, know — they have striped skin.

Apocalypse

"Fallen! Fallen is Babylon the Great
Which made all the nations drink the
Maddening wine of her adulteries."
Revelation 14:8

Drunk, we gasolined the world again,
set it alight, to watch the explosions light
the liquidating rains on fire.

In once ravaged Saigon not a building
was ever built by Americans that stands today,
only more than a million graves.

We blore, howling behind boulders,
our black weapons hung upon broken branches,
and avoid the spalls of flame.

Nudity is just another costume
left to us, the last, after swaddling clothes,
high-school jacket, graduation blacks,

green Army gear, our wedding coat,
all those three-piece suits we wore to work
all those bathing suits we had,

after exporting all that duncery
of war. After slaughtering endless Vietnamese
and drubbing Iraq to rubble

we're in retreat, pottled with wine
naked in the dirt pile-driving the last tarts
who've stayed to take our money,

our hands, our hair, wet with gas.
This is no building. We're in a brainless wood
with nothing all around not fallen,

all those clothes in piles of grass
do not matter. They burn where once we stood.
That's the seventh trumpet calling,

Mrs. Couture's Long Walks

Mrs. Couture, the parvenu, going through
a low point in her life, looking at her hairy husband
and seeing nothing but a brain of clunch

found it gave incentives for long walks,
alone, which she undertook on more than one occasion
by nosing around her neighbors' yards,

measuring their incomes with her eyes,
noting the amounts of mail in their filled mailboxes.
Next door they built a barn she loathed.

It threw a dark shadow across her self-
conception from the very first week that it went up
and once she thought of stealing lumber.

But how? You need a truck for that.
Envy is another way of hating yourself, she saw,
and so by wearing a sleeveless blouse

one night which accentuating her boobs
gave the mesomorph a drill only lust could follow,
the extent of consciousness in him,

by guile got him to take out his BB gun
on a week that she learned the abutters would be gone
away and watched him shoot a window.

The incentives then on all her walks,
what became a high point in her life, was seeing
the zero where the zero made a hole

The First Flesh

Did not Christ at the resurrection
return in human flesh to the sky
declaring to all his earthly connection
by dint of never having to die?

What did they think in heaven above
when he to those heavenly ramparts returned
wearing the body he offered with love
and being seen whatever was learned?

When for example he took off his shirt
were the holy angels filled with surprise
awed by the muscles with which man was girt,
struck by the beauty of human eyes?

Would Jesus not have needed to shave,
preparing his ruddy cheeks to lathe
and with manly arms a razor to wave
over his chin he then wet to bathe?

Who cannot have been eager to witness
the power of what was a carpenter's arm,
the shoulders, the buttocks, the fitness
of the body of man and its physical charm?

Why after death would he alter his being
when to his Father and the Spirit He rose
or consider in any true sense of freeing
Himself from the nature of human repose?

Our Savior included without exemption
what he had to become according to plan.
A significant part of Christ's redemption
was giving to heaven a true view of man.

Prayer Wheel

"God knows our hearts."
  — Sarah Son-Theroux

Who can deny a wish is a prayer
understood by a God always there?

If what we desire we must declare,
pleading aloud to make it clear,

are we not presumptuous to dare
to utter words that heaven may near

and in the process fail to beware
no one deserves particular care?

Who can deny a wish is a prayer
understood by a God always there?

Dr. Young Son

No minister was ever truly more a man,
offering up your life in several ways,
from the errands in God's name you ran
to helping your children to nurture and raise.
Then in Korea with a school called MTI
you founded a place to educate the young
for present and future generations to try
their best wherever God's glory is sung.
An adventurous life worthy of a book

you led in the shadows in order to meet
the obligations you found but never took
the plaudits the worldly seek to greet.
you've traveled the world in every part,
but ever remain in the home of our heart.

Whatever the Forest Its Color Will Never Be Uniform

Whatever the forest
its color will never be uniform.
  Camouflage is checked,

  not the way when wearing
scrambled patterns big bold gunners
  expect linear rules

  stalking a young royal
through forests running with freaks
  like hummels, switch-horns,

  and old back-going beasts.
A forest shuffles outside of its lines
  with whooshing winds

  and scumbles solid color
by the most unlinear trees and leaves
  that, checkering chromo

  and making irregular
what stalking conformists expect
  by way of alignment

  while wearing patterns
running with freaks like hummels
  and switch-horns,

camouflage the forest
whatever the forest, by which alone,
   alone, makes it boom.

Red

Red is the terrain of guilt.
We're boiled in it in a flash the way steam
   scalds wind-milling lobsters.

What brindled cat won't shriek
at our brutal, swatting hands when drunk
   with wet-eyed red we rage?

I intuit God's barbecuing hand
whenever I pass red rooves, a bloodied head,
   that salvia in mid-scream,

see a rabbit's frightened glare,
the blistering heat of chilies and Thai peppers,
   stop signs threatening arrest,

a fifty-lek note, boiled bricks,
cherries, rusted pipe, the ruddy lips of a pedophile,
   all infections, all infarctions,

the Fry-O-Lator chromosizzle
we are all doomed to a one to have to try to flap
   out of in some igneous hell

where we will be tormented
by scaly gigantic devils with red pointed ears,
   debauching us with forks.

The way red warns in lights
and snakes, like condensed hate, signaling threat,
   but also in bland bathing-suits

when young girls go scarlet
as the murderous sun beats a beach down flat
and makes wetness fry red,

cooking tiny embedded crabs.
My mad aunts in their vermilion shoes flashed
fury, so did sweet Dorothy Gale,

for the color having a howl
headlines scold, barks, shouts, screams, bellows
stop and triggers a finger

through which in dread red
no firework fails to set off terrific gongs in me
like the martyrdom by guilt

of all my accumulating wrongs
that shock me merciless in hot steamwater
like a flammable crustacean.

The Hearse on the High Plains

A nightmare, the hearse on the high plains,
beckons every one of us to have to climb to witness
what lies there and how we are responsible.

Did Edmund Hillary defeat Everest or win it?
By climbing it did he for example avoid it in the way
that by not climbing it we do not avoid it

and so have its burden? Climbing exalts
what slays in a public version a private darkness
where tall men, madly desperate to crow,

stand in the light to put us in the shade.
O Lord, I am depraved with sin here in this world,
studying the hearse on the high plains,

a soul being bundled to yet another height,
out of visual clarity, to be judged while frozen,
   suddenly gone like a blown oboe note?

   Could that be where the Elect really are?
Or are they humbly low, avoiding where the prideful
   live, not and never to be seen on high?

   My seriousnesses all remain unnoticed.
I stand shot on my despotic shores and feel rarely sane
   down here with all the hectoring failures.

   Didn't Augustine tell us every man seeks
peace by waging war but none seeks war making peace?
   Faith surely has need of all the truth,

   and I is the name I give to my mistakes,
avoiding what I need to know I do not have to face
   so that I can sleep through what awakes.

YYYYYY

   Do you know what this odd license plate
told me with its juddering replication of whys? Simple.
   Disintermediate all authority

   and race to question everything!
How else keep tyrants, fools, fascists, powercats, and nags
   from writing all over your soul

   their filthy declarations in ink?
Seek original truths *within* you, their rehabilitative force,
   the only way to come to see the light

   There is not a single stereotype
for any authentic conversion experiences in all of Scripture.
   Check to see! Zacchaeus, Matthew,

Lydia, Paul, Titus, and Timothy,
rummaging their blessed hearts for whys and wherefores,
could all have been driving that car.

The Sins of David Ricardo

"Let the rich get richer with celebration!
Grow fat your wealth fat high exultation!

Compassion is wasted on the working man,"
asserted Richard Ricardo, economist and Jew,

to his pal Malthus, a non-practicing prelate,
a command repeated in his obscure prose

that exuded the stink of sulfur and proved
by math that pity was wasted on the poor

and damaging, as it accelerated population-
growth by which both were then brought down.

"Do you not know the 'iron law of wages'?"
asked the MP-cum-stockbroker in the Exchange

who left bite-marks on all widows and waifs
who suffered all as he twiddled his safes.

"Give workers the minimum, nothing more —
Let all of them shit in a frozen basin!

Landlords, shove up your rents!" Dickens
did not adopt this slime-bag for his Scrooge,

nor use him systematically in many a tale,
nor circumcise Ricardo with his icy loupe

to put this contemptuous weasel on display
who freely offered the rich their formulae

for ignoring the misfortunes of the poor?
"Save the poor? Dun the filthy burkes!

Hold down wages! Hold down the population!
Ennoble the rich who support the nation!

Look to your ledgers with celebration!
Grow fat your holdings with exultation!"

Audible

We all should remember today
how the embers of genius flickered
when Manet inspired Monet
at whom art critics once snickered.

If you choose to point to delay
with determination to scorn
with Monet not worshiping Manet,
the slower he'd have been born.

But I swear it is still hard to say
without expecting a glitch
when referring to Monet and Manet
which of the two is which.

Frog Eyes Goes to the Movies

"To be a Negro in this country and to be relatively conscious
is to be in a rage almost all the time."

– James Baldwin

We face the night a thousand ways, but
in the dark it is generally always the same

When Jimmy Baldwin watched Bette Davis
in 20,000 *Years in Sing Sing*, he saw,

not without the silvery revelation that
takes place upon looking into a mirror,

that she had big pop eyes just like him
and, just like him, was ugly! That day

he raced home to tell his mother, it was
so like a compliment, although it wasn't.

Later, he did imitations of the actress
in school to crackling laughter, guffaws

from the kids who called him "Frog Eyes,"
snarky bits especially from the last scenes

in *Of Human Bondage* in which the ophthalmic
Davis was so sinful and lost and hopeless

that, to knowing Jimmy at least, she did not need
to have pop eyes. She could have been black.

Absalom's Monument

"I have no son to carry on the memory of my name."
— Absalom II Samuel 18:18

Absalom, having no issue and feeling dejected,
decreed for himself to have a pillar erected,

the height of which made the prince overjoyed,
— and all this, two thousand years before Freud!

But if he was in fact a connoisseur of height,
in every respect a brave lad and worthy wight,

how when riding a mule in open air and free
could he manage to catch his hair in a tree?

Cycle of Sin

"I know that nothing good lives in me,
  that is, in my sinful nature. For I have the power
  to do what is good, but I cannot carry it out ...
  when I want to do good, evil is right there with me."

Romans 7:18-21

I have always bitten my fingernails
from anxiety or fear I never knew,
and if, comparing neuroses, the scales
weighed heavily on it as something to rue
I honestly felt it never my lot to say.
My father waxed furious over this vice
of mine which his nerves began to fray
and gripping my hands as tight as a vice
at my trembling fingers he would glare
as if nothing more he could deplore
which, making my fate seem more unfair,
grotesquely only made me do it more.
The cycle of sin, weirdly unremitting,
sadly commits us to go on committing.

Louise Nevelson at the Dump

"The shadow is as important as the object."
        — Louise Nevelson

Who could deny a huge irony upon seeing
Louise Nevelson, bag lady from Shushneky —

with her wackjob bandanna, gypsy bracelets,
from some screwball chapter of Dolgoruky,

double-long fake eyelashes, chinchilla coat,
a blue denim workshirt, purple Indian vest,

big sand-hog boots, some cockamamie shawl
fake sepal ear-rings, jockey cap dung brown,

red farcical make-up, eyes rimmed with kohl,
parading Second Avenue like a circus clown,

— that all her sculpture, wooden and blunt,
was meant to be viewed from only the front?

Louise Nevelson's Wall in the Chapel of the Good Shepherd at St. Peter's Lutheran Church in the Citicorp Building on Lexington Avenue

Asking her friends to roam the ports
finding wood she could nail together,
she cobbled a wall with the broken orts
sprayed it with paint to give it weather
then hit the dump for shards and plates,
tiles, broken forks, and furniture parts,
doors, splintered windows, parts of gates,
electrical spools, half-wheels of carts
eggbeaters, spatulas, cooking utensils,
staves, old posts, and splintery shook,
flex, fish-bones, tips of chewed pencils.
Whatever the fucking thing could brook.
It stands there today the essence of qualm
where it's advertised an "oasis of calm."

Louise Nevelson Pauses with a Spray-can in Her Mitts

At what point exactly
>
> when Louise Nevelson painted old toilet seats gold
> did they become art?

There is no mystery
>
> from the foods and drinks we consume in the body
> in expelling a fart.

Dogs

> The perfidy of sisters —
> forgiving them even the coarse fat
> they wear to defend
> the disgust their unregenerate malice makes —
> creates dogsbodies
as ceremoniously unfit
as the dogs
that they trot out on leashes daily to parks
> just to watch them shit.

Mr. Deuteronomy Deals

"But whatsoever is dead of itself, eat not thereof.
Give it to the stranger that is within thy gates, to
eat, or sell it to him, because thou art the holy
people of the Lord thy God."

Deuteronomy 14:21

"Of the foreigner or stranger thou mayst exact it
[debts owed you]: of thy countryman and neighbor
thou shalt not have power to demand it again."

Deuteronomy 15:3

"Lobsters I just parboiled," said Maggid the butcher,
holding up two sagging beasts of orange imperfection,

rubbery wrong. They'd croaked in the filthy tankwater
three hours before, limp, two baskets of infection.

"I'll sell them cheap, Mrs. Shanahan, for you alone,
say nutting to nobody, *nu*? Betwin you and me, hokay?

You want I should throw in steamers ten dollars more?"
he asked and rubbed his hands, "Cracked, but no way

after you wash out the sand they don't smeck good,
trust me." He snapped the mottled paper from a roll,

wrapped the trash quickly, taped it with a slap, and
shoved it over to the Irish lady as if a ball to bowl.

So the things reeked? So Mrs. Cohn and Mrs. Franken
and Mrs. Pushkar would throw them back in my face?

Business is business, thought Maggid with a shrug,
need is need, selling is selling, and race is race.

The old lady opened her purse, took out her money
to pay, a bit confused by the amount of the bill.

Pushing his Borsalino back, Maggid counted the cash
did so again to be certain, and waved it into the till.

"By the by, we hev to settle somethink else today
before too late, Mrs. S. and you head out the door."

If Mrs. Cohn got a shin bone free today, enough.
"Last week for that cut of ham? Six dollars more."

Mrs. Grewsome Bares Herself

She felt she needed to record something of herself
in those perverse years, oh, just around the time

fondue pots and forks were all the rage and hustling
thirtyish couples in Washington, D.C. waxed political

and gossiped with pulled faces all adroitly captioned
and over black coffee one morning — Evelyn Waugh

smugly considered it an especially vile Americanism
not to say "a *cup* of black coffee," or so at least

her ex-husband, a pompous ass himself, pointed out
more than once — she opted at last for the lyric essay,

for that is what one read on NPR, with a familiarity
that always allowed for irony, which she thrived on,

the way, say, she wore her eyeglasses on top of her
head, repeatedly said "sort of," as did Oxford dons,

and, sipping stingers, snapped off quips. Born in
Monterey, she was gray now, fattish, although she

still wore plaid wrap-around skirts, worked on a book,
and had an affair with an oik named Henry Mosstaw,

an owlish balding minister who carried a man purse
and lived in Hanover, N.H. and wore a trim goatee

and whom she prayed people would not take for Jewish.
No brutal scission, if it meant gain, meant a thing to her.

Shedding a pound was hard, never shedding a husband.
It was time for a memoir — rain in March told her so.

How she adored those fruity, self-cherishing, affected
voices of that fey reporter on "All Things Considered"

— what was his name? — and the witty women who went
on air and gave such knowing accounts of their busy lives

like how fruitcakes palled, holidays galled, autos
stalled, and, she recalled, shoes never fit, cats often bit,

and how life, sort of, you know, life never quite
rang true, at least not the way we all wanted it to!

But back to that lyric essay? She might even write
about coffee! It has become such a religion these days,

sort of. To sound harried on NPR, ironic Mrs. G
in a plaid skirt, sounding off — with insight! —

became her self-fulfilling dream this rainy March
so she could finally bare herself. Fun? *Abso-lutely!*

Amerigo and Ansgarius

for Ned Rorem

Young Ansgarius and sweet Amerigo
on a sunny day in Londinium
caring not who in the city might know
swapped a daisy and a delphinium.

Said one to the other in passion
of the sweet traded-off floral treats,
"I love white but still follow fashion:
this pale color my toga repeats."

"Which is why I gave it to you,"
whispered Amerigo, hurt to the core,
lowering then his flower of blue,
for to him that color was pure.

"You see how you follow sobriety?
I offered you a flower of blue,"
said Ansgarius, disliking piety,
"our passion, dear heart, to renew.

Plus it matches your toga tint
which being blue is so brightly gay
and to sex gives more than a hint.
See, white doesn't work that way."

The sun above seemed no longer warm
as they faced each other that day,
for in the heart of youth a storm,
it's proven, rarely soon goes away.

Now Ansgarius was given to wonder
if lust alone ruled the heart,
while Amerigo started to ponder
if pureness at all played part.

"I believe purity central to love.
You would give passion that power.
The whiteness of a daisy, a dove,
by which hue I intended to shower

on you, Ansgarius, my affections,
not only offends your aesthetic, I see,
but reduces to pious confections
my love, throwing shadows on me.

How do colors signify fairly
for you but not me in kind?
Is it just that you see so clearly
while I am considered blind?"

Amerigo wondered in love if lust
should ever prevail in the end.
Ansgarius thought lust was a bust,
though it cost him even a friend.

Meanwhile, folks in Londinium saw
the young men there in the street
talking as if, engaged in a draw,
no one but these two should meet.

Amerigo, always so touchingly twee,
then kissing his friend said with glee,
"Why then let heterogeneity
over homogeneity be — "

and batting softly his hot blue eyes
" — at least as to togas and blooms!"
He claimed Ansgarius as his prize,
but just before they retired to rooms

each returned his flower by right.
Ansgarius took his delphinium back,
and his companion his daisy white.
Both happy lads now felt on track

for exchanging pureness for lust
is to take it but be no less pure,
as the ultimate meaning of love, to be just,
is to give and keep giving more.

Loch and Lake

Stillness of water defines a lake,
in and of itself entirely composed;
neither goose nor loon nor drake
will ever find it metamorphosed.

A loch never stops running though,
an inlet and outlet never without;
a bird some drift will feel below
and surmise it the pull of a spout.

Lochs, unlike lakes, are always cold
from their turmoil always in shift;
the chill is blue and hard and bold
in its drive and insistence for drift.

Unmoving waters tend to be warm,
serene in the way they nothing await,
and show the preternatural calm
of glory at ease in a natural state.

Jennifer Guest

She pretended to give me her very best
a condescending smile
it was implied I file
under Generosity: read Jennifer Guest
around the time the word *absolutely*
rather stupidly substituted for "yes."

She resembled the foolish slang she used
employing adverbs the way
language is what you say
in the farcical fashion that one is enthused
by appearing to seem like a victim abused
while me with her vapid smile she accused.

She concluded our meeting and walked away
using disconnect as a noun
and not a verb, as a clown
will assume a pretension in trying to say
she was leaving the circus but, looking gay,
hoping that she'd be remembered that way.

Black and White

"Aim above morality"
  — Henry D. Thoreau

I crave whiteness and wind, pack ice,
the refuge of freezing Antarctica, the vast tundra
sterilized by quantities of ultraviolet

radiating through the frigidation!
No measles, no mumps, no chickenpox, nothing
in the way of colds or flu where

the wind blows forever northward.
I'd live on seal meat, lightly boiled or fat raw,
lap blue glaciers to slake my thirst,

swim in the foaming seas to see
a daring aquamarine me. I shall put on the new
man, finding sleek sanity in cold,

for no way will I kneel in a church
again in the black dark, funereal candles alight,
the hooded confessionals beckoning

me to spill my guts and weep down
contrition to once again find another, newer me,
holystoned by rehabilitation.

It is unbafflingly beyond cupidity,
ascetic, yet as art formed Yeats' gold Byzantium
and guaranteed a gelid virtue.

What of darkness speaks of God?
I yearn for wind and white and wet and light!
The transfigured Christ I seek

who on that severe mountain high
revealed himself at night in incandescent white
when it was only me was bleak.

Sad Lonely Lesbian Hoping To Be Taken
for A Socialite

Horse-faced, all decked out, a sour pucker ready
with one of those marble, oh-no-you-don't chins,

alone, rained on, why do you never have a date?
You sit sourly, a solitary figurona. Is it *fun* to be

waiting for some partier who never ever comes
just to be photograsped that sad way in *public*?

You insist on attending Tribeca Film Festivals
and those annual *Vanity Fair* Oscar parties, all,

dressed to the nines compulsive in black tie,
not really the mis-step someone should make

who so resembles the Cowardly Lion, pouchy-
eyed, fat lips, just *scads* of mistrustful archness.

No, homeliness is not a crime. Bold and brassy
demivierges yearly cozy up to king and court,

yet as the adage says, "The eye can cross a long,
long river." Desire goes far beyond the possible.

I never saw a sharp Anderson & Sheppard suit,
Hilditch & Key shirt, or Manolo Blahnik shoes

do so little to help a given soul. While you fight
to feign indifference, perched there in a corner

on that neglected couch, French cuffs a-link,
nursing god-knows-what kind of grievance —

trying hard to concoct witticisms would be
my guess or with bold premeditated flourishes

ostentatiously pretending (but to whom?)
that you in fact have been ready to leave —

you seem also driven to court photographers
as if perversely to record the studious neglect

you suffer there without fat Harvey Weinstein
howling at your ear or editor Zuzu Zinnabar

or the perky Rhodopsin twins, half-looped,
or little Mr. Ponceau, hairstylist to the stars.

Why? So that in your rented duds and boots,
you will be reproduced, postage-stamp-size

in some far tiny corner of a gum magazine
in your extra-sad, over-dressed loneliness,

there in white tie and gray XL waistcoats?
I can tell you exactly why you are there

You are badly looking for — face it — courage.
all that sly bluff and concocted fashionola

is only saying, *"Put 'em up! Put 'em uuup!"*
Look, wear your hair and just stay home.

A Poem for Sarah After Her Departure for Estonia

(November 23, 2007)

Sarah my dear
As you took to the air
To follow your Fulbright star
I returned to the house
Like an orphaned mouse
And wept alone in my car.

I followed procedure
And tried to read your
Notes on how best to cope
But with you not there
To show me where
Things were I felt a dope.

Few would rate
Any man's estate
Higher than functioning well
But your disappearance
Gave full clearance
To super-add dumb to bell.

The cheese is hard
And reeks of lard.
Coffee? Best call it swill.
I jimmied the locks
Misplaced my socks
Lost an important bill.

The days feel cold
The skies grow cold
Because of your missing smile.
Since you went away
I really can't say
That living isn't a trial.

Since then it seems
My waking dreams
Are filled with thoughts of you
You drift into sight
Directing me right
Yet you are a ghostly hue.

But this I can say
While you are away
And loneliness I explore
Though we are apart
— and this from my heart —
I love you even more.

Nipmuk Makes a Canoe

Nipmuk on his knees snouting the beaver pond
rose and with a hatchet quickly brought down the Tamarack.
His tough, pliant, slender muscles shone tawny

this morning as he yanked out its looping roots
and laying them on the papery strips of tough, pliant, slender
birchbark took his tawny needle of deer bone

and sitting cross legged sewed the bark tight
with the needle looped with Tamarack roots making a canoe
as tough, pliant, slender as the tall tree.

No Woman Hated By Her Mother's Sane

No woman hated by her mother's sane
Who ingesting all the bile she's got
Vomits up the hate and scorn and pain
On everyone with whom she's fought.
A savagery the duplicating daughter
Like the mother viciously repeats,
As if by doing so she sought her
Choice to echo all that bitch's bleats.
A daughter apes her mother to a T,
Can never mask by guile her real face.
Neither wants the option to be free.
It's toward the final villainy a race.
No monster of a daughter as a scold
Is not taken from the mother's mold.

Apologize When You Are Not Wrong

Apologize when you are not wrong
and confirm the offender in her fault

who concludes where you were strong
that now you are weak so rubs in salt,
and so reboldened with double the vice
she blames you the more by lying again
as flames of fire are followed by ice,
ever ready to register either strain.
There is a guile in the wily offender
who extorts contrition in order to blame
like returning mail to the loving sender
once having assessed a letter came.
Innocence darkened can never right
when what's left is guilt to make light.

The Walls of Jerusalem

Was Jesus crucified outside Jerusalem's walls
for sacrificial reasons, as Leviticus 4:12 demanded bulls
     be brought "outside camp" to be burnt,

     past your squat towers fortified by Uzziah
and those gates never to be opened until the sun grew hot?
     I saw blank faces watching from the walls

     no cleaner than the bloody bulls baying out
like the gormless Hebrews who once got hacked by invaders
     pouring into that unfortified flavescent city.

     Jerusalem was always attacked from the north
because it was most vulnerable there. Nehemiah led the
     rebuilding with funds in fifty-two days,

     putting stone on stone, hanging purple curtains,
all to be ripped down again in 70 A.D., sacked by Romans
     which the tears of Jesus predicted years before

     you took him out from camp, way beyond the walls
past the hot gates, runty towers, stone on stone, and purple
     curtains, cravenly to slaughter like a bull.

An Estonian in the Virgin Island

"I'm freak that I don't enjoy swimmink and sun baths
but that's it," Ants wrote us on a postcard showing

a pith-helmeted cop and palms. "I canst change myself."
Ants Leukoplast in Trunk Bay? We could only guess

what he looked like, bald, pale as paper, a Soviet
electric shaver in hand without a matching plug.

"Is unstable to expect weather hold?" He motioned to
a black waiter, "Give der childrens here citrus fizz!

Have you also *kartulipealsed*?" Pause. "Potato tops?"
No one moved who should have. So he pointed to a roof

and cheerfully exclaimed, "We also to have the stork!"
A spoon-headed waiter behind him grinned and grabbed

his crotch and walked away, flapping off a dirty parrot
which flew onto and badly rattled a tin Coca-Cola sign.

A purple sun can scald anyone from Tartu or Tallinn
where all men fishbelly-white know only shade and dark

are meant for them, but suddenly carting off your wife
to Siboney on an economy flight? Where greenfinches

sing in palm trees above a plaza? Hot maroccas rattle?
Steel dented drums are loudly beaten by goofy elves?

So immense is the misery of humankind that snow
more than sun creates a comfort when in a billowing

bathing suit it seems sadly far more false to try to talk
and be a dork than keep mum. I see Ants in living color,

preparing in dreadlockland to ask for postage stamps,
sweating, sheepish, blushing, thumbing over idioms

in a tiny book he bought with kroons in icy Estland
to memorize the English words for *lemon, umbrella,*

hot sexy girls, crabs, how far is Charlotte Amalie?
commode paper, shark alert. It had to be all uphill,

despite the crashing surf. "We *also* to have the stork*!*"
wildly cried Ants, pointing to the crest of a red roof.

He would know the waiters (or whomever) mocked him
(I sensed rue and bitterness not only in his tourist postcard

but in the sharpness of his black cacography) as they laugh
and snort, "Shithead no see Mr. Bird is just a fucking rook!"

It Is Not That I'm Smart. People Are Dopes

It is not that I'm smart. People are dopes,
They sit on their pile of dumb,
Rather than read.
On ideas try to feed,
Each just sits on his bum
Idly to twiddle his thumb
And when walking abroad he but mopes.

I get hugely praised for the size of my brain.
In the course of an average day.
"Oh, you're so bright,
You must read through the night,
But I can't make hay
With books and must say
To me they seem nothing but pain."

Crows at Night

A crow's lone enemy is the Great Horned Owl.
They make crows draw their heads from under their wings
　　to sit in shivering misery until morning

　　out of vigilance. Crows do not see well in the dark
but roost with an ache and burble and mutter through the night
　　until in extreme cold weather this results in frozen eyes

　　and blindness, where death by starvation is only
a matter of time. What one crow learns, the rest of crowdom
　　shortly knows. What crows in black jackets also

　　know is it is always night whether their heads
are under or over their wings. Guile without eyes is tough
　　enough to blacken any wing. What is being said

　　to them is that life so horned and cold and wet
with but a fragile blackwing, even if dark, to protect a bird
　　will only last until after waiting it is dead.

Parable of a Potato

　　The potato, until the Mayans tamed it,
　　was a deadly green and poison shade

　　like tobacco, bell peppers, hot nitrates,
　　but its roadworthiness, the way it paid,

　　was it endured, for in any empty hole
　　you dropped it, land flat or any grade,

　　there tuberous it sat about to sprout
　　the toxic leaves you sat before afraid,

　　and its distinction, after it was tamed,
　　lay partly in the method it was made.

Mash me, nutso! Boil me, bake, or fry,
of my vegetable soul never be afraid.

How Did You Find Your Way To Me Through Those Black Rooms?

How did you find your way to me through those black rooms
where on my pallet I lay sinful as Nineveh, repeating endlessly

how plots had been devised for me to fail in what of faith I owed,
bitching how binary choices came to seem so burdensome to me

when faced with an existence I preferred to blame on you, O Lord.
only one of my many demurs? I was proud myself with awfulness

who refused your grace. I like Job deserved stricken plant and worm
for disobeying you who asked only that I but obey to show my love

broiling in the heat of my fixed and fatal concepts, shadeless, ill,
working for the ministry of cretins in this world instead of you.

Room after room receded, atrabilious as my life was small and dark,
unfit for salvation, where unhappiness signified exactly what was lost

to any soul who listened to your holy call. but in the hone-black rooms
of wasted days I lay. Who would harrow hell to someone so undone?

Yet, behold, it was you alone who sought for me among the glooms to
raise a soul who by your love finally saw the goodness of the sun.

Balthazar and Oscar Goings

No Civil Rights folk ever bothered to mention him that I recall,
who seemed, to most. nothing but a chalk statue at the manger,

representing with a *soupçon* of black witchery the voodoo set,
him and the two other majestic dudes with their nibbling camels.

What did he know of slums, screaming neighborhoods, the "Man,"
and exactly what of protest, drug-busts, the world of minking hair,

did *he* exact? They all looked like veteran house-guests for a night,
no one bad or electric with rebellion. "He Sage, the Yo Yo Champ!

Know'm sayin'?" I heard Oscar Goings bitterly quip, flicking off
his butt ash as we passed a crèche one Christmas ago in Medford

back in 1958, figuring from the crown he wore he owned poodles,
expensive watches, and in that hay was strictly out of his element

or, as my black friend put it — when I went to put in one good word
at least, tentatively, for integration — "Like from nowhere, man."

A Tanzanian in Tartu

Jews from Pskov were welcome
even in the Tsarist days but a cold frost

Greeted Wilfred Bgoya from Dodoma
when in Tartu he muttered "Jambo"

to a man in a reindeer-hat
who did not so much scowl as drop his jaw

when again he blinked to see
a smiling black head as perfectly as odd

in that snowy Estonian city as seeing
the devil! Mr. Kauplema almost shit!

"*Tumm! Trumm! Trummeldama!*" he boomed
and made a few quick applauding claps

to snatch the attention of three runty
passersby, one a truculent harridan

carrying a cane — people gathered —
and all now began regarding Mr. Sambo.

"*Praak*!" said Mrs. Uha, cane high.
"*Scrap!*" "*Löötspill*," screeched another,

miming an accordion. Wilfred, bug-eyed,
in the meantime with true delight

in the icy darkness of the Old Town Square
at noon looking at Mrs. Bgoya

reached down to present two pigtailed
Bgoya girls twining through his legs

to show them they liked music, *too*,
drums and horns and big accordions

but not before two dwarf men cachinnating
awfulness the way a beggar begs

began bouncing up and down,
one making fat lips while the other gave

as if to brush his face. Horn-hat hissed.
"*Valgeks värvima*!" "Paint it white!"

A Tiger Is Liquid

When tigers clawing trees to sharpen both choose
a tree, the favored one is the *biga* which exudes

astringent blood-red gum. The beasts love blood
running down the trunk. Bark is savaged into hair

in insistent horror, and so the trunk is fluid twice.
A tiger walks as if it had no bones. It tends to hunt

by tides, as well. Where motion is, no one is ever
quite prepared for the abruptness of a sudden stop.

Scream, shout? Its damp presence eats the echo up,
as with a baleful stare the beast sifts scent through

the roof of his open mouth and drools. An ocean
of hot muscle ripples through his waving stripes.

A tiger is liquid, can disappear behind a single
blade of grass, instantly appear from nowhere,

in a way is always wet. Where it flows its motion,
even if a stare, leaves strips of blood and hair.

Song for Sarah

"Say it," the girl said. "You don't know how important
things that are said are."

Renata in Ernest Hemingway's
Across the River and Into the Trees

I awake in a place
In vastness like skies
And kiss your sweet face
And kiss your soft eyes.

Your name casts a spell
Like a dream held by sleep
Like a voice down a well
Like a secret I keep.

All the tales I can tell
All the letters I write
Only deepen the dark
Only sweeten the night.

If you went away
The world would dissolve
You alone define day
And the nighttime resolve

I yearn for your beauty
The strength you define
And love and not duty
Is what makes you mine

So all you are, Sarah,
Makes a world full of rhyme
It is wide and not narrow
And as endless as time.

Vera Nabokov Hurts an Animal

"She never compiled a list of her dislikes, at least
on paper. Had she done so her catalogue would have
included... cooking, housekeeping, untruths, cruelty
to animals, even in fiction...Giving the time of day to a
philistine."

— Stacy Schiff, Véra

"I played soccer — the great love of my life."

— Vladimir Nabokov

As all I read of you came to rest
in a book where I saw you said
you hated to see animals suffer

by any means, even in movies,
comfortably offering all of that
with whom you thought you were,

I recognized that something
most uncomfortably sat next to
what suddenly I then recollected

of the person you really are,
coldly having returned a book
I mailed to Montreux years ago

(along with some butterfly stamps)
for your husband to inscribe, where
you stated coldly, "VN does sign

books for just anyone." Crushed,
I looked to see the book unsigned,
when out fluttered the stamps,

and I saw you added in your note,
truthfully — I'll give you that —
"Besides, the stamps are canceled,"

which is exactly how a philistine
would respond at any time of day.
Who *wouldn't* chose soccer over you?

Movies are Lies With Peekaboo Eyes

"What's in a name? That which we call
a rose by any other name would smell as sweet"
                        — *Romeo and Juliet*

In the noir movie, *The Blue Dahlia*, which is a nominal merry-go-round
in which aliases have been adopted where true names all remain hidden

— the sleazy nightclub owner Eddy Harwood's real name is Bauer,
for example, who is a robber wanted for murder back in New Jersey —

when Johnny Morrison tells Joyce Harwood his name is Jimmy Moore,
(which is also Alan Ladd confessing to Constance Frances Ockelman,

who, although she had peek-a-boo hair and a sexy smile, for the sake
of her baby-blue eyes alone was denominated Miss Veronica Lake)

he is lying, inviting her, seeing the "J.M." on his suitcase, to conclude
that his actual name might really be (why not?) Jeremiah McGonigle,

and although he replies, "No one was ever named Jeremiah McGonigle,"
that is only a continuation of the chain of exuberant movie fibs, in fact,

for while it is well beyond doubt any flower can serve as a movie name,
in this particular movie in keeping with the theme that nothing is exact

there are no blue dahlias — that is just another lie, like Santa and the Easter
Bunny — so until the day dahlia genetics are altered, we're stuck with red,

white, yellow, purple, orange, and other blends or variegations thereof
that we happen to find or even try to grow in the soil of our flower bed.

Edith

May I ask why you
(don't call this harsh)
read the novels of Ngaio
(born Edith!) Marsh?

Melanie *et Cie*

I bothered to seek
the muses on the mountain
but saw only a fractious
bingo-winged female agent,
thin with rage and sawgrass hair,
as she grackled on,
cawing cant, with spite lines,
chinned, with teeth like combs,
talking at mad cross-purposes
with short nail-headed editors
whose wide-ties billowed red
with little but kerfuffling comedy
who never had a word to say

of art, merely action (sales!),
pawing my pages to peddle
to base-hearted reviewers,
and they all came up — count them! —
both close and far,
little gray molehills.

Boston Bruins Cracker Jacks

When I opened my box of crunchables,
munching by the handful what sounded nutttily good
in sweet, explosive noises,

milan lucic, zdeno chara, tuukka rask,
miroslav satan, vladimir sobotka, mark recchi, david krejci,
johnny boychuk, andy wozniewski,

I suddenly realized as I swivel-chewed,
the sounds were the roster of the Boston Bruins, 2010 —
A surprise in every package!

Godfather Drosselmeier's Tears

"But, dear God, please give me some place, no matter how small, but let
me know it and keep it."

—Flannery O'Connor, in prayer

I who knew it badly wrong to quit a venture
when it became routine knew I'd do what Noël Coward would,
like any neutral, yawning Laodicean,

and so big God, tall and eye-patched to avoid
having to watch my incorrigible fears and boiseried corruptions,
disordered, corrupt, larboard-leaning,

opened no goatbag of shiny gifts to me,
lest by pride and vanity I falsify the Scriptural pages I thumbed,
    no wiser than a blunt-muzzled capybara,

    figuring if Absalom was the handsomest
man in the Bible I would settle to be a knave of hearts, anything
    remotely blessed, a squire with fox-red hair,

    say, some pomeroy in a stiff collar and tie
allowed to arrive at some small certainty, raise an eyebrow or two,
    not necessarily invent the wheel,

    prove, for all my workaday baseness,
I merely be not fooled in this life, penalized by commonness,
    be no feeble houseguest on this earth,

    even if no apostle, a fool but a fool
to make a difference, somehow, to rise above the life I was handed,
    some bravo to frivol with a little fire.

    Tinfoil-hat alert: I asked God for more,
sharpening my quills and gathering reams of paper to write books
    as an antidote to all I was not!

    A work of art offers itself to everyone
but belongs finally to no one, according to Baudelaire. It gives
    itself away indiscriminately in the way

    any two-act ballet belongs to any boob
perched in any seat in any row in any theater he claims, and I
    secretly hoped that art and love, partaking

    of the same self-surpassing generosity
through which God gives himself to the world, might find me
    worthy who would also co-create.

    Wasn't I competent enough to count,
show God I was not just another queer quidnunc in this world
    a stupid chew toy, a right prat?

I who carried thoughts in my head
the way Henry Thoreau carried botanical specimens in his hat
to pluck them out at will?

Was it so haughty of me to need
to interpret my own life as other than a formulated creature,
the product of a syndrome,

lest in my own charmless eyes
I become objectionable to the very me parading the black halls
my pedestrian self walked?

I sought to write pages to be loved,
preaching through personae, odd multi-voiced puppetry
masks that grinned and groaned

through whatever infamy narratives
that might outlast me lest love be locked out, so was I too odd
to succeed on this planet?

Couldn't others see I had a stage mind,
nearly photographic recall, selves to share? In dreams I anticipated
coming perspectives of development.

Was Marx correct when he said of legal institutions
they cannot stand higher than the society that brought them forth?
I've always been a famous version of myself

with a word to the fates not to be a symptom
of the times I wished to transform. I saw I was a law unto myself,
not above nor below, only beyond my peers.

Who cared what kind of shirt or shouting slogan
the murdering party wears, whether it is attacking working slobs
or in-bred toffee-nosed silver spoon wankstains.

Life, I saw, me left an anthropophobe,
still I *insisted* I be saved even if through those sins and sorrows
I abjured in and by desperate repentance

to be worthy of the God that made me
and my face and my vagrant need to expend my talent and tact.
   I badly had to matter in my mind.

   That there is no description of Christ
in the whole of the New Testament bade me feel I myself
   may shape-shift a fit semblance,

   transcending the impossible illusion
that I had to be what, when looking down at me as bloatware,
   people surmised I would be nothing else.

   I have milled about with the precariat,
watching fools ambush market their mediocrity to the world
   bowing low and scraping. And me?

   Art was my salvation to *remake* what I
in the world inherited, whether hare-drummer, Fritz, gnome,
   mouse-king, or Nutcracker soldier.

   I prayed I that I could signify just enough
to make heaven weep for me and my blunders. I would count
   myself justified even by God's pity.

   I pled only not to be a donkeystone.
St. Augustine declared, "Love means: I want you to *be*!" I was —
   or, I swear, at least pretended to be —

   and so that gets me nothing? I who *swore*
I need not have been a soldier in full-parade uniform, nutcracker cute,
   expected no Clara or Marie to buss my bum.

   Moses boldly killed a man, and so did David,
and the good Godfather, reaching into his grab-bag of dolls and dollars,
   allowed them solid profiles the world adored,

   so why let the poor Gringoire I am, I asked,
be a dry ball of failure? I will play any role you offer, Councilor Grand,
   please let me only be a nut that cracks!

Ho Chi Minh Visits the U. S. in 1917

"Don't drop those trays, chink!" shouted Bob Yaw,
head baker at the Parker House where, in the kitchen,

Nguyễn Sinh Cung, 22, worked all night baking rolls
with Wallace Lines and old Jeremias Molds, Negroes,

who were hot-footed by two drunken Irish sweepers,
the moronic Burke brothers who called them "cueballs"

which Cung remembered seven years later in Moscow
in his pamphlet, *La Race Noire,* from notes he wrote,

bitterly critical of prejudice, on a bench on Tremont St.
where delinquents mocked his stook of odd black hair.

Miss Frostquilt stepped aside when she saw the little man
come round a corner, and Dickie Trickle lighting a cigar

for his gay young friend, Forrester, threw the hot match
at the dirty quilted coat and bellowed, "Yellowballs!"

Cung wrote his sister, Bếch Liên, of mobs and lynchings
of Negroes in the South and of the sheeted Ku Klux Klan

shown in photos in the Boston *Globe* he'd snipped out.
He lived for a time in Harlem in a room, working for

grumpy Arnold Metzger in a photo lab, touching up
pictures, for $3.50 an hour in order to pay him rent

for an empty waterless flat. "You don't like it, leave,"
barked the photo man's wife, Lil, snorting down her beezer.

"No one here's asking you chinks or nips who eat cats
who no different than blue-gums to stay here, okayyy?"

Groups, troops, crowds, marching armies of men, unions
swarmed the busy streets, barking, shoving, reeling.

Always alone, he walked the streets. A harmonica
in a pawn-shop fascinated him, and he learned to play

"I'm Always Chasing Rainbows." Sleeping outside
was common for disenfranchised hobos on 125th St.

but when Nguyễn went to help one on Christmas Eve
a cop named Slinger broke his wrist with a nightstick

assuming the Asian was filching a flask of cheap wine
or rifling the pocket of the drunk there in the gutter.

He went to movies, holding his hat in his hands, and
watched Chaplin in *Easy Street* in the flickering light

showing tramps, drug addicts, dire poverty, and thugs,
and saw newsreels of worker-strikes against the war

and the barbarities of American capitalism from which
he made a slim volume of poems later published and read

by firelight to Pham Van Dong, and even once a play
Le dragon de bamboo, finished in a Chinese prison,

which flopped on stage in Paris. *Thirteen black soldiers*
were secretly hanged at dawn at a military camp outside

San Antonio for their parts in a Houston race riot: so read
the headlines of the newspaper he saw shoveling sidewalks

for Hodler's Smoke Shop to pay for groceries and heat.
"Don't throw your fucking slush on me, for chrissakes!"

barked Harvey and Hilary Willcockson to the shoveler
behind the huge drifts, to see two strange eyes peep out.

Olive Bagni, passing, said, "They're everywhere, no?"
to her laughing friend, Carla, going, "Ahhhhh, sooooo!"

Dancing Hassids on West 47th Street threw fruit at him
when panicking he broke through their connected hands.

"It was patriotism, not communism, that inspired me,"
said the revolutionary, later, when he spoke of groups.

Epitaph for Alexander Theroux

He was W.H. Auden in conversation,
Talent not nearly the same,
But he was envied by *les pauvres*

Who kept him from public recognition,
Never mind fame.
Such is the malignity of dwarves.

Who's That Standing In The Orchard?

Who's that standing in the orchard?
Why does he lurk by the trees?
What shape can have such a shadow,
its hands hanging low as its knees?

How it does blacken the trees!
Three fingers pull hard at the bark,
clawing to spy through the leaves
the better to see through the dark.

I see bowlegs, a beard red as sin
above eyes that seem but to stare,
and when the shape draws forward
sweat drips from wet minking hair.

A face I glimpse briefly fleshless
as the foot of a decomposed bird
and a tongue I suspect is foreign
fighting hard to whisper a word.

Listen! There some coins clankle.
Men gather, torch-lit and stark;
A noise of swords drawn rankle
to shock the donkeystone dark.

A figure steps quickly forward
as a hand as if making a claim
shapechanges, becoming a finger,
to point to an object of blame.

The shape as if following fate
slinks from the gathering band
and slips through the garden gate,
thirty pieces of silver in hand.

Crow Meat

"O man of God, there is death in the pot."
— 2 Kings 4:38

Creak, beak, feat, meat, stink, who eats the bold black bandit?
The flesh tastes like acid, as non-songbirds should and would.

What do crows ingest? Anything. They tear windshield wiper-
blades off iron cars with red savagery, gnash the rubber to bits.

A murder of wild black fish-crows shot and floured and fried up
would taste shitty as the filthy roosts they slant on to screams.

Kebob it you say with cherry tomatoes and peppers? Fry it up?
Fix up crock-pot crow, stir its inky gouts with a wooden spoon?

Elisha piously purifies such a deadly stew in 2 Kings 4:38,
pressure-cooked in the desert. No stringy crow-meat there.

I suspect a crow's godawful caws badly strain its body, rawness
pulling at its thin being like a slingshot, bad blue-black flesh.

Edward Bunyard rated plain grouse the tastiest of all birds.
André Simon added woodcock, partridge, pheasant, snipe.

Roast peacock was served at royal banquets in the Middle Ages.
Ortolans, so prized in Europe, are eaten whole, eyeballs and all,

pace the legs. Brillat-Savarin deemed the figpecker the finest
of small birds. "If the figpecker could grow as big as a pheasant,"

he proclaimed, "it would be worth the price of an acre of land."
What Elisha cockily did with a fist of flour, ordering everyone

about in the foul, famine-ridden slums of Gilgal and showing off
his powers, like raising floating axeheads and multiplying bread,

could not have worked to make impalatable crowcrap savory, try
as might the man. A mouthful of that black shuck, creak, beak, feat,

all stinkmeat, would find you spatter-shitting in the very black hole
the crow now perched on your raucous roof is waiting to devour.

Woody Allen and Alan Dershowitz

It is my unswerving belief
that Woody Allen and the Dirt,
two chinless nerds with yellow teeth,
look just alike enough to skirt

the belief that both are ugly twins.
For true ugliness, by the dose,
Dershowitz hands-down clearly wins
first-prize, but Allen is close.

It is Embarrassing To Have To Die

It is embarrassing to have to die,
somehow routine,
like a broken ladder that gives,

gets crunkled and thrown away,
like it's never been,
I would rather never have lived

than be, briefly be, and then
like nature's fool
to go falling flat on my face,

get pitched blithely aside
like a dried-out hide
dispatched, degraded, disgraced.

A Fat Man Stands Before A Wall

"I'm in despair...It's because everyone can see what a fraud
I am."
—Mark Rothko

Deracinated, sweating, stirring a pot of black,
trying to make negative things do the work of positive ones,
fat worried Rothko turned his back to the wall

of the sacred Houston Chapel, where
his devoted Catholic benefactors, the privileged de Menils,
paid him well to do murals, and hissed.

He swore he would not violate the spaces
with graven images. But the fact of the matter is, he who
disparaged "skill" could not draw a *cat*.

Religious ikons became monochromatic
elongated black and plum voids which he called perfection.
He could put no faith in his brush,

so all visual phenomena went wetly
disintegrating into a series of equally material squirtage.
An abstract faith is misunderstandable

in one who, spiritually eclipsed, stares
into a monochrome where mere paint cannot recapitulate hope,
and, dropping his brush, starts to cry.

Dungeons and Dragons

This lovely, fragile little-yellow-idol centenarian was once a dragon
who beat cake batter in a bowl with angry swipes.
How in earlier years her howls of imprecation shot echoing screams
through my soul even at 10, twisting it into gripes.
When I wet the bed like a leaking fool every black night of the year
she spit such fury at me my skin got actually braised.
No one knew my fatter mother well who failed to see her dash water
onto rumpled shirts with that scalding-hot iron raised.

That we ripen, grow old, and eventually fade was never my thought
whenever she hung a rubber sheet around my neck
It was all I could to try to outrun her shit-storms of exaggerated fury
just to exit my teens and not be a nervous wreck.
She once had the horn-strength to strap us hard with her red Italian hands
that flew skyward with her crazy immigrant cries.
I will get drunk, stand on a plinth, and loudly recite "On the Extinction
of the Venetian Republic" on the very day she dies.

Evelyn Fish

As a teen I knew few verities. Evelyn Fish in her plum
-colored bathing suit rarely ever looked my way. Still I wistfully longed
for the fragrance of her arms, as the slick magazines

put it. Answerlessness silenced me on every front
back in those junior high school days, although reform was on my mind,
even when she came into the A & P where I bagged.

Shaping up. Striving to do things right. Making lists
filled with earnest resolves that I fondly hoped would bring me success.
   There was a secret, I believed. One big one.

   My parents' speeches encouraged that faith. Orphaned
very young, Confucius could never sit straight, unless his mat was straight.
   That pretty much explained me, having tropisms.

   I was looking for the magic key. Now I'm seventy.
and no closer to any of the secrets of life than I was then, except perhaps
   that there are no absolutes on life whatsoever. Well,

   be decent, hurt not a soul, never undercook pork,
let bygones be bygones, learn to forgive, obvious as that sounds, and no one
   was sexier than rumpy Evelyn Fish in tight plum trunks.

On Photography

A photograph never, never lies,
   we are assured, for everything it copies
   of what nature happily supplies:
   faces, fences, pontoons, poppies,
   anything perception will permit.
   The camera with its double senses,
— whatever line and light will hit —
   it quite perfectly condenses.
   But then every true phenomenon
   has an infinite number of aspects,
   more in its pictorial noumenon
   than merely light and line collects
   So since it sees only what it spies,
   a photograph always, *always*, lies.

Hell and Damnation

Thomas More thought eternal damnation too cruel
to be a divine plan. Was his God Santa Claus? I know in battle
  many die of heatstroke, albinos cook white,

  we sneeze when exposed to sunlight. Absorbing
radiation now, half the seawater in the world is red-purple lit
  with disordering horror. We are scalded

  everywhere, enough to see how retribution
follows us for inexactitude, one definition of sin, if you will.
  I detect hell at *every* conceivable angle

  and, as to wider plans, none ever conceived
failed to figure in how, because every question is a quandary,
  we must face facts when they go awry.

  Burning, deprivation, isolation, darkness,
huge gloating mad disasters that tell us what we've lost remind
  me going forward of divinity's damnation.

Egon Schiele and the Color Blue

  When Egon Schiele and his dying wife
caught their fatal virus, it turned them ghastly blue, though
  it was never a color he loved, and spitting blood

  they were gone. He was only 28, flickerer
of knives who scrape-painted all of those tortured figures.
  His blue was slate, like the skies that pandemic

  wrought, felling all like a gas-house of cyan,
ending all the conscious self-elation of the hearty Hapsburgs.
  His "Houses with Colorful Laundry" has only

  a trace of blue, as museum-goers know.
They should also know he tried to nurse poor baffled Edith,
  unfocussed, questioning, surely lonely —

her flocky hay hair worn up, twisted
like that bewildered look we patrons forever know her by —
holding up for days a candle by her bed.

Was it in apology for his trysts with teens,
as coughing blood, azure-faced, he watched Vienna fade?
Cyan is a complement of red.

Notes from Vienna, 1933

Money didn't work. People bartered their shirts to eat.
Paper money was worthless, rising consumer prices led to gleeful extortion.
96% of Austrian children were officially classed

as "undernourished." The harsh winter of 1918 palled.
There was much quarreling over food. Touting prostitutes in black-net
widow's veils walked the Ringstrasse in wet shoes.

You were looking for garden allotments? Dances?
The delights in a celebrated theater of butterhorns and kaiserschmarrn?
I would have sought a sixteen-fold revenge

for the Hungarian and Czech embargoes alone,
taken out of their skulls my hungry grief for all we saw and suffered.
as the trains all slid to a stop in the freezing snow.

I was but a young boy in those Hapsburg days,
waiting in that unstable republic of where all the soldiers had gone,
until I realized that they were all dead,

two million dead, more than two million imprisoned,
three million wounded, darkness, misery, a cruel settlement that left us
colossally ruined. My teary eyes squeezed shut.

I wanted to fly a swastika flag fifteen years later,
wave it proudly from my hands, and then one day when joy came back
I saw Hitler driven past me in a touring car

and when I waved I began to cry for I had seen
the future take wing in the way a singing lark flew out of my heart,
knowing the world will once again make sense.

Never Date a Woman with Big Teeth

"I'll get bitey when I damn well want!"
— Marjorie Main

"All women who insistently try to justify
all they do, no matter how irrational, have big teeth."
— Dr. Flummerfelt

Never date a woman with big teeth
With big teeth, she can't pronounce
When she can't pronounce, you can't hear
When you can't hear, she'll get angry
When she gets angry, you start to argue
When you argue, you grow bitter
When you grow bitter, you split up
When you split up, you end up alone.
Thanks ever so much, teeth.

Neglected

Whereas once I had no other choice but to accept it,
now I like it over here in the shade and write for myself.
Being granted no recognition sharpened my quill. Light
can blind. My personal saint has always been Simone Weil,
although it was her people in Manhattan, the Isle of Joy,
who, clannish, resentfully saw to it, less by bad reviews,
than by ignoring all my efforts, that I went nowhere,
selecting, flattering others for all awards and prizes,
but I have nothing like her goodness, her guilelessness,
her grace. Quilps became my critics, biting hard wires,
little hunchy villains whose calumnies pointed nose-like
to their own insufficiencies. All children draw by looking

first, then proceed by *envy* to make another world appear
that constitutes the only real art that they prefer to know.
There must be some apt Shakespearean line out there
to fit the spite of those who write the history they choose.
Reviewers, agents, editors who by whim alone select
which will *not* be the chosen people, which are Jews.

The Oklahoma Sky is a Dragon

The Oklahoma sky is a dragon,
its gaping mouth an updraft looking to make a bite.
What in circulation seems unjust?

The way it keeps seeking where
in a fearful rotation we were taught, except in a wall cloud,
a motion had a meaning

in no way lessened the dark,
the barking blackness spoiling out of our flat land in May
where I saw never a jot of sense,

only the menace of a snarling beast
dropping a funnel of atrocious turds and roaring urine
like racing, boiling diarrhea.

I have come to loathe robust nature,
But in a well-defined super-cell storm which is a bowl-hell,
rude filthy rain, a yellow busty wind,

ripping off the faces of whole towns
the size of Kingfisher, Pottawatomie, Osage, and Caddo,
look for no maxims or meanings,

only a smoking wyvern, fire-breathing,
rising up on its sky-blackening haunches and awful claws
that are far beyond all scales.

Mont Blanc Brings Whiteness to My Soul

I can see Mont Blanc from my window
where on a winter morning it gives off a pink glaze
from its sharply pointed snowy peaks.

But then I saw its light had changed
as faster scudded the clouds across the frozen sky
into my poor muddled soul, it seemed,

for on certain days its glaze is blue.
I often sat before it feeling wistful *I* was not found
in such correct, discernible ways,

changing as I myself have during days
but feeling never touched with anything of light or color.
It was this temperament of mine

that brought me here to Chamonix
where — I feel driven to have to confess this as I write —
I badly yearned to harm myself,

that is, until with passing months,
I watched through my window the sanctifying lights
of those glazes pink and blue

on the cold high snowy peaks
and what it taught of what I see I myself consist of
in my own impermanence,

changing as I have, seeing what I do,
I learned to see and saw exactly what those colors
said to me — and immediately knew

that impermanent is what we *are*
in our own dimension by those very clouds that race
which then became my joy in Chamonix

watching all those pinks and blues
through both the enchantment of the changing light
and the tears of my transfigured face.

God

Matter into energy can be transformed
and the reverse is also provably true;
when energy transformed into mass,
the solid bodies of our universe grew.

Now energy is required to create matter.
But the matter in the universe we know
attracts other matter, now made negative
energy by the very law that makes it so

— which is immutably equal to the energy
necessary to create the matter of the world,
so the total energy of the universe is zero.
Once into matter all of energy unfurled.

But know that once the matter is created,
the energy of the universe was never lost
for energy exists *in* the matter it informed
and is embodied in the universe, its host.

.

The energy needed to create the big bang
— the explanation here is deep as it is odd —
came from the very universe that it created,
and who would deny that energy is God?

413

The King of a Rainy Land

Baudelaire's verses are heavy as weights,
laden in the way that shouting in fury makes us breathe deeply,
accumulating far too much of ourselves,

making what we bellow we squeeze.
The way he called down God, seeming to grow vegetative
in black wrath, leek-rooted in intransigence.

"There is a smell of destruction here," he cried
in a beer house, confusing the acrid smell of a cabbage soup,
   with the blocks of some infernal city

where no one else could. Heaviness in a way
can be worn in a poet's mind like the faces of evil in flowers
   and detect disintegration, carnage, abolition

even in perfumes ("*Se mêle dans mon âme*"),
cats, confessions, iron, cities, cement, broken bells, and spleen.
   The king of a rainy land never finds gold

to extract from a tainted element where
groves, adorned with fleurs-de-lis, are actually dark graves,
   deeper than breath after shouted fury,

for the Demon he swallowed burning his lungs
added weight to all he wrote and, like a badly reddened throat,
   drags us down like the stones of weighty poems

laden with emboldened images and words
that, like cities smelling of iron and cement, accumulate in blocks
   that when we bellow seem to squeeze.

A Motswana of the Batswana in Botswana

A Motswana of the Batswana in Botswana
   took me by jouncy Jeep to Orapa
where on the blue ground I squinted for diamonds,

not ilmenites or garnets or coarse gabbro but the shiny stones
   that flat Orapa held
where blue-gummed Motswana sorters with bowed heads

rolled the carbon chunks beneath their palms
   that the blue laws in Orapa,
where the tribal Batswana in their preoccupying sheds,

allowed no Zuma-big glittering dreams they could afford
  at least not in flat Orapa
where blue-eyed me in rich Botswana ran my errands

The Crocodile Smiles of My Nieces and Nephews

Since you can all identify yourselves,
no accusing finger pointed at your faces,
— where shallow, no one ever delves —
singles out a decent person's graces.
The crooked served you. Nothing straight
you ever swore was reinforced by proof.
Deceit and guile could alone equate
with what you would fob off as truth.
But who can't spy the paradox of trickery?
Age is old where youth is never young.
Yes, hypocrite smiles were offered me,
but lies that filled your mouths became a tongue.
By moonlight assassins always shadows track
but wait for darkness to stab you in the back.

Nelson Bodfish

"There is something mysterious, even ghostly, about cranberry bogs,
They seem lost themselves, out-of-the-way, like much on Cape Cod.

Haunts mostly," said Nelson Bodfish, shaking loose an old wet glove,
the better to pull his collar tighter, as the ocean winds blew in sharply

from the Sandy Neck hook. "Somewhere back there in the woods,
real old timers tell me, was a sanitarium for the mentally touched,

but no one," Nelson paused to laugh, "ever talked about it much." He
snorted, laughing, shook his head, deftly sliding a hand into his glove,

and looked up to the weather. The sky darkened and wind blew colder.
"You hear claims of spooks. Howandever," he chuckled. "Howandever.

They found a dead body over Cotuit way in a bog, uh-uh, oh yeah,
a Finn it was, turned out to be Matti Huhtanen. 'Hoot.' I knew him —

well, nobody really *knew* him. A drunk. Carved decoys. Around about
when you bought over there on Willow St., just about the same time

I bought this old Makepeace bog you're lookin' at, when the bed here"
— look," he said, snatching up a small twisted plant, "weak uprights —

was full of damn good runners and nobody but nobody knew but me,
no one." Nelson swirled his rake and looked away. "You still writin',

— books, right? You oughta write about Hoot. Like I been tellin' you,
mystery and ghosts go with bogs. All seem lost in themselves. Sooo,

that's six bucks for your berries. Them old boxes is all red-stained,
but you writers don't care, do you?" He leaned in to grin up at me

and winked and rap-tapped one of the box-rims — "'Taint blood."
I smiled. "West Barnstable got lots of old skeletons," he muttered.

"How long is it you been livin' here?" I told him forty-one years.
He pocketed the cash, called back, "Oh, you still a wash-ashore."

Leon Uris and Herman Wouk

Whom do you judge the biggest mook,
Leon Uris or Herman Wouk?
With names reversed they even bore us?
Leon Wouk and Herman Uris.

Such names surely invite a rebuke,
Leon Uris and Herman Wouk,
especially when coupled in chorus.
Hoople the Wouk and Loople the Uris.

Two of a kind, spirit and spook
Leon Uris and Herman Wouk,
With or without a useful thesaurus,
Horrendous Work and Lost in the Forest.

A person can virtually predetermine
with a Uris of Leon or Wouk of Herman
prose with the heft of a brontosaurus.
Herman Wookie and Leon Ignore us

Hard to determine the greatest fluke,
Lumpy-Lou Uris and Humpy-Poo Wouk.
since *both* were hacks and *both* were porous.
Hermie P. Wouk and Leonie M. Uris.

So if both authors force you to squirm,
Leo the Ure-man and Woukie the Herm,
Enjoy, like me, a nominal tour — with.
Woukie the Herm and Leo the Ure.

You But Swam Through the Sea, Now God Has Sent His Gulls

When you are rising eighty-six, death is drawing near
to put its blackened claws upon your waking dreams.
It is not age you see deep down, but rather basic fear,
scrying pecking beaks, wings whirling mad as freams
at your incandescent terror that b-b-begs you to despair
there in a soiled nightshirt crumby and stained as sin,
nothing making sense in that little room as ugly as bare
where no scream matters, "Let me out!" or "Let me in!"
Wildly waving, mad as Lear, your fingers crinkled white,
being pecked, your face a bloody plate, regret and remorse
made more painful by the feelings that you have of spite
and the filthy truth that on this earth gain was only loss.
The truth is that none of this horror your existence annuls:
you but swam through the sea, now God has sent his gulls.

John Evelyn and Samuel Pepys

John Evelyn and Samuel Pepys met each other in 1665
and maintained private diaries made felicitously alive.

by logging their daily habits, wherein that particular age
came brightly alive in entries alternately silly and sage.

They once set off for Bagshot riding a coach and six,
walked, dined happily many a time, argued politics,

collected books, loved numismatics, popular at the time,
prided themselves on keeping gardens tidy and sublime,

also bought Indian curiosities and Chinese *objets d'art*
studied hard the ways of the head and equally the heart.

Sammy was chubby and lusty, while John was rather thin
becoming a vegetarian who abstemiously passed on gin.

An expert on trees, he saw that well-grown timber could
provide the British navy with generous lashings of wood,

and since Sam ran the Admiralty for a number of years,
which the traces of his distinguished legacy still bears,

they fitted well each other's fancies like fingers in a glove
a mutual union in separateness, affection joined with love.

John lived down in Deptford, Sammy in Clapham-town
with his wife, Elizabeth, with no children of their own

— he suffered from impotence — while John had fully eight,
all of whom had died, but one, Susanna, a 17th-century fate.

In 1703 when Sammy died, for the solemn funeral call
among the first to be asked was John to carry a pall.

A long forty year friendship was theirs in London of yore,
and we've the correspondence that very comradeship bore.

A mystery's why for all their invention not a mention
is given to the diaries of one another. Had apprehension

of a threatening sort exacted a silence we can't explain
that could only recognize work of the others' with pain?

Can we say, of emotions so personal, does the fiery arrival
in one's pages kill the love of one's double and diary rival?

Admissions

When we take her upstairs in the attic,
it's as much a crossing over
as a going up, erect, like Bozo clowns,
for children in the tide.
And the running after noon to call
sweet hellos and coos to her
is as much a lying down for us, renown
as much as children for a ride,
in joycarts, on a slide, or for a fall.
And all the thrashes, mysteries,
the Easter lurches we take unfrightened,
must become a dancing in the dark
as well as moaning in the night
when our apple-chested ladies, benighted
with our ribbons and our cozy flesh,
know so little of our attic,
or its ladder lying down or set aright,
that they don't dare chance one remark.
No, it's all geography and promises;
I'm afraid, the happy dancing over pears,
the boo-hooing dance when ordered to our bed.
We stand erect, we lie, or duck around the bend,
but running up a ladder,
like making love,
is running toward the end.

419

Alexander Theroux

I fear my name
As fear my name I should,
For sibyls say
(It's quite the same)
A strange and silent motion's
Also found in wood.
Alexander let's discount
The great I couldn't, the great he could.
My surname's but
An ur-name, shut
To all discerning eyes and good.
The hero buried deep within
Without is shrouded by
Clumps of consonants and vowels;
And it we can't espy.
The rue I fear.
The rut its smut
One easily detects.
A surface has its symbol
As a galley ship its decks.
The royal r-e-x,
One notes,
Is threatened by a hex.
A sibyl's not frenetic
To find the static so kinetic;
The *truly* enigmatic
Is the syncategorematic,
A truth at once accessible and new.
Pronounce it *throw,* pronounce it *threw,*
Thorough, thorax, Thoreau,
Whatever thing emphatic—
But when you find a route
You find a rue. I fear my name
As fear my name I should;
For sibyls also say
Effects must fear their cause.
And what mostly gives me pause,
Mostly fear and mostly stir,
Is not the rut, the rex, the rue.
It mostly is the her.

Amelia Earhart (1998)

I've always loved your smile,
Your eyes of gray, the bell-like
Cheekbones of your face,
Your tapered hands,
A symbol of your flying grace,
Your tousled hair, the soft full lips.
What model out of *Vogue* ever showed
Such elegant slim hips?
Your were known as "The Girl in Brown
Who Walks Alone" in several
Of the high schools you attended.
You had your own principles.
You wouldn't carry a comb.
You were a dreamer,
Needed to be free;
I don't believe a love affair had ended.
No doubt you were alone for want of me.
(Can I not dream dreams as you,
 Rue as a man what as a woman
 They said you couldn't do?)
"I'm still unsold on marriage,"
 You once wrote.
"I don't want *anything* all the time."
 I would have understood.

I've memorized your habits
 Like the name that in repeating,
 But which you mocked, I love.
You hated hats (for which I'm glad),
 Would not drink tea or coffee,
 Disliked hairpins,
 Had a penchant for cotton shirts.
Particularly short-sleeved ones
Colored plaid,
In which you looked too thin.
You loved your Lockheed Vega,
Red and bold as you were shy.
Your avoirdupois aloft was gasoline
In a sort of perpetual duel;

Going against the precept
Virtually constituted a sin.
"Six added pounds" (I know, I know)
"Offset a gallon of fuel."
Did always keeping windows closed
In the cars and planes you drove
Indicate anything of dread?
"I don't like to be mussed up,"
You once, I thought enigmatically,
Made it a point to be said.

When you worked at the Settlement
On Tyler Street in Boston,
Denison House I knew,
Why couldn't I have been alive to bring
Your lunch, buttermilk (your favorite)
And sandwiches just for you?
We would have found a bench.
I would have let you rest your head
On my knee, right there, to pass the time.
I could have read you poems,
Which defined as much as clouds
What in your too brief life you held sublime
In those mile-high worlds above
Waiting for you to explore.
Is it so vain of me to think
What you were looking for,
When in that plane you flew so high,
Was really love? Why then,
Let vanity go on to say,
If at the end it was your fate
When falling from the sky,
If it had to be
And I could not have caught you,
I wish it was for me.

Andover Spires

You stand, old school, bright upon a hill,
Distinguished by two centuries' long reach,
But what of fools now hired there to teach,
Indifferent to the students that they kill
By snobbery, sloth, political intrigue?
Drones who rarely read, are voted pay
Not by merit or degrees but length of stay,
Conspirators to only those in league.
Spires are declarations of intent,
No more signs of education than
The poles effected to support a tent
Can guarantee who'll gather there by plan.
No need, Sam Phillips, however, to repent.
A blackness even Eden overran.

Anecdote of Santa Fé

On the reservation
Oné and Noné make posole.
They love each other
And so will stay

Together in the way
That blue needs brown
And brown needs blue
In Santa Fé.

As blue needs brown
And brown needs blue
Oné is as much a part
Of Noné in that way,

But though they stay,
Together Oné and Noné
Are neither one
Nor none in Santa Fé

Are the Skeletons of Fat Men Fat?

How find joy enough to survive
Our daily pain? No black-hat chef awaits
With tricks to pamper us with anything

Other than with refuse meats,
And that is Mr. Death with his umbrella
Unfurled above our every hope,

Frayed, sieved with holes,
A mockery of the bluer, higher vault
We wish of heaven's dome.

What awaits at the end of all things
Awaits by definition at the end of each,
So how then do we all imbibe our joy,

This fragile self with but
Fat enough for seven cakes of soap,
A spoonful of sulphur,

Iron equal to a one-inch nail,
Lime enough to whitewash a small shed,
An ounce of various metals,

Phosphorous for 2,200 matches,
Carbon equivalent of a 28-pound bag
Of musty unimpressive coke?

There is no cool capillary action
In the spirit. A skin forms, for instance,
Where moving water meets the air.

Surface tension. There is always
Someone in front, someone always behind.
But there, *that* is why

No heart is a Marianas Trench.
Just enough of hope resides to prevent
The weak neap tides of the heart

In knowing happily that next to us
Are only more fleshbags, whitewash, coke,
More fat for soap, sulphur spoonfuls,

Iron nails, more funny phosphorus
For the many kinds of flames in front and,
To tell the truth, more pink behinds.

Ars Poetica

What polishes, like gold
Transformed by art from moron metal,
Is what alone will shine.

Don't wise old cooks suspect
The way fluidity is always flux?
The liquid that they pour

Into their snouted spoons,
Exenterated by an artist of a kind,
Is not as wonderful?

Making's not what's being done
But rather finished. What we contain
In an array, to make perpetual

And true as a solid form of grace
Must first have transformed from potency
To act, a process of arrangement

No doubt Aunt Susanna Seacat
With her long fabricopediac fingers
May call it art. But is it?

The stuff of lace and lancets
Trundled out to while away an afternoon?
Becoming isn't Being any more

Than what necessarily we're large
Enough to finish in those complications,
Giving substance forms. Oh Cellini,

battilòro, such coin and shield
And buckle! Your beauteous pizzopizza
Make me cry! Poems are tribute,

Each one a sacrament, a *caelum,*
Hosts in gilded monstrances like mandala,
Rose windows all ablaze.

There's nothing wrong at first
With faking what you fumble to fist in clay.
Forge what isn't forged. But

Stay close to the scheme of God,
Otherwise what is fashioned is not made.
Poems are hammered and distinct

Of what once of course was molten
Precious and fluid and light and sweetly gold
As sesame oil in Szechwan.

Assumption

Found nowhere in the Bible
Is a single verse to justify
Mary being crowned in heaven.
Should we assume it's a lie?
Why do priests so fabricate?
To compensate by drama what
their own lives lack in scene?
Not to care what's corrupt?
Why not simply say she lived
in a house somewhat content
after a complicated public life
like any aging beauty queen,
praying, fasting, remembering

before she died a natural death
she gave birth at age fifteen
to a dark-eyed boy with a destiny,
survived for a quarter century
his death at thirty-three,
then sat outside the door?
Why any different from any mom
who understandably missed the son
she couldn't make gnocchi for?

Auden's Face

It was cracked like a Weetabix.
A pound, like ours, of funny dough
Thumbed to a play-face, nostrils to wicks,
The widish ears, appended last, for show.
Then was it cooked. A simple noun
Animated by the heat of verbs
Which best describe it, make it renown:
Runneled, tunneled, words that disturb.
Some say, old dackel, that all those frets—
An apple creased, a steppeland parched—
Were scored by the smoke of smoking cigarettes.
Your biscuit cheeks, so antique, starched,
Are those smirks? Frowns? A worry each line?
How with such wrinkles shows something so fine?

A un romancier de ma connaisance Qui ne mesure qu' 1m 70

A la saison des Nobels, au printemps,
  Pour la gloire, le prestige et l'argent,
Naitront pléthore de voix,
  Mille sentiments de choix,
Des hourrahs meurtrissant les gorges qu'on deploie
  Il en sera le seul parent.

To a Novelist I Know Who's Only 5'8"

At Nobel time in spring
   For glory, fame, and pelf,
Will come a plethora of votes,
   Sentiments of a thousand notes,
Cheers as if from aching throats,
   But only from himself.

Billy the Kid Questions the Dark

Young Henry McCarty roamed the Lower East Side
Stabbing boys and thieving coats from Chinamen
Virtually every week.

Don't killers stand before us all like questions
Calling to the jackal deep in the darkness
Of our own hearts to speak?

He beheaded cats with a broken pocketknife.
That someone could do such a thing to another
Involves us all in a way.

He developed a skill at monte and changed his name
Soon after murdering something like nineteen men
And settled in Santa Fé.

Who can't confess given this fallen world
That we all share in the desperate crimes of others
When darkness is all we know?

Where the healthy tear the sick apart
Nothing hale applies, and one quite calmly
Remains another's foe.

One day he went to Fort Sumner to visit a girl,
Called out "*Quién es?*" in the darkness there.
Nothing more was said.

What does anyone find who questions the dark?
Anubis wearing pointed sheriff's ears
Tearing away your head.

Black Racist

to Dr. Pouce, child spychologist

What head isn't filled with feathers
that's black because it isn't white?
Yours, you say? Don't make me laugh!
Rhetoric is monkeyshines, like
anything else. As if ventriloquists
don't mutter like their cats, Mr. Pouce,
you with your show-rooming barks
and yowls while waving white *mouchoir*!
You can talk to me about compassion
without showing any to me, bleating
for pity with your watermelon whines?
It's a fact that bigotry has paper walls.
You naughty nitwits with funny hats,
public forums, and wagging cravats
who spoon tar with the best of them
are no different than any nobodaddy,
including you with all your ballyhoo.
Dummies, for all their wood, fare
like all the rest who by manipulation
cack racial obloquies from a wooden head
and nothing on earth can make them
seem less real or right
sitting on their owner's shelves
than words that they expect from you
that they love to cockadoodledoo,
that they use to constantly boo-hoo.
but never use themselves.

Blackwind at Prayer

Blackwind kneels in silence all alone.
He paints with yucca tips on skeletons of cows.
Bones are real. To him those bones are real,

like boulders that inside us as we kneel
measure our mortality, not might. But art endows
with blessings men who color bone,

who dare approach a surface hard as stone
and leave on doleful dryness what the wind allows
to whiten after giving sol its meal.

Boogie Man Blues

for Clarence "Frogman" Henry

I'm a nightstick man, gone canoninize yo bitch.
I got a cat's black fever, enough to make you itch.
I scairt you born at the crossroads, caint you tell?
You howl night and day like my dog Idabel.

We live in the Nickel thowt no coat and hat
Use to greens n possum skilletfried wifout no fat;
Don't make no matter, I takes what comes to hand.
When you strut by I plunk yo elastic band.

I'm a watchwitch, lowdown, bluegum chocolate boy.
When I bop yo booty you gone ring-a-ding-ding with joy;
I barefoot with love which fill my guitar-case heart.
Yo can dig my mojo rising in the cotton cart.

I gone saltfish yo heart, come down like summer rain.
I gone disclose existence, cayenne pepper yo brain.
I gone dicker, dodder, doodle, n dodge yo jelly roll.
I got kisses like a screet-owl's sweet momma got soul.

I got the two-stage warble, got me a lion's mane.
I got a goosefoot root like to drive the mommas insane.
I gone plink, plank, plunk-a-doo-doo like a mumbo man,
I can cling, clang, clunk-achoo-choo jiggity jan.

I got sly boots for the askin', baby, turn it up.
I gone be bustin' thoo yo walls to walk yo pup.
I make yo seedpods scatter, make you think.
We shake midnight, Momma, kettle and sink.

I got the magic motion in my poontanging fingers fo fun.
Get you loney dogs for lunchtime, RC Colas and rum.
When you hot pot dog trot, baby, I wan mess with you.
You be wantin' to start bout when we getting through.

Boston Irish Pols

You were not brought up on A Street
As much as spawned, ignorant as the dawn
Only the insincere get up to greet.
When you swept the wards by cadging votes
From lackeys with your coal-scuttle hands,
Who was shocked you wiped them on your coat?

You hate each other like the running pox,
Urban bog rats, unprincipled pimps of graft,
Greener in your envy than your shamrocks
When another of your kind succeeds.
"I knew him when he was *nothing*," comes the sneer,
To best assure (according to your creed)

No one, saving you, be seen as God.
You've been on the take for donkey's years,
Pulling strings for phonies, fakes, and frauds
Feeding like a pink pig in a sty,
Burrowing in dirt beneath the State House
Searching out another dug for sucking dry.

Gifts, free tickets, bribes to pass a bill,
A pension huge, a car at state expense,
A parking space for you on Beacon Hill,
You jig and amble on Saint Patrick's Day
And play the stage buffoon to guarantee
The dopes supporting you remain that way.

Sexless faces, empty speeches, lies,
A narrow mind as thick as two short planks,
The Irish pol in Boston only tries
To fill his pockets. Therefore understand
His perfect description as an arse upon
Which everyone has sat except a man.

A Boston Marriage

Miss Amy Lowell was butch,
Miss Ada Russell was femme;
Lowell was mostly apple,
Russell was basically stem.

The former loved smoking cigars,
Chewing them down to the root;
The latter loved shopping on Tremont
In a perfectly tailored suit.

Amy was big-bummed and hefty
As she wrote her Imagist poems.
She ignored society's dictates
To attend to her chromosomes.

She referred to Ada as "Peter,"
Kept a favorite mustache cup.
Given to sleeping all day,
She many a night stayed up.

When Amy and Ada went walking
On Beacon Street now and again
The couple quite symmetrically
Resembled the number 10.

"Her work's not creative," said critics,
"Only reproductive," they said —
An irony not lost on two women
Who explored each other in bed.

They intentionally flouted convention,
Traveled the whole world round;
They had friends all over Europe:
Aldington, Lawrence, and Pound.

The man who wrote *Lady Chatterley*
One night peeked into their rooms
And saw, through a haze of cheroot smoke,
They slept in the fashion of spoons.

H.D. once gave them a gift
Of some lavender beeswax candles,
Which in turn Amy gave to Ada
While Ada held Amy's "love handles."

That masquerade ball in Venice?
Strong roles must balance the weak.
"I'm Queen Christina," said Amy.
Whispered Ada, "I'll be a leek."

They usually got along well,
Their spats uncommon and few.
"Turning?" asked Ada, indignant,
One time in a Trinity pew,

When Ada, holding a hymnbook,
And this before dinner at eight,
Moved to give berth in a gesture
As if criticizing her weight.

"You are no better than Sappho
Or Joan of Arc!" Amy snapped,
Stressing her martial behavior
(The allusions were hurtfully apt).

What can you expect of a woman
Whose lifetime was given to verse?
Ada Russell, coolly indignant,
Replied, "At least I'm not worse."

What could be truer in Boston,
The home of the bean and the cod?
Nobody's anything, trust me,
If they're not particularly odd.

It would never matter to Amy,
And the same goes for Ada, as well,
Which of the two had the ding-dong,
Which of the two had the bell.

The Sostenuto of Brahms

Do the high violins of your Symphony No. 1
    in C Minor, Op. 68 confess
in the isolating loneliness of what I hear
    matter not of wails or tears,
but when we're facing sorrow how to cope?
    The calling horns like voices
announce mysteries, distances, extremes
    that sorely make me tremble.
Are you telling us, like Henry James's Strether
    or Wittgenstein in Norway lonely
with his deep but deteriorating mind, to *live*?
    Does being alone at least provide
the need to face inner life, a working means
    to cope, to hope, when something
is not there to teach or is not there to learn?
    The future, becoming past so fast,
leaves us only where we were to suffer loss
    It takes great strength to live alone,
and is often more than I can find to bear.
    If that courageous music in the face
of what you know and I suspect in the world
    must first increase our pain, as beauty

often calls up loss as if it were its equal share,
   try to comfort us at least with what,
when we all find ourselves alone, like you,
   we see we have to learn to gain.

Bridalveil Falls

for Julie Sexeny

I had never once seen you,
Missed nothing I never had,
But the day that you came by
I died in my heart for such beauty
As we paused staring eye to eye.

When the morning broke
I woke in the wild of my bed,
Impaled by the moon's white beams.
Had you come to my soul in a vision?
Had I met you there only in dreams?

I roamed the outlying hills
For endless months with words
That formed in my heart like pain.
It seemed I traveled the land forever,
Though you never once came again.

If I believe you existed
I wonder since you have gone
As, deserted, I stare at the wall
If I should mount curses or blessings
Over the fact that I'd seen you at all.

By the Waters Now of Doom I Sit

By the waters now of doom I sit
Feeling with the sand my fingers,

Historical and long.
There's no memory forgotten,
I'll be sure, from Egypt when
The aching Jews with dripping clouts
Flitted through the night:
Adam's people's stirring to be free,
Psalted,
Infected,
Null and void,
Just too damn tired of hammering
With nut-like fists
The granaries of tin.
Pharaoh unsuspected them, clammering,
And glugged his shandies off his wrist
Amid his women's cordial groans,
When—zap!—like dough shells
All the Gypsies bleated in their shower caps
And died.
Things that happen fast are
Very often meaningful, and linger.

By the waters now of doom I sit
Feeling with the sand my fingers,
Historical and long.

Café du Télégraphe Anglais

What cook who makes a poisoned pie
will agree, by what he does, he doesn't dream?
I told you, mediocrity's a cinch.

The argument we had in Tangier
made two reflections on the subject, not one,
but upset less than two people,

Our love was so confused by talk.
The very act of doing does away with thought,
like Arabs being bilked by traders,

their noses close to coins as scrolls,
who ignore their pain to fumble up their gain.
But being in the desert dreaming of God

is not eating dessert of spotted dog.
We need each other to contest what otherwise
is killed by what's ignored.

I can even take your theater French,
Amy of America, to sad things unexplained
and left to die like that.

There are dracos in the darkness,
Arabs in burnooses who color the air they run,
like shadows. Isn't talk however hope,

even if it hurts? White tainted pies,
like lies, by talk and thought can be examined,
not so when being wolfed.

Deliberation brings illumination to the mind.
Forget the waiter. You know what's important? Knowing.
And even more. Knowing knowing's.

Camera Lucida

1.

Bowls of snibbled beans,
A slave in muslin padding down
An alley wearing tchipships,
A kiss in the Joe Pyeweed,
Striped awnings, São Paolo in the rain,
Some Carpathian prince.

Every form correctly seen
Is beautiful, concluded Goethe,
Not a photographer

But a man who knew a poem
Contrived itself around a way of looking
Out of who and what you are.

Hard? It's only a camera,
Not the Gofriller gamba you pretend it is
Waiting for your touch,

Though you unshy shutterbugs
Make up quartets of pains-in-the-ass
Just by being yourselves.

Few people have the imagination
Of reality. Few dare imaginatively
To glimpse it as it is.

Any craptoad in Andover
With sheets of just-wet snapshots
Can make claims for art.

The camera is cold. The eunuch
Behind it if unable to impose meaning
Beyond that through which he peers

Adds no poetry to what he sees,
Only saves to sell for stupidity to see
Paper crammed with gewgaws.

2.

Ho, Nutrix, feed me.
No muse is a meddler, no intimacy
Ever really unearned.

Make me by myself be me,
So by the occasion of being what I am
Not be the gist of what I make

But making out of what I see
Transform reality by making me meet
What I alone can transform.

No ice can set you on fire
But yourself, as Turandot well knew,
Yourself with a singular soul,

Unlike that quack in Andover
With his sprockets, snoots, and strobes
Who fakes what he can't find.

Product is not the point.
It is not a question of making art, but
Of making art of what you do.

What Lithuania without bears,
However, can be made to have them roaring
Just by fancy dreams?

A mind that is too flexible
Is powerless to restrain, I've seen,
The dialects of its own moves,

Although for want of a bear's
We can substitute a boiling ocean's rage
For roaring in a cage.

When is there never a taste
Of nothingness itself in the roar
Of a crashing ocean?

3.

Talent can be horrifying,
In the way a photograph becomes a secret
Of only yet another secret.

We are always more or less
Than what we create by vision or void.
We run like fright, for artists

In being set apart resemble slaves
In low dry deserts or princes up on mountains
Where few decide to pup their tents.

Imagination also makes us live,
We who would create, in states of heightened
Crises that disturb and kill,

As we bide time in darkrooms,
In attempts at finding comfort with solutions
Even if they can't be seen.

Everyone suffers from the limitation
Of being only one person, while art requests,
Suggests we be more than what we are,

Lest dreams become an odd defense
Against awareness in a certain kind of mind
And never help or heighten it.

Images are there for us to see,
For such as those who look beyond excuse
To see above their fat equipment.

Forget Andover and its pedant.
Thought, remember, is a motion that divides.
Look hard, for palmary subjects abound.

Wends. Sorbs. Slave. In no matter
What Carpathia are counts and princes
Boasting to be real.

Cat Noises

Who makes a kind of crowing, clacks it teeth at birds
Like maracas, chiclets, blows notes in flatted thirds?
Cats! Night's the sax. Egypt with its cult of cat
Worshiped all those mutt-whines, owl-howls, bat-spats,
Creaking doors, sounds a guitarist plicks with a plack,
A bumming top's spin, the winding of a watch's stem.
I once heard one even moo. Hectoring is big with them.
Leave one for a day. *"Bite my bum!"* he'll quack.
Mine once lost in the woods became an electric drill.

A throaty wire-drawn-out whine like stretching twine
Which soon becomes low thunder accompanies a kill.
Yours, for example, which would frankly suit them fine.

Catharine

"The truth that's told with bad intent beats all the lies you
  can invent."
                                                — William Blake

Your alias might have been
Miss Harriet Brown,
The serviceable shoes, peevish cats,
The way you ate,
Your jutting jaw,
Your glasses out of date.
Then math, your books,
Your hair too thick,
Too low a forehead for
Orthodox good looks.
No play of fancy ever lit your smile;
Your pinched-out emotions,
Graceless and tight,
Resembled for me the falling of night.
Your silly brother whose calendars
You feigned to love at Christmas
Just to keep him sane
Loved hockey, worshiped teams,
Bought tickets in the pouring rain.
The fool had a passion —
At least give him that.
You measured tit and gave only tat.
Surely no one like you becomes so cold
Without the benefit of a shaping mold.
What of your parents?
Queer father, promiscuous mom,
May I ask, was your divorce together,
Even half as bad
As what separately you've become?

Or was it what you caused
Over what you grieved?
A dope of a son,
So earnest and so bent;
A daughter who believed
The less she wrote
The more she felt
You didn't deserve the letters
That she never sent.

Chirico by Chirico

Original men must have wandered through a world full of
uncanny signs.

—Giorgio de Chirico, *Mystery and Creation* (1913)

The steeple clock marks half-past twelve.
The sun is high and burning in the sky.
It lights houses, palaces, and porticoes,

Their shadows on the ground describing squares,
Rectangles, trapezoids of so soft a black
The burnt eye can refresh itself in them.

What light. How sweet to be able to live
Near consoling gates, porticoes, arcades of
Black and white. No color. But what light.

And the absence of storms, of crying owls,
Of seas. Here Homer would have found no songs.
A hearse has been waiting forever.

It is as black as hope, and waiting forever.
There is a room with shutters always closed.
Somewhere is a corpse one cannot see.

The colonnades are empty, black and white.
Shadows both console and fail to console
In the way they fall by the way we feel.

A want of life awaits in colonnades.
Everywhere the sun rules. Shadows console
Sometimes. Precise geometric shadows

Of such starkness. Once cannot count the lines.
Sadness. Nothing. The endless walls and arches.
The soul follows and tries to grow with them.

A garden gate is making you suffer
By premeditated geometries that run
The length of shadows right to left.

What is the way of refuge can we speak of
When we speak of porticoes and colonnades
That are empty, black and white?

Ancient lines, fitful lights and shadows.
The sun is setting. It is time to leave.
The clock marks twelve thirty-two.

Percy F. Snofax and the Miraculous Calendar

"God always takes the simplest way."
—Blaise Pascal

Old Mr. Snofax, a cobbler in Fremont, Maine
who'd kept a small shop in town had died a hundred years ago
    tonight with the lights out in a snowstorm.

His son had married, fled Maine, served in the war,
lost two children, then his wife, sold their house, retired, grew old,
    moved to Boston, lived alone, was ignored.

Percy, a studied precarist, had had no faith
but lived on the edge of his memories, concealing himself
    from recognition. Had he really lived a life?

Nothing connected him to reality anymore
and seeing his face in a store window on Christmas eve
he reflected that his now long dead mother

had sadly only dipped her finger in India ink
and made a visage of it, him, in another lifetime back home
when he was born. Tonight he remembered

— *why*? — an old print in his father's shop,
a print of *The Martrydom of Crispin and Crispinian*,
by the painter Aert van den Bossche

that had hung above his father's stool.
He had stared at it when a boy and knew much of the story
93 years ago! Its images now flooded him.

Percy closed his eyes and wept.
His heart bulged! That panel of pain this was also his life,
all lives, all pain, all color, all existence,

horses, water, work, food, faces, cruelty,
ice, trees, all recorded, dogs, children at play, death, a span
of life, gardens, faith. He stood in the snow

and his scalding hot tears of remembrance
positively filled his soul with a kiss of sudden faith and never
again was Percy F. Snofax alone.

"Circle" Burke

"Circle" Burke was a nasty piece of work
    And smelled. Even as a boy he weighed
    Over two hundred fifty lubberly pounds and was fatter
    Than the food he fed on, wolfing doughnuts,
    Ring-Dings by the fistful. And Moon Pies.
    At fifty-two, he lived alone. He was Irish,
    Never married. When he got depressed, he'd
    Crawl up into a ball and hum show tunes.
    He was impotent. He found dead gods.

He ate everything, pizza especially.
At midnight he often went for slices
By himself, sweating in this undershorts,
Soiled, heading down to the bar.

I was reminded of him recently,
Reading somewhere that the oldest letter
In our alphabet is in fact the letter O,
That prodromic nightmare, certain oaf,
Having held its round unchanging shape
Since the Phoenicians formed it in 1300 B.C.
Isn't character destiny? Fate what we are?
One night I slept with his ex-girlfriend.
Whereupon he creepy-crawled her house
And punctured my two front tires in spite,
Coming to despise what first he hated
Strictly because of what he saw he was.
Round things he hated. And fat.

Cocaine Cat

Shoot it, baby,
You can taste
A doctor's office
In back of yo throat,
Was all I said.
I handed her the set of toys,
Syringe, needle, and tie,
And say Merry Cripmas.
She hot for boy, do you
Understand was all?
Get me some cold fruit juice,
Motherfucker, she say out the open window
To no one, and grind her teeth.
I took a hit myself
And put away the toys.
Things stiffened.
She feel funky? Good.
I slam-dunked her

Wif my lovemonkey.
She cried, see
What I'm sayin?
Then the bitch
Died, like
Jumped.

Cochiti Love

Gravures are kisses.
And then those hoops.
Cochiti make patterns
That go in loops.

Love's not straight.
Court with an eye
For pueblo designs
On pots that dry.

Colloquy with Miss Rita Hayworth

When you touch me, there is silver up my back,
a dance down Hollywood Road, Chinese nights,
racehorses poised like shotguns behind hot gates,
ready to break. There is no questioning it, manductress.
It is skylight, measurelessness in my mitts,
a gaze for the grace that is unaware of itself.
Won't you count the ducats piling in my heart,
swap gold, only for your fingers there to tease,
twiddle values out of me like coin, that you might
buy me cheap, naked as night, your slave?

Communion Tongues

Were you ever an altar boy
And had to pass the plate?
(The phrase is '50s Catholic
And probably out-of-date.)

Each and every communicant
Knelt there stiff as a post
Sticking out his or her tongue
To receive the wafer, or Host.

Such an array of tongues
A monster movie could claim,
Most of them frankly disgusting,
No two of them quite the same.

Sizes, all colors, and shapes
Ran the entire spectrum.
Some huge and puffy and swollen,
Other small as a plectrum.

Coins, checkers, phalloi,
U- and V-shaped and wet,
One or two loomed like a helmet's
Plume on a fat majorette.

Some fairly resembled slugs,
Bulbous and smooth and pink,
Others were fissured and grooved
And white as a porcelain sink.

Look at that wagging white one.
Is it a tongue or a beak?
Half a ruined Napoleon?
A piece of cracknel antique?

Stocky men had blunt ones.
Spinster's tended to fork,
Children's were round and rosy,
Fat men had loins of pork.

Sickly kids displayed
Tongues red as a new Toyota,
Old folks broken moonscapes
Like the badlands of Dakota.

Pretty girls showed seedcakes.
One boy flicked his like a lizard
Which, stained from a purple gumball,
Gave it the look of a gizzard.

Far too many were icky,
Membraneous and coated with yuck;
Some hadn't a trace of moisture,
Dry as a corn in its shuck.

A certain tongue seemed chamfered
On the tall and angular sort
Whose cross-hatching patterns recalled
The mazes at Hampton Court.

Many seemed bisected by
A parapsidal furrow,
An uncanny sort of trail
Recalling a gerbil's burrow.

Betting chips I saw,
Complete with fissured edges.
Two poked out like cheeses
Triangularly cut in wedges.

A lot looked just like coasters
While other not so flat
Revealed the wimbling tip
Of a hideous vampire bat.

Point ones seemed evil,
Sharper than winery bungs.
Another horror included
Senior citizen tongues,

Dry and rumpled and green
Like the floor of a witch's hovel.
And what about those protrusions
Long as a biscuit shovel?

Want to hear a confession,
Kind of climax to a play,
Of how I was even affected
In a personal sort of way?

Years later at the drive-in
When I was a teenage boy,
Though I was never a prude,
I suffered delimited joy.

My urges were healthy and normal.
I promise, I wasn't remiss,
Except for this single stricture:
I would never French-kiss.

Love's Law

Love cannot be asked to be returned,
In the way that one may give to get.
It may be echoed freely or be spurned
And whether it we hold or leave to let
Depends entirely on the lover's mind.
Zeal can stifle all for which it yearns
Seeking hotly, and by guile, to find
What it more properly must wait to learn.
To want and therefore simply try to own,
Which one must know is never ardor's seat,
Disallows the chance that love be shown,
Thus killing hope to guarantee defeat.
We must learn from such a law as this
To see by what love isn't what it is.

Counterparts

Spare me the girl whose best friend is her mother.
Ready with the word to set her right;
Let a lad appear, and she can't find another
Reason for disliking him on sight.

I knew a woman in New Jersey once
Whose husband was a burden on her soul.
After their divorce this banking dunce
Left his bitter partner in a hole.

By this I don't mean money was the thing
That came between the woman and her kids;
It was the low suspicions that she'd bring
To every small activity they did.

She had affairs with half the men she knew
At work, in school (she took a course at night);
So how could she avoid staining blue
Any subject that initially was white?

The evil here, implicit, is the blame
Passed on as if by magic to the daughter
That in each circumstance she'd do the same
And any man involved? No less a rotter.

Jilted, jaded, homely, out of sorts,
This woman's life became what she conveyed;
No daughter, when face with such reports,
Conceives of anything but innocence betrayed.

The danger in relationships like this
Is that the daughter then becomes the mate;
Responding otherwise would seem remiss,
And so becoming partners is their fate.

Thus like a married couple off they go,
For dinner, shopping, partners to the mall,
A week in Bermuda, to a Broadway show,
The daily expectation of a call.

No wonder then that love as it's defined
Can never penetrate the daughter's heart;
She deeply hates her father in her mind;
With her lamprey of a mother she can't part.

There are so many who another's freedom want,
And many of those content to pass it on;
A ghost prefers an empty house to haunt,
But both are equally forlorn.

So having lived, mother knows what's best,
Advises daughter just what not to do,
And what does daughter think to pass the test:
Why, Mom, become a cripple just like you!

Creeping Judas

A very thin premeditated ghost,
he seems more predator when acting host
than some hyena blinking in his lair
who's at your side before you feel him there.
A hand like fog he slides around your waist,
with fingers cold that touch as if to taste.
Many roles he plays, like traveler wide,
political pundit, companion at your side,
critic, confessor, even acting dumb.
He's best by far at buttering your thumb.
A stiff uncanny stand-off air belies
the pink ambition in his shifting eyes.
He wets his finger and holds it to the air
to ascertain the proper face to wear.
A questioning informs his walking pace,
as he glides without a shadow, not a trace.
Scheming like Polonius he easily leads
willing messengers to do his dirty deeds.
He subtly seeks to keep his reputation
simon-pure from every connotation
of public censure or any public wrong,
needing to be lord of every public throng.

He visits gardens, funerals to boot,
goes to concerts, sports a tailored suit,
flatters widows with his nasal bleat,
smiles at every herbert on the street.
On Arbor Day he yearns to plant a tree
in a public square for everyone to see
his motives high. He also tends to go
on Sundays to a Negro church for show.
He'll mock a friend to titillate your taste,
then snicker at the victim he's disgraced
behind his back. He couldn't care a jot.
Once you begin to care, you care a lot.
Snatching any pious chance to preach,
he's keen as spit to open up a breach
between you and anyone he has the chance
to lure into his arachnoidal dance.
Your virtues he will praise aloud to friends
yet lest a hand of friendship they extend
in your direction as he puffs you, be advised,
drops darker hints of you to be surmised.

Success, you see, is not enough for him;
others have to fail, remaining grim.
He'll say for your advancement he is keen,
so takes your side pretends to intervene
in arguments where you've a lot to lose
and then by cunning twists of logic choose
to say the reverse of what will do you good,
blurting out your faults in your defense
in mock attempts at trying to make sense.
If your suspicion leads you to complain,
then his reply becomes the queer refrain,
"Why, doing just the opposite, old blue,
Is a form of imitation, too!"
Martial never flattered more than he
or worked so hard in public to agree
with any fool who could advance his schemes,
be the method craven or the means.
A friend to all who knows no loyalty,
he becomes for each just what they want to see.
Conformity becomes him like a drape
which he wears satanically to ape

the kind of simple guilelessness he seeks
to murder by the havoc that he wreaks.
Truth and honor? Oh, for heaven's sake,
what's virtue when appearance is at stake?
He'll loudly threaten to resign the club
of drunken sods who tendered you a snub,
then turn around and suddenly appear
on the club committee he later comes to chair!
The treachery beneath such evil ways
Can plague a person to his final days.
Suppose your luck should take a bitter turn,
for instance, and the penalty you earn,
leaving you to mount the gallows bleak,
is so extreme you're not to live a week.
The state sets out to find among the mob
a hangman suitable to do the job.
Who will be the person that they bring
twitching with a hempen rope to swing
you like a silly bolo to your fatal end?
Can't you guess? Why, everybody's friend!

He's as he was and is and long will be,
your comrade true for all eternity
If proof you need to have that he's sincere,
a phrase, say, or gesture of his care,
He'll smile at you, the rope behind his hips,
and hissing *"Hail, Rabboni,"* kiss your lips.

For Roy Campbell

Criminal Man

"Whether it's murder, rape, or the S & L scandal, crime
costs about $300 billion a year ... a national tragedy. Why is
crime essentially a male pursuit?
> — June Stephenson, *Men Are Not Cost-Effective*

For all the violence men create
Women are surely involved in the way
They flirt with whomever they mate

Like flash in electrical wire.
What more can one go on to say?
If prison inmates are 90 percent male,
Were they not first webbed in schemes,
Related to eros or love as frail
As hopes are entangled in dreams?
The sexual act is give and take,
When glowing hot flesh lights up
In passionate charge and abrupt
To fashion a fire with flames
Racing madly like me through you
And consuming us both in a pyre
Where nothing at all remains.
Isn't it true that men simply do
While women prefer to make?

Crow

Black flags, black rags,
Waving out of the nesting woods
High above the crags,

Be ever watchful when
Flying too low over rainy roods
Of trees and fen.

Men in blinds await
With no other thought but to kill,
As though your fate,

Being left to us,
Should be determined by our will.
Disposed of thus,

You're living proof
That we can bravely bring down heaven,
Vulnerable roof,

Kill what we can't face,
Less to justify than leaven
Our theology of waste.

Darconville's Sonnet

Love, O what if in my dreaming wild
I could for you another world arrange
Not known before, by waking undefiled,
Daring out of common sleep adventure strange
And shape immortal joy of mortal pain?
Art resembles that, you know — the kind of dare
Nestorians of old acknowledged vain:
"No, what human is, godhead cannot share!"
But what if in this other world you grieve,
Undone by what in glory is too bright,
Remembering of humankind you leave
That which pleased you of earthly delight?
Out then on art! I'll sleep but to wake —
Never to dream if never for your sake.

A Daughter's Confession

It wasn't him
I hated
Or any of the boys
I dated
To whom
I said good-bye
My head is haunted.
It was my father's death
I wanted
In Quinton, N.J.,
Where he
First took his breath.

It wasn't them
I disliked,
All the girls
I knew
To whom
I never wrote.
Wrong waters fished.
It was my mother's death
I wished.
In Salem, N.J.,
Where she
First took her breath.

Deliriants

"Make me a child, stout hurdysturdygurdyman"
e.e. cummings

Almost old as powdered white
I left Athens late at night,
Tired in my rumpled suit,
Wishing in my hands for love,
For love had just relinquished
My powdered cracking hand,
Doom-eager, white as goat cheese,
Late at night in Athens,
Mad and quiet in its winking lights.
Smells of stone and burning meat,
Age, terror, promise. A *sirtaki*
Echoed from the outer dark.
It reminded me I was alive, chasing
the child in me.
I had left my coal brown Opel
Parked in Italy. I was taken
For a bummish messiah in Patras,
In my shorts, black from sun,
With my raven beauty,
Her there swinging her sandals,
Me a malicious enough cartoon.

We kissed in hooded doorways
Until she had to say good-bye.
Nothing to recount for others.
No parliament of friends would ask,
Bank on that, they wouldn't.
Silence, nightwind, lights.
There were no longer crones in black
Or cypresses standing sentinel
As I went trainward to Italy
And toward my coal brown Opel
Under a mandala of a moon
As round and bright and far away
As the imprint on my mouth
Of burning Grecian kisses.

Departmental Secretaries at Yale

You were both death on a bun,
Two bitches with bums spinnaker-fat,
Your white bryony hands, dead creepers,
Killing whatever you entwined, your perfume
Cheap as the envelopes you dispensed
With more spitting rancor than Alecto.
Not for you to hand out stationery,
Pencils, light bulbs free. Your mouths
Were bigger than your twats and those
Acid green supply cabinets you defended
Like phylacteries from Philistines.
"Paper just doesn't grow on trees,"
You'd snivel at five o'clock, rushing
With your hair like tortured midnight
Out to meet your wistful husbands
Standing there like damaged penguins
Waiting by their cars out front for you
In the gloom of a New Haven dusk.
"Can't you meet with your students
In the corridor?" you once snapped,
Denying me an office, penny stamps,
A telephone, shoving your face at me

Like the dark blue thumbtacks you
Slowly, parsimoniously counted out
As if diamonds from the Ritz.
(Since you are the same, you are both.)
You disliked each other with an intensity
That suggested you both recognized
Something of yourself in what you saw.
Too used to being mean to feel
The need to kill, you found
Quite happily that pettiness alone
Sufficed to get and keep you high
Like those cheap orchids
You pinned on your tits at Christmas
Which forced to it, believe me,
We chipped in grudgingly to buy.

Emily Dickinson's Bread

In quiet Amherst
You cooked many munchy meals
And were good at it, too.

At supper table
Your stern father ate no bread
Not baked by you.

You lowered gingerbread
Eccentrically down to urchins
From an upper view.

When you won 75 cents
At the Cattle Show in 1856
With the money you drew

Did you buy some bones
For large and grumpy Carlo when
Barking himself blue?

Eveyone's Fat Friend is First to Coo

Everyone's fat friend is first to coo
love through the trebles in its face
rising like a cock to crow its song;

it is the sidekick that rubs lusts,
bold and armored with its *tho* and *chan,*
ribbon-lipped to smooch the darkness

that it swabs, not as if it had a soul,
but as if it had a heart, for flesh
by law has no soul even fit for darkness

of a kind, or of that kind it rises
to spelunk like a fool with its fat funds.

Tableau: a fat acrobat swings to thrust
its trick above the nets surrounding it,
dumbly to perform. And though I stand

459

on him and am so high, so far above him,
still I worry that he brings me down,
for just as I gather myself to love,

my fat friend phones from where all phalloi
hug, from fountains where all huggers love,
and he is first to coo.

Février

La neige, c'est cette tige étrange que l'on coupe a l'été:
Elle a un goût de noire écriture fine sur une page blanche.
Ce texte des foulées qui gaufrent le vélin
Fleure le quart d'eau de puits, au juillet chaud.

L'hiver balaie des dunes brûlantes de sable sterile
Et me rôtit la face comme un chien au désert.
Blanche, froide, une cendre légère descend du ciel aveugle,
Atterrit sur mon gant, cri aigu, doux, bruit mat.

Alors que le vent éveille ma chair d'un claquement,
Je plante mes bottes dans la saison blanche et noire.
Sachant qu'au moindre arrêt, je disparaîtrai dans le neige,
J'entraine ce mois à l'abri du premier seuil venu, et je souffle.

Fiction's Fun to Feign

Fiction's fun to feign. It mutters up the sleeve.
Aren't we mostly critics, failing to admit in masks
What our faces must reveal, of what most we hate
And so critic of ourselves? But answer what we ask?
Beleaguered by foolish sons and begging in-laws,
Didn't Dickens simply wire up with all his taints
Flinty Scrooge in the fury of his being bilked
From the bitter bile of his personal complaints?
Snatching sibyl's leaves often skews the sight.
"Easter Parade" is a secular song: Berlin kept it so.
"White Christmas" has nothing to do with Bethlehem.
It has to do with winter, it has to do with snow.
Dr. Seuss's Grinch is only Mr. Geisel's Jew
Irked as much by Christmas as by Gentile greed.
All writing is confession, duplicity in session.
Our imagination's more than anything our creed.

Formal Theater

Your eyes please keep
Above the puppet Man
And weep

But spare the rod
The operator's wrist
Is God.

Francesca da Rimini

Does the poetry of women lie
In being conquered? In the *Inferno*
You're far too ready to comply,
Crying, "*O animal grazioso e benigno.*"
The tone, the adjectives of crouch,
To me reflect the nature of your soul.
The sin of obligation you avouch.
If Paolo's body won yours whole,
Brought about the fatal kiss that doomed
You to the windy space of hell, know
At least a man's fair form consumed
Your heart before the cold below.
Passion today has lost its purity:
Woman swap their bodies for security.

Fr. Mario

"The infant will play over the hole of the cobra, and the
young child will put its hand into the adder's den."
Isaiah 11:8

Fr. Mario used to visit our house.
His eyes were crossed like a shit-house mouse.
He put me down for his own scenario.
A wicked priest was Fr. Mario.

He was our uncle and jimmy-jawed,
Pugnacious, tiny, and deeply flawed.
He drank bottles of Moxie, case upon case,
And spoke to people an inch from their face.

His collar was white, his mind was dark.
He once on a stroll to Webster Park
Stopped in the street, pinching my arm,
And hissed, "You're doing your mother harm!"

I wet the bed which he wouldn't forgive.
He sucked cigarettes like a Broadway spiv.
He sent us on errands across the street
And gave lordly advice with a nasal bleat.

He pinched girls' bottoms, squeezed our hands,
Took thirds at dinner, gave brisk commands,
"Study Italian!" "Don't fork the bread!"
"Get an afternoon job!" "Try using your head!"

He knew all the perks of being a priest,
Took subscribers on tour to the Middle East,
Collected Hummels, finagled free roasts.
Meeting Franco was one of his boasts.

He bumsucked the rich, cadged tickets for shows,
Kept shelves of good whiskey, row upon row,
Got turkeys at Christmas, sometimes the trees,
And of course for Mass cards took standard fees.

From all that he told us he ran the Church.
People in Rome if you wanted to search
Knew him at once, he said, merely by name.
Was it for me to question that fame?

My weaknesses, anyway, got him quite vexed.
He constantly shamed me on the subject of sex.
"Sissy," cried Mario, wagging his knife,
"Get married, you? You'd pee on your wife!"

"You think a woman will turn a blind eye
While you hang a wet mattress out a window to dry?"
My heart almost stopped, missing a beat.
"Sleep on a bed with a cold rubber sheet?"

His mockery more by far than his screams
Polluted my nights with nightmarish dreams.
The church I soon saw, when I came awake,
Was as tricky and cruel as a ten-foot snake.

At family gatherings for the longest time
(I never go but know chapter and rhyme)
Thanks are made to the good God above
And someone is chosen to discourse on love.

The homily's Mario's, now pathetic and old,
And he offers up prayers like a hypocrite bold.
He'll die in a bed surrounded by candles.
His coffin will shine and have real brass handles.

But in hell when he's screaming, almost insane,
And he calls upon someone to lessen the pain,
Howling for help from the hole in his face,
My dream's to appear and administer grace.

It's a symmetry due him without any reserve,
A fate one can't say he doesn't deserve.
Let eternity balance time and degree.
Dante himself would be quick to agree.

I'll locate the priest in the midst of the fire,
Roasting like Dives in a scorching hot pyre.
Seeing me suddenly, what will he think?
There'll be no Moxie to give him to drink.

Why not then do what I'm good at, OK,
That which he knew me for day after day?
I'll prove myself useful, if somewhat uncouth,
Stand on his head, and say, "Open your mouth."

Gesture of Vanni Fucci

As reasonable as muffins
But sinister for all,
Rather than beginning,
One's begun, that's all.
I lay as flat as quiet,
New as color in my nudity,
Then sick at heart and sad,

Tucked asleep in pins,
Sketched in hair
And wet as snow in my lanugo.
Incepted, bleak, and charred.
With holy salt
I grew in size,
Became brown with the best of them,
And fought my private wars,
Enjoying for the nonce
The paper stars I won
For more than being me.
I wait for number three
To see if I'll be sane.
I began when the Second War began
And left for Europe on Bloomsday
Carried by the plane.
But if all that's said is ever done,
I mean, inceptions—
If they're repeatedly deceptions,
I know enough of figs to give them one.

The Girl Who Makes You Cry Is Always Love

The girl who makes you cry is always love,
    As dear as laughter,
    Expensive as your heart,
When night becomes as close as she,
    Embraces sweet as hair is warm
    Around her neck prompt the tears
That make a cry and therefore love.

The cry that makes you love is dear,
    For after hurt the laughter isn't there
    Nor the girl reflected in the song you sing
But only mirrored in the light
    Of what by broken hearts
    Is consequently learned of care
Which makes you cry and therefore love.

The love that makes your laughter real
    Is a cry that's kissed upon the mouth,
    The girl you taste and love,
A warmth you've hurt as close as night
    Who's angry from the eyes,
    Expensive as her heart, as dear as tears,
And makes you cry a laughter and a love.

God

Even the greatest man has to live in his own century.
                                      —Ortega

When I take God upstairs,
Flip the light on, and
Provide him with the towel
Of my suggestion
To wash from the bowl on the stand,
I step downstairs, and he feels great harm
Like all old men,
And, whimpering, he stops with his cane
Until I take his plastic arm.

465

The Good Old Song

"Wahoo-wa, Wahoo-wa!"
the University of Virginia fight cry

Bitcoin, half mad, stood before the Rotunda,
speaking of the coming Resurrection, but then stopped to sing,
inspired that music begins where words fail.

Was not Charlottesville a wonder for us all?
Didn't T. Peter, pissed as a cricket, go howling "God's Grandeur"
walking through the "Grounds" in a snowfall,

white as the general hope that general change
would come only from messengers who began to rave in the way
we knew time ripens corn and rusts iron?

We loved and lived that poem, *heard it*,
in the lyrics back in the Sixties, that musicologically informed
the few of us we were on a mission from God

and so woke to daily visions of a sort. Buried
in a yell was something from throats blessed by St. Blaise himself
and his gathered gallimaufry of creatures.

It was a gallery of rogues: Boustrophedon.
Fussheim, little Boray, *Le Pêche Mangeur*, the Psychodynamist
who wore an actual hairnet to sleep at night,

grim "Charlie Starkweather," Surfing Jesus,
Ann Dior, The Corpulent Philosopher, Ms. Cherry Chmatch,
black Clarence Daphne, The Nashville Idiot,

Funcheap, Wallace the Pinhead, Mr. Reuter,
the cheering joyful Hitler Jugend of The Jefferson Society,
Moskeehtuckqut the Mad Wampanoag,

Wuxtry, the Cagone, Poloponyhead, Bloaters,
Ray ("The Pinnacle of Cynical") Garland, "Merry" Kretschmar,
The King of Unobtainarium, Mr. Argue,

Carl "Area 51" Potts, John "Turkey" Anderson,
Nancy Anne Cianci, the Human Swingsong, Russ the Mormon,
Clarence ("Dash of Lavender") Daphne,

dumb Aphra Behn, The Human Question Mark,
Loighnde Boigerdoine, The Danaë, Weird Man Fuchsiste,
"Mousie," Wallace Parsnips who could juggle,

Fartdog, The Intrepid Norwegian Sailor,
Dupo Evers, the Barfonya Twins, The Red Fairy who was gay
and would never say the word oxygen

if he could say "dephlogisticated air."
"I smell Being in the air!" cried one delicioso, waving his arms,
for questing we were rabid! Eurekoids all

indeed sought the shining of shook foil
and did cry, "The world is charged with the grandeur of God!"
as if we stood right there on that very soil!

The Harvard College Tinies

1

O Swung Tree,
Your servant oranges
Hang from you,
Terrified.

2

Do you love me
Or do you not?
You told me once
But I forgot.

3

Corpses are buried,
Cadavers un-;
The distinction's pointless
In terms of fun.

4

Girls have mothers
Upon their backs to bite 'em,
So girls grab boys
And so *ad infinitum*.

5

A lexical man came to marry
And erred for the trull's mood did vary.
The rosy-cheeked bride, feared a Uxoricide.
Prevail, sturdy man, through the parry.

6

Holy Divine Providence
Did one thing odd;
Allowed a cruel absurdity
The name of God.

7

In a wordly law as it is built
He was innocent of guilt.
Explain now the nature of this offense:
He was guilty of innocence.

8

The piece of foolscap
By a poem enhanced
Is never completed;
It's only advanced.

9

Of the two main reasons why earth exists,
Walking on it is one, says the prophet;
But among his number you needn't enlist.
So proceed, dear friend, to walk off it.

Harvest Time

Autumnal days make me believe
There is in leaf-meal musk, apple smells,
A mood of something like prevision.
Yesterday kicking through the leaves
I brought a bottle of wine
As a gift over to my new neighbors,
A lovely young couple who knew I was a writer
(How? All my books are out-of-print).
It suddenly stuck me walking home
Reflecting on their grateful grace
That given the small celebrity I have,
The kind that in my village that goes for something
But not of course too much
They would one day be at my funeral.

Haves and Holes

Like a novel, like a sequel,
Marriage is that equal:
Halves, but one half previous,
The other, somewhat devious,
A counterpart, say, in the following way:
As a workweek equals a Friday's pay.
Two stones grind in an ancient quern;
One stays static, one will turn.
Nothing in nature is equal quite.
Jaws don't match in a single bite.
Your ear on the right, your ear on the left—
Some will say "reft," some will say "cleft":
The words to that queer inner porch both apply.
The cave from the darkness who can descry?
The terms are the same, but not so the ears,
With shapes as different as smiles from tears.
A push, you say, is only a pull?
A glass half empty is a glass half full?
The riddle's the riddle of number two;
The one call me, the other you.
But a couple, alas, is not a pair.
Love's disappointment's precisely there!
If a simple kiss is what one wants,
Turning the cheek is the others' response.
The vision you'd share can never be,
Not to another who cannot see.
For the singular act of creation
Absolves the other of obligation.
Love letters sent, countless and grand,
Parch the pen in the other's hand.
The fair, they say, requires foul;
An owl is cognate to its howl.
And if with love you see your fate,
Why, be prepared to suffer hate!
In the duchess you wooed at the midnight hour
Claws a black-faced bitch mad to devour.
You seek to select and select what you see,
But is what appears what then must be?
The nature of choice *itself* is sin,

Where one must lose and one must win!
One eye's inaccurate, two we need
To watch, to learn, to know, to read.
One image is gotten of those two:
But is it real? And is it true?
Distinctions! Differences! All life long!
You can't do right if you can't do wrong.
The bride, the groom on a nuptial bed?
Spills one white, spills one red.
Yet each fulfills defect in each,
The epistemology of stone and peach.
(But when it comes to the hungry lip,
Are equally praised, the flesh, the pip?)
A paradox, say, that can never be:
The strange conundrum of lock and key.
Man's "too much" he boasts to show;
Woman's "too little" down below
Incorporates as best it can
The larger half of her messmate, Man.
A large half? Ay, there's the catch.

It's the deathless quintessential,
The flint, the strike, the spark sequential,
That fires every human match.

History is Made at Night

Deception is the price too many pay for love.
A knife beneath the tongue, a vow above
As thin as lies,

Lost to whatever dreams when young it hoped to find,
In innocence it sought to bind
With honest ties.

How can ever love transform a soul, redeem
A spirit unalert to all but its own scream
Of greed?

The self that fights for gain itself is fought,
Content to fill its own and not
Another's need.

There are plots as red as witches in our heart,
Turning love to schemes, and schemes impart
A living blight.

A blackness that infects us soon can make us shade.
I think what's often said is true: history is made
At night.

The Hollywood Rag

Hand me my populuxe hat,
Give me my rancho mirage cane,
Sing me a parody, instant hilarity,
I've got a yen to be vain.
> *O, O, O pink villas and palms,*
> *Sweet loving baby, open your arms,*
> *Doing the Hollywood Rag.*

Put on your Malibu tails,
Don your flamingo-beak shoes,
Drive me nutty, turn me to putty,
Tell me only good news.
> *O, O, O pink villas and palms,*
> *Sweet loving baby, open your arms,*
> *Doing the Hollywood Rag.*

Make up your insincere face,
Wear silver earrings that peal,
Wing me a wing, fling me a fling,
Let's try and pretend to be real.
> *O, O, O pink villas and palms,*
> *Sweet loving baby, open your arms,*
> *Doing the Hollywood Rag.*

Kick up those art deco feet,
Extend your Clicquot Club arm,
Let's be tacky, drive me wacky,
Turn on your boulevard charm.
  O, O, O pink villas and palms,
  Sweet loving baby, open your arms,
  Doing the Hollywood Rag.

I Think of Death at Times

I think of death at times,
I mean my own, the one
I dream of and wake up
choking on a dry tongue,
wish for when the woof's
too tight and nerves snap,
whiplash, tangle at the
edges of my moving frame.

Sometimes on summer days (I am alone),
lying in the snap,
lying in the sand, all life
cooked out of me except
a violent consciousness,
I plan the whole affair,
or try to, but never get
beyond the crusty scene of Wiglaf
sprinkling water on my
beautiful face.

Iliad

We all heard the mad birds
Telling us to kill
Our loves
With murders and by schemes
Unheard of since Achilles

Broke Hector's spine in thirds:
Sing out a wild adeste
To those very birds
Who shriek bent songs,
For who denies the questions
Will be answered
By the dreams we have of Priam,
The lovely graces of his and our
Beautiful faces,
Our winking jewels,
The deaths
And small, but real,
Resurrections.

Imagos

for Sue Collins

What I thought
the most wonderful
butterfly I had ever seen,
daubed double, yellow, white,
winged, shuttling straight up,
and from flower to flower,
was, when I came
close, two.

Folie Circulaire; or A Meditation on the Nature of Prayer

"Likewise the Spirit helps us in our weakness; for we do not know how to pray as we ought, but the Spirit himself intercedes for us with sighs too deep for words. And he who searches the hearts of men knows what is the mind of the Spirit, because the Spirit intercedes for the saints according to the will of God."

Romans 8:26-27.

for Fr. Benedict Joseph Labre,
Fr. Titus Brandsma, and Rev. Dietrich Bonhoeffer

I received a much needed check.

It made me feel grateful.

This was one of those times to thank God you read about, I felt.

So I whispered a halting thanks to God only because it seemed one of those times to do so and because it occurred to me that that is what obligated people did.

But my words seemed such a craven gratitude as I expressed my thanks, feeling that it sullied the recognition.

Also, I was looking for credit.

I spoke words like pulling a slot-machine lever, watching coins rattling down into an aluminum gambling tray that rang with reward.

But the echo died.

My words seemed vain. Can we actually bridge the gap between a mighty God and ourselves even though the most intensive and frequent prayers, at least the mutterance I made with uncommunicative smugness, are a *quid pro quo*?

As I spoke, I heard the whining of a lost Corgi.

What tumbled out was a ruckus of words, hubbub, clamor, commotion, racket, din, cacophany, a noise that became only preamble to a smiling approval of self, and in amirror of pathological nurturance I saw my complacent face smile, then sorrow-soften in my supplication, like the supple glove a fop detaches finger by finger blithely to say hello.

My voice

And a reply from Isaiah 59:1-2:

"The Lord's hand is not shortened

That it cannot save, neither is

His ear heavy that it cannot hear.

But your iniquities have separated between

You and your god, and your sins have His

Face from you, that He will not hear.

I always heard in my prayers splenetic clowning, half-hearted doubt, someone else's voice, ventriloquial goofery, the push-pull of implicit requests as bargaining. Since a web of implied intent, challenge, and constraint surrounds every communicative act, I felt as I spoke a role of shame in calling forth a sublime forgiver

Isn't to supplicate to solicit?

St. Paul knew how to pray because he did *not* know how to pray. Might we not propitiously draw from this confession of that Apostle the conclusion that those amongst us who act as if they knew how to pray, do not know how at all?

2

Didn't I love the money more than I sought to give thanks? Love the thanks as much as the money? Admire the love I gave to God with a seeping expectation that my acknowledgement deserved credit as a just requital worthy of large recognition?

Greed *prompted* my damn thanks.

I am a public smiling man!Prayer is to be chaste, solitary. We are adjured to pray in secret (Matthew 6:6) so as to give ourselves no chance to fool ourselves on our motives, just as Christ did in the Wilderness (Lk. 5:16), at Caesarea-Phillippi (Lk. 9:16), in Gethsemane (Mt. 26:36), in a Solitary Place (Mk. 1:35),all night before choosing the Twelve ((Lk. 6:12), after the Feeding of the 5000 ((Jn. 6:11), before the Raising of Lazarus ((Jn. 11:41-42), in the Temple (Jn. 12: 27-28), before his Transfiguration (Lk. 9:28-29), for the Disciples (Jn. 17), on the Cross (Lk. 23:34), at Emmaus (Lk. 24:30).

None of my feelings seemed pure in that while I felt mercantile of mood for bargaining. the narcissism of seeming good in my own eyes struck a metallic note for which I blamed God in making me a needy and pathetic mercenary.

I sighed and lost all respect for myself as prayerer.

What a belief-drenched farce I fear I faked! No, according to St. Paul, prayer is humanly *im*possible. We talk to somebody who is not only nearer to us than we ourselves are but proceed to tell something to Him who knows not only what we tell Him but is aware of all the unconscious tendencies out of which our conscious words grow. This is the reason why prayer is difficult, awkward, nonviable.

Were we not taught that it is God *Himself* who prays through us when we pray to Him. If God Himself is in us, which is what Spirit means – spirit is another word for "God present" – isn't there something in us which is not we ourselves that intercedes before God for us, walking before us like a hooded ghost of protection? Questions, questions, questions. I tally them up and am mortified! In the Gospel, however, Christ himself asks 290 questions, so many that T.S. Eliot in "Choruses from the Rock" refers to Our Savior as a "questioner:" "Oh my soul, be prepared for the coming of the Stranger. Be prepared for him who knows how to ask questions."

475

Since nothing we ask for is anything we have, isn't desire perversely an aspect of ownership, capturing us in its importunistic grip?

Our psychic bandwidth which is shaped to own, to be gratified, unlocks a history of our personal struggles – who would deny it?That our sense of place, our locus, our domain, and the centrality of it makes a demand for justice is at the root of prayer and seeks requirements with our words, and yet we surely bewilder even ourselves in the answers we expect. Petitions, petititions, kneeling prostration, I fall forward in desperate *salat*.

Know why the shape is, not what the shape is. How distinguish Wyoming from Colorado, both rectangles yet vastly different?

Reverse speech may be involved, for when we ask what we need we not only state what we are missing but manipulate what we expect in our craving to gain. Invocation is an act that seeks to activate a rapport with a deity — *calls him out!*

I swear I once heard a cat desperately say "Out!" causing me recall that a therapist at Harvard University once told me, after I recounted much of my life for him, that I was always trying to withdraw from the world, evacuate, disappear.

To pray is ask that something be revealed, be made clear, be brought in the open, disclosed, divulged, in the way saw Christ called out of Bethlehem:"But you, Bethlehem Ephrathah...out of you will come for me/one who will be ruler over Israel." (Micah 5:2)This is the only pleace in the OT where it is specifically stated that Christ would be born in Bethlehem

4.

All prayer is importunate, with words revolving around the tongue by Mr Dunandunate.

In Psalm 4, seeking relief in his prayers, the Psalmist virtually demands that Jehovah heed his words, effectively saying, "Discern, please, what I myself cannot say!" – in other words, save me! Inarticulate, we call for flutes, lutes, tambors, as this Psalm does, to accompany us in our bid to God to restore our soul.

Aren't Buster Brown with his harmonica singing "Fannie Mae" and Wynonie Harris jiving with "Lollipop Mama" and Big Bill Broonzy playing "Bricks in My Pillow" and "I'm Gonna Move to the Outskirts of Town"all fervently praying as hard as grumpy,dogged, pertinacious, and overly solicitous Jeremiah in Lamentations who complained that God, studiously ignoring him and his prayers, "had covered himself with a cloud that no prayer could pass through"? If mutterance is prayer, isn't silence rebuke?

Are we to understand, nuttily, that an atmosphericologist has the key to celestial communication? Even if confession doesn't in itself make amends, may one ask is it preliminary to reparation.

Is recompense compensation? Atonement repayment? Apology indemnity? I want to *feel* redress when on my knees I'm howling with abjection, hear the ache in the sycamores like a merciless, bum-drumming wind.

But in that everything attests, everything prays. Nature so affirms, corroborates, certifies. The heavens, the sky.Being, alone, is prayer. The Psalmist sings,

"The heavens declare the glory of God; the skies proclaim the work of his hands.
Day after day they pour forth speech; night after night they display knowledge.
There is no speech or language where their voice is not heard.
Their voice goes out into all the earth, their words to the ends of the world. "
Psalm 19

I speak without capability but culpability, both, in my faux prayers, in the same way
that because in an argument my wife will not go away my invective increases.
But if the symbol of God interceding before Himself for us says that God knows more
about each of us than that of which we are conscious, does he not anticipate our
worth in that and make prayer irrelevant and bless speechlessness, the unspoken?
Is prayer then *silence*?

5.

Consider the most mysterious part of Paul's description of prayer, namely, that the
Spirit "intercedes with sighs too deep for words."
But wait a minute, *had I not sighed*?
Had I recognized a level of consciousness by blundering effort in which something
happens that cannot be expressed in words. Is it possible the essence of prayer is
an act of God working in us and so raising our whole being to Himself?
St. Paul refers to "sighing." It is nothing less than an expression of the real
weakness of our creaturely existence. We are told only in terms of wordless sighs
that we can approach God, and even these sighs are His work in us.
If I cannot find the words of prayer and remain silent towards God, was this a
lack of Spirit? Or was it silent prayer? A sigh which is too deep for words. He who
searches the hearts of men, knows and hears at least those sighs which are *too
deep for words!*
At last I understood and, sighing, smiled.
So I pocketed the check.

Insect

So awful is the vice of incest that no noun exists for the person who
practices it.

— Alexander Theroux

What would you do
If your sister once said
Visiting you

That your brother
Tried to take her to bed,
Tell another?

To *someone* you
Must find yourself led.
My question is to who?

In the Children's Parks is Fun

In the children's parks is fun
But more than that a pleasant motion.
When the squeaky rubber ducks are pushed
Beneath the water up they come.
The little girls like pencils
Know what the slide delivers
When from the top the shove brings down
Like a golden puff of pistol
A little tyke, all coos and stripes.
The kite that jerks with bastardy
Up in the air with ughs and swoops
Will surely fall tomorrow
And wasn't up there yesterday.
Look at the swings, they're back and forth,
A rolling roiling motion;
The kiddies know when it goes south
It then has to go north.
The kiddies bounce in the frosty air
At the balance, but there's more:
If a creature's ripped from a momma's womb,
A papa must go to war.

Job

Where are the truths you wanted to hear
But couldn't for the lies the doubters told?
Though Bildad called you guilty, Eliphaz queer,

In the face of all destruction you stood bold.
The promise made, that He that keepeth Zion
Should not slumber, should not even sleep,
A faith emboldened strong enough to die on,
Gave a faithless nation promises to keep.
Now, Israel itself is lost once more,
A persecutor in the very way it hurt,
Tells the very lies it only heard before,
Grinds another nation in the dirt.
Why ask again the ways of God, His mystery?
Palestine's impaled on Israel's history.

The Voice of Joni James

Nobody could love you
For yourself and not your voice.
My own angel couldn't have
Stranger, refaned, more quinchful diction
In her song, though my choice
When I meet her in the sky
Is that she try.

La Compagnie Idéale

Pressant,
A demi-submergé
Monte sous notre vie
Un désir de compagnie idéale.
Ce désir n'est pas l'idée
Qu'existe telle compagnie;
Il est cette compagnie.
J'avoue que peu m'importe
De rester assis a observer le monde
Si le monde ne m'importune;
J'ajoute que jamais je n'ai trouvé
De compagnie
D'aussi bonne compagnie que

Le solitude qui donne forme
A ce désir, et donc,
Pour l'essentiel,
A moi-même.

Perfect Companion

An urge
Beneath our life
Is the half-submerged wish
For a perfect companion.
The wish is not the notion
A companion can be had;
It's the companion.
I can say, I don't mind
Sitting and watching the world without
The world bothering me.
I can add, I've never found
A companion
As companionable as
The solitude that makes
The wish, and so me,
Much of what
I am.

Le Bruit

"Noise is the most impertinent form of interruption."
— Arthur Schopenhauer

Take those Dadaists with frying pans.
Le bruit with its banging tins and horns,
Typewriters, rattles, kettledrums, and bells

Shook awake the capital of Paris.
So, a table's not its wood and nails
But, as you say, the mere idea of it.

O Tzaraites, you're something premature,
For isn't noise produced by every movement?
The soul itself in nature is volcanic,

The very opposite of what theologians
With their platitudes of Plato claim,
That we in being virtuous must be quiet.
But what in a person awakes to be approved
Whose vitality announces little but that
Noise is rich? Chocolate will kill a dog.

I prefer girls doing elegant bascules
In silence, shimmering like the sh-sh-sh-sh
Of the silver leaves of the poplars,

The secret thoughts they hide to harbor,
Dreaming, the manias of moans they save
For silken beds they plan to quiver in.

Little League Parents

Squinting into the sun,
You both watch from afar,
Bellowing for the team in the field
Wearing blueberry blue,
Eating fistwiches, wedges of pie,
The carboy of lemonade nearby
Gone warm by inning two.
Your screams at little peewee
In right, wearing his cap down low,
Can't compensate for the fact
He's whiffed three times in a row.
You're spread out on a hummock
Like Litvaks on a beach.
Good that that fucking umpire
Is conveniently out of reach.
Smoking butts one after another
From the pack perched on your knee,
Isn't your face-shaking fury

Exactly what half-pints shouldn't see?
Aren't you as badly out-of-shape
As your anger is, as unpromising
A parent to fumbling Freddy
As his bat angle is to me?
And when I see you waddling
Moose-slow into dusk
With your lawn chairs
Across those empty fields,
I wonder, can anyone doubt
Specifically how
Beyond here and now
That little boy struck out?

The Lollipop Trollops

Matsu, spread out your netsukes.
A good one has no sharp points.
It can't. And it must also stand.

What in any particular arrangement
Doesn't show to the derelict mind,
Capable of missing what it sees,

Patterns forcing thought on us,
As the past exists to be summoned,
Painful as points and placement?

The poet is a veteran of the night,
Method the soul of his management,
Drawing lines that you might dream,

Indeed surrender to your dreams
But not without the working mind
Sharply shaped about its themes.

Knowledge isn't often what you like.
It may by truth more than in disguise
Surprise a tragic shadow in your eyes.

A poem must reach, as a blowing wind
After constant rain manages somehow
To bring summer somehow in again,

But along with birds a bleaching heat
Against which we must interpose of course
White sombreros and cold umbrellas.

Praise enough for sunny Solomon.
David having lessons in his wrists
Sang twice in giving sense to song.

But poetry should please as well.
Blow your fat trumpet, senator,
To those didacticians at your feet

Who've given up magic and shadow,
Becoming eunuchs for the jobs they want.
"I've been too harsh on Brother Donkey,"

Cried Saint Francis on his dying bed.
His spirit needed pleasure, too.
Rip off your sleeves in spring!

Isn't high seriousness for sects?
Mormons don't want masques, pinwheels,
Silly cats, noisy flats, party hats.

As trollops singing "Zuk Zuk Zuk!"
Heedless as their clients are un-,
Poems to that extent are fun.

Forgive the painted trulls in heels
If only for the sad disclosures they
In hocks of laughter are intent to hide.

A simple lyric makes us as unaware
Of time as time is of itself in passing.
Can't sense be made of only what we feel?

The pleasure that we seek in them
And often find makes poems like boxes
Lovely as Italian bijouterie.

Jubilo! Jubilo! Jubilo!
Skip into sheets of driving rain with me
So we can lick our faces and laugh!

* * *

 But who remains the same
After no matter how little knowledge makes
Of us as much a mood as a man?

A different cowpoke
Walks out of a crepuscular cathedral
Than who went strolling in

By definition. What indirection
That you seem to take, squandering time,
Fails to matter? None, *none*.

We are never twice ourselves.
Whether read for sensuality or sense
A poem must disturb,

Badly reminding you, spintry
And spintressa, of your need to be
Surely more than what you are.

Smug students, reading to have
Themselves confirmed, ignore or wave away
Despair like ditzy drones,

Refusing to see we progress
Precisely by what low logo of misfortunes
We are willing to face

And face to know, like Alexander
In Tashkurghan, rousing himself from bed
To survey the hostile hills,

Leaving in a sweaty pile of pelts
At way past midnight alert to sudden danger
A naked and disturbed Roxane.

Lost Friend

Most of him recalled for me
One of Puddn'head Wilson's remarks,
Which were rarely kind,
Although they got a laugh.
"I wish I owned
Half of that dog," he said.
"I'd kill my half."
Why form friendships
Over which one must then reluct?
I once knew a guy
Who though some of him
Was nice
Much too much of him
Sucked.

Lost in America

I searched for you in Critical, Mass.,
Won't, Wash., and Eightnine, Tenn.,
over every last road and mountain pass
of Lo, Cal., and Ball Point, Penn.

You went skipping about in Tra La, La.,
in each suburb and city park
of the palmy reaches of Flip Flop And, Fla.,
Junior, Miss., and Noah's, Ark.

Doctors were called in Chekhov, Md.,
Ex, Conn., and spacious Big, Al.,
Pro Nobis, Ore., and Ravish, Me.,
and the deserts of Silent, Cal.

Eeny, Meeny, Miny, Mo.,
seemed a logical place you'd be in.
Same with dark Agememnon, Io.,
Either, Or., and Waita, Minn.

You rented a car in Miner, Va.,
uncaring that you were remiss,
and took as you sped out of Areyou, Ok.,
a motel in Nowmakea, Wis.

Racing through Luc, Ky., one night in snow
you decided you wanted to try
to avoid my pursuits by trying to go
from Pho, N.Y., to Dontaskme, Wy.

You tried Salaam, Al., found nothing to see,
then apparently traveled as far
as the lawless outbacks of Givitto, Me.,
and freezing Looknohands, Ma.

Who was it saw you in Do Re, Mi.?
One newspaper in Valhal, La.,
had you living half naked up in a tree
drooling in rural Ga, Ga.

You were never right after the day,
or so went the rumor mill;
you spent two weeks on a fatal stay
in Suddenly Taken, Ill.

Gossip quickly had you trans-
ferred to a living hell,
a barmy house in Bottles And, Kans.,
some whispered in Infi, Del.

Enough of this crazy fantasia about
what sounds like a chronic disease.
Allegorical paranomasia! Watch out
for accompanying medical fees!

I despair, do you hear, because I have landed
no closer than when I'd begun.
I'm doomed I see to stay where I'm stranded
in the terrible state of the pun.

Love, 1957

The only way
I could like her
was to feel bad
about myself
after hating her.
The only way
I could make amends
for berating her
was pitifully
to start dating her.
The only way
I could feel right
with myself
was to marry her
after creating her.

Loverboy

"After the loving',"
  croons Engelbert Humperdinck,
"I'm still in love with you,"
  as if it's a bloody miracle
in the process of getting through

he still can manage
to feel in his heart
for the woman lying unkempt
anything resembling love
and not just merely contempt;

but were I
that she to whom he sang
those rubbishy words in bed
I'd sever his flaccid tool
and slap him upside the head.

Wittgenstein's Proposal

After two weeks she [Marguerite Respinger] left for Rome
to attend her sister's wedding, determined that the one
man she was *not* going to marry was Ludwig Wittgenstein.
— Ray Monk, *Ludwig Wittgenstein*

For me
As I hope for you
Discovering a sentence
Has no means
Of verification
Is to understand
Something important
About it
But not to discover
That there is nothing in it
To understand.
Will you
Give me your hand?

Mary Snowfire

All the boys knew Mary Snowfire,
Who wore lipstick at thirteen and a pout,
More than by the Ping-Pong photos
Snapped half in a booth, half out.
At night she dawdled at Hickey Park.
"I see France," she once said.
Of the heat that so held me in thrall
For others who smirked in the dark
Though my life was cold as December

No whisper fails to enter my head
And most of those girls I somewhat recall
With a memory not always up to the mark,
But Mary Snowfire I remember.

We slicked down our hair with Vitalis
To dance in the gym at the junior high
Where Miss Bigwood kept us an arm apart
And we avoided contact by eye.
I waltzed in silence with Shirley and Clare
In my boxlike shoes and I ached,
Never quite knowing to stop to start.
I had combed and wet-parted by hair.
A number of girls I knew from the hall
With breath sweeter than birthday cake
Brought a blush to my cheek like an ember
And many a one of them I can't recall
To whom I'd have given all of my heart,
But Mary Snowfire I remember.

Medford Kids

He combed his hair, proud,
        and,
with large fat sighings,
dillydaillied about.

She took out a Lucky
        and tapped it on his
arm.

Furious with each other,
they kissed, lovely.
He with his pomade;
She with her funny
truncheon.

The Meeting of the Heads

The meeting of the heads with eyes
Prevents the murder love attempts.
There are the perfect fingers
Lovers use, the snatches in the dark.
And it's awfully brave of some
To pile on lovely in the sheets
When murder smells out loud for them.
No, not the glugs of life passing out,
The quimmy tugging of the gluey sheets,
Is it we should think about;
But the ripe wet daggers that commit
Along with hugs, our heads.
Then the eyes: acrobating like feathers,
There are the pouncing things,
Hopping beyond the mammaries, and
Even the slope of chin and armatures;
Cellulose or beady, likeable or red,
It's the eyes the head brings soft to love,
Walleyed and warranteed, like eggs,
To crack and flutter and spill.

Megabucks Ticket

A winning Megabucks ticket worth three-quarters of a
million dollars, taken out at the Swan River Market in
Dennis but never picked up, was invalidated today, one
year after being purchased.
—*Cape Cod Times,* June 19, 1991

"Your thermocouple's broke,"
The plumber muttered,
Face up in the cellar
Dark and cluttered,
Grunting, clucking, exhaling sighs
Under the water heater,
Getting cinders in his eyes.
"Got a scrap of something

On you I can light?"
"I might," came the helpful reply,
"I might."

Mens Sana in Corpore Sano

Dr. Nathan Pritikin
Who told Jim Fixx, "Take heed.
Stop eating meat;
Your veins are clogged
And running doesn't help
Unclog them,"
Was right of course,
But when he died —
Nate, I mean (who shot
Himself in the head)
Not Jim (who jogging
Fell down dead) —
His veins were clear
As a twelve-year-old's
Only his *mind* was clogged.
How many the miles
His spirit never logged?
So much for hopes.
Weightlifters never read.
Professors
Are physical dopes.

Milagro

Why cut your braids
in Quito, brown girl,

when others with hope
to win their loves

offer Santa Niño
in his shadowy niche

old medallions,
sacred vows paid,

of bone wood stone
gold shell clay?

O, give up your
tiny tin heart

to El Niño, girl,
in whatever way,

but never those
long dark braids.

Mill Stream

What is the secret said
In what unable to be held
We love? Spillways, pools,

The sea itself. Water moving
Has become for me, as much
As for Heraclitus in his mind,

While somehow proving,
The symbol of mutable beauty,
Masquerade as performance,

Form transcending flux.
Why can't flowing water,
Above its supernal duty,

Beyond its natural task,
Stop briefly meandering
Long enough for us to ask

May we *ever,* standing far above
The heart of what its secret says,
Come to hold what we love?

The Miracle of Fasting

Fasting makes a face that lights an onion up.
Three days without a morsel turns the stomach

Out as if it were a limp and laundered sock,
Scrimp and empty as a Dutchman's bummock.

I have often tried to supplicate my soul
By concluding that the body I was given

Is the worthless brute I know it is.
For mastery of self I long have striven.

Fat forces flesh to fast in cutting ways.
Fasts cut through fat and flesh obeys.

The hours drag. You're white as paper,
Can smell a pie some forty miles away.

If melons were a woman you would rape her;
For a tart in any sense you'd pay.

Our stupid flesh can never comprehend
How deprivations elevate our being.

Fatness is in fact a kind of blindness.
And fasting but a special way of seeing.

Monsieur Trinquet

O red-wigged wit from Tambov,
Everyone's favorite poet,

You came with the family Harlikov,
sponging at the name-day party

like all poets full of pride
content to let the others pay,

and dance with their spinster
daughter out of obligation.

Not a word that was recorded
did you exchange with Onegin '

that we know of. In your one
appearance you sang off-key,

worrying about your stanza
with an aesthetician's fears.

I only want to know was Tatiana
Larin as beautiful as they say,

Or were you too busy to notice,
Filling your face with éclairs?

Moses the Lawgiver

"We give our word to the Palestinians we want peace."
　　　　　—Yitzhak Shamir, Prime Minister of Israel

Moses murdered a man, flat out,
Though this was against the law.
He saw an Egyptian, took up a knout,
And left him without a jaw.

Then Yahweh announced "Do not steal."
Try guessing who first got the news.
But did Moses believe what he had to reveal
Of the law he passed on to the Jews

When during the course of several nights,
Preceding the Exodus bold,
Egypt was robbed by the Israelites
Of its jewelry, silver, and gold?

Look in vain for a sign of remorse
After the thieves got the boot.
The Golden Calf was fashioned of course
From mostly Egyptian loot.

Another commandment was then handed down
To Moses who waited in dread
On a misty mountain above the town.
"Don't bear false witness," it said.

So Moses spoke up to Pharaoh
And his very first *word* was a lie.
Knowing full well he'd never come back,
He promised that he would try.

A very short leave was requested
For the people of Israel dear
To pray, have a feast, and get rested
In a wilderness really quite near.

What later of Moses's assurance
The feast would last only three days?
Or the worth of a prophet's endurance
Who can break laws in so many ways?

His word was as barren as sand.
What honor to all kith and kin!
They stole every valuable and
Their asses were gone with the wind.

One moral's as good as another
Of the many there are to be had.
Laws are made only for others.
Whatever you do can't be bad.

If Scripture's literal, anything goes.
Crime often pays. Laws are pied.
Savagery's sanctity fighting your foes
If you boast God on your side.

Rules without any exceptions
Are basically written for saps.
Truth depends on deception.
Another commandment perhaps?

One fact is undoubtedly certain
If you must call Moses a saint.
You view him through a gauze curtain
And persist on seeing what ain't.

That, and, however you pose it
If you still deny Moses a sinner,
History, as any fool knows it,
Is written, in fact, by the winner.

Mother Gideon

Once, my god, we allow for accusations
    Watch out for things female and dirt brown,
The terror stance that ducks us under bridges,
    Puffing and white with swollen feet.
The pipewife, Mother Gideon, in my nightmare
    Cabbaging her way through forests
Grimly held her torch and wolf for me.
    What of what she spies infuriates her face?
It's the truancy she hates, she do,
    Your failure as a member to erect
Underneath your braided spread. She looks.
    You have spread out all your comic books.
With a vicious pointed stick accusing
    She has waited for a boy who died.
Or so she said, moving toward your bed.
    Isengrim the wolf snaps terrified.
She wore a stocking cap of medieval brown,
    Burrowing toward you in her circus clothes.

Hideously, she was what most you feared
   For accusing her of what you felt
By dreaming of a mother with a wolf
   Who seemed about to kill you
In the way people said you were born.

Mrs. Mixter

"And what judgment would step from this to this?"

— Hamlet

"She's really not a bad sort,"
 Someone who knew her once said,
"And yet" (a pause for this report)
"Married four times!"
 It left a vivid picture in my head.
 The beautiful is *one,*
 Presents itself as unity,
 Fullness, not community,
 Chooses, is, has done.
 The ugly is multiple. Life
 Nourishes the whole,
 As a husband should a wife;
 Oneness is the beauty of the soul.

Why speak of parts that never fit,
Messiness as neatness?
Not divided, separate, or split,
Beauty is completeness.
Ugliness betrays degrees.
If the ugly were complete
(The way soul and body meet)
Without a trace of beauty,
It would for that very reason
— by definition and by duty —
Cease to be ugly, discrete,
To itself a treason:
A woman who weds once,
And not in every season.

Mussolini

"The mob loves strong men. The mob is a woman."
—Benito Mussolini

You loved to strut,
Made your buttocks even wag,
Though you stood no more than 5'6"
Searching the crowd,
Looking for a girl to shag.
They were one and the same,
You say, easy to conquer,
Being easy to sway.
You shaved your head
To look like Caesar,
Saw yourself above the Pope.
But was that really you?
When you curled your lip,
Wooing women to your bed,
Scowling, head flung back,
Didn't that aloofness
Indicate far less cunning
Than a low IQ?
Braced on your feet,
Hands on your hips,
Standing in your scarlet Alfa,
Romeo, your peasant face
Mahogany dark, livid lips,
Bulbous with a cretin's eyes,
Your lantern jaw thrust out,
Completing a lump,
Half provolone, half *melanzana*,
Who but a woman
Could fall for that?
But if what makes a mob
Makes a woman, as you say,
Women give tit for tat.
So why expect less passion
From those harpies, moulinyan,
Who stung you up like a ragusano
In that piazza in Milan?

And when lifting up their skirts
They urinated on your upturned face,
Which they squatted just above,
Why bother to deny,
With what you know of mobs
And how they're just
Like women
It had less to do with love?

The Night of the Niflheim Dwarfs

for Steven Moore

There were cobblers, cocktails, white cups, and flips
    Neguses, nectars, and wet juleps.
And out danced the dwarfs in a dance so true.
      O, that night on the sward the sward was blue,
      For blue is the sward at night.

There were sangarees, nectars, shrubs, and slings,
    Smashes, catawbas, and Bimbo stings,
Around hopped the dwarfs in their nighties new.
      O, that night on the sward the sward was blue,
      For blue is the sward at night.

There were liquors, absinthes, and blood red ports,
    Toddies, mulls, and arrack orts,
Through their magic cheeks the dwarfs then blew.
      O, that night on the sward the sward was blue,
      For blue is the sward at night.

There were brandies, drams and sputtering nogs,
    Juniper gins and buttered grogs,
From the fire leaped a girl of heavenly hue!
      O, that night on the sward the sward was blue,
      For blue is the sward at night.

There were ching-chings, malts, and spiced radish ales,
    Fog-cutters, whiskeys, and bottled pales.
Then up on one dwarf their black crow flew.
      O, that night on the sward the sward was blue,
      For blue is the sward at night.

There were bishops, filled tumblers, and bitters queer,
    Mother Shiptons and bumbable beer,
"Marry her! Marry her!" the cruel bird crew.
      O, that night on the sward the sward was blue,
      For blue is the sward at night.

There were punches, brown mums, and bottle jack,
    Antique barley wine and poker-hot sack,
But what the dwarfs wanted the girl would not do.
      O, that night on the sward the sward was blue,
      For blue is the sward at night.

There were claret, grappa, flosters, and sops,
    Furious cognacs and worts with hops.
The dwarfs in a cluster all angry grew.
      O, that night on the sward the sward was blue,
      For blue is the sward at night.

There were parries, caudles, and cider nips,
    Black-stripe mixtures and calabash sips.
As the girl screamed in pain the dwarfs screamed, too.
      O, that night on the sward the sward was blue,
      For blue is the sward at night.

There were sifters, moonshines, and muscat casks,
    Aqua composita and barleycorn flasks,
The rejected dwarf's eyes grew scarlet with rue.
      O, that night on the sward the sward was blue,
      For blue is the sward at night.

There were meads, tall bourbons, sherries, and hock,
    Pitches, rosins, and murderous bock.
Then flashed a knife which one them drew.
      O, that night on the sward the sward was blue,
      For blue is the sward at night.

There were squashes, tokays, and mystic stouts,
 Spirits of wormwood and devil-get-outs,
Their funeral grins shone through the night dew.
 O, that night on the sward the sward was blue,
 For blue is the sward at night.

Padre Todopoderoso

I am fat with vision,
A cleric transubstantiating hosts
With a *hoc* and a *poc*.

My creed is all things
Are to be seen to be understood
To be known, Scotus,

To be good. *Creador*
Del Cielo y de la tierra! Ink's a drug.
I have titquills, paper, hands

Strong as a fruit tramp's
To wield a pen to circumscribe
The fat round wholeness

Of the vast compossible.
Big jumanna! No fat blue marble
Is more real than dreams

And I am sitting one off
You at dinner, Sleepy and Dumbo,
Taking notes. Wake up!

Part of Loving's Leaving

for Patricia Scoppa

Part of loving's leaving,
Just as part of leaving's love;
For lovers part, it's right.
What's left is happening
Beyond belief or out of sight,
And yet between the loving:
The lover's word's parole,
A predictable control
That makes love's leaving
Loving just the same,
To word itself apart
Softly as a candle weaving
Carbon from a flame.
But know departure when it's there,
For up and down and north and south
And logically is built the stair;
The mystery that swings a door
Makes loving far or leaving near.
Yet words also mean parole;
Parole means that there's more
Of words, like flames
Within a burning coal.
We loving leave and leaving love;
Hello then, as it must,
Eventually becomes good-bye;
The harmony of fire and smoke
That joins the earth to sky.
There's down below and up above,
For part of loving's leaving,
Just as part of leaving's love.

Patriotic Bigots

The racist, bigoted, anti-Catholic nativist 'Know Nothing'
Party, an oath-bound secret society created in New York
City in 1849, was originally called the Order of the Star
Spangled Banner (OSSB).

Celebrate, America, and crow.
You've never been cursed
With being bombed
Or seen planes flying low.
I love the way big guys with guts
Talking in the post office,
Their faces like fists,
  Cry, "We'll kick their butts."
"Bomb Baghdad,"
  Sing the jingoists,
"Put it to the rack!"
  Where did you ever see more
  Of nothing?
  The empty desert
  Isn't only in Iraq.

Yellow-ribbon wearers
Approve as kin do kin
The flag fetishist
With his patriotic pin
  Prominent upon his dress
"They don't value life as
  we do," said fat Marlin Fitzwater,
  speaking to the press.
"Bomb the A-rabs,"
  Sing the jingoists,
"Scorch the bastards black!"
  Where did you ever see more
  Of nothing?
  The desert
  Isn't only in Iraq.

Passacaglia for an Italian Witch

For Camille

"I don't *do* blurbs!" you screech,
  howling, wagging your short dark arms,
  like some mad *spaventapasseri*.

Who the fuck are you, zoticona,
  strega with murderous mouth and mustache,
  ragout of draggled ideas,

not to crow or cack or comment
when that's all, mortrewer of quips and quotes,
you're known for ever having done?

What's a carping critic but blather,
boustrophedon, banter, bullshit, total blab?
Your rage is only sad flirtation.

Who more bitter than a low-bred crone
writing words like plaiting rotten straw
claiming it for either gold or art?

You're no more after privacy,
vecchiacchia, then your fog-horning fancies
cry out to us to be ignored.

It's only in your ratty reveries,
in the muttering insistence of your mind
you're as important as your acolytes,

all five or six or so of them,
laughably insist you must insist you are,
middle-aged culture-humper!

What hideola of a critic with her bags
of half-assed hoodoo can't be counted on for blurbs?
Aren't blurbs all you fucking do?

Pathology of War

Proclaim this, you people among the nations, "Sanctify war!"

—Joel 3:9

I have a certain sympathy with war,
it so apes the gait and bearing of the soul.
Murder fighting mercy is a kind of law.

The longing need to love that keeps us whole
also summons what it cannot abide,
for what we fear it from a part of manhood stole.

We fight to prove that we refuse to hide
the dog in us that gentleness rubs raw,
lest what or whom we kiss the killer might deride.

To Henry D. Thoreau

Peasant Festival

"The Middle Ages were run by and for adolescents."
— Arnold J. Toynbee

In memory of Pieter Bruegel the Elder

All the chunky little men turn red as we catch them before the act of ruin.
And as the melodies play on reeds, the huffing red men hop alive for us,
ninnies in fat hats and grins, running hither and yon with piles of cake.
Medieval towns are full of woody halls, as breakfast girls in blue sailed in
with wet red meats, bread, grapes, eggs in sweaty piles, frothy yards of beer.
Little kids in pie-wide hats run around in crazy circles goosing cats, and
old men fart and holy nuns walk by as pryncocks boys with poop and glee
make themselves so windy and so round that when they yell from faces
it comes across as lusty song. We thrill to find them, knowing well the men
of red who rumple-rut like goats to tinny bells and beefy-shaped violas
live in a present they never betrayed by looking at the past or the future.

I think about the hedge priests and their buzzardry, the silly puffy trolls
and trouncing elves who skip about on Whitsun through forests green
and barge into their high-kicking oyster wenches and globe-titted wives
and bouncing gammers and tongue them who run silly through the snow
in the pudding of their socks, celebrating dugs, mammaries, and paps
that drive them crazy with shapeliness. These are the chunky dancing men,
the tubby sons of square-thumbed grannies, the dirty shitter-louts and
able thumpers, bold as ax-headed woodmen with bulging codpieces,
brothers in the knolls of Flander, great gross heavy-waisted baronbums
who rise at night to gnaw the brains of sleeping cows, to moon-yowl,
and hop the ha-has and hit with slingshots birds and fall on their faces
and sleep on hair pelts or on the dewy swards and meadows of green.
They never jam their frothy pewter pints on table-wood until they laugh
with Jesus, hard, with prickling jokes and huge. Bells spoke to them,
but hopping was the game, to trilling notes, to silly yelling into winds,
in baggy pants and greasy caps. After the chunky men turned red, we
have the luck to see them glad, briefly, before we catch them ruined.

Phantom of Werther

The question we ask of death is a fair question.
                    —Theroux, in drink

With his pistols
Werther must have wondered,
Having just been spurned,
If water thrown on fire
Isn't firstly burned;
And faced with that
Craziest of crazy dooms
Which of which
Initially consumes.

Wally Screechbald, the Traveler

"Never go on trips with anyone you do not love"
— Ernest Hemingway

He traveled to parts where the quechee bird skrawked.
where the Zulu drank *maas* and Joe Chinaman hocked,

to the far Andaman Sea where green turtles spawned
and to the far furthest reaches at the back of beyond.

He voyaged wide and alone, for his favorite mate
was himself, half second-fiddle, the other half date.

On tip-toe and stridently he peered at the world
to see who, where, how, and just what unfurled.

Travelers mainly return with notes that they jot
but Wally's intent was to write more than a lot

and be famous for *books* on how Patagonians kiss
how Greeks flip komboloi and orangutangs piss,

say how Pygmies fart, where anthropophagi dwell,
and how every single Afghani is as lazy as hell.

Wally doggedly wrote with the bit in his teeth
as page after page of screed gave endless relief

with volumes he offered the middle-brow reader
punched out with the zeal of a cattle stampeder.

After a life of such effort, what could go wrong?
An old vaudeville adage says sing but not long.

He traveled on trains, buses, and kayaks and such,
but like poor Arnold Bennett he wrote far too much.

The moral? Next take a mate on a typical trip
and frankly someone who is worldly and hip

and dares to suggest you, without seeming rude,
give some serious thought to a brief interlude

between published books, your profile to soften
— face it, no real writer is interesting that often!

We all love ourselves but to truly break through
when you pick that companion *don't make it you!*

Pimp

As a literary agent
you hustle books like flesh,
a working burke for money,
an English snob in a coat,
2 percent castle, 98 moat.

The difference between
the preening you and a pimp,
since both of you are frauds,
when the arithmetic is done,
is simple: there is none.

Poem for a Christening

The new soft bells tune in anew
Your child, a yawn and able arms,
To pass a dream,
The whole earth through:
Let the water be as much a kiss
As blessing;
The whispered prayers the lute
Which brings to consciousness
The loves and yes
We have, we've had;
And the salt reminder that a dream,
Small Tarquin,
Is often lost, is often sad.
So, if and when you're far from home,
Unfold, re-read,

And try to understand
The whole earth through
The meaning of
The bells and prayers and salt
And find again
In this poem I wrote for you.

A Poem in Which is a Celebration by Negation Or, a Repartee on Jeopardy

If on a friend's bookshelf
You cannot find Joyce or Sterne
Cervantes, Rabelais, or Burton,

You are in danger, face the fact,
So kick him first or punch him hard
And from him hide behind a curtain.

Yale University

Look down, Elihu, we're all right,
still echoes your boola blue chorus:
faculty women have faces like night,
professors go mincing like florists,
padlocks on buildings, empty graces,
shallow youth with missing faces.
The colleges rise like broken rocks.
Its stone like frozen sleet is cold.
The tower thrust of Harkness mocks
the eunuchs who in classrooms old
twist literature of noble breadth
into verbal games, like living death.
I pray heaven's azure is a different hue
than Yale's, asphyxiation's ghastly blue.

Transkei Beauty

No white woman and no African girl
who has grown up in town walks as those country women do
    beyond the Kei. The Pondo girls

    burnish the wind shinily black
as they walk the dry roads, clicking turquoise and red beads
    on their breasts, clad in layers

    of rainbow-hued clothing surmounted
by the heavy patterned blankets round their strong shoulders,
    each with her own white unique

    knotted turban headscarf. They walk
slowly and deliberately through fair weather or madly foul,
    as though made of something denser

    than normal flesh. Sauntering belies
their measured pace, part stroll, part amble, a meandering
    wander, with something of drift.

    The pert progressive pace and the
large amount of physical space they can occupy despite not
    being of great stature amazes.

    However much of a hurry you are in,
forget the idea of overtaking them, so you may as well
    slow down to their dark speed,

    if the word speed at all applies.
There are aeons of experience and a long, long history
    in that steady purposeful walk.

    Had perchance Virgil also seen it
when, insightfully as was his gift, he distinguished a goddess
    from a woman by her walk?

Muizenberg, South Africa

August 2013

The Raven

(A parody written as a requirement for election to the
distinguished Raven Society at the University of Virginia, 1967)

Twice within the week so given, to this assignment was I driven,
    To fulfill my obligation to a curious *per favor*.
I was forced, despite resistance, with a curious insistence,
    Not at all unlike persistence, a persistence I deplore.
  "Write a parody," they muttered, "with some substance, that's your chore."
  Nothing more was added, and I murmured what a bore.

Now you may think it craven that I want to be a Raven,
    But a member of the working class I've always been.
So with little exhortation, and as little information
    To inform this incantation, I began my recitation
Like the Jingle Man who did it way back when.
    And though the people laughed, I didn't care a yen.

There seemed no need for muses or any of the magic juices
    Which the poet sometimes needs to make him budge.
Everything was effervescence, a massive bundle of excrescence,
    But my lack of phosphorescence and its insistent presence
Made me seem, like Poe, a poet of sheer fudge.
    I ran madly towards Parnassus, but found I had to trudge.

My lines bunched like tangled rigging, me a madman madly digging,
    Talking, mocking, wigging, jigging
In a strangely private, no way to describe it kind of semaphore,
    But I continued at my scribbling, driven like a rival sibling,
Reading back my words of rant and lexic quibbling
    As my wretched poem did everything but march up to the fore.

A verb, a noun, a bit of chatter, nothing, nothing seemed to matter,
    For in my poem the endless clatter just became a thrum.
There was no real epiphany or remotely good polyphony,
    Only sheer immunodeficiency, a failure of proficiency
    In a lyric not a single creature could ever hum or strum,
    Which is sadly how you tell a poet from a bum.

So here I sit above my silly verses with a maximum of curses,
    Suffering reverses I never thought I'd know.
And somehow it's demeaning to try to impose meaning
    While I sit here keening on a fowl so overweening
That I find it nothing but a foe, a silent upstart crow.
    Whose baleful shadow only brings me low.

The nightingale of Keats was the greatest of his feats,
    And for Shelley's noble skylark every heart has stirred.
We have praise unapologetic for Yeats's golden bird magnetic
    But what strange brand of emetic did Poe use in his aesthetic
That leaves me a moron groping in these verses so absurd
    To conjure up but one poetic word?

The waterfowl of Bryant was a perfect little client,
    And the albatross defiant came on the scene as something new.
But Edgar's bird cannot hold a smidgeon to Coleridge's pigeon
    Or that ferocious, precocious, grandiocious symbol of religion
That Father Gerry Hopkins sent up in the blue.
    For these, ah these, yes these are all too few.

Sorrento has its hoary doves and they fly so high above,
    And Noah with increase doubtless loved his bird of peace.
But to make a sweet mosaic on a bird so damned prosaic
With a face so pharisaic is like singing of Passaic
    And that unprepossessing city's flocks of oily geese.
Oh, that I might have legitimate release!

Our feathered fiends are nice, for eating they suffice,
    On Thanksgiving, with some spice, they'll get the nod.
But should not some propriety in this august society
    Allow for sheer variety and far less contrariety
To hand me next a topic with more justifiable reward
    And make the subject matter—God?

Reveries of Children Dying;
or,
Some Recollections after Hypnosis

I poked about for friends in winter,
   was blinded in my pajamas by the moon-man,
blinked lucky at the icicles,
   jagged and Norwegian like skis.

The carnival wheel had sparks along
   its cutting edge, and blue-honed gears:
midgets leaped for their private toys,
   like fireworks ignited from the ground.

Zap was the noise of my fist in the chocolate box,
   done in daisies like my clown hat.
It is the wet mouth of the trumpet, we remember,
   and the arrowhead of doughnut in the drawer.

Was I different to expect the story of a cow forever?
   The rubber in my shoes began to sicken me,
like the awfully funny print of Joseph in his coat,
   giggled off by his brothers for a hole.

There are the cracked and pointing shoes, out,
beneath my room, smelling like iodine marks.
   I dreamt of jelly baskets full of threads and needles,
the hint of a French horn down the street.

It was as much my roasting oatmeal bowls, piping,
   as the endless pocketful of snow,
and the misery cones I nibbled in the park,
   that gladdened me beyond measure in my chair.

We all have dreams the mild susurrus of the babies,
   in inchlings placed in rows like blackboard chalk,
their talcum fumes too, and the lilac of our teacher
   who took attendance in the darts of rain.

Silent and foxy but mild, we spilled onto the floor
    each peg of language; my socks were green that day,
when I thought in the mirror: was it for me to march
    into the kitchen and demand a cookie?

I received my red and orange fife for Christmas,
    the fat pencil I was bound to give away.
Laughing, I tugged madly at the bowl of plastic fruit
    and imaginatively left for the stairs.

We hold our breath and try with delicacy to touch
    our fathers, there in shouts and hair,
eating paltry lunches at the foot of cellars.
    I loved the way I held his hand by the finger.

I walked on treetops fashioned from my dreams,
    as real as most of them promised to become.
Every night through starlit eyes I saw,
    obedient to me, my bath, and my bready mother.

Then my pastel book I knew, and Kristina,
    dimpled in her leggings and her gold,
who walked me through the windmill on the hill,
    and never startled at my footsteps.

No one seemed home when I had my nickel-plated dimes,
    the counting silver on the gum-colored magazines.
I watched for treasures in the meadow
    and was more than glad with my crunch bars, and my soup.

A muffled shout from the pantry made me stop
immediately;
    sighing in my flannel shirt my giggling friend
beeped a nice hello, proving there was no dead child
    lying amoung the spices and the recipes.

First the penny on the counter, then the finger
    pointing through the iridescent glass.
We hear the door slam, but with our courage,
    march out with clucks while holding our sweet ribs.

It can't be called a gasp, but rather gasping:
    the pink of the nursery diminishes the squeak
of terror, the wide-mouthed rage we have,
    too small, in knickers, as we look ahead.

Romard

What, sculptor, do you see
Within what's missing that
You have to mold to make,
Shaping thin from fat?

How does the hammer arm
Not lose the tender touch
In what it takes from life
To give to art so much?

Which transfigures better
Out of pain coming twice,
Adding, subtracting,
Chiseling fire, cutting ice?

Why is the fragile soul,
Burnt like molten steel,
Ignored by critics
In what it dares reveal?

Where goes the self,
Relieved of what it feels,
Giving to the idle metal what
From the heart it steals?

Who is that strange enigma
Given the gift to make,
Artist consumed with fire
Or martyr burned at the stake?

Samoan Brother

You might think perhaps that a bully,
not having grace, rising in his cockpit of bombast and fat
like some tempestuous conductor with his haystack hair
to write you nasty letters, is not sentimental.
But no: he is a hog of tears and flowers
For his daughter, shallow wife, an aria or two,
views of old Samoa, and is easily forgetful
at just such times and not regretful—
or so is my surmise—when not punching someone blue
or dreaming to, he feels good enough to eat
something of his size.

Sarcastic Middle-aged Women

Don't they find their faces hatchets?
Are clawing and pawing all they know,
Sharp-elbowed cunts all they ever want to be?
Have they ever read a single book,
Prayed with their minds, knelt on stone
For no one but God above to see?
What frost is colder than their looks?
Are the muscles used to sing
The same used by women to give birth?
I only wonder why neither are popular
Among these pants-wearing tarts I know
With mustaches and mouths like chainsaws
Muttering through their focus and cigars,
"I love to break and tear. Beware!"

Six Limericks

When Charlene Pigg reads the news?
Man, it's Henry Mancini on blues.
    I don't mean to be harsh
    but call Jordan Marsh
and find work for her fitting shoes.

You want a conception of dumb?
Take a pen the size of your thumb.
　　Charlene's brain is as thin
　　as a refill put in
with some added leeway to strum.

Charlene? A girl with an attitude,
not the slightest conception of gratitude.
　　But think of the strain
　　of having a brain
beta-blocked with her kind of fatitude.

Let's buy Charlene a strong anorak
to parade in faraway Kodiak
　　or cold Lackawanna
　　with a helmet-cam on her
or the stews of beleaguered Iraq.

For Charlene's replacement we choose
Anyone—the station can't lose.
　　Just get a droolie
　　to sit on a stoolie
and drawl, "This is the 10 o'clock news."

You want to buy Charlene a lariat,
A ring, say, some boots, or a chariot?
　　Mail the woman the gift
　　and you start a rift;
Your ass is intended to carry it.

Sneezes

Most compound consonantal sounds,
odd to the eyes because taken from the Greek,
we legitimately try to avoid on the grounds
comprehending them takes more than a week.

Cnidoblast, Ptychodera, Bdellostoma,
Mnemotechnic, Xylem, Ctenophora

To pronounce such words next you are led,
with a nose that twitches as if smelling fescue,
and though you manage to get the word said,
the corresponding response is "God bless you!"

Acanthobdella, Gnathostomatoa, Psammobatis,
Cnemial, Zygaena, Pneumatophore

Snobbish Women at McDonald's

But you wouldn't be seen there, Dale.
Where swaggarts eat? Where comedy is food?
Where jingles jangle your nerves?

Not for you the common muttwich, reeking
of heat spattering fat, Happy Meals for goofballs
nauseous wafts of fracedinous meats.

Ronald looks insane, for one thing.
It's not so much that you in your elite disdain
are mortified with all your pride

cartoons have become American gods.
You don't want it known your mouth is wide,
you're urgent, resigned to get in line.

Little kids buried under snowfalls
of hot fries, wolfing mouthfeel, are too common
with their shouting to be loved.

You have no weakness for curious episodes,
Miss Glass-ass. No backyard vegetables for you.
You won't eat with Bedouins, lesser breeds

of finch, smouts with mustard on their noses.
You want dignity, not chubby fingers arrayed around
something round and wet like waferbeef.

Down with Tuna Colorado, hot as heated hands
and smelling like the dump! Vile untouchables in
booths! Suricates munching ghost crabs!

How priggishly you turned aside
the way royalty in red rouge would sniff at oranges
processing among the benighted.

Let them pronounce ketchup in Wyoming.
You choose never to appear hearty for anything you eat.
A whopper through a window in a wagging fist

mocks you like a motley clown reminds you
with his foppish foolery and frock only of yourself
howling to a waiter for another drink,

clashes with your choosy charm. Your hair.
You want rich décor and linen tablecloths and violins,
opera-length pearls, a curving stair,

a dunce to dance attendance on your needs,
celebutantes, posh friends, walletfuls of funshine,
like movie stars in silver ogled from afar

in limousines coursing through the night
through streets of an expensive dark to Rollo's
for champagne and salmon caviar.

These blue potatoes are not *pommes
de terre dauphinoises,* nor a richly colored Merlot
that paper-cup of fizzing piss.

Attitudes can thrive only for a time.
Your insulting scream for us both to eat hot death
is cruel to all crumb-bummery,

and fortune can reverse. Things change.
When, poor ditchwitch, cruel fate being what it is,
you should begin to fail, to roam about,

muttering on roads in your aluminum hat
and ripped old sneakers' or shoeboxes for shoes,
looking for a dog to greet,

fummaging through dirty barrels
for a rusk, no longer golden, your arches fallen,
remember well the food you snubbed.

The Spittoon Has Gone Ceramic

"I like to think how easily Nature will absorb London as
she absorbed the mastodon, setting her spiders to spin
the winding sheet and her worms to fill in the graves, and
her grass to cover it pitifully up, adding flowers — as an
unknown hand added them to the grave of Nero."
                                —Edward Thomas, *The South Country*

The spittoon has gone ceramic,
The parade ground mossy.
Once, in a mid-afternoon, I thought
We know our bargains.

There's a glimp in the tear,
A crimp in my shin; I hurt
For the huge afternoons
When packs of flowers were laid at my door.

Nowhere is the lovely bassoon
That etched out funny notes at me.
The tumbling kids of my mother
Now square themselves in boxes.

In front of me my friends, the kids,
Jam their thumbs past their teeth,
And question each moment of transfiguration.
Swivel-eyed, they beware of things.

And so as I brush memories from the corner
Of my head, wait pleasantly for the needle
To slip into the groove, I fright at the
Lost big things that have made me turn on my heel.

It does no one good to fill up on bread
When the Hallowe'en children ask for meals,
Nor can one feed lovely little shadows
That tattoo glee-steps on your front door.

But when did I deny, though this was fleeting,
That this was love?
I tune my ears willingly to the corduroyed
Boy ready with his trumpet for me.

And though standing like a blue doll in my room
For the smacky knocks for candy
I cannot forget: remember my own
Thatching hair and wide wide glimpse.

Oh yes, I have danced on the stones;
I have bounced into the bright water of the sea.
But still I watch out for myself in the rain
And wait for the link between world and toy.

The spittoon has gone ceramic,
The parade ground mossy.
Once, in the a midafternoon, I thought
We knew our bargains.

The Star-Spangled Banner

The choral group from Somerville
Swaying from side to side?
The goon from the local Moose lodge
Who steps to the mike in one stride?
Irish tenors, young starlets,
DJs who claim they can sing?
On a bet from the bar the moron

Who thought he'd give it a fling?
Those VFW fascists,
Mainstays of the Sunday School Choir,
Painfully sucking in air
Crazily breathing out fire?
Miss Muttjack who suddenly came to
The difficult "rockets' red glare"
And reddened just like the rockets
And virtually tore out her hair?
The Italian boy whose accordion
Wheezed like the doors of a bus?
Montes parturient;
Nascetur ridiculus mus.
The opera singer from Eboli
With pesto sauce on his breath
Made me prefer to living
An instantaneous death.
The chubby lady who howled it
Spotlit on an ice-cold rink
Who snatched at the hem of her dress
That might have been cut from zinc?
(The echo alone of her voices
As she practiced some in the hall
Sounded to me like a gang-bang
In the parking lot of a mall.)
The Negro hipster was charming
Who did it in flatted thirds,
Though he sang the "twilight's *glass* gleaming,"
And the haircut from local radio
Quickly forgot the words.
Look, no one can do the Anthem,
Whether singing it soft or loud;
A law should be passed in America:
No one should be allowed!
I'll gladly abridge one freedom
Despite what our forefathers say;
The "Land of the freeee," forget it.
And the "hooome of the braa-aave"?
No way.

Strange in My Hencoop

Strange in my hencoop
Was the frost that killed.
I waited all alive as usual
Braving off in mittens all the cold—
Translations of my body
White now in the frost.
Three friends also were alive,
Not as wordy but as nice;
They'd come to hammer on the breaded screen
To tell me of the frost,
Warning as they should
To stamp freely in the cold.
(Once, we jumped on hens.)
It had been warm once;
We had had the fun warmth brings
The days when foolhood was acceptable
As awful chickens,
Rotten in their offal, in their skulls
As blue and light as ounces.
We weren't so frost-faced then,
But positive as music in our trousers,
Firm as decency, alive as coals,
And clever in our faces, then.
We wasted time with easy persecutions,
Glad as girls with our advantage
As we stoned the chickens
And pulverized the hens,
Sticking with a passion we would never
Ever understand
Golden pins into brainless hens
Prosperity, however, freezes;
One must know his hencoop,
Surely, to make advantage work.
I wait in the ice of my hencoop,
Feel with gloom the icy nettles
Underneath my boots,
And wait for friends, both thin and jeweled,
Deliberate as frozen,
Exclusive as I'm chilled,

Jumping to the fence with my hands,
My eyes as wide as doors, and scared,
Pouncing now on feathers and on blood.
There are no chickens now,
For they're all dead
And beaten into dust where
Strange in my hencoop
Was the frost that killed.

A Philosopher Questions Night-Blooming Cereus

White is a dissembling color, strength
never foolproof or as stalwart as a cactus also is not.
Don't be fooled by a mock orchid.

The night-blooming cereus, queen of night,
is large but opens only once, in darkness, and then it wilts
and dies, never letting the light of day

into its bosom. It is believed the wishes
of those who pray to God while the flower is blooming
will be fulfilled. Tears run down by sides

of the eyes of everyone whose fond hopes
are so often dashed in the terrifying desert of this world.
How the cereus resembles a dead bush,

inconspicuous, so rarely seen in the wild
by anyone but for one midsummer's night each year,
when it opens briefly, to close forever

with the first rays of the morning sun,
and yet for that it is exquisitely scented unlike eyebright,
japonica, red peonies, or the gentian,

that beautiful wild flower of autumn.
Who can find the flower to get any prayer in on time
to ask the living God who sends us

the paradox of a lovely white flower
born as it dies, hot tears, desert flats, perfumelessness,
   the brevity of beauty, dead bushes,

   shrubs like creosote, night itself,
indeed this world so often filled with forlorn hope
   why, why, why, why, why, why?

Tammy Wynette Waves to the Rabble

I'll never forget,
Your waving at me from the stage
One hot July night
At the Barnstable County Fair.
So I forgive you your many husbands,
Don Chapel, Georges Jones, and Richie,
Chaw-chewing Euple Byrd,
All those flings with other men,
You were desperate and hurt:
Why else would a woman take up with Burt?
You needed love, like as not,
Ever since you stole your first kiss
With A. G. Stepp
When you were only thirteen years old
(What I was is not what I am)
In the balcony of the movie
Thee-ay-ter in Red Bay, Alabam.
Think of the pain of this country queen!
Gallbladder surgery, electric shock,
Kidney infections, a ruptured spleen.
The lurid locutions of trouble and strife
Echo Ralph Edwards on *This Is Your Life*.
How many pregnancies? Beatings, as well.
Then headlines! Abduction! Another seduction?
You're given up for lost! *She's dead!*
But then you appear —
Who can explain it, no motive was clear.
("Try six kids and a country career!"
The Nashville cynics said.)

But music's about those you make glad.
There's Aunt Princie Hambly, loyal and true,
Uncle Harrod, and Hollice, your dad.
After all, it's the family that counts
And multiple marriages needn't be sad;
Your mom—Ms. Mildred Faye Russell Lee Pugh!
That lonely feeling? When few seem to care?
Didn't I feel it myself,
Walking home all alone
From the Barnstable County Fair?
Hey, Tammy, you do what you can—
You stood what you could,
Even if not by your man.

Thanks for the Memory

Thanks for the memory
Of New Jersey's lovely shores
Moorestown and its bores
The piano bits you tried to play but buggered up the scores
How lovely it was!
Thanks for the memory
Of rainy afternoons
Meals with dirty spoons
Talk with you that seemed less eloquent than Icelandic runes
How lovely it was!
Many's the time you got weepy
Over your father's odd life
Your mother's sexual strife
No eschewing their wrongdoing.
And thanks for the memory
Of your brother's pompous pride
Which no one could abide
Mother Teresa would have killed him
But I took it all in stride
So thank you so much!

Thanks for the memory
Of humor not too swift
Not your biggest gift
Asking stories be repeated to which you never got the drift
How lovely it was!
Thanks for the memory
Your mathematic skill
Rarely fit the bill
But if murder's ever called for it's a perfect way to kill
How lovely it was!
Your friends I never met
Not a matter for regret
I thought caring partly sharing
But thanks for the memory
And when you got the blues
Calling me became you ruse
Yet I've had fortune cookies
With more fascinating news
I thank you so much!

Thanks for the memory
Of always being late
Your dresses out-of-date
The company you work for, the biggest polluter in the state.
How lovely it was!
Thanks for the memory
Of meals you tried to cook
Even following a book
That cassoulet you turned out tasted like burnt rook
How lovely it was!
The sports you couldn't do
Set your jaw with bitter rue
After a year I couldn't care
Yet thanks for the memory
Of every mousy curl
Skin that felt like burl
I swear I could have whittled
A more congenial girl
But thank you so much!

(With thanks to the Paramount Music Corp. and acknowledgment of the original version, words and music by Leo Robin and Ralph Rainger © 1937.)

Three Questions

Why do grebes with a clutch
who ask nothing of Tibet
feed their young with feathers?
Even pundits cannot say.

Who's to blame when empty
they should fall from the sky
when they feed on what they fly —
the grebes with a clutch,

the pundits who can't say,
or something in or of the sky
that makes them fly and fall,
from feathers they weren't fed?

Tiresias in Mushroom Town

"The Honourable Stephen Tennant arrived in an electric
brougham wearing a football jersey and earrings."
—William Hickey, *Daily Express (1927)*

We all have the chances
our centuries give;
we meet with its old men and dogs,
and the days we now see
the women are fee,
and the men go forth in their gowns.
In the beautiful, beautiful mushroom towns,
In the beautiful mushroom towns.
We inherit with glimpses
surrounding modes,

the habits of our time are safe,
girls waddle to work,
with a masculine shirk,
the sweet boys continue their rounds.
In the beautiful, beautiful mushroom towns,
In the beautiful mushroom towns.

We stand mute and accept
the available times,
never letting the question arise:
Is a man somehow less,
if he's wearing a dress,
or weeping when watching a clown,
In the beautiful, beautiful mushroom towns,
In the beautiful mushroom towns.

To Sarah

Because your eyes light up what in
my life makes spring of what's begun
the warmth you give creates a dream within
and so till now I have not seen the sun.

Because that light like sun creates in bliss
a passion warmest seasons fail to bring
it wakens dreams where lovers always kiss
and so till now I have not seen the spring.

To the Eight American Women Soldiers Slain in Vietnam

How you went involves
No longer why you came,
But that you did,
Ten thousand strong,
And by those dying men
Who lost their lives

You added yours.
There were eight of you.
A memorial now stands
Along the Washington mall,
Name upon numberless name.
A sadness comes in reading
Anyone's name on a wall.
A sharper pain is felt
Among them finding you.
Can anyone explain?
Could it be that you so few
Who were so brave
Intensify the pain?

For Eleanor Alexander
Pamela Donovan
Carol Drazba
Annie Graham
Elizabeth Jones
Mary Klinker
Sharon Lane
Hedwig Orlowski

Turkana Girl

Sweet black pharaoh,
With your finely
Chiseled face
And graceful nose
Flatly shaped
For looking down,
Milk your camels
In Nadikam
Without a sound.
In moonlight
Toying slyly with your beads,
Flirting with me
Up and down
You slide your hand

Along their leads.
I dream of you
Moaning *ululu, ululu.*
Whip me with your rat-tail hair,
Goddess, dressed, unlike you,
Naked, hot as Kenya,
Open legs in passion,
With the mixture of fat
And black earth
Out of which
Girl of the dark
I choose to think
That you, like
The shadows of
Your dreams,
Are fashioned.

TV News in America

"An empty cab pulled up in front of 10 Downing Street and
   out stepped Clement Atlee."

—Winston Churchill

Don't be fooled:
The trick is
To tell them
What you've told them
And then to show them
What they have to see
To be told.
("He just ran for a touchdown,"
Howard Cosell said,
Who looks like an insect
With earphones on this head,
But that handoff, that long run,
Hadn't we just seen
The *ana* and *katabasis*
In the picture on the screen?)
Stupid is in,

Not out,
Dollars in accounts
Receivable, no doubt.
War is ratings,
(Not on the battlefield)
Emotions only aped.
Sex, death, violence.
("How did you feel
When your daughter was raped?")
That bite, maybe we can
Add an ad, you know
To show with it?
Go with it.

Vinyl Junkie

What did
Gaynel Hodge and the Turks
Who sang "Fathertime" (Keen)
So great
Know in 1958
That made them so fine?
Or the Pearls
With "Jungle Bunny" (Dooto)
Back in 1959?
The Five Thrills on Parrot,
The Clovers on Atlantic,
First gave me a picture
Of white girls frantic.
What first moved my soul?
A dance, a deck of smokes,
The Harptones'
"Sunday Kind of Love" (Bruce),
My hair in a roll.
The Olympics, the Penguins,
The Acrobatics,
Little Augie Austin and the Chromatics,
Chubby and the Turnpikes,
What satisfaction!

Throw in Zodiac Mindwarp
And the Love Reaction.
I want you to know
For what you went through,
Practicing wage slaves,
Old auditoriums, drafty halls,
Broken contracts, unanswered calls
To teach me
Love was bop,
You reached me.
Doo wop.

White Kidneys

What does my wanting to be
like someone — anyone —
tell me about my desire?

I've dreamt of you as if
you were — somehow —
a being somewhat higher.

By telling myself the truth
do I grow — like you —
or condemn myself a liar?

When the Circumcision Screams Die Down

When the circumcision screams die down,
The gingerbread licks quickly off the finger.
Remember the attic with its shadows
And the boards that smelled like Christmas
Where we slept in rows like elves?
I had for play a riddle of a rattle
And let the monkey with the plastic face,
Furrowed like sweet old granny's shank,

Squirm in beside my knee—you know,
The small fur thing I kept nearby
For safety's sake? We jabbered late
After being read to in our trundles
And twirled for fun the radio dials,
Upsetting dear ol' Dad and toasty Mom,
Who kissed us covered in our bunting,
Where I felt safe in my short bed,
My thumb locked on my monkey friend,
A peppery little gnome between
My dreams and that dark wall I saw
And studied when I couldn't sleep
For joy, the moonlight in my face.
I wonder was I any less a fairy tale
Than what I dreamt of when I wished?
Every wondrous thing that I imagined
I waited hopefully to see come true.
I'm sure I blundered as I slept,
Lost beneath blanket and pink puffs
After hearing stories in the night
To find them echo in my dreams,
Reverberating everywhere it seemed
But when I awoke to morning light.
Of what we never had we knew, yet
Heard so many tales we never cried,
But when we crack open the rattle,
What is left a person but to stare
Outraged and bewildered and sad
At the tiny bead inside?

An Apologetical Thought of a Literary Student One Snowy Winter Afternoon in Graduate School

When Wordsworth charged us to see
that we are all greater than we know, if a man "erect
himself" above himself he can reach

to his primal sympathy," a delight
that allows us, not Rousseau's plangent yearnings
to escape the world, not angry Shelley's

intemperance or insolent rebellion,
but "a grandeur in the beatings of the heart," a glimpse
into "man's unconquerable mind,"

I realized how, although some insist
that Jesus looked very much like other men of his time,
simply because Judas had to kiss him

there in the garden of Gethsemane
in order to single him out to the Roman guards
— if he had been tall, light-skinned

with long flowing hair and beard,
is it likely he would have needed to be identified?
a question detractors like to pose —

that it was the glory of his holy *self*,
the sacrificial strength that shone amidst all others,
an incandescent radiance of mind,

that, blazing like a sun, revealed him
alone as unlike other man, predestined for the cross
to which for us he was resigned.

535

When You're Looking with Your Right Eye

"I thank you with all my heart for your gallant generosity in writing
 to me of that which I've longed not to lose the so terribly twisted
 clue to."

—Henry James

When you're looking with your right eye,
Your left eye isn't there.
I watch the elephant in girls,
Alone and masticating treacle in the movies,

But they become Snow White and tenderness
When I turn and watch the gum machine
Kicked and rolled about by floozies,
Bold in their nylons and plumpy in their dress
And smirking funny in their swatches of hair
Because when you're looking with your right eye,
You left eye isn't there.
Appendicitis hurts; it's bad.
But it's moonlight and balloons you say
When that baby's in the groin,
The upshot of your hubby's play.
Though he's able to paint on Saturday morns
The whole of your house and its dome,
Weeping and blinking in his underwear fumes,
Your freaky son mopes home:
Six feet in the second grade, far too much he grew.
Yes, right wrongs in the librarian's eyes
When the book, all right on a Friday night,
On Saturday is overdue.
Some call meat a flank and some a loin;

My granny may call some things false;
My grampy maybe true.
At once a woman becomes a whore
When her goofy partner, through,
Whistles happy out the door and leaves behind a coin.
Some say it's an ogle and some say it's a stare
When you look with all your might;
But let's forget my granny and ask a question here:
When you're looking with your left eye,
Then what about the right?

John Wilmot, Lord Rochester, to His Mistress, Lady Funnel

Your urgent hand at dark of night in bed
when you no longer find yourself with me
softly quivers like young leaves in a tree
as you thrash about your perspiring head,
yet in my passion I approximate that tree,

as fully hard as you are soft and spread
within that orbit where your fancy's fed
and ever borne aloft on wings of ecstasy,
and so your rainy wetness is a part of me
for in the bond of tree and quaking leaves,
where here conjoins and there so cleaves,
we meet as one, no longer me and thee.
May your urgent hand be as loyal in oath
and my solid passion be true to us both

Who Isn't What

for Dale

A woman's properly beautiful
Only if something she does
Adds up to something worthy—
It's not simply someone she was
Or is, as if heaven-sent.
Why insist on maintaining
That beauty obviates training?
You are a near cadaver now,
Older than New Hampshire dirt,
Ass-fat in your matronly jeans,
Sea-otter homely, if less alert,
But take heed of what I say.
Worth means accomplishment.
You find it hard to agree?
If so, expect a petunia
To assume the role of a tree.
Nelly Ternan, a mistress,
Being what she was,
Simply never became what she wasn't;
She was what she was *because*.
She was born, had great beauty,
Painted her face, wanted fame;
Why discuss what she wasn't?
Fucking was mainly her fame.
She wasn't a surgeon general;

So, tell me, what else is new?
Is it so complicated
To see what we are's what we do?
No better example emerges
In spite of feminist dread
Of the Christian exhortation,
"Let the dead bury the dead."
Nell merely proceeded by choices
As dust comes only to dust
And hung herself
As an ornament
(Ignoring Victorian voices)
On Mr. Dickens's lust.

A Widgin of a Thing with a Face Like a Gun

A widgin of a thing with a face like a gun,
    her nose between the glass and her idea for blood,
was sent home by her son on Christmas.

After the airport, bumping though the air made blood
    fluster to her neck, bitten like the tree of Christmas,
holding her cream cup, she wanted no umbrella but a gun.

Sonny didn't care, the foul ball who peed on Christmas
    many a night, and wasn't ready for cracky hugs or blood
relations, now—a man who knew nothing of the gun.

Lubricia

"To speak the truth, there must
 be moral equality"
— Robert Louis Stevenson

I love you, promised Lubricia,
Much more than you do me,
The veracity of which
let me leave it for you to see,

If it is not already quite clear
In words that hardly seem meek
That we are considering someone
With a competitive streak.

She was carking, to begin with,
And more often than not aggrieved,
Which made me when I was with her
Yearn just as often to leave.

At forty, she'd already seen
A lot of her hopes go bust.
She hadn't a smidgen of faith
And, sadly, even less trust.

Although as a word fidelity
Was in constant use on her lips,
Two husbands and many affairs
Had left her in partial eclipse.

A fading, middle-aged woman
With rabbity-bright blue eyes,
Lubricia once said she was selfish
And didn't try to disguise.

Unshaven men attracted her,
She said with a wink of her eye
But something about it told you
She told it to many a guy,

Like her handing me a bottle
Of spicy *Obsession* cologne
Though we hadn't said forty words
And those were over the phone.

She had a little program
For whoever new was in tow,
As if men to her were generic,
Coming along in a row.

I had met her and husband two
Sometime the previous year.
I had some wear in my fabric
And she the occasional tear.

She divorced, brought me home,
And cooked dinner that very week
But couldn't disguise though she tried
She had an irrational streak.

She flew airplanes for a living
And had an estimable view
Of herself and her house on an island
And all that women could do.

She had never become a captain,
Although women much younger than she
Had done it. So what was her boast?
It was something anybody could be.

She was rich, she insisted, then poor
With debts of all kinds incurred.
Her concept of independence
Was always completely blurred,

For she needed a man around
As a duchess needed a carriage,
And although she'd failed at it twice
She was totally sold on marriage.

She wasn't a reader of books,
Didn't garden, have pets, or collect
And rarely sent off a letter
One didn't have to correct.

I cannot stand stupid people,
Tasteless, or stubborn as stone
Whose plans for you in their lives
Involve robbing you of your own.

Far worse is one who demands
Attention because she is bored,
Whose mind, unsheathed in its scabbard,
Has decayed like a rusty sword.

The hills and valleys of love
Characterized most of our days,
Though I had never deceived Lubricia
By infidelity's ways,

Although she once rifled my desk
And found a note I was sent
By a woman (a friend of some years)
Which to her a liaison meant.

It is my firm belief that people
Most hate the sin they commit,
And will forgive even worse sins
If they are the sins they omit.

I gathered several letters
Of that woman's, all I could find,
And presented them to Lubricia
And asked was she out of her mind?

An irony here let me mention:
She flirted with men all the time,
Strangers, neighbors, construction
Workers, shoppers in line.

As time passed, we made an effort
And hoped, as it did, to see
Something of worth in our being
Together of solidity.

A Sunday the following summer,
When I had been visiting her,
A car was heard on the gravel.
She suddenly didn't stir.

A look in her eyes of panic
Led her straight to the door,
And I saw mounting the porch
A bald man extremely cocksure

Of exactly where he could be
(And where he had been a lot?)
Of my automobile in the driveway
He couldn't have cared a jot.

Their conversation was brief,
But its gist I quickly took:
"It's not a good time to be here"
here a significant look —

"Alex has just happened by."
Though we'd been together all day,
"Can you come back tomorrow?
It would be better that way."

I smelt her deceit in an instant
Summed up in her sudden gloom
And of this bald prat had questions
When she reëntered the room.

Can someone say I love you
With joy, a smile, and a shout
And then start seeing a man
She never once told you about?

But on that Sunday in August
I knew I had seen full well
That Lubricia was suddenly caught
Like a nasty coyote in hell.

He was unshaven, I saw, so knew
He'd had his *Obsession* cologne
She'd been at work on her program,
The game plan he had been shown.

I pulled on my trousers in anger
For a tee-shirt was all that I wore
And white briefs, mainly the reason
That man was kept at the door,

For she was the type to outface,
So self-promoting she was,
Even that desperate meeting
By bluffing it over with gas.

All I know was their whispers
But lasted a minute or two.
Yet I can say in a minute
Yours truly up and left, too.

A month passed. I never saw her,
Though she called on my birthday to wish
Me well, though her lack of apology
Fell on my ears like dead fish.

Then my conscience started to nag
And my feelings for her to grow.
Why had I been so jealous?
She had had a visitor. So?

Maybe he was a neighbor.
Why always the worst did I seek?
Hadn't I heard of friendship?
What if she'd known him a week?

So exactly thirty days after
The very day I had walked out
I returned unannounced to inquire
What this whole thing was about.

I waited all day on that island
By her house on an outside wall
As speculation increased in
Her absence and spread like a pall.

I slept all night in my car
And had nightmares under the moon
Of a person always precipitate
For once not acting too soon.

She never came home that night.
I had no doubt we were through
Or where she was and what she was
Or how and exactly with who.

As her car was in the garage,
I opened the door without hope
And looked in the glove compartment
And found there an envelope.

It contained a brief epistle
And a pair of earrings not new.
"Richard," the letter began,
On a sheet of a bluish hue,

"I take it from your silence
That this is to be it
Concerning our affair?"
My pale hand trembled a bit.

"Regardless of what you believe,
I was completely faithful and spoke
Nothing but truth to you
From the start." Was this a joke?

It was he who had jilted her.
Her iciness made it quite clear
To her house he had never returned,
For I saw that in seeing me there

He had, just as I, felt betrayed
And that Sunday saw with a sigh
She was not only a liar but he
Had been duped as fully as I.

Richard! Lubricia had now
Something few women could claim:
That name was one of her husbands'
And a previous lover's name.

A pilot named Dick she once lived with.
She had married a Dick, and so
With another Dick in hand
Had had three Dicks all in a row.

Oh, she had told him about me,
Versions, no doubt, of the kind
That we were nothing but friends
Of the sort you generally find

Who might share a casual dinner,
See a film, you know, no romance,
So fancy his seeing me there
In her house and wearing no pants.

Richie was top of the totem,
At least she had had him believe.
Then to be left on the doorstep
Without even a by-your-leave?

I wondered when she had met him
On that fateful August the first
And how in keeping us both apart
She had managed never to burst

The bubble of total secrecy.
By acting with total deceit
She had managed to court us both
By the act of being discreet.

Whenever I chanced to be in,
Me she had charmed without doubt,
And this was simply because
He on that day had been out.

She lived on an island, you see,
And what with the ocean tides
Preventing access, she could act
Like one of Poseidon's brides

To whichever of us was there,
Though I lived an hour away,
On Cape Cod, but Richie, on hand,
Lived within sight of the bay.

She breathed never a single word
About this ongoing intrigue,
But now I remembered when asking
Her out she had pleaded fatigue.

Whenever a date had been cancelled,
Regretting Lubricia's ill-luck,
I couldn't have known those nights
She was blithely dining on duck.

Her scam had approached perfection
That had kept us apart so long;
She had temporized with a view
To see who deserved to belong.

Then suddenly into the driveway
Came a car with Lubricia inside.
It wouldn't be Richie, I knew.
An airport cab was her ride.

It turned out she had been working
And had flown the previous night,
No Richie was there to bonk her
That month. Nor was I in sight.

She was astonished to see me.
I dissembled and, hugging her, asked
For the truth, to see how she lied,
Which was never a difficult task.

She told me she told him about me
Right from the very start,
Completely omitting the detail
To him she had promised her heart.

I said I suspected someone,
Privately thinking a week
Was the maximum someone like her
Could manage being a sneak.

That detail I needed to know
The better to ascertain
Not whether she was flirtatious,
Crippled, or simply vain,

For I knew for certain I'd never
Trust this person again,
No, I wanted to see how long
I'd been kept in the pouring rain.

The length of time would determine
An obvious way to see
Exactly what she was worth by
The extent of her perfidy.

Self-righteously she sniffed
And dramatically lowered her head,
To wait for the full effect
And spoke of a letter she'd read

That was sent to me by a woman
From New York at the turn of the year
And with reference to a phone call
Accused *me* of such an affair.

With someone I never met? I asked.
It didn't matter, she said,
A person can have an affair
With someone inside of his head.

I'd received a flattering letter
From a reader of something I wrote
And in response to that missive
Injudiciously answered that note.

In spite of the fact that I had
Over the course of a year
Never once bothered to see her
But phoned once or twice to be fair,

Thus proving my point, but it
Did nothing to shore up my case
For defending her misalliance
She threw deceit in my face.

That, I was told, was the reason,
And there wasn't the hint of a tear,
That she had been sleeping with someone
For fully (I gasped) half a year!

Why never did she confront me?
It gave her sanction to cheat.
What's the point of seeking
The truth when it means your defeat?

She denied it was an affair,
Pretending she loved me instead.
I kept mum and refused to confide
About the letter I'd read.

I saw only a pitiful woman
Up to her mad eyes in mire;
A thief you can watch; however,
Not so a psychotic liar.

She had not even the grace
To confess in the end and say
Truth might be a beginning.
I needed to get away.

But if my belief is that people
Most hate the sin they commit,
And will forgive even worse sins
If those are the sins they omit,

Where does that leave me here?
What sin is mine, you may ask?
My sin was the vain assumption
I could do an impossible task,

To construct a human Babel,
With mortal shovel and pail,
And seek with pride to foster
A relationship doomed to fail.

The writer's vice, overreaching,
Is what I loathed in such lice.
And yet I found in her duplicity
Myself — and wearing her vice.

I saw myself quoted exactly
And confess in my sin to say
Upon my first seeing that woman
I should have hastened away.

The writer's vice is he gambles
On disaster and walks on the ledge,
Failing to weigh the real chances
Of falling over the edge.

Let this poem, if ever she reads it,
Preferring truth over sloth,
Prove only we are both sinners
And in need of confession both.

Andy Warhol's Art: A Sonnet

"I like boring things."
                          — A.W.

First, blow up a common Polaroid,
with you as the sun, the solanoid,
having selected a subject's face.
Do not add or subtract or erase.
To a silk screen simply apply it,
then with wet paints test and try it,
two colors, say yellow and green;
after pouring them onto the screen
grab a plain house-painter's roller
and walk like a Manhattan stroller
spreading paint of a chosen gloss
to saturate the photographs across
dyeing each image bottom to top.
Then? Hawk them at $25,000 a pop.

Sacred or Profane?

Baal in compounds
denoting places names
implies the omission of Beth.

Religion by creed
fostering opposite views
to the world brings only death.

Trouant's Island

"Perhaps she would not have considered evil to be so rare...had she
been able to discern in herself, as in everyone, that indifference to
the sufferings one causes, an indifference which, whatever other
names one may give it, is the terrible and permanent form of cruelty."
                                                      — Marcel Proust

A confirmed compatabilist, you loved insular
life only for the charm you craved, not for anything you ever gave,
  — the difference between supine and prone —

  unlike original souls who mainly live on islands
as a way of avoiding the quidnuncs of the world who task them,
    boring monotremes rapping at one's door,

  all the gossips, fools, pecking cormorants,
labile half-wits waving in the wind like wagging garlic scapes
    with time on their hands to interrupt.

  What was all that bollocks you scared up
about looking for an island sanctuary to protect you from the evil
    of the world, lurking ghosts and thieves?

  Any grinning crowd rubbering toward you
would be a thrill, so of course I could never bear your awful company
    no matter how detached, secluded, separate,

  you deludedly claimed it was you were, you
being obstinate and narrow-minded in the way all needy islanders
    remove themselves, then look to see who cares.

  The topmost spring of a hemlock, predictably,
also bends to the east, and on shore I spy you there in isolated waters
    simply truant, merely toxic, never ever true.

551

The Poverty of Christ

'The Spirit of the Lord is upon me, because he has anointed
me to bring good news to the poor. He has sent me to
proclaim release to the captives and recovery of sight to the
blind, to let the oppressed go free, to proclaim the year of
the Lord's favor."

— Jesus Christ
Luke 4:16-19

Christ was born in a manger, not his own.
Over our loneliness his sacred light shone.
Come ye all and hosanna sing! Noel, Noel! [Refrain]
Jesus Christ is born! Play trumpet! Ring bell!
Lift up your hearts for by His sacred merit
And holy poverty full richness we inherit

Christ was raised by two people, not his own.
He walked humbly over hill and through town.
[Refrain ff.]

Christ bore all of our burdens, not his own.
He lived for thirty years virtually unknown.

Christ slept in lowly houses, not his own.
He laid his tired head in places unknown.

Christ was sustained on food, not his own.
He prayed and fasted with never a groan

Christ preached from a tiny boat, not his own
He calmed all water raging, all wind blown.

Christ was lathered with oil, not his own.
Some protested such worship was shown

Christ wore a seamless robe, not his own.
It was woven in one piece and never sewn.

Christ rode to Jerusalem on a mule, not his own.
His disciples had borrowed the beast on a loan.

Christ was ridiculed on a seat, not his own.
The priests in Antonia laughed at his throne

Christ was crucified on a cross, not his own
The prosecuting soldiers broke not a bone.

Christ died for the waiting world, not his own
He died for our many sins that he might atone.

Christ was buried in a tomb, not his own
After three days he passed through the stone

Christ was born in a manger, not his own.
Over our loneliness his sacred light shone.

Come ye all and hosanna sing! Noel, Noel![Refrain]
Jesus Christ is born! Play trumpet! Ring bell!
Lift up your hearts for this day we inherit
By His holy poverty salvation's sacred merit

Blue Jewels

I recall your sparkling blue jewels,
how proud it was for you to iridesce the night
with whatever they were,

tourmalines, spinel, kyanite,
rainbow moonstones, tanzanite, agates, topaz
apatite, sapphires, aquamarine,

and that they replaced your passion.
It is quite fitting how we find blue unappetizing
in our workaday cuisine,

its scarcity as worthy nourishment,
I will allow myself to speculate in reverie,
quite fitting when applied to you.

My worst dreams of corrupt Jezreel
are nothing next to the decadent way you needed
they stand attendance courting you, .

Jezebel, at every turn of the wrist
and throw of hair as you flashed your earrings
and twiddled your necklace

and lead me firmly to believe that
what naturally does not occur as nourishment
offers surely nothing of health.

A Sonnet for the Marriage of Michael and Kim

August 24, 2013

Mightiest of truths anyone can find
In the paradox of love we all must face,
Crucial for the heart in being kind,
Hoping to convey the maximum of grace,
Asks one to *sacrifice* and in the finding
Each soul receives by what it learns to give;
Love's secret's thus a way of binding
Kim and Michael, lovingly to live.
All you grant in love redeems what's yours.
No sail in wild and windy seas or still
Dares ruin of a ship with such a chart.
Kisses given, a reception so assures.
Indeed, what's freely offered of your will
Measures the distinction of your heart.

A Date at Au Lapin Agile

While sitting at Au Lapin Agile, footsore
on the hill, drinking calvados, speaking of painters, she asked me,
"What did their black portfolios contain?"

I saw how on the terraces of the Rat Mort
Renoir, Degas, and Pissarro quarreling across the marble tables,
alternately listening in the dark,

while lesbians crooned "*Viens pou-poule*"
and "*Caroline*" and "*La Petite Tonkinoise*" and "*Circassiens,*"
and quietly demoralizing each other

with sibling-like observations and quips
that repeated shadows are not brown or black but are colored
by various objects around them

and reiterated how "local color" in views
is modified by the light and reflections of what surrounded them.
They each intuitively knew as adepts

that while light is an elevated form of color
the black matter of logic and law misuses itself to generate heat
   instead of becoming radiant.

   Evil is light that refuses to shine.
How else can the paradox of light hidden under a bushel
   make any sense to us at all?

What their black portfolios contained
was the singular truth that madness is genius that shirks its calling,
   which is to say their paintings

   filled their portfolios, and I knew tomorrow
when my swollen feet hurt less, in spite of my apple brandy hangover,
   I best rather write my book than flirt.

Circles

"The circle is a symbol of rest."
                — John Ruskin

   A caruncle ruins a turkey's symmetry,
   offending its full roundness with excrescence.
   In Africa, bushmen always work

   in a circle, if possible. Ramparts,
   say, the comfort of huts where fireplaces
   are always located in the center,

   just as their huts are found in circles.
   Visit a kraal where cattle and turkeys in rings
   squabble in looping coos. I have seen

   spoon-headed children in Sierra Leone
   without use of compass, caliper, dial or gauge
   draw perfect circles on the ground

   as round and full as the moon,
   hoops, nooses, ovals, spirals, twirls, whorls,
   convolutions that explain how

symmetry is a necessary comfort
with ends insisting on implicit beginnings
as a way of making sense

and why all the bushmen there
when speaking to you always begin with "yes"
when the next word is always "no."

Johannesburg, South Africa

Mr. Coit the Travel Writer

Let's simply say my faith in you was like a lack of faith,
reminding me of what Santayana said of William James,
through whose weird imagination flitted witch and wraith,
exacting of his fearful spirit no end of sinister claims:

"He did not really believe, he merely believed in the right
of believing that you might be right if you believed."
Your tortured lack of honesty with me was always slight
that left your lying, if never once your loyalty, relieved.

The World as Will and Idea

"I have not gone and done anything, Mother. I have gone
and *not* done something. Which very much needed the *not*
doing."

— Jerome Lawrence and Robert E. Lee,
The Night Thoreau Spent in Jail

1.

You have a name
Before you even scream
Carried on your head

As heavy as the leaden years,
Tumble into playgrounds
Where someone waits to beat you up
Because of your squint,
Wide ears, or folded lunches.
It's all been there before,
All the news,
Tired old proverbs, old debates.
Face, feet, desperate hunches.
What in life isn't thrown at you
Like clothes?
How many Christmases
Happily took place
Before you had a chance to be?
We receive our lives
Like broken sets of plates
For six, except we're one.
We inherit all we have.
If nothing is new,
Even worse
Nothing more awaits
Under the sun.

2.

I hate the world
For what in being what it is
It isn't. The wet, the wind,
Vacant yards, broken gates,
Fistfights, not enough light,
Man both debt and debtor,
Animals, weeping, locked in pens,
You couldn't imagine better?
What, waiting lifetimes for a tender kiss?
Who with any brains
That can't foresee a better world
Could be satisfied with this?
Face it, there *isn't* any truth.
We're no more preconceived
Than if our fathers at a fun fair
Plopped a coin in a machine
And out bonked a Baby Ruth.

History makes of teachers
Something obscene.
I look at piles
Of ragged sheet music
Fifty years old
And think: *dead people,*
Names in the night,
All gone, basically sold.

3.

We are born
Against our will and die the same,
Depend by strictly chance
Upon the wife we meet,
Fail to succeed for her,
But still must take the blame.
This is the way
You say it has to be?
Raving half-mad prophets
Running quaquaversal
Throughout the streets,
Drooling hobo harridans
In dirty doorways curled,
Two-thirds of a population
Revolving in a starving world?
I prefer to be told
We find our fate, our fortune,
In the street.
We all are tempted
By our dreams
Of what could be,
The way they come,
But it's only the daring
The brave, the truthful,
Who succumb.

Italo Calvino on Cesare Pavese,
or,
I am Developing a Piranesian Headache

Many novels revolve around deep hidden themes
with frankly something unsaid, much of the time,
looming the solidest part of the author's schemes
which can only be fully signified, putting it fine,
by way (here's the trick) of not giving it mention
and so, reading, we bore through a tissue of signs,
— many of which have a secret side, a convention,
meanings with polyvalent or inexpressible designs —
which prove to count more than the obvious ones,
but the full central meanings all lie in relation to
what binds them to what an unspoken theme shuns
in the matter of fictionally passing the plot to you.
So while you descend try to feel you have arisen,
like breaking *into* a fictitious atmospheric prison!

559

The Whirligigs of Pretense

for Robert Hatch, critic
quisnam est narro

It was Jean Genet's
intention in his play
The Maids,
in which two tweenies,
Claire and Solange,
are discovered
rehearsing the murder
of their mistress,
that real boys
should portray
false maids
who as real women
enact a false hate
that is inextricably
confused with false love,

as a circular alternation
of truth with falsehood.
But is not a play
what in life we portray
the truths we won't say
reality to stay?

Claire is playing
the mistress,
and Solange, her sister,
is portraying Claire,
and by a transmission of roles
Claire can both revile
and caress herself
in the person of Solange
and Solange, both hating
and fawning over the mistress,
can at the same time
loathe and fondle Claire,
her alter ago.

The servant
is the image of himself
reflected from the master,
as is the servant.
But is not a play
what in life we portray
the truths we won't say
reality to stay?

So a metamorphosis
can be proliferated at will.
In the end, when the mistress
(actually) comes home
to discover the maids,
Claire drinks the poisoned tea,
thus committing
in a real suicide
a symbolic murder,
and assuming in death
the identity of the personality
who gave her substance. It is all

a conspiracy
against the spectators,
and the hostility
flows strongly
from stage to auditorium.
But is not a play
what in life we portray
the truths we won't say
reality to stay?

Saint Teresa Transported

"I saw in his hand a long spear of gold, and at the iron's point there seemed to be a little fire. He appeared to me to be thrusting it at times into my heart, and to pierce my very entrails; when he drew it out, he seemed to draw them out also, and to leave me all on fire with a great love of God. The pain was so great, that it made me moan; and yet so surpassing was the sweetness of this excessive pain, that I could not wish to be rid of it. The soul is satisfied now with nothing less than God. The pain is not bodily, but spiritual; though the body has its share in it. It is a caressing of love so sweet which now takes place between the soul and God, that I pray God of His goodness to make him experience it who may think that I am lying."
— Teresa Sánchez de Cepeda y Ahumada (March 28, 1515 - October 4, 1582), Spanish mystic

Matter calls to spirit as a flower to rain,
rain to wind, the blowing wind, shaping landfalls, shifting seas,
the afflatus of the designing Paraclete.

Gian Lorenzo Bernini's "Ecstasy" shows
just such a cry when in ecstasy Teresa's heart was pierced
by the fiery arrow of divine love,

her head thrown back as in a swoon,
eyes half lidded, her lips parted, as if caught in an unguarded
moment of sexual fulfillment,

less a flower to rain than any burning
to the touch of love, a moan of matter answering to the spirit
like a kiss that makes the two caress.

Scripture is Silent about Bananas

Scripture is silent about bananas, but if mentioned they would be in
a bunch — and blessed: *"For where two or three gather together as my
followers, I am there among them." — Matthew* 18:20

Baana of course doesn't count, son of Ahilud,
one of the twelve men appointed by Solomon to get provisions
for the great king's family, but surely

foraging in the vicinity of Megiddo he saw
something like them — Mohammed was familiar with the fruit —
even if with fuzzy skins bubblegum pink.

Nor does Baanah, a son of Rimmon,
a stalwart in his kinsman King Saul's army where he was chief
of the raider bands. He cruelly beheaded

Ishbosheth, a son of Saul, bringing the head
to David and was rewarded by death and dismemberment.
Peeled and exhibited in public disgrace.

David was king after the death of Saul
and was then followed by Solomon, clustering all and curved,
scarlet, yellow, purple, and green

I am speaking of bunches, at least. You can
see that? It is a Wolof word anyway, *banaana*, African and
passed into English via the Portuguese,

starchy and vulnerable and cultivated
gathered but even if in bunches, like Saul and Ishbosheth
and Rechab, not always blessed.

Sermon to a Jawsmith

A principled man sees
what is everybody's
   truth
when he is alone
   that
a humble man knows
that he is nobody's
   answer,
not even his own.

The Political Realism of Henry Kissinger

"The emigration of Jews from the Soviet Union is not an objective of
American foreign policy. And if they put Jews into gas chambers in the
Soviet Union, it is not an American concern. Maybe a humanitarian
concern."

> — Henry Kissinger to Pres. Richard Nixon
> March 1, 1973
> (Oval Office tapes in the National Archive)

While humanitarian matters may be a fit subject for any slob who burns,
the global aspects of *realpolitik* are what frankly speak to our concerns,
issues around which any true leader's (and secretary's) reputation turns,
despite the bullshit for which every bleeding heart idiotically still yearns.
May I therefore recommend this profitless meeting immediately adjourns
before another variation on this truly boring subject idiotically returns?
I spied coming into the Oval Office a table with a phalanx of sauternes!

Bouquet for an Ex-Girlfriend

Mushrooms have the stench of semen,
as does the Linden and Tree of Heaven.
Cranesbill smells enough like mutton
to cause one's bum to fully unbutton.
Carrion-flowers resemble a corpse,

exuding an odor that utterly warps.
No arum is not a fetid mess
whose origins bleak are anyone's guess.
Horse Shoe Vetch reeks so badly of cheese,
it can foist upon one a terrible wheeze.
Lizard orchids smell rudely of goats,
short-tailed weasels, and filthy stoats,
Mountain Ash smells of a witch's teat,
Dittany smells badly of gas,
Purple Trillium like rotting meat,
the Dragon Lily a monkey's ass.
Rafflesia is as mephitic as shit.
The turtleback plant with its sickly shine
gives a resinous kick like turpentine.
A shrub Ephedra pungent of alkaloid
with a bitter whiff could make her void.
Black Hellebore can summon a demon.
Marigold's like a pissing pit
Sour Flaxinella like bitter lemon.
Bradford pear hints of rotting fish,
its white flowers half-dead skink.
Skunk Cabbage smells like marijuana,
the Butterfly Bush pure stink.
Paperwhites smell precisely of urine.
The Stinking Root parasite palls.
Above Titans are disgustingly foreign
with an odor of something that crawls.
Lobelia which is also called "pukeweed"
is most vilely used as a medicinal herb;
gagroot, wild tobacco, and asthma feed
— other names it goes by — also disturb.
A Carob tree smells like a hippo's duff,
the Hawthorn could twist off a nose,
like Yellow Alyssum and Candytuft.
Crown Imperials are an anti-rose,
their orange utterly stinking of lice,
as if they'd been, with their hideous pew,
criss-crossed with hyena feces and mice.
Cherry tree foliage, rhododendron leaves
a toxic inhalation quite easily achieves;
the same with leaves of an elderberry plant,

a fate the common oak leaf will also grant.
Now wrap all the blooms in a lovely bouquet
with some delicate ferns and some rue,
— appending perhaps a tasteful card
with an added line of romantic lard —
ring the bell, bow, and then happily say
(being quite ready to go on your way)
"None more deserves this than you!"

Asyndeton, the Omission of Conjunctions

Our arithmetic teacher, bald and old,
— he taught us function and fraction —
was Mr. Asyndeton hoary with mold
and we soon detected his attraction

to fat, spinsterish Edna Mae Creech
who, wobbling her head when she spoke
of Latin grammar and figures of speech,
became the occasion of many joke,

as nasty rumors ran through the school
that after hours in a room they'd lock
Edna Mae and Mr. A broke many a rule
with the lights out so nobody'd knock

where mathman, now exploding with lust
thumbfumbled off her buttons and bows
and despite a libido riddled with rust,
snatched like a fiend at her inner clothes.

We all gleefully rolled in the aisles,
recounting tales of salacious surmise
about how Mr. A suffered from piles,
fitch, sciatica, and wet dripping eyes,

post-nasal drip and painful arthritis,
memory loss and toe-flaming gout,
prostrate enlargement, chronic phlebitis,
hearing loss, and severe mental drought.

It was then time to make crucial bets
as to their progress, making quite sure
to verify facts and with nervous frets
posted a guard in the closet next door.

At first came coos, brief little squawks,
curious noises of an ambiguous sort;
then wall-banging noises — aftershocks? —
followed by a definitive snort.

Imagine our shock as things fell out!
The union, if the correct term that is,
ended with, "What a hideous sprout!"
— then silence like a flattening fizz.

The final story that everyone heard
was a woman half-naked was seen,
bolting the room in a manner absurd
accompanied by high-pitched scream.

It was clear Mr. A., the poor geezer,
had darkly infuriated his better half
by failing to raise up his Ebenezer,
mocking the phrase the *faculty staff*.

Now we were heeding Creech's lessons,
whatever of grammar she had to teach,
and as the result of her classroom sessions
had memorized every figure of speech,

always hoping the bell would free us
as the afternoons darkened outside,
while studying Dido and Mr. Aeneas
until our brains nearly ossified.

And so it became our sadistic delight
to apply with joy all we had learned
and to spot Mr. A with juvenile spite
was to call him what we felt he'd earned

regarding the aspects of human malfunctions,
and whenever we saw Mr. A we'd mutter,
"Asyndeton, the Omission of Conjunctions!"
adding a knowing smirk — and a finger flutter!

Amos

"Sacrifices do not make up for bad deeds," warned
the prophet Amos, a sycamore fig farmer who was unclubbable,
and delivered only a single sermon in his life,

insisting God demanded righteous conduct
and not the slaughtering goats and rams, contrition-less bollocks
like bouquets that cads send gullible women,

cheap girdle-salesmen looking for absolution.
"I hate, I despise your feasts," he told the Jews, "and take no delight
in your solemn assembles." Only lonely

outliers alone can have a pure voice,
Amos belonged to no machine, no union, no lodge, neither the Elks
nor the Rotary, no Moose, no K of C.,

no guild of dervishes, no Playboy Key Club.
He despised Wall St., Goldman Sachs, Lehman Brothers; Thalmann
& Company; Lazard Frères; Kuhn, the Loeb Group;

Speyer & Company; Knauth, Nachod & Kuhne;
Hallgarten and Co.; Ladenburg; J. &W. Seligman & Company,
and all those rat-souled regulatory agencies

killing the poor and making the richest richer
but it wasn't only weasel zippers and bald conniving miscreants
he hated, for religious ecstatics also left him cold.

Amos was a rough shepherd, a humble dresser
of sycamore trees from Tekoa, and well knew how summer fruit,
    lovely within could be so rotten without.

He had little say or influence on his people.
for the Hebrews blew him off as an annoying crank to be ignored.
    So who is surprised that such a holy man

who said God was not only independent of Israel
but in fact a universal God of justice for all men, Gentiles included,
    was slain by Amaziah, a priest of Bethel?

Telephone Conversation on November 6, 1994

"Truth does not do as much good in the world as the
semblance of truth does evil."
Đ *François* de la La Rochefoucauld

I find I need several men and
Cannot see to being your wife,
Yet if you claim that you love me
Why can't you be in my life?

Loving you makes inconvenient
My decision to grow, but you
Can prove your devotion to me
By approving whatever I do.

I have to admit I am selfish.
Let's put the facts on the line.
But have you so many friends
You reject the offer of mine?

Here is a grand opportunity
For you to show that you care.
How can shutting me out of
Your life now possibly square

With my continuing needs
Of looking for my inner light?
Why with love must you paint
Things all black and all white?

Half-measures work, I've seen it.
Compromises and looking away,
I'll see you when it's convenient,
While I proceed on my merry way.

I am talking about my needs
(love, you tell me, endures);
Be patient, will you, with mine,
And I'll try to overlook yours.

I'm older, a practical woman,
A flyer, not patient, it's true.
With me if something takes time
I can blow it away and renew

Acquaintance with what will work,
A car or a boat or a man.
You say now I'm black and white?
Hey, a woman does what she can.

I've never cared about logic,
Delays, or the ways of grace.
Whomsoever's is nearest mine
Becomes the prominent face.

So if you love me, take heed.
Let it support me, not kill
Affairs I prefer to keep private.
Just let me do what I will.

There are too many obstacles
For us, down, below, and above,
One, I'm afraid, is you and
Sadly, one of them is love.

J. M.W. Turner Discovers the Secret of Primal Light

"All is without form and void. Someone said of his landscapes that
they were *pictures of nothing, and very like.*"

> — William Hazlitt on Turner

He found storms in wilds of Dorset,
wind and rain in Wales and rising squalls in Bristol, chasing
them with his watercolor box

with a young man's passionate need
to take them down, cold moonlight showing boats in peril,
twilight, nightlights, bat-light glow

and glare, what is glimpsed, spied out,
for light is a kind of temperature that warmed or cooled
the brushes he wielded to record

all he saw, snow falls, breaking sun
in air, ripping gales that shook the passive earth through which
ran temporal slants of etiolated light,

but what he discovered in Italy
was a luminescence, evanescent, a shimmering golden steam,
a radiance all belonging to him

— resplendent — born out of chaos.
It was here he saw there could be a *storm* of light, by which
a solid object in a shadowless flash

of incandescence might be consumed
in a way different from their evaporations in the cooler flux
and darker radiations of the north.

What he captured was the elemental light,
that God saw was good in the beginning as he separated light
from darkness, *pictures of nothing,*

as it were, light in the very abstraction
of what it illumines and obscures, reveals and conceals, and
this was the vision given to Turner,

to have discovered the aboriginal light
that was parcelled out to the sun, moon, and stars in the vast
   vital exhalation of our primal creation.

Turning Dangerously Handsome

"To look *almost* pretty is an acquisition of higher delight to a
girl who has been looking plain the first fifteen years of her
life than a beauty from her cradle can ever receive."
—Jane Austen, *Northanger Abbey*

I turned dangerously handsome in my own mind
at a party in the basement of David Bianco's house

when I was thirteen and heard "Charmaine" playing
on the radio. I saw angels in the beauty of the oboes,

if that is indeed what they were, although I know
violins could be heard. What exactly did alcohol do

in a hair tonic? I used tons of it to stiffen my quiff,
and when I experienced my very first kiss (Italian girl,

brown sweater) making certain in a circling maneuver
to rub her back, round and round, like Victor Mature

did in a movie I remember, just to drive her crazy
and prove myself irresistible — we were in a closet —

it seemed that, the oboes, violins, my mad marcel,
that Vitalis hair oil, Eleanor Pelosi wearing brown,

and the gentle strains of Mantovani's lovely song
by way of a single intoxication that gave me sheen

conspired at once (all of a sudden) to let me belong
as I turned the unpredictable corner of age thirteen.

Grammar of Murder

In their invidious bigotry,
eight weighty neighbors freighted on a sleigh
set out a thief to kill,

for when a jealous eye, you see,
an enemy spies it cries *aye-ee* and seeks to slay
its opponent and his will.

Schicklgruber and Djugashvili

Solely in terms of mood and your soul feeling chilly,
which freezes it most, Schicklgruber or Djugashvili?
I mean in the blot-out-able sense of a spot-remover,
what name is worse, Djugashvili or Schicklgruber?
Say between two voices, one hoarse and one shrilly,
which would you take, Schicklgruber or Djugashvili?
A choice above ground or below, like tomato or tuber,
select one or the other, Djugashvili or Schicklgruber.
The question is political, please, so don't say it's silly,
vote for one or the other, Schicklgruber or Djugashvili.
See, one name may seem rude and the other one ruder,
but the options are these, Djugashvili or Schicklgruber.
So which is it, far Right or far Left? Save your breath.
At the extreme of whichever you choose awaits death

The Perspective of Oliver Chinpoint, Painter

O. Chinpoint is interested solely in the truth of the *unguarded* moment,
when a sitter has never a chance to put up a front or rearrange his face,
hoping to find the clue to his character by way of what he hopes to hide.

It is to snap-capture a person's eroto-physical candor, if merely a trace,
to penetrate a person's offhand being and catch details pullulating inside
as a clue to his character. The subject posing before you is an opponent!

Truths on the surface, in the matter of import, you will find rarely abide
— no spy won't assure you this central weakness is a human component —
for it is our divided nature as we pose and preen every fault to displace.

Root of Jesse

"And there shall come forth a rod out of the stem of Jesse,
  and a Branch shall grow out of his roots."
  Isaiah 11:1

  As Christ boomed wildly
out of Judaism, the United States loomed out of the
  stem of the British Isles,

  growing like a sturdy branch
in a suddenly bright and singularly new majesty,
  sporting new styles,

  diminishing the mother
and the father who watch in shock to see a vision
  no longer a child's.

Did My Honey Kiss Me Off For Good?

A 1920s- style song for ukulele
  for George Formby, Gene Austin, and Dick Robertson

  Did my honey kiss me off for good?
  Am I once more in the trough for good?
  She seemed awfully in a rush
  As I felt a breezy brush.
  Did my honey kiss me off for good?

  Did my honey kiss me off for good?
  Shall I my hat no longer doff for good?
  When I reach for an embrace
  I find only empty space
  Did my honey kiss me off for good?

Refrain:
There is melancholy in migration
When all the birds have flown.
Only simpletons call it a vacation
To be left there on your own

Did my honey kiss me off for good?
Has returned my winter cough for good?
Farewell the soothing balm
in that hint of L'Air Du Temps
Did my honey kiss me off for good?

Did my honey kiss me off for good?
Is mine the echo of her scoff for good?
I detected in her eyes
It was goodbye to lullabyesI
Did my honey kiss me off for good?

Did my honey kiss me off for good?
Has she dropped me as her prof for good?
Irrelevant is fail or pass
Since she's no more in my class
Did my honey kiss me off for good?

Did my honey kiss me off for good?
Have I had my final boff for good?
Odd, I find I have great fun, saying,
"Darling, you can bite my bum!"
Did my honey kiss me off for good?

The Equation That Ushered in the Information Age

Must I seriously care about data for efficient codes
for whom over a struggling lifetime syntheses vex?
$$H = Ð p\,(x) \log p\,(x)$$

Forget all those lossless encoding or compression nodes
for is not the secret to all solutions and its sequels faith?
$$Ð p\,(x) \log p\,(x) = H$$

Metrosexual Froings; or Upon Perusing *The New Yorker* After Thirty Years of its Decomposition

Stupid folk who feel reassured by the might
of a selling institution give high marks to *The New Yorker*,
   fad-surfing its glossy pages for the up-to-date

   but finding among the standard urban priggery
only the usual meaningless cartoons, lack of moral clarity
   in its mockery of Christianity, presaged by

   those relentlessly secular covers (Easter bunnies,
goofy cross-eyed Santas, etc.), spates of endless articles
   all written by conniving in-house favorites

   week after week, year to year, infomediaries
from the in-crowd while every new, any new aspirant
   is plutoed as a parvenu, and always poems

   by the same tame lamos or Eastern bloc poets
with names like Witold Zxgycvhskijipo and Misha Smirt
   and Yavo Popo, some dead Lithuanian Jew,

   to say nothing of the insidious cosmopolitanism
in pieces denying traditional identities and moral principles
   in gay celebrations with showering confetti.

   Am I now a Russian, revolted at pinch-points
in a magazine that recapitulates what's happening in the West,
   rejecting old values with its decadent hauteur

   and approving policies that equate large families
with same-sex partnerships, running photos of metrosexual
   jumpatives kissing in front of City Hall?

   I flip through this magazine as through bumph,
revolted even by the new dead look of its computerized pages
   and tinkered-with type-faces, neutering the lot,

a redesign with its structured grid in the layout
as damaging in its visual butchering as the editors themselves
are dopes. Receptivity, however — openness —

was never a value in those starchy ramparts,
so high in elevation that actual belief in God is mocked
with the accepted primitivism of a rude *éclat*,

despite its frictionless presumption, comically
held — what ego is not blind to its own awful excesses? —
it is the "Best Magazine on Earth," a boast

so vulgar in its swaggering self-conceit
that one can only conclude by algebra the opposite is true.
No Christians agree with Kafka who said,

"The meaning of life is that it stops."
See, back again to stupid folk. This is getting momentous.
I have more important things to do.

Discrepancies

"Is God willing to prevent evil, but not able? Then he is
not omnipotent. Is he able, but not willing? Then he is
malevolent. Is he both able and willing? Then whence
cometh evil? Is he neither able nor willing? Then why call
him God?"

— Epicurus

The scandalous
discrepancy on earth
between the cossetted
and the many
who are
clawed,

in that it reveals
by demonstration
the dice-throwing cruelty
beneath
the essential
fraud,

forces us
simply from love
and any sense of decency
not to
believe
in God.

Benedicite Dominum, or the Canticle of the Three Young Men

(Daniel 3: 57-88 and Psalm 148
form the core of this Canticle)

When I prayed as a young Trappist novice and first heard
this song, my heart burst with joy over God's every word.

O ye Sun and Moon, bless the Lord: praise Him, and magnify Him for ever.
O ye Stars of Heaven, bless the Lord: praise Him, and magnify Him for ever.
O ye Showers and rain, bless the Lord: praise Him, and magnify Him for ever.
O ye Winds of God, bless the Lord: praise Him, and magnify Him for ever.

A vision of earth's multifarious beauty rose before my eyes,
revealing God's eternal glory under vast immemorial skies.

O ye Nights and Days, bless the Lord: praise Him, and magnify Him for ever.
O ye Light and Darkness, bless the Lord: praise Him, and magnify Him for ever.
O ye Lightnings and Clouds, bless the Lord: praise Him, and magnify Him for ever.
O let the Earth bless the Lord : yea, let it praise Him, and magnify Him for ever.

The wildness of God's awesome power in everything that we know
brought mystical, musical proof of God's heaven to us down below.

O ye Fire and Heat, bless the Lord : praise Him, and magnify Him for ever.
O ye Winter and Summer, bless the Lord : praise Him, and magnify Him for ever.
O ye Frost and Cold, bless the Lord : praise Him, and magnify Him for ever.
O ye Ice and Snow, bless the Lord : praise Him, and magnify Him for ever.

What I had witnessed that moment beyond all I had ever dreamed
was that through Christ's holy sacrifice all of *mankind* is redeemed.

O ye Mountains and Hills, bless the Lord : praise Him, and magnify Him for ever.
O ye Green Things of the Earth, bless the Lord : praise Him, and magnify Him for ever.
O ye Seas and Floods, bless ye the Lord : praise Him, and magnify Him for ever.
O ye Whales, and all that move in the Waters, bless ye the Lord : praise Him,
and magnify Him for ever.

Fire Sluts of New England

Choose your metaphor. A weyr of dragons. A cloud of bats.
A scourge of snipe. They gathered in covens. I think of crows

brooding, creosote-dark, on the branches of a leafless tree
— *burble, burble* — in a comfortless December in the rain.

It was as if discontent were a raging virus spreading overland
to spread flammable infections and scalding fevers in its path,

as, furious at their fathers, these titless intemperates came roaring
out of New England with red-rimmed eyes and sharpened claws,

meeting fire with fire. A damaged life is the sole occasion of revolt,
fit to any firebrand. Rage was their offspring, borne of empty wombs.

Who is surprised that Lucy Stone, whose screeches could scorch
a smeltery, was the first woman in New England to be cremated?

Or that with her iron chin activist Lucretia Mott of Nantucket
raged with nut-like fists against the very bonnet that she wore?

Or that Susan B. Anthony of Adams, Mass. hurled venomous
rebukes against all the clergy and called her work the gospel?

Or that Frances Perkins from Boston grizzled at politics the way
incendiary Mary Wood slashed Sargent's portrait of Henry James?

Or that voracious Mary Baker Eddy ate up men like peaches
whose stones she threw away as she did her one ghostly child,

for whom the woman never had so much as an ounce of feeling
and who had been sent out to relatives all his life. Horrid corvids!

Who cannot create will always destroy. It was as if in every case
they all paraded to a dark forbidden hill where a pyre awaited each

victim and executioner, both, they screamed with crazy delight
in the midst of their own immolation, match, fuel, faggots, self,

and as they became unglued by the heat of their smoking wombs
it was fire alone as the consuming element that marked their tombs.

Midnight Tango del Floridita on Duval St., Key West

I dance nightly with you in a purple caprice,
    jeté, *relevé*, and glissade,
which lets you deep from within to release
    a rush of hot silver aubade
just as our hot tears coalesce in plush streams
    beneath a sky fully starred
after a dark corridor opens wide in my dreams
    which you enter ever hard.

Pastor Stoneseed's Sermon

There is me, bespectacled, stubbled chin,
scribbling notes on the sermon that rainy Sunday morning
on mankind's value, virtue, vim, and valor,

with my dear wife who though she knows
my habits well cannot help but think my woeful inattention
more pronounced by my shuttling pen.

I who never held (a Protestant locution)
with tut-mouthed Pastor Stoneseed or his atrocious ideas
that fallen human beings are "worms,"

mere "trash" frostjacked by idiotic Adam
and totally depraved, fully enslaved to the service of sin,
always knew in the pew of my kneeling,

while I bowed to the need of God's grace,
that he who defends the Creator must defend the creation
who reflects his glory as the pale moon

does the light of the incandescent sun,
and I, like Abe Lincoln who to fix something in his head
always wrote it down and by following

the Evangelists in addressing the Word
at least proved, if nothing else, some worth on this earth
by the act of faith it would be read

if only by me, no worm, and my resolve
to pray on it (another Protestant locution), despite the tears
running down the window, only gave me joy.

Winter, 1978. Cape Cod

Analogy for a Day Lily

On temptation, if I may,
I have often found myself disgraced
  as I myself betray
  while looking silly
with resolutions humiliatingly erased,
  yet a flower of a lily
  lasts but a single day.
If equal are they partners both in waste,
embracing one, the other be embraced.

So why then the piper pay
since both of these are rapidly replaced,
  the peccadilloes I weigh
  as I proceed willy-nilly
with my resolves so terribly displaced
  and this frail floral frilly
  that goes equally astray?
If on nature all natural logic's based,
blessing none, neither can be graced.

A Homily for Twins

for Shiloh and Shenandoah

Twigs or branches of trees grow either alternately or opposite each other.
Maples, ashes, dogwoods, and chestnuts have branches that are opposite,

as do shrubs like a burning bush, viburnums, winter creeper, and privets.
There are far less trees with opposite branching than otherwise. Why so?

What is being said of anything at all that alternates or stands in opposition
in the branching habits of common backyard trees that we can take away?

Can one say aesthetically that one opposed is therefore more symmetrical,
and yet as far as constituting beauty is such symmetry always good or bad?

Alternating branches can make an equal claim in their staggered balance
of a pattern that in its beauty exceeds in looks the dual shape of twinship.

Must a limb perforce have bilateral symmetry like the flatworm planarian,
an interdependent mirror image? Yet what is such an image if not a clone,

in a servile way a mindless duplication that in every sense merely mimes,
matches like a reprint to correspond in some pathetic equivalence of envy?

Is there hap in the way of nature's arrangement of limbs, or is a plan afoot,
and may one say a limb nourishes which stands opposite or acts the rival?

It depends if we argue that what is opposite is antagonistic or corresponds,
is contrary or compatible, works in the way we see something as complete.

Do not both act reciprocally, interchange, follow in turn, and act the mate
by way of alternation and due exchange? I say bless, accept, and foster fate.

Blue John Goblet

Look at the bands of purple-blue
in the goblet there on the tavern mantle torn from
mines with walls of fracture

bruised by the squeezing terra
as if with its hurricaning ripples wet by the ocean,
sphalerite, fluorspar, mineral,

which it matches wave for wave
blue-white-purple-banded it irradiates and seems to crash
amethystine chunk, drunk,

that has blue-bloomed with lead
down in the dark Derbyshire mines, so tell me please,
why then does it seem at sea?

Terribilità
of
Tuna and Tarpon

Have you munched on a tarpon?
And did you gag on its bones?
Are they not fashioned to sharpen
Your red vitals like flinted stones?

Nothing of tarpon is valued for food
When caught it is often thrown back.
All anglers delight in the savage feud
Found in its fight as a sporting hack.

Strangely curved is a tarpon mouth,
Whereas a tuna's gob is all straight.
A tarpon's all scales, north to south,
While a tuna is as smooth as a pate.

Tuna are notably chinless of face,
Tarps show prominent lower jaws.
Tuna are bigger and fatter and race
Like tarpon and leap for applause.

The flesh of the tuna is heaven sent.
It is solid and salty and red as blood.
We preen at a catch huge and spent
To be displayed like raising a rood.
A tuna landed is hung head down
But a tarpon is hung by the head.
What is said in a flaunted crown
Is a thing that should not be said,

For no manly boast in a battle rare
Should mock a beast that you kill.
The human trick is to take a dare
And fix with delight on the thrill

Of trumpeting it o'er hill and dale,
The proven glory of our expertise
In hanging proof, both head and tail,
As we proclaim it in mortal grease.

We must master the fish we fight
To show (as in photos) we've won,
Raise them in public, trophy height
In the brightest of all possible sun.

Tell me where does the difference run
In the shape of the creatures we slay?
In killing to eat or to slaughter for fun?
Should we not be shown how we play?

I see Prussian might in a trophy raised
And the craven need for a victory roar
No victim, with its executioner praised
and smiling, is not a metaphor for war.

Venus is Hollow

The rising and falling atmosphere,
a "breathing" action,
seems to indicate
that as a planet
Venus
is hollow.

From all we know of human passion,
its ups and downs
who is prepared
to soon discover
emptiness
can follow?

I have witnessed in the loving heart
how confidence fulfilled
prevails in love until
a cold reversal
makes
you wallow

The Sun

"The visible photosphere covers the actual surface of the
sun,much as the earth's oceans cover most of the surface
of the earth. Inthis case the sun's photosphere is very
bright and we cannot see thedarker, more rigid surface
features below the photosphere withoutthe aid of satellite
technology."

— Hippolyte Fizeau

The sun stands fixedly still
fierce, unchanging, inflex,
allowing by savage effects
an everlasting power to kill

by a terrible lack of motion
around which all revolves
while servile man evolves
a slavish fawning devotion

less for its immoderate light
or the broiling heat conveys
than that *rigidity* it relays
as God's most terrible fright.

The Man with the Fenestrate Shoes

for Jane Birkin

"The bread of my twentieth birthday I buttered with the sun"
— Charles Causley, "Cowboy Song"

I remember, I remember still
I felt the just sun in my bones,
the volumes underneath my arm,
and watched the symptoms of a grin
on the spooning cook's face
for the girl from Fiesole I loved
who could be read on me

as I walked and walked and walked,
and the brown lace of the Arno
flowed through my beautiful soul.
If La Rochefoucauld was right
with his ironic remark about love,
that very few men would fall in love
if they had never read about it,
I would not know, for I had found
what I had read about and delighted in
what I had found!
That day, it was so miraculous!
My bread felt good in my pocket.
The hand need only poke about
to feel the glory of the yeast,
flour, flowers, beaten, warm,
to be eaten near the water
by the naked umber walls,
past dark men and churching women.
I pass in my hat, Assyrian cap,
speedy with my holy lunch,
giggling at the time on my hands,
almost guilty from my joy.
I was lighter than heart-song,
ready with my dreams of lyrics
for the girl I leaned less upon
than against the walnut trees
all afternoon above the city,
letting my heart fill to the brim
as in that special place I walked upon
the sacrament of special moments
and felt the pentecosts promised
through the hole in my Italian shoe

Adolph Gottlieb

"We are going to have perhaps a thousand years of non-
representational painting...The social realist wants to
charm you or win you over. But the abstract expressionist
says to the public (more honestly): 'You're stupid. We

despise you. We don't want you to like us — or our art…'"
— Adolph Gottlieb in Selden Rodman's *Conversations with*
Artists

There is another buyer with a head of feathers
pondering my spadiceous and sorrel melange

in circles sloshed onto sandpapered hardboard
that I circular-sawed for panels, got two, three,

with an actual hardware store mop, $4.75 tops.
Whorls, all just wide enough to contain others,

— out-mouthing many of my own angry rants
shouted out in my cold-water flat-cum-studio

that my customers are only ugly cormorants
with cash — look impressive in puce or purple,

intertwining loops for fruits, ovals for assholes,
who because they jiggle change in their pockets

think they impress me? I squirt-squeezed lime
slashes, then crossed them with a chopped liver

vertical that could be any bitches' long cervix
for any dumb representational-seeking *pisher*

and this I turned out Sunday morning in, what,
fifteen, twenty minutes, had lacquered by noon:

and called it *Potshkit No. 47*. Love of painting
makes men stupid. What they deserve, I give;

remind me there is something else but cash,
when you have time, OK? Meanwhile, look

what I'm painting out of cheap pots of nacarat,
after leaching oil through gesso? Fungo shapes

slit with a razor blade, black drips, miceshit
bio-wrenched with colored milk cereal I pock

with tit-quills, fucking nibs, man, a dime per,
and this is — crazier than a Frank Stella fart —

Fungoofunshineana 444, and I state, why not,
and you know what it's telling you, wise guy?

It's telling you you're a fucking woodcock,
like I give a care. But, hey, you want squares,

I give you squares. You want fungo shapes,
you get fungo shapes. Why? You're a cluck,

Whorls, you want whorls, I'll give you whorls,
buy them all, dummy, and then go fuck a duck!

Cant

"Go to the ant, O sluggard; consider her ways, and be wise."
                                                — Proverbs 6:6

Since masses of ants
can flow like a liquid
and then bounce back
like a solid,
why in comparison
does the swarm of men
so brutally inflexible
seem so squalid,

and worst of all
when facing that fact
shrug in cold indifference
to remain stolid?

A Jew Looking at Fraktur

A Jew looking at Fraktur always grows anxious,
seeing in the type-face what, rinsing his bowels,
goosesteps across the page on a march of vicious
glyphs hammered out by gouges, knives, trowels,

a black-letter font known as *Gebrochene Schrift*
— "broken," halt, crippled with letters in ligature,
carved in an antique way, textbook heavy, no lift,
on any given page a kind of fractured furniture —

declaiming Wagner, *Neues Volk*, a Prussian fist
in its evil black, whether printed large or littler,
with dread echoes of victims on the Kaiser's list
and evocations of the broadcasts of Herr Hitler.

Red Dahlias

With their long purple stems too machined
with stiff gay piping like the jeans of Provincetown hustler,
red dahlias make me skeptical, blooms

— which yield not a scintilla of scent
as intricate and coldly repetitious as those geodesic domes
of Bucky Fuller, eyestrain heaven.

A bee will never approach that gold
central button, frigid in the over-crotcheted petals there
and tighter than a duck's rectum,

until it opens, and even then it is too small,
lost within that sculpted dodecahedronal efflorescence
that preens so cockily day and night,

all through summer. We love endurance,
in a flower to justify not merely the money we spent on it
but for all the extra work required by us

to squire it down like an overfussified nance
into the warm winter quarters of our dark cellars all winter,
husbanding it, so to speak. Truman Capote

in thick sweaters never needed to be coddled so.
Nothing rigid in a flower makes for warmth when delicacy
Is what the thing asks to be understood by.

Zucchini

On the morgue floor lay
Paul Castellano, murdered

mobster who, being impotent,
had had a gooseneck lamp

implant some years before
a rival gang shut the door.

An oddity in someone shot,
paradoxically so,

Little Pauly was ready to go
Big Pauly was not.

The Disease of Romanticism

The Romantics' deep self-immersion in dreamlike scenery
kept the entire lot of them all floating in ethereal greenery

with rare passion for nature, long vistas, hermits, and monks,
myths, Gothic ruins, twisted old trees with gnarled trunks,

scary forests, bare churchyards, hopes aflame and Teutonic,
chalky heights, mountains fierce rising high and symphonic

where dreamers wandered pondering problems insolvable
filled with strange urges, distortion, and layers improbable,

and seized with fevers of heart in the grip of mad passion,
brooding with inexplicable moods of unattainable fashion,

in rainstorms, wild and naked, they imbibed the imperious,
feeling the mystical, the fantastic, the strangely mysterious.

They rediscovered the lore at the core of old Germany wild
all that it honored, prefigured in darkness, and all it defiled,

tossing seas, morning mists storms, crosses, weather at war,
all found in Caspar David Friedrich and Eugene Delacroix.

Something in such worship pagan has the call of the fiddler
to dreamers unchecked. Did Wordsworth give birth to Hitler?

All Actors are Mentally Ill

"We're actors. We're the opposite of people."
— Tom Stoppard

"Pacino appeared on 'The Merv Griffin Show,' and, in
front of a television audience of millions, he froze. He just
couldn't do it," [Israel] Horovitz recalled. He felt he had
nothing to say. He was humiliated by his own presence. He
wasn't the character he was playing—he was Al. Pacino's
devotion to acting is, in a way, a defense against that self-
doubt. Having a script to work from gives him, he said, a
kind of license. 'I can *talk*, I can *speak*, I have something
to *say*,' he explained. 'You don't need a college education.
All the things that you were inhibited to talk about and
understand—they can come out in the play. The language
of great writing frees you of yourself.'"
— John Lahr on actor Al Pacino

Justin Archestrate flunked out of school
but, failing upwards in his dreams even as a kid by dint
   of craving hugs he felt badly due him,

now lived dorsoventrally to proceed
by what he could pretend to be by working front to back,
   so in a queer way actually succeeded

by flatly refusing reality as one sees it,
for anything one imagines can come true even if, a dwarf,
   one sweatily insists he is a giant

while not a one of them has even close
to anything like the isometric heads of sane folk use, trundling
   off to jobs in the real workaday world.

But, tell me, what vaulting hambone
in an asshole's hat is not on his way to some kind of
   casting-call in this world's auditoria?

Actors of course are all mentally ill.
What don't they crave? Audiences of lackeys and love
   howling in heat to watch them strut

and fiddle and fop and tock and preen
in skin-tight peacockian pants across white klieg-lit
   stages brighter than a thousand suns

are not enough to fill their empty holes
or anything like shill-bidding hankering for glory.
   Applause-freaks heave their hearts

at us with such abandon they prove
that excess alone comports in the end to one long
   suffocating bout of mother love.

How else does Hollywood fashion
falcons out of buzzards and set them soaring high
   above the air for fucked-up fame?

To crave accolades? Acclaim? Cheers?
Approbation for what? Shapeshifting some dumb role
　like a prehensile color-changing lizard

　into a million dollar life-style to give
the country only another girdle-salesman, more godfop
　for the slick gum-colored fan mags?

　An actor can play thirty different people —
it is less therapy than a desperate escape from himself —
　but, whatever role, he is always Don Juan

　playing up to an audience, all virgins,
with the flirtatious hidalgo wagging his phallus,
　seeking a monstrous sort of love.

　By moral law he should suppress
whatever accustoms the mind to applause and spend
　a week in a mud-hut once a year

　without books, money, agents, or any
amenities in order to meditate, as H.G. Wells suggested in
　in *A Modern Utopia* we all should.

　As taxi drivers divide the world into fares
and pedestrians, actors recognize only fans or fools,
　the filtering fools of any playwright

　who states the area of the personalities
that they adopt in order to learn to know what to give
　by way of the vanities they also borrow

　in changing their names, capping their teeth,
learning to speak, bob their noses, curry their bodies,
　and then dare to call themselves real.

　Any performance is not a production
but a contest for adoration, a narcissistic love affair
　by fabliau archetypes for themselves.

What is not certifiable in the craven
desire to be a model or go on television, capsizing
    when not being massaged by hordes,

and say it is not a disease? Pursuit alone
is not suspect in itself, draping itself over the world?
    Need: greed. "*I insist I be overpaid!*"

cries Thespo, who calls himself a ball of fire,
and if he reaches the top, befriending fat producers, glozing,
    apologizing to mirrors for his shallowness

in order to seem real, he calls room service
in some Louis XV Suite with bottles of Roederer Cristal
    on ice by a bed with opossum coverlets

and ivory linens as fine as Swiss hankies
demanding, first, a *pâté de campagne* and a plate of
    salad with *only* baby vegetables,

then a *cassolette de queues d'écrevisse* and
some crayfish in a delicate buttery bath (for the two dogs)
    followed by a bottle, make it 1975,

of, indeed, an expensive Romanée Conti,
then later in a wasted stupor in the midst of drunken dreams
    when his face falls into the salad bits

he can pretend, when he can see and is still
sentient, an artichoke is a not thistle, barley is not grass,
    and wet, weak watercress is not a weed.

A Thought on Lobelia Cardinalis

The French "impressionists" all knew
that a touch or two of red in a garden
    made the pastels sing,

in the way supermarket shopping carts
when unreturned in parking lots prove
  — and in censure bring —

an eyesore and that many lazy Americans
deserve neither a Monet nor, in my opinion,
  a single goddamned thing.

Christ the Laborer

Give me Christ the working laborer,
  the man of hammer and nails,
whose compassion extended especially
  to him who stumbles and fails.

I seek the flogged Galilean to love,
  friend of leper and whore,
he who gave hope to the working man
  who built, to open, the door.
The man of sorrows owned not a thing
  who suffered whip and thorn.
No gentleman was a ever a God for me,
  none unfamiliar with scorn.

For you who walked the thoroughfares,
  forgave the world without pride,
and hung on a cross to be speared for us
  I kiss the dear wound in your side.

Easter 2014

Goodbye to All That

"If the Bill of Rights were put to a vote, it would
  probably lose."— *Earl Warren*, Chief Justice of the United
States

When I'm on my deathbed remind me
lest by happenstance I should forget
and through nostalgia alter my plea
to flee this world without any regret
that men now marry men at the altar,
the Nativity crèche is a public taboo,
each corner bank is a potential defaulter,
family traditions as such are all through,
grass-fed beef is now sold as a rarity,
ponytails are worn by middle-age men,
income-tax forms are wanting in clarity
and filing them more complex than Zen,
boys find romantic their pants hanging off,
showing their shorts and much of their bum,
crudeness in movies is as pigs to a trough,
our south border crossings are all overrun,
news a day old is called "breaking news"
and half of the stories broadcasters invent,
rare is the sight now of real leather shoes,
what we manufacture is not worth a cent,
there is cheating on income taxes galore,
true faith has been supplanted by doubt,
no set of rules for dating exist anymore:
in fact it's referred to as just "hanging out."
It is bigotry now to say "Merry Christmas,"
mental disorders now rate higher than ever,
outsourcing's the key to all major business,
today finding a job is a hopeless endeavor,
ocean levels are rising up over our lands,
all rivers and ponds full of algae are silty,
Congress does little but sit on its hands,
thieving bank execs are never found guilty,
teenagers bring loaded rifles to school,
paper money is now made of plastic,
insider-trading on Wall Street's a rule,
no political speech is not bombastic,
our economy keeps hitting the skids,
Army women are engaging in combat,
a pastime for priests is molesting kids,
music now alters from format to format,
taxi drivers in cabs can carry no money,

property taxes are as high as a mortgage,
most stand-up comedians rarely are funny,
tuitions are raised for football in college,
Republicans all thrive on hating the poor,
while Dems look to throw money away,
the high national debt continues to soar,
prohibitions in school prevent you to pray,
baseball players are all millionaires,
Arabs are openly mocked with impunity,
What's manufactured in America wears,
political parties are defined by disunity,
television is killing the national soul,
Spanish in places has English replaced,
going on welfare is everyone's goal,
all seven seas are filling with waste,
rap music is now considered harmonious,
the crappiest books alone are best-sellers,
feminist rants are now seen as euphonious,
fish sold in markets are all bottom-dwellers,
pornography pollutes the World Internet,
athletes take steroids and perpetually lie,
black people rarely are met with respect,
junior school students their teachers defy,
American children are allergic to sweat,
all actors get paid as if they were sheiks,
both unions and owners production beset,
we learn government truths only through leaks,
talking in libraries is now standard behavior,
churches no longer stay open all day,
lobbyists can literally purchase a favor,
men are wusses and women now bray,
airplane seats are all smaller than books,
unaffiliated female clerics abound,
big city mayors are guaranteed crooks,
gas and oil prices rising daily astound,
correctness in grammar's a thing of the past,
single parenthood is considered the norm,
morons on cellphones are yakking full blast,
all President's birthdays are now uniform,
atheists are publicly revered now as gods,
there are presently two living Popes,

Mid-Eastern countries are forever at odds,
our Congress is run entirely by dopes,
the most serious source for authentication
is now [quote] *"I saw it on television!"*
Our savings are rocked by constant stagflation,
men who are honest are met with derision,
pro bikers and racers all secretly cheat,
most human beings cannot write a letter,
politicians not wealthy can bank on defeat,
every new generation is deeper a debtor,
talking-haircuts on television never shut up,
Wall Street has purloined America's teeth.
Which national institution is not corrupt?
What was on top is now sadly beneath.
We have found to our horror a culture respelt
in what I would call Rumplestiltskinian ways,
where so little is thought and even less felt;
the colors of autos are all indistinct grays.
Let this explain why at this solemn hour
when I'm called upon to exit this world
you'll not see me fight to fate overpower
as I lie here a helpless near-fetus encurled,
for I have witnessed the world out of joint
and the lack of all graces a pitiful sham.
No, only the *living* will fate disappoint.
As to my passing, I don't give a damn.
Bless me with Extreme Unction, please,
and a compress apply to my fevered brow,
but I plead with you not to stay my release,
No matter why, when, what, where, or how.

Woodpeckerness

On a train like a log to Bridgeport I see faces like bark-dependant birds.
There is Mr. Titmouse, ever reaching around to fold his paper in thirds
Hel*looo*, Ms. Rowbottom! You with that bag again, label: *Buenos Aires*
— to me you're a blue-headed vireo, munching bars of fruits and berries.
I find that fashioning ornithological names to passengers I repeatedly see
allows me some time on this boring haul to indulge in much personal glee.

There is odd Mr. Cobblecod, a tiny Eurasian nuthatch in an old gray coat,
his pen perpetually raised above his crossword, seeking an apposite quote.
Across is a seed-eating chickadee, munching a scone and spraying crumbs.
Why is it that on this bark of winter trunk my brown creeper never comes?
But wait, she's there, a tiny woodland nymph up front — and see her flaunt
by the bald junko whose whinnying sneeze sounds like that of crazy aunt.
I call her Susan Cheatgrass, all in secret fun. Baldy's name is simply Pferd.
A crow punches my ticket, Mr. Ollie Poopsaint, a great dark shuffling bird.
Carbonaro has a northern cardinal's scowl. Bugfuck is a spectacled finch.
I suspect the former's Italian, the latter with a penis no larger than an inch.
Up suddenly gets the chickadee, Stuffeta, heading once again off to the john,
wearing a suit of brown that resembles in color the mud of a rainy dawn.
There is Creamsicle Pants, Snazzel, Major Hoople, Amarillo — cowboy hat —
sleek Clive Christian, a perfumed gay, and Pot Roast who is walloping fat.
The Fartcushion's a tubby lady-with-hat who resembles a lesser flamingo.
House sparrows are seated everywhere: Nosehair, Mr. Feedbag, and Ringo.
See the punky pileated woodpecker with a wet DA haircut just getting on?
I hate him, despite he looks to me like an Everly, you choose, Phil or Don.
Is it any wonder, when boarding, I see this lot heading to their New Yorks
that in terms of sound in the car I've come to hear not voices but squawks?

Impossibility of Limits

The edge is not me.
Where I have gone to the farthest
proclaims no dares.

Outside of me
where I notice my dreams biggest
are scarlet warnings

but never refusals
that notify of boundaries farthest
not being mine.

Limits may measure
and not. The boundary of bodies
are neither a part

of the enclosed body
nor show any surrounding buries
any atmosphere for me,

so no limits
mean no measures, only bounties.
I pay no fares.

Strumpet

"O adulterous people, do you not know that friendship with
the world is enmity with God"

— James 4: 4-5

Why, if Esther to be queen was willing to fuck,
to move on up, hide her dark Jewishness to thrive,

perfuming her hot flesh with purple oils and myrrh,
and watch among the Persians wily Mordecai connive,

taking a full year and more to study bedroom tricks,
the better to seduce a king and share his might,

sashaying before him naked on her furry mules,
with jellied smirks for every tongue of night,

a cosmetic whore shelving all the sacred rules,
why then cannot victories await the rest us

who, stifling secrets that may hinder our advance
and swapping by intrigue our chastity for lust,

yearn for the world's success — and is it wrong?
There is a horny, bejeweled Ahasuerus who awaits

anyone who would advance by dancing in a thong.
But while his hot and hairy appetite he sates,

more than a body's yet required, truth to tell,
for such a greedy Jewish girl to reach her goal.

Be prepared, anon, unlike Daniel in his cell
or Joseph in his filthy den, to sell your soul.

Forked Tongue

Jews say they own *all* of the land
as the will of God as defined and literally recorded,
   in the pages of the Bible,

   but then *all* flatly refuse to accept
blame for literally screaming for Christ's crucifixion
   and call it anti-Semitic libel.

The Malebranche

The twelve vulgar, quarrelsome demons from Dante's *Inferno*, whose
duty it is to force the corrupt politicians (*barrators*) to stay under the
surface of a boiling lake of pitch, have all gathered together in Hell
to meet and greet the twelve warmest advocates of torture, their evil
counterparts, in the George W. Bush administration who chose to employ
the "*verschaerfte Vernehmung*" techniques employed by the Gestapo during
World War II in order to pry information from imprisoned victims.

I.

Satan's Introductions in Hell

Malacoda, the leader ("Evil Tail"), meet President G. W. Bush
Barbariccia ("Curly Beard"), meet Richard Cheney, Vice President
Cagnazzo ("Nasty Dog"), meet Condoleezza Rice, Secretary of State
Calcabrina ("Grace Stomper"), meet Michael Hayden, CIA Director
Ciriatto ("Wild Hog"), meet Donald Rumsfeld, Secretary of Defense
Draghignazzo ("Big Nasty Dragon"), meet Senator Joseph Lieberman
Farfarello ("Goblin"), meet John Yoo, Deputy Assistant Attorney General

Graffiacane ("Dog Scratcher"), meet Alberto Gonzales, Council to the President
Libicocco ("Libyan Hothead"), meet Paul Wolfowitz, Deputy Defense Secretary
Alichino ("Harlequin"), meet Jay Bybee, Federal Judge on Court of Appeals
Rubicante ("Red-faced Terror"), meet David S. Addington, Legal Counsel
Scarmiglione ("Trouble Maker"), meet John Bruce Jessen, Air Force
psychologist and designer of "enhanced interrogation techniques"

II.

The Demons Welcome Their Visitors

Malacoda sporting with George W. Bush shoves a rocket up his ass.
Barbariccia locks a helmet over Cheney's head made of heavy brass.
Cagnazzo, the Nasty Dog, yanks out Condoleezza's wagging tongue.
Calcabrina fatally throttles Michael Hayden with a sold rubber bung.
Ciriatto castrates Donald H. Rumsfeld to become some devil's wife.
Draghignazzo slices Lieberman's head in two with a Santoku knife.
Farfarello snips off John Yoo's little penis to make a ballpark frank.
Graffiacane makes Alberto Gonzales eat it — shriveled — as a prank.
Libicocco hangs Paul Wolfowitz, blinded, upside down with weights.
Alichino locks Jay Bybee in a room with cobras pouring out of grates.
Rubicante releases rabid raccoons to chew off Addington's fat feet.
Scarmiglione fills Jake Jessen up with creosote so he cannot excrete.

The Mating of Mountain and Forest

Something of gender is proclaimed in mountain and forest,
sensual pleas in power and patience, grandeur and growth,

sensual interdependence of bush and light, roots and height
and layered space and hot bearing that intermix and modify.

It is not for me to determine just how, as seeds develop here
and soaring occurs there or the way water courses through

the roots of trees that rise up to spread across a mountain
where loft and layered space and bearing mold and modify.

Mountains are all of them darkened by their mystic forests
which have for centuries been a favored location for them.

and while few soils are truly hostile to trees, no boggy soil
nor loess nor silt can ever serve trees or craggy mountains

or the concept of either. A forest may colonize poor soils
because as it slowly grows another soil it slowly makes,

particularly when it consists of leafy trees, which produce
rich humus, which only then can rise to meet a mountain.

Noirfontaine, the *Montenegro* in Yugoslavia, *Bois Noirs*,
The Black Mounts in England, the enchanted *Schwarzwalds*

are all colonized by an open light that soon evokes darkness.
Trees that come to grip the ground then create shaded areas,

making a black of colored space as each receives the other,
tree after tree joining a mountain, it receiving tree after tree

which as we watch them in an after-imaging embrace must
watch as inevitable darkness makes them majestically one.

Verbal Threads

to Prof. Hugh Hennedy

"The next day," "I myself did not know him,"
"After me comes a man who ranks ahead of me because he was before me,"
"I saw the spirit descending." Verbal threads

in the Gospels told by the story-teller, details,
an inside account, assure us he was an eyewitness who remembered —
— and recorded — special historical moments.

"Where are you staying?" "And it came to pass."
"And so it was, that, while they were there, the days were accomplished
that she should be delivered."

When I was a boy I was *yanked* into books
by reading what I suddenly saw with a flash I badly needed to know,
   and being so compelled so decided me.

A raven was the last animal to leave the Ark. (Gen. 8:6)
Goliath was a full 9 ½ feet tall, and the iron point of his spear alone
   weighed a heavy 15 pounds. (1 Samuel 17:7)

David had beautiful eyes (1 Samuel 16:12)
In Biblical days, men closed a deal by exchanging sandals (Ruth 4:7)
   All animals have to answer to God, too. (Gen. 9:5)

I love the high specificity of narrative
"It was about four o'clock in the afternoon" we are told of a day
   when two disciples first meet Jesus

late in the afternoon, a lectionary reflection
— fabulous aspects — only the truly passionate reader can cherish
   when Jesus hearing their footsteps asks,

"What are you looking for?" They know not
how to answer but simply ask the first question that comes to mind.
   It was bold. *"Where are you staying?"*

"Come and you will see," Christ replies.
"It was about four in the afternoon." That is, it was the tenth hour.
   It was those details took me to His house.

The Clawing Winds of Nebraska

"Plongez au plus profond du gouffre, où tous les crimes,
Flagelles par un vent qui ne vient pas du ciel,
Bouillonnent pêle-mêle avec un bruit d'orage."

Charles Baudelaire, Les Èpaves

There is nothing to cut the sharp winds in Nebraska,
gusting insanely over the endless and flavescent plains

through the arid sand hills, scarfing trees and shaping
into noses like sharp pinocchionian dowels small hills,

birdless over the interleaving scapes. It is mindless,
beyond its blind whim in what striking out it fails

to reckon, and in its uncalculated abruptness betrays
no more intent than the flailing arms of the tortured.

Where begins the conceiving rage, the thrust, of wind?
In what hell is it gathered to wreck the very air it rides?

Women with broom-dry hair hear shutters bang and
see washing disappear, jostling delusions of all kinds,

as they wait silently beneath precarious rooves lifting ,
like flimsy hats above the juddering, shuddering walls.

Wind, irrupting, can be stronger than dreams and so
leave nothing in the head but brooding melancholy.

605

In the midst of one blow, Godiva Ealing, 17, distraught,
hanged herself from the crankshaft of a raised car in a barn

and was found swaying above the blowing whorls of hay
she often pitched, now all unbaled and loose in fierce chaos.

Vilate Poel walked out of his 1940s Socony gas station
one day and never returned. Blistered with rusty pumps,

the broken windows of the place, empty as blind eyes,
are vacuumed by the sucking sounds of merciless wind,

just the tall grasses, keening, sound their odd threnody.
Wind here is called whining by more than one farmer.

It drove Oren Crayonstone raving mad, an old soldier,
cracked, who ended up leaping in vain, as daily he did,

at the bent"Railroad Crossing" sign out by Worsenville,
trying to nix – rub out! – the central black double S's

he misunderstood in his dementia to be secret Nazi code,
even as rolling trains with their endless lines of boxcars

curving down the rails from the Powder River roistered
through his brain like the shells that battered the Bulge.

Transgrounded by the void, what can one do but wait?
In its cruel, insistent, unweathersensing mercilessness,

must we not ask how wind in its featureless emptiness
could the Holy Paraclete define for all that is missing

in the nothingness of the uncut sharp winds in Nebraska,
gusting through the long flavescent plains to the sand hills?

Provincetown Chat

How can a sex
With an entrance
No matter how one directs it
Choose not to be willing
To oblige another
With such
A convenient exit?

When has sex
Please tell me
Even in places of lenience
Been ever aligned
To a process
With something
Approaching convenience?

Suicide Woods in Japan

Mr and Mrs Mokusai wept on their table
after a post-war American couple inhabiting their rooms
 by way of requisitioned housing in 1947

 had covered every inch of woodwork
in chartreuse paint before they left, indecorously howling!
 Where was the flat-sawn grain they loved,

 their chinaberry doors, gently fumed,
those unsanded Japanese larch borders with their oily feel
 and distinct resinous odor? Gone, *gone*!

 All those lovely spalted maple cabinets
with their massaranduba knobs, beefwood beech closets,
 shelves of teak and paper birch,

 slubbered by ignorant *yanki zuwari*
with outsized buttocks, enormous shoes, and huge hooting
 knobs for noses.! *"Kusottare!"* "Shit-drips!"

 shouted Kuri Mokusai, squeezing his fists,
"Baka!" "Noroma!" "Dasei!" Ijiwaru!" and *"Chikushō!"*
 Kaide screamed, *"Orokana amerikahito* !"

 No western mind can ever quite know
how much Japanese love wood in its pure natural state
 and find the act of painting or staining it

 a crime. It is not merely bad taste to do so
but ugly, crass vandalism. No enameled tubs for them,
 only scalding water, never cold,

to bathe in a box of wood, un-pigmented,
square, like the Mokusai's petrified wood-sink which
   the *Ba ka na nyūyōkā* had decaled!

Wood in Japan is never ordinary lumber.
The planking in their lumberyards is catalogued like books
   in a library, with every single board,

   carrying identification. Like book pages,
every board that is cut from the same tree is sold together
   with an eye to pores, interlocking grains,

   patterns, flecks,tight curl, and natural age,
bird's eye, quilted, curly, slab-sawn, fiddleback, and burr.
   The refinishing loons left the Mokusais

   suicidal who could not sand deep enough
to get paint out of all the tiny cracks. They tried by hand
   for weeks, crying, and still didn't get it all,

   they who had courted on the Nihonbashi,
the lovely Tokugawa-era wooden bridge replaced in 1911
   by the present-day concrete *bashi*,

   the very one on a dark rainy afternoon
as if out of ritual obligation holding hands and in tears
   the two of them despairingly jumped off.

   It had been painted, you see, overshadowed
by the Shuto Expressway by the old canal, unlike the sacred
   Sea of Trees, too revered a spot for sacrifice.

Evgeny Rood, With Knife, On His Wild Hunt for Dandelions

Free greens? Open hunting! Nature's wild market basket sale!
It is Spring and Evgeny, a bald lawyer (ret.) madly trundles off

to Oak Grove Cemetery with his favorite cutting tool, a knife
and big colander for dandelion leaves, their lion's jagged teeth

a miser's delight! "The vitamin C in these plants alone is gold!"
he mutters to himself, fast on his old knees snapping up plants.

"Rich minerals to be had for nothing! Iron, potassium, and zinc!
Complimentary, gratis! All for zip" He had bored people rigid,

crowing about such finds for years. people who tuned him out
back in the 1970s. "All on the QT! Weeds! Pick 'em young, see?

The leaves I use to add flavor to sandwiches, salads and teas.
The roots are used in some coffee substitutes, and the flowers

And the flowers? Just perfect for making wine! Free! All *free!*
Tiny patches on a hill show traces of his cuneiform syllabery

as he haunches back and forth on a kneel-hop with a drilling eye,
poking his way among the lichened gravestones and fallen urns,

snatching up fistfuls of leaves the second he is looking for more.
Retirement offered no rest when riches could be had for nothing,

not for Evgeny, a skinflint all life — "To be had for the asking"
was a phrase, a key, that vitalized his every dream, aspiration,

despite the fact he was a multi-millionaire with endless acreage,
three homes on Cape Cod, and a rolling farm in rural Virginia —

now he found he had nothing to do but wander old graveyards
like a wizened Rumanian *bunicĐ* in a kerchief simpling for herbs,

greenery no Coleridge or Wordsworth could have valued more
who in their many splendid songs to river, flower, bush and tree,

wrote not a word that could more have lightened Evgeny's heart
than that paramount thought he'd love — to wit, that nature's *free!*

My Heart is a High Belfry

My heart is a high belfry
where carillons play and swallows fly
that looks out upon a coast

but acts as well a fire-watch
to guard against odd fancies that can rise
within and serve a ghost

to haunt both stone and height
with what can murder music when it plays
and whatever bird that flies

No one who is not prepared
within to guard the ramparts of himself
goes unready when he dies.

The Red Bulls of Çatalhöyük

6000 B.C.

Cannibal Toygar, his big teeth
jagged with sickle shine, bold restive hands,
cultivated hoe-like stones

he licked after rubbing them
to kill wild pigs with thuds until with sticks
fashioned out of bones

he craved to draw red bulls
on man-made walls in clay Çatalhöyük caves,
the copied cattle, auroch clones,

so sporting real his people met
there in fur to mime them lowing, chewing, and
to give them, dying, groans.

Mr. Feenamint

Try as he might, he suffered from thought as it rolled in his mind
for he could not mix his thought or the result of it with his feeling
and could only think about feeling, as if to all thought he was blind,
which then, divided, left part of his mind, part of his heart congealing,

but if he *thought* about feeling, he could only conclude he thought,
so if feelings were the product of thought who would deny he felt,
despite the fact that every thought his feelings excluded as if a clot
automatically prevented the flow of one wherever the other dwelt.

Thoughts, it seemed, compared to feelings were far easier to change,
but then again did not changing our thoughts change the way we feel,
and therefore did not feelings as subjects let thought itself rearrange
what seemed borne as much of eternal confusion as personal appeal?

As nothing seemed to solve a dilemma that made him look like a fool,
he ingested instead a powerful laxative and sat out the day on a stool.

611

We're All Off to Pimlico

Mo, get on your moped
Joe, get on your joped

Mike, hop on your bicycle
Bike, hop on your micycle

Esther, jump aboard your vespa
Vespa, jump aboard your tester

Kooky, hop on to your suzuki
Suky, hop on to your kabuki

And we're all off to Pimlico for cream![repeat refrain]
Zipping off to Pimlico, Pimlico, Pimlico!
And we're off to flaming Pimlico for cream!

Bonda, spring upon your honda.
Honda, leap upon your bonda

Pursuing, pursuing,
Whipping off, zipping off to Pimlico, Pimlico, Pimlico!
Pursuing our elusive dream,
Nipping off
Tripping off
Zipping off to Pimlico for cream!

Tawdry Ball

Earth! I will not bring a child into the cold
cacophaginous sadness of this waste-filled midden, broken,
    poverty-ridden, starving, washed up.

Dirty Tom Masaccio portrayed our parents
creeping out of Eden like child molesters. Look at Crazy Eve,
    out of step, consider Adam, red-haired goon.

Where should I will what I want to save?
I see nothing for my heirs but rolling bones, designs of evil,
    charred witnesses of blackest crimes,

the caretakers of this dark poisoned garden
standing by with long rusty rakes to cover over orts and offal.
    That my mad books were written to last

alone makes a mockery of the kind of time
nothing humanly created deserves with its pretensions to eternity
    and blasphemes the very idea of hope!

I will therefore neither write for you nor ape
the fatuous idea that posterity awaits, merely mock the enterprise
    of blooming until final winter arrives.

Christ and Bread

That sheaf of grain near the manger bed
in Hugo Van der Goes' *The Adoration of the Magi,*
which is bigger than Christ, could be another child
and is in a real sense Savior to our eyes,

for Jesus told us, "I am the living bread
which has come down from heaven, if anyone eats
of this bread he shall live forever. This bread is me,
is my flesh. Grain,yeast, dough all rise.

Christ is — embodies — what we are fed.
The very name Bethlehem *means* "house of bread."
He gave of his body as much as he gave his blood.
Pray to living Christ. Bread complies.

The Specter of Ravensbourne

I am the Specter of Ravensbourne
who walks by the docks of the sea
seeking to mourn all hearts forlorn
who have summoned eternity.

The darkness, fog, and the mist
which combine as design in me
silently lead to those who plead,
both appointment and appointee.

Time in this place is up for them
as they stand by the strand or quay
to help me decry those who apply,
to leave time and no longer be.

Cloth of Gold

American Indians loved buttercups
and would boil their roots and eat them or make a flour
   from their parched and tiny seeds,

   and share them with partridges,
voles, mice, chickens, cattle who grazed for the seed-heads,
   and geese who yanked the weeds,

   but never with white men, vain swains,
who plucked their leaves solely to see if they were loved
   or young girls walking the meads

   to see if they'd soon be married
if the shiny flower cups reflected yellow on their chins.
   Squaws squeezed juice from its reeds

   as a yellow dye for their blankets,
but weren't Indian, whites, and beasts looking for sunshine
   plants to fill their personal needs?

   for Henry Bernatonis

Three's a Crowd;
or,
the Fateful Tale of Harry Napoli, Cleaving
Rappleye, and Ms. Carson Potter,
(A Novel)

to Frans Masereel

Napoli
happily
Rappleye
called,

leaving
Cleaving,
seething,
appalled.

Carson
Parson
McPharson
stalled.

Average
marriage?
Savage!
Recalled.

Canary
Harry,
wary,
crawled.

Lies
guys
devise
galled.

Potter,
hotter,
plotter,
evolved.

Rappleye
unhappily
sloppily
bawled.

God Doesn't Care What We Do

Shoot old ditso granny down dead,
admit you're a Trotskyite red,
drive a purple screw up a black chimney flue,
pitch off Mt. Blanc on a sled,
bite fully in half a cross-eyed giraffe,
For God does not care what we do.
He couldn't care less what we do.

Want to waggle your weenie at women,
dispatch a nun with a poison persimmon,
commit Zadok the Priest to a zoo,
change your name to Harley McCrimmon,
throttle a dog or go gigging for frog?
I say God does not care what we do.
He couldn't care less what we do.

Drown your troubles in 100-proof liquor,
chug down wormwood or watery ichor,
to your wife prove untrue on a boat to Peru
with a tart with a tongue like a flicker,
shove blow up your nose by using a hose.
See, God does not care what we do.
He couldn't care less what we do.

Detonate the entire National Treasury,
to a gay say, "Bend over and pleasure me!"
Puncture every canoe of the radical Sioux,
have your way with an innocent Kashmiri,
serve to a group bowls of vile cold chalk soup.
But God does not care what we do.
He couldn't care less what we do.

Pity poor church-going believers
gnawing on Scripture like beavers,
hoping heaven to view as they stand in a queue,
to a one of them underachievers!
Imagine the waste of living life chaste!
No, God does not care what we do.
He couldn't care less what we do.

Black Heart

I saw one winter the grave at Novodevichy Cemetery
as I meandered down a beaten path under a cloudy sky

of Nadezhda, Stalin's second wife, who had once drawn
a tattoo of a black square over her heart and pointing to it

told her young daughter, Svetlana, "This is where the heart
is." It was the very spot in which she shot herself in 1932

after a public spat at a dinner party. (Some claim the revolver
was found beside the hand she did not use, indicating a frame

-up, for many in Russia allege that Stalin killed her himself.)
Stalin and Nadya had became angry with each other. Irritated,

Nadya started dancing with her louche Georgian godfather,
"Uncle Abel" Yenukidze, the official in charge of the Kremlin,

who often boasted of shocking affairs with teenage ballerinas.
Stalin was also flirting with Galya Yegorova, the beautiful wife

of a Red Army commander, a brash movie actress well-known
for her affairs and *risqué* dresses. "Why aren't you drinking?"

Stalin asked Nadya, tossing an orange peel at her. "Hey you!
Have a drink!" "My name isn't 'hey'!" she retorted, stormed

out screaming. Stalin well knew blackness of the heart, where
each resided, both blackness and heart, without a drawn tattoo.

To shoot yourself in the heart , or coldly to be shot in the heart,
is however a personal death either way. One dies of a disease,

from hunger, by violence, with malice or not, and for another,
but direct, empirical, firsthand, and immediate is — especially

to show your daughter, was my thought at the Novodevichy
as I walked there under clouds — where you draw the line.

On the Rope Ferry at Bablockhythe

On the rope ferry at Bablockhythe
    I saw a pale maiden fair
who coming out of the watermeadows
    seemed to be shedding a tear.

I fell in love with her by the footbridge
    at the site of the lower weir,
but she strangely was gone of a sudden
    as if never a soul did appear.

Was it the river took her away from me?
    No boat had removed from the stair.
My heart disappeared from within myself
    and my soul I once held dear.

I return to the Thames intermittently
    all alone with a heart full of care
and by the bridge ovelooking the meadows
    live with my unfulfilled prayer.

Dramatis Personae

"A mask tells us more than a face."
        — Oscar Wilde

Those twin masks, side by side, scandalized me as a boy,
the Fool and the Frown, cheek to jowl — a matching toy?

I feared to see the pair of them fronting a theater marquee,
or on a cinema poster, barbaric grimace next to insane glee,

when holding my mother's hand she took us to the Loew's
where in darkness we'd thread blind through the seated rows.

They were *never* mirthful eyes, not on the face of the Fool:
idiotic risibility has ever since for me come across as cruel.

I saw only the taunt of Dionysian madness, kindness none,
the mock of a grin, a sadistic mask, that never stood for fun.

The mouth of the Frown looked badly torn, a rip in a bag,
upside-down, *puuuulled*, as if yanked low by gravity drag,

and its mad eyes — its, hers, theirs? — are filled with agony,
as if being tortured, in actual pain, to some violent degree.

A mask, whether for protection, novelty, bluff, or disguise,
by the fears of childhood reckoning speaks basically of spies,

and carved on the plinth of a theater or arch or vault or flue
the Fool and the Frown can be descried often surveying you.

Monster from another monster from other monster's weaned,
two disembodied heads, fiend behind a fiend behind a fiend,

this worthless, unrelated, ruminating twosome seems to judge
all human creatures whom they observe and find them sludge.

No child in its contemplations can't locate the face of threat,
however, for ferocity by its own odor calls up a mood of fret;

innocence by dint of purity sees the visages of empty souls,
the smell of demons, the danger of beasts, the hearts of trolls.

I hate those cretinous faces, portrayed at the human extreme,
as if it is somehow memorable to see oneself in mid-scream,

And as an adult it isn't much different attending a film or play
I notice that passing a theater portal I still tend to look away.

The Transfiguration of October

Each dark warm October dusk
holding enchantment in the air
reaches to our deepest dreams

beckoning ourselves to dare
in finding nothing as it seems
to breathe in the magic musk

as the mystery of nature deems
to pass through our bodily husk
and assume anew a spirit rare.

Wise Men Fish Here

for Alec Stansell

Fish in your own blessed world!
Which of us can't hire snipe-faced guides with grips
to wade with us in the Miramichi

or rent a fishing charter to ogle
tarpon chasing down a top water plug in aerial shows
in Boca Grande or Islamorada?

I knew a master dibbler who could cast
his line in a dumpy, urban pond, a bend in the channel
tzzzz*plp!*- and make of it a honey hole!

Didn't William Caxton fashion books
with his own devices? Thoreau not love the millponds,
races, and lakes of rural Concord,

his small domain? To Kant Königsberg
was his sole dominion. Manufactured mother love,
where she woos you to love her,

not her to love you, is falsely pathetic.
My fret of snobbery obtrudes when I beseech you,
not only to fish local ponds for stripers,

but of refraining from sending me
beery letters with smatterings of bought anecdotes
from hellholes metropolitan to vaunt

your friends. Be an apprentice always,
holily real. Silliness originally meant innocence,
a lovely styptic to coarsing vanities

that would have you boast you are first,
fitter, superior, better than being last, not and never
the advice the Lord in his wisdom

gave to his avid apostles, fisherman,
who on the stormy sea of Galilee angled for barbel or
biny, sardines, scaleless catfish,

musht fish with their few small bones,
catches of majesty enough in that conceits are put aside
and tastier for being of your world.

Possess your small pond, take pleasure
in your small fish, prize their small bones, treasure
the small place you're in, on, near, with!

Something Wicked Comes This Way

But it is not grim death that we're taught to shun, the end,
that dark horror we receive as if legislated by committee.

Only the timid roturier — a common person — fears death.
Life will be far, far better on the *other s*ide of life. A pity

we read Enoch and Elijah never died. Where did they go?
Translated? Lost in a whirlwind? Gone to a galactic city?

To live with our God on the ramparts wide? As vistas soar
consider space of timeless blue. Ponder the joy of eternity!

All of life's navigators, adventurers, poets, artists, and minds,
history's geniuses, intellects, souls rare and endlessly witty,

explorers, wanderers, sculptors, true holy men, and trekkers,
kings, true wits, court-jesters, princes, women who are pretty.

I await the hour I fly through space, a better world embrace,
to kick away with joy all traces from a valley gray and gritty.

Desperado Prayer

If bamboo grows up to an inch an hour
and soars fast enough quite to see,
why in the world, then,
regarding a hateful ex-girlfriend
can't I by some whirlwind
from that nightmare get fully free?

Fr. Motherway's Absolution

Loneliness makes for a fierce coldness in a soul, a hard-
bitten rue redder in priests than the sins they are asked

to absolve day after day, night after grim night, a cesspit
of perversions, dark adulteries, queer angular creepshows.

What had Fr. Motherway but celibate nights, living alone,
among shiny ciboria, amices, manciples, copes, and stoles,

and a nutty Irish maid who did the beds? Clerics live alone,
with not a soul to whom they can become attached, save Mom,

simpering Sodality ladies who cook them awful casseroles,
male organists weeping in the dark with dents in their heads,

and desperate middle-aged gay collection-taker-uppers who
hang around, sibilating, arranging flowers for the side-altars.

They are not permitted to live, to have a life, and therefore
the lives of others for them are not of the same consequence

as they are for normals. The hardness of the church! Steel!
No wonder priests ask for unheard of sacrifices, demanding

cash for weddings, baptisms, flatly refusing good couples
birth control, howling for tithing, living large on lobsters,

even asking God in whispers to understand touching boys
should be allowed for them for all that they have given up.

Fr. Motherway sits alone with wibbling lip late Saturday
drinking whiskey sours with Lou, a teenage lad from camp,

and although seeing reflected in a the dining room mirror
the wretched, half-mad Judas goat he has become knows God

for a charity that although he in his fierce hardness himself
cannot deliver by grace can be delivered him who's so alone.

Wound within a Wound

"Hitler created Israel"
— Dr. Henry Makow

I've always badly bitten my nails;
as my angry father always knew.

Did early nerves and fears of mine
like some foul odor emit a clue?

It was a filthy habit he despised,
creating a fury that in him grew.

But I also nightly wet my bed
as if some fate guaranteed I do,

and father howled at me in anger
which scorched me cobalt blue.

Mornings he would grab my arm,
catch me reeking, and shout, "Pew!

You're killing your own mother!"
And I knew his words were true.

It crushed me and worse, I felt,
enrolled me in the devil's crew.

"We should tie a rubber sheet
around your neck — on view —

exactly like a public signboard!
Who deserves it more than you?"

But that was *why* I bit my nails;
as in fear I felt my brain unglue.

I woke in horror every morning
to discover once again with rue

my self in soaking wet pajamas,
cold, waiting in a ghastly stew,

desperate to devise some plan
in my sad humiliation to outdo

any possibility of confrontation
and some clever scheme construe

until all my family left the table
when breakfast was all through

to let me sneak into another room
and dress as quietly as I could do.

I tell you it was like a crucifixion
to watch every brutal dawn ensue.

I never had the nerve to tell him
how one fault had became two,

accepting how misfortune let one
vice of mine another yet accrue,

but let me here confess right now
and all that childhood pain renew,

defending my own childhood self
from the sorrow of limited review,

edgy, tense, and apprehensive still,
in high-strung words surely overdue

why from mad anxiety I bit my nails,
nipping them all brittle as if on cue:

"You should have known who caused it,
father, O dear father — it was you."

March of the Tomato Cans

"The murderer is always the victim's inferior."
                              — Vladimir Nabokov

Pitchers throw at hitters in baseball, a macho extremity
no gentleman would consider fair. How did this begin

is not a question for low-brow fanatics who exult in such,
wild, yowling cretins in the stands who live for "payback."

when in any truly elegant sport — for sport is about grace—
unforgivingly hurting an opponent charts an all-time low.

A coward needs his tiny satisfaction in revenge, the dwarf
becoming a giant in his midget dreams for rude retaliation.

Tradition-mongers, in which the sport of baseball's crammed,
receive the way they think and so, never questioning habit,

moronically go along with this brainless loyalty of tit for tat,
exactly what no true professional athlete could ever condone,

but many imbecilic ball-players also play to impress their fans,
and they war-brand in a dopey exchange of reciprocated farce.

Fans have weak predictable minds, catch the drift and hold it;
like common pop-ups. Tomato cans. *I've got it! IIII've got it!*

All those unenlightened half-wit players who run out to fight
en masse, emptying dugouts, just to throw out airy haymakers

should all be loaded onto the slow buffoon train to Bushville
where you can punish an opponent instead of beat him fair!

Retribution? Revenge? Even the score, not by taking vengeance
with a 97 mph fastball to the head, but by talent, you rumpswabs!

Crow as Looking Glass

The crow, thought in Sweden to be the ghost
of murdered men haled from the otherworld and proscribed
a respectful greeting wherever it may land

— in Islam it's one of five animals for which
there is no blame for anyone who kills it, for Hindus evil
carriers of information darkly come to hand —

although black itself, as swart as India ink,
is terrified of anything *else* that is black it spots to scrutinize
and from its shelter is atrabiliously banned.

It seems it cannot bear to look at what it is,
guiltily to encounter terror mirrored in a tulip, tar pits, rotting
food, tornadoes, charred and blasted sand,

rotting bananas, volcanoes, cats, mambas,
skunks. But night must ever fall and so engulfs and catches
it, the archetype of every shadow scanned

Sketch of a Sinful Life

My sign was fire and the whole world at war
   When I came into the world.
Soon a drab devil's flag like a quarantine rag
   In my personal life unfurled.
It was said with astonishment I was incontinent
   In so many words at three.
To some evil condition I had given permission
   By refusing to get up to pee.

There was some refuge yet in my reveries
   Born of pitiful hopes and my books
Where various shapes mimicked robbers and apes
   And the hands of pirates were hooks.
Such daydreams of mine were a substitute shrine
   To worship and not look away,
Lest the truths of reality with all their brutality
   Shout loud and a sinner betray.

When I wet the bed it was as if I were dead
   As I stood in a darkened back hall
Prayerfully hoping that my family were coping
   Elsewhere to make me not stall.
I have stared at disgrace quite full in the face
   Taking the sad tour through life,
But appearing defiled when a sensitive child
   Cuts deeper than any sharp knife.

I walked through thick weeds to study the creeds
   And spoke through the high naves above
Where floated my dreams among many crossed beams
   To soar to the heights of a dove.
A church perfume of dread that illogically fed
   My fancy more than my fears
Sat deep in my soul like a shining white bowl
   Which brought perfect joy to my tears.

But just how I was scarred in many ways barred
    Any normal aspect of growth.
A cruel uncle who shocked me constantly mocked me
    And adjured by an annual oath
That if I should wed I'd forthwith soil in bed
    Any woman I took as my wife,
And so in bleakest remorse as a matter of course
    I selected a celibate life.

There is that in a priest of something deceased:
    He must forgo having a mate.
I partook of that gruel, an unquestioning mule,
    And forged what I thought was my fate.
But I soon had a vision of a deeper precision
    That told me to leave and pursue art,
In which to make sense of my mingled intents
    By writing the things in my heart.

We have sadly the proof of the ongoing truth
    Signs of fire and war never end.
I've accepted that ghosts are my personal hosts
    As the past and the future contend,
And though different in kind they serve to remind
    and to teach and to preach — *all* of me —
That every tomorrow has its requisite sorrow
    In both time and eternity.

Shaking Hands with Poe

Only in stark moonlight
turning the world misty bluish green,
  refusing all time to exist,

  with the center of the rainbow
becoming the shadow of my head
  to give it a magic twist,

  was I able to walk on rubber
or foam and go tilting with delight
  as if on an aurora of snow

and then by the rare telenovela
of a rare force preternaturally right
able to shake hands with Poe.

Hedy Lamarr and Winona Ryder and Bess Myerson

Shoplifting is a deed of need, like acting.
We all need love, which is a need to *own*.
Emotions in anything can be exacting
in someone unimportant or renown.

Misses Kiesler, Horowitz, and Myerson
were Jewish girls with remarkable looks
So why, even if poor as any dyer's son,
did they all turn out to be crooks?

Here's a paradox of glory and guile:
look at me high on the silver screen,
but while I am shopping in any aisle
I feel sheer terror in just being seen.

Were they greedy, sinful, cold, or cheap?
I swear as long as there's a God above me
I believe, in movies or weeping in a heap,
they were simply asking, "Just love me."

African Flag

In winding Zungomero
are roads of dirt as red as any Christmas fare
and cattle boldly black

which form altogether
into a chromic vision like a scarlet tanager
and nothing of glory lack

while along the banks
bananas bunch as green and as glistening rare
as any emerald stack.

Confrontation Freak

Mrs. Shang Nyun, filled with no end of anger
for a lifetime of complaints, real or imagined, lived to refuse
to back down, to go away, to admit faults,

and when she chased you through rooms,
barging forth as hard floors thundered, howling and fury-blind,
gog-eyed, shaking her thixotropic cheeks

and wagging chubby arms like yo-yo poles
there was never any place for you to go! Pursuit of the sort
is a kind of murder. "*I will not be denied*!"

was Lucifer's black ontological yowl
imported into every thick female Korean head as if by fiat
but no ochroleucous face turning devilish

can match the marching, big-feet charging,
no-end-of bulldozing, stampeding zoom of this turbulent scold
to square accounts even she could not explain!

I once in the desert met a madman, a loon
strabismic with one blue eye and one infuscate, six fingers,
who chewed fury as he spit at the sun,

changing his voice as if with a tongue-chip
in rancorous execration that went positively reedy at the top,
nor would he go away as rubber-bouncing

he spent himself cold. I would take a bus-ride
with him to Oregon, manacled, than with this Asian harridan,
don't dare to doubt it, dawdle for an instant.

Shiloh's Birthmark

On the cheek by her ear
of minutest size
like a sweet angel's prize
with the tint of cafe au lait
sits a birthmark so small
almost nothing at all
that for life Shiloh will bear.

It is fetching not odd
on her small girlish face
with nary a trace
in its gentle display
of blemish or blitz
and yet there as it sits
it resembles lovely Cape Cod!

La Bella Dama Senza Pietà

She walked like the flash of a shine in silver,
    her laughter rang like a peal of bells.
Love pierced my inner heart like a sharp stiletto.
We paused on the Palatine in that ancient ghetto.
Her kiss tasted of light white wine from Orvieto
    with a message only an angel tells.

She looked past my eyes with that Duccio face,
    as pale of skin as the breaking dawn.
Doubt in the hanging silence rendered me mute.
We froze like two souls in pain white and acute.
She then vanished like dusk with no final salute
    when I saw I myself had gone.

Rome, 1965

Once in A While Forever

Once in a while forever
are days as they come to us,
in spite of human endeavor,
no matter our force or fuss.

No lasting wish whatsoever,
whether of pleasure or gain.
can possibly last forever
which only in dreams remain.

Expect nothing forever after
but triumph followed by trial.
You will find joy and laughter,
not always, only once in while.

Always is closer to never
in the way of the human plan
no matter how wise or clever
we brood on a future span.

I've often yearned for eternity
of things to preserve but then
find them mine with this certainty:
once but then never again.

What comes must go, the flow is
the nature of time and its style.
All we can possibly know is
forever, once in a while.

And the Child's Name is Anthony

My father was known for his sayings,
all of them original, spare, and strange,
repeated through his life to his progeny,
often as lessons, generally earnestly put
but never idly or with cynicism or irony.

Examples occur to me without number
of phrases kept like tools in his mind,
adages that seemed to keep him company,
inventive, eccentric, and non-conformist,
all of them open yet closed to scrutiny.

Whenever he finished a job well done,
for example, he would predictably say
always with a settled sense of harmony
as if calling down a blessing on his work,
"And the child's name is Anthony!"

637

"For I am convinced that neither death nor life, neither angels nor demons, neither the present nor the future, nor any powers, neither height nor depth, nor anything else in all creation, will be able to separate us from the love of God that is in Christ Jesus our Lord."

Romans 8:38–39